DEBUSSY

DEBUSSY

A Painter in Sound

STEPHEN WALSH

Alfred A. Knopf · New York · 2018

THIS IS A BORZOI BOOK PUBLISHED BY ALFRED A. KNOPF

Copyright © 2018 by Stephen Walsh

All rights reserved. Published in the United States by Alfred A. Knopf, a division of
Penguin Random House LLC, New York. Originally published in hardcover in
Great Britain by Faber & Faber Ltd., London, in 2018.

www.aaknopf.com

Knopf, Borzoi Books, and the colophon are registered trademarks of Penguin Random House LLC.

Library of Congress Cataloging-in-Publication Data
Names: Walsh, Stephen, [date] author.
Title: Debussy : a painter in sound / by Stephen Walsh.
Description: First United States edition. | New York : Alfred A. Knopf, 2018. |
Includes bibliographical references and index.
Identifiers: LCCN 2017059045 (print) | LCCN 2017058738 (ebook) |
ISBN 9781524731939 (ebook) | ISBN 9781524731922 (hardcover)
Subjects: LCSH: Debussy, Claude, 1862–1918. | Composers—France—Biography.
Classification: LCC ML410.D28 (print) | LCC ML410.D28 W35 2018 (ebook) |
DDC 780.92 [B]—dc23
LC record available at https://lccn.loc.gov/2017059045

Front-of-jacket images: (background) Stage setting for Afternoon of a Faun by Léon Bakst,
Paris, 1912. Photo 12/Alamy; (font details) Debussy's six planned sonatas score cover.
Music-Images/Alamy

Jacket design by Jenny Carrow

Manufactured in the United States of America

First United States Edition

For Chuck Elliott
incomparable editor, neighbour and friend

Contents

Author's Note

Money

Exact equivalences are, of course, impossible to establish but certain parallels can be made, especially since, before the First World War, European currencies were stable. The franc was common to France, Belgium, Switzerland and Italy, one for one, and the pound sterling was worth 25 of them. In 1900 a good average restaurant meal in France might cost 4 francs, a medium-class hotel room about 6, and a second-class rail ticket from Paris to Lyon 38. To post an ordinary letter within France cost 15 cents. The 250 francs a month Debussy earned playing Wagner every Saturday for Mme Escudier thus seems fairly modest, especially as it was more or less all he was earning at the time, and his later, much bigger advances (25,000 francs for the sale of *Pelléas et Mélisande* to Durand, 20,000 for *Khamma*, 20,000 for *Le Martyre de Saint Sébastien*) had to be set against the 3,600 per annum maintenance he had to pay Lilly Texier, his expensive Bois de Boulogne apartment, the lifestyle that went with it, and the fact that these sums were island peaks in a choppy sea. Needless to say, his medical treatment in his final years would have had to be paid for. He never received an adequate regular income, liked luxury and was a poor money manager.

Translations

Unless otherwise stated, all translations from French and Russian are my own, including in cases where published translations by others exist.

DEBUSSY

A Biography of Sorts

He rejects all heritages and is repelled by those construction kits that so often turn the composer into a make-believe architect; for him, form is never given; he was constantly in search of the unanalysable, of a development in the course of which surprise and imagination retained their rights; he had nothing but mistrust for architectural monuments, preferring structures in which rigour and free will intermingle: with him words, keys, all the paraphernalia of scholarship, lose their sense and relevance; the usual categories of an outworn tradition are inapplicable to his work, even if we extend their meaning.[1]

PIERRE BOULEZ

Pierre Boulez's image of Debussy as a composer in constant rebellion against musical tradition has to be understood in the light of his own rejection of the past. But it's by no means a distorted picture. The one thing it lacks, perhaps inevitably, is any clear sense of what Debussy took from the musical environment in which he grew up: what he accepted as well as what he rejected.

I spent the first dozen years of my money-earning life as a freelance music critic, an activity that positively forbids specialisation but forces you to confront and find words to describe whatever the repertoire and your editor is pleased to throw your way. There was already a great deal of Debussy about in those days, the 1960s and 1970s; but there was plenty of other French music as well, the music of the world into which Debussy was born and against which, in his student years especially, he fought. Of course there was *Pelléas et Mélisande*, but you could also catch a production at the St. Pancras Festival without the extended interludes (the form in which it was composed, but never played in Debussy's lifetime). There were operas by Gounod

3

(not only *Faust*) and Bizet (not only *Carmen* and *Les Pêcheurs de per-les*); there was Massenet (not just *Werther* and *Manon*) and Chabrier (*Le Roi malgré lui*, *L'Étoile*), and Lalo (*Le Roi d'Ys*), and Dukas (*Ariane et Barbe-bleue*), Chausson, Fauré (especially his chamber music and songs), wall-to-wall Berlioz after his centenary in 1969, but also Alkan and Franck, Saint-Saëns, even d'Indy, and plenty of the earlier French music—Rameau, François Couperin, Destouches—that Debussy complained was neglected in the Paris of his youth.

It was easy even then to identify all these composers as in one way or another French (with due allowance for the Belgian Franck), much harder to put one's finger on what it was that they had in common. In the introduction to his book on French music, Martin Cooper had provided a lucid explanation of the differences between the French and, for example, German views of art. After quoting a remark of the critic W. J. Turner that "it is the sublimity of the soul that makes the music of Beethoven and Bach so immeasurably greater than that of Wagner and Debussy," he pointed out that "to seek in French music primarily for a revelation of the composer's soul or for marks of the sublime is to look for something which the French consider a by-product . . . The French composer is consciously concerned with the two data which no one can question—his intelligence and his senses." And Cooper added, "The regarding of a piece of music as an artefact—a thing of planned shape, dimensions, colour and consistency—rather than as an expression of an emotion whose end is in itself, brings the French composer nearer than any other to the plastic artist."[2]

This strikes me as a perfect description of the attitude of Debussy to his work, and indeed of the work itself. But it doesn't exactly fit the other composers listed above. Or rather it fits them only in part, and it is precisely this hybrid character of so much nineteenth-century French music—its partial fulfilment of the aspirations that, in Cooper's analysis, would make it truly French—that explains the context against which Debussy, first as a student, then as a composer and music critic, found himself rebelling. The problem, in two words, was German music. From Gluck to Wagner, the German influence on French composers had been irresistible and, in Debussy's view, profoundly damaging. "The influence of Gluck on French music," he wrote in *Gil Blas* after a performance of Rameau's *Castor et Pol-*

lux, "is well known, an influence that could only have manifested itself thanks to the intervention of the Dauphine Marie-Antoinette (an Austrian)." Rameau's music, he goes on, is

> compounded of a delicate and charming tenderness, precise accentuation, strict declamation in recitative, without that German affectation of profundity or the need to double underline everything or explain everything with a breathless "you're a collection of particular idiots who understand nothing unless forced to have the wool pulled over your eyes."[3]

Gluck had famously pontificated about the nature of opera, and aspired to turn what, in Lully and Rameau, had been an essentially artificial, hybrid spectacle into an integrated, high-minded moral allegory of life and death. And Gluck had been one of the favourite composers of Berlioz, whom Debussy, in turn, called "the favourite musician of those who knew little about music."[4] In an early letter he called him "a prodigious fraud who came to believe in his own hoaxes," and he later accused him of "aiming madly at effects, which is what makes a lot of his music so intolerable."[5] Berlioz, he remarked in *Gil Blas,* is "so in love with romantic colour that he sometimes forgets the music."[6]

So it turns out that, from the start, French music of the nineteenth century had been deflected from its true path by the influence of German grandiloquence and the Germanic soul. Berlioz had in fact been a cul-de-sac, at least as far as French music was concerned. But something far worse had befallen French music, and that was Wagner. In some ways, the extent of Wagner's influence on French music is curious, not least because it reached its height in the decades after the disaster of the Franco-Prussian War, when one might have expected there to be a serious reaction in France against anything remotely Germanic. It was almost as if there was some conscious self-abasement before the master race.

The Wagnerian origins of French Symbolist literature had preceded the war in the person of Baudelaire, and were in any case highly selective, a matter of philosophy and aesthetic atmosphere, and without specific technical consequences. But for composers it was something altogether wider-ranging and, in Debussy's view, correspondingly damaging. French musicians flocked to Bayreuth for the first festival in 1876 and the several festivals of the 1880s. In Paris the short-lived *Revue wagnérienne* started up in 1885, with predominantly literary contributors; but the influence of Wagner was everywhere apparent in French music in the 1880s, especially, though not exclusively, in opera, which in France had always been the touchstone of musical excellence. Composers struggled to absorb Wagner's technical prescriptions without being able to match his control of scale and continuity or his orchestral brilliance. Devices such as the leitmotif, the long-breathed chromatic harmony, the heavy mythical, quasi-symbolic subject matter, were adopted like costumes out of a dressing-up cupboard, without ever working their way into the essence of the musical or dramatic thinking.

For the young Debussy, as a student at the Paris Conservatoire in the late 1870s and early 1880s, there was another crucial aspect of musical life that had effectively been appropriated by the German way of thinking. The teaching of harmony and counterpoint (*solfège*) and of form was deeply rooted, as it still is, in the music of Bach and the classical Viennese masters. True, the elements of counterpoint were derived from Palestrina, but the author of the system—the *Gradus ad Parnassum*—was an eighteenth-century Austrian, Johann Joseph Fux. To add insult to injury, the teaching of piano, from the ground up, was dominated by the method of yet another Viennese (admittedly of Czech parentage), the Beethoven pupil Carl Czerny. All this pedagogy was imbued with concepts of system and logic that Debussy made up his mind were alien to French ways of thinking and feeling, though it's fairly clear that what he actually objected to was the connection between the theoretical apparatus and the great monuments of German music, culminating in the overpowering music dramas of Wagner himself. After all, logic as such was just as much a French (Cartesian) purview as it was German (Kantian-Hegelian). The difference was largely one of atmosphere and, if truth be told, *amour propre*.

Debussy's changing attitude to Wagner is bound to be a recurrent topic of a musical biography such as this. Almost alone among French composers, he managed both to love Wagner's music and to escape the more pernicious aspects of its influence, while pinching from it all sorts of isolated musical images—chords, fragmentary progressions, what one might call musical situations—and recycling them in a way that expressed his personal idea of sensual beauty. Partly for the same kinds of reason, he tended as a young man to avoid the company and conversation of fellow musicians, and to prefer that of poets, writers, cabaret artists and, to some extent, painters. He was one of the few musicians at Mallarmé's Tuesdays. There was a brief, intense friendship with the composer Ernest Chausson, himself a somewhat detached figure musically, but an artistic connoisseur with a house full of beautiful pictures and strong artistic connections through his painter brother-in-law Henry Lerolle. Chausson had been a keen Wagnerite and an early visitor to Munich and Bayreuth for Wagner performances. But Debussy's greatest Wagnerian friends were not musicians but writers, notably Pierre Louÿs and the Swiss journalist Robert Godet, one of the founding committee members of the *Revue wagnérienne*.

In rejecting Wagner, Debussy was thinking a kind of music that prioritised what he saw as the virtues of French art, "its clarity of expression, its precision and compactness of form, the particular and specific qualities of French genius." In fact he achieved a great deal more than that. He might after all simply have followed Nietzsche's (insincere) injunction to "méditerraniser la musique"[7] in the spirit of Bizet's *Carmen*, a masterpiece that breathes freshness and vitality but hardly reinvents the language. Instead he not only discarded the heavy northern gloom of *The Ring* and *Tristan*, he threw out most of the grammatical infrastructure that had supported Wagner's immense narrative frameworks. Suddenly there is a concentration, a focus on particular ideas and images that is, as Cooper implies, somewhat painterly. This is not a question of taking sides in the whole tormented issue of whether Debussy can or cannot be called an Impressionist. It has more to do with the way in which any painter handles the motif within the limits of the picture frame. In much of his music, Debussy seems to work like this with motifs and frames, rather than with the evolving, novelistic discourse, not only of Wagnerian opera, but of the whole symphonic tradition of nineteenth-century music. He was perhaps vaguely aware that, working in this way, he was proposing a significant change in the language that would have consequences in the work of other composers. Or maybe he was simply joking when he told Louis Laloy, "I've at last got a 75-centimetre table for writing things that have without fail to revolutionise the world."[8] He was in a hotel by the sea near Dieppe in August 1906, trying to work on the second book of *Images*, pieces such as *Cloches à travers les feuilles* and *Et la lune descend sur le temple qui fut*, which really do, in their quiet way, turn the language of music upside down.

What follows is a biography of sorts, but it is a biography with the difference that it sets out to treat Debussy's music as the crucial expression of his intellectual life, rather than, as one finds in many Lives of Composers, a slightly annoying series of incidents that hold up the story without adding much of narrative interest. This approach inevitably involves a certain amount of musical talk, though I hope nothing impenetrable to a willing non-specialist. The existing literature on Debussy is rich and extensive; there are straight biographies and there are studies of the music, either in whole or in part. Much of it is on a high level of excellence, and there is work of real brilliance. Obviously I have depended to a considerable extent on much of it, always I hope adequately acknowledged. But I am not aware of any book that adopts a strategy quite like mine.

Working on Debussy, his life and his music, has been the greatest pleasure imaginable. Few composers ever had so precise an image of the music they wanted to write, and even fewer have been so ruthlessly meticulous in the search for the exact expression of that image. Nineteenth-century composers (to say nothing of their predecessors) had worked with a set of routine procedures that would theoretically have enabled them to produce music by the yard with barely a thought, though needless to say that isn't a fair description of what they actually did. It is, nevertheless, more or less what conservatory students were taught to do, and it is what Debussy rebelled against. In the end he was having to formulate every detail of his music as he went along, judging sequence and continuity, structural design and balance, more or less afresh for each piece. In the twentieth century this way of working became more and more the norm. But Debussy did it first, and nobody since has done it so skilfully or with such beautiful results.

I

The Prisoner and the Prodigy

I t is never easy to locate beginnings, since even beginnings come from somewhere else. Even the big bang had its causes. But if we want to argue, as some do, that twentieth-century music began with Achille-Claude Debussy, then it is by no means absurd to suggest that it actually began in the prison camp of Satory, just south of Versailles, late in the year 1871.

There were naturally causes of this cause. If an aspiring young composer by the name of Charles de Sivry had not somehow got himself implicated in the activities of the Paris Commune in the spring of 1871, or if Manuel-Achille Debussy had not lost his job as a print worker with the firm of Paul Dupont in November 1870 and in desperation taken work as a siege provisioner at the *mairie* of the first Paris arrondissement, a seemingly innocent post that led inexorably to his promotion to the rank of captain in the 13th battalion of Communards less than six months later, these two more or less insignificant pebbles in the stream of Parisian revolutionary history might never have collided, and life might have taken a very different turn for Manuel-Achille's supposedly but not yet demonstrably musical nine-year-old son.

It's true that a certain fecklessness in Manuel's character had already had the apparently unrelated side-effect of introducing music into young Achille-Claude's existence. When he was two, his father had abandoned his unsuccessful china shop in the remote western suburb of Saint-Germain-en-Laye, moved in with his mother-in-law in Clichy, and turned to selling household goods while his wife, Victorine, took in sewing. Four years later he changed tack once again and became a print worker.

But even before the disasters of the Prussian war of 1870, the terrible siege that followed the French defeat, and the savage ten weeks of the Commune in the spring of 1871, the family's situation had become so precarious that Victorine had haled their three children off to stay with Manuel's sister, Clémentine, who had recently married a hotelier in Cannes. There, because Clémentine was a moderately well-to-do bourgeoise with the normal aspirations of her class, the seven-year-old Achille[1] was given piano lessons with an Italian violinist called Jean Cerutti, and perhaps even encouraged to take up painting, since Cerutti and his wife shared their house with two or three artists. Unsurprisingly, the violinist failed to detect any particular gift in this somewhat uncommunicative child. But the lessons must have made an impact, because by the time Manuel spoke to his fellow prisoner in Satory he was proudly talking about his eldest son as a musical boy who could play the piano.

Manuel himself knew nothing much about music and had taken little trouble over his children's education. Achille had not gone to school, and his only lessons had been with his mother, the daughter of a cook and a coach-builder. Probably Manuel mentioned the music only because de Sivry had told him he was a musician himself. So it must have taken him by surprise when de Sivry announced that his own mother was an accomplished pianist, a pupil—she claimed—of Chopin himself, and insisted that little Achille be taken to see her and her advice sought. The suggestion can hardly have been prompted by any evidence Manuel was able to supply as to his son's unusual talent, and may simply have been intended to give pleasure to a father at a low point in his life.

It turned out to be life-changing. Manuel remained in Satory until the summer of 1872, but long before that Victorine had presented herself, with their son, at the Montmartre home of Mme Antoinette Mauté, Charles de Sivry's mother by a previous marriage, and arranged for Achille to go to her for piano lessons. This Mme Mauté is a far more interesting and significant figure than has often been made out. Her claim to have studied with Chopin, who taught mainly society ladies of fragile ability, has usually been taken with a pinch of salt. But Debussy accepted it and always spoke respectfully of her teaching and her playing. More than forty years later he passed on what she had told him about Chopin's advice on practising, advice that rings true: "He wanted one to practise without pedal, and, with very rare exceptions, not to hold it on [even in performance]."[2] She revealed Bach to him, he said, "and played it as it never is played today, putting life into it."[3]

She may have impressed him, too, with some vague bohemianism in her personal charm, as hinted at by the poet Paul Verlaine, who married her teenage daughter, Mathilde, in 1870 and later described his mother-in-law as "a charming soul, an artist of instinct and talent, an excellent musician of exquisite taste, intelligent, and devoted to those she loved."[4] Verlaine, who eloped to Brussels with Arthur Rimbaud soon after his young wife had presented him with a highly unwelcome baby son, was hardly a man to praise the conventional charm of a suburban mother-in-law. In a backhanded way, his view is borne out by a police report on Mme Mauté after the defeat of the Commune, towards which, as the artist mother of a republican suspect, she was assumed sympathetic: "A woman of about forty-five, of light morals, especially formerly, giving piano lessons, despite her husband's 10 or 15,000 francs income. *Free thinker*, anti-religious, sometimes acting the honest woman in the noble company her piano connections have procured for her."[5] The voice of the establishment will always make a crime of individuality, but its instinct is sound. Mme Mauté was a woman of spirit, independence and taste who, in happier times, might have played host to an artistic salon. She surely taught Debussy more than just the piano.

It was at her suggestion that Debussy's parents put him forward for entry into the Paris Conservatoire in the autumn of 1872. It seems unlikely that they would have had this idea of their own accord, and still more unlikely that they could have found among their own acquaintance any musician of sufficient standing to act as an effective sponsor or referee to that august and deeply orthodox institution. Yet a sponsor was found, in the distinguished person of Félicien David, the famous composer of *Le Désert*, a member—since the death of Berlioz in 1869—of the Institut de France, and, conveniently, an examiner on the board of the Conservatoire. Why David should have taken up the cause of this still raw ten-year-old remains a mystery. It's true that at this time David was living in Saint-Germain-en-Laye, but that was hardly a connection by 1872. Somehow he must have heard the child play, and read between the lines. For the fact is that something exceptional in his playing was already to be detected by an experienced ear. At the audition on 22 October 1872 he was one of 157 candidates, most of them no doubt a lot older than he was. Only 33 were admitted, and Achille-Claude Debussy was one of them.

Adult or near-adult virtuosity on a musical instrument at the age of ten is unusual but by no means freakish. Musical performance, like mathematics and chess, is an activity at which precociously gifted children can emerge, apparently at random, and outshine all but the most brilliant grown-ups (many of whom will themselves have been prodigies in their time). It seems almost incredible, though, that Achille, barely two years after his first piano lessons, can have become a pocket virtuoso of this kind. His contemporary in the piano class, Gabriel Pierné, had started at the Metz Conservatoire at the age of five. Fluent Achille may indeed have been. But his first piano teachers at the Conservatoire, Antoine Marmontel and his assistant, Alphonse Duvernoy, picked out other aspects of his playing. Duvernoy commented on the boy's touch and sound quality, and both he and Marmontel were struck by his intelligence. In the second year, Marmontel noted his "real artistic temperament," by which he surely meant that Achille did not play like a brilliant child but that he sensed more elusive qualities in the music and knew how to bring them out in his manner of playing.

As well as piano, he had to study what the French call *solfège*: theory plus practical disciplines such as sight-reading and aural training, which included writing down music at dictation. Achille had probably never done anything of the sort before, and he struggled at first, especially with theory, which, because of its desiccated character and weird terminology, is the last thing a naturally gifted person thinks of when he or she thinks about music. Sight-reading came easily to him, and he soon got the hang of dictation, which, if you have a good musical ear, is simply reverse sight-reading. It quickly became apparent that Achille's ear was a gift from God, but theory was something he had consciously to learn, and in due course this, for him, would be a launch pad for rebellion.

Achille's upbringing thus far had hardly instilled in him any particular grasp of the virtues of practical, or even moral, discipline. Schooled by a dutiful but not notably powerful, affectionate or well-educated mother; his father wayward, ineffectual and for a time in prison, and his only proper music teacher a gifted but somewhat bohemian lady, he seems to have understood how to discipline himself to achieve what seemed to him worth achieving, but to have had little patience with the impositions of others in matters that did not interest him.

On the face of it, the Paris Conservatoire was the worst imaginable school for someone of his background and temperament. Its whole pedagogic structure was built on the perpetuation and recycling of sets of principles derived by theorists (some of them of considerable antiquity) from past music whose composers mostly did not adhere to them or even, in many cases, know they existed. For instance, the study of counterpoint—composition in two or more independent parts—was based on a system extracted by the eighteenth-century Austrian composer Johann Joseph Fux from the music of Palestrina, who would certainly have been astonished to learn that his style could be reduced to a dozen or so simple rules. Harmony was based on grammar-like rules of progression and combination that had remained essentially unchanged since Bach; form was that of a classical tradition handed down like the Ten Commandments from Mount Horeb. Moreover, these principles also governed the teaching of actual composition, though it would be several years before Achille confronted that particular version of the pedagogic mentality.

The curious thing was that this fossilised approach to the study of a fine art was put into practice by a body of exceptionally talented and for the most part humane men, one or two of them composers of genius. When Achille started at the Conservatoire, Ambroise Thomas, the composer of *Mignon*, had recently replaced Daniel Auber (*Fra Diavolo*, *La Muette de Portici*) as its director, and César Franck had just been appointed professor of organ; a few years later, Jules Massenet, the future composer of *Manon* and *Werther*, joined the teaching staff for composition. Achille's own teachers were lesser lights, figures of purely local distinction, such as Marmontel himself, who had taught Georges Bizet and Vincent d'Indy; Ernest Guiraud, the composer of the once famous recitatives that had replaced the spoken dialogue in Bizet's *Carmen*; and pure academics such as Achille's first *solfège* teacher, Albert Lavignac, and Lavignac's successor in that role, Émile Durand.

One might expect such men to have been intolerant of a student as self-willed and untutored as young Achille. In fact they recognised his exceptional talent from the start, and even expressed what one might call unofficial admiration for some of his musical deviances. In Durand's class, for instance, his harmony exercises would be littered with (presumably deliberate) breaches of the most elementary rules, and then he would take delight "in seating himself at the piano when the class was over and producing monstrous successions of weird, barbarous chords—that is to say, chords that were not classified in the official treatises of the Conservatoire."[6] Correcting the exercises, Durand would rage at Achille and cover the page with angry crayon marks; but he would then reread and say, "Obviously, all this is hardly orthodox, but it's very ingenious."[7]

One should probably understand this kind of incident in the context of the extremely tight rules that applied to the harmonisation of baroque or classical melodies at the Conservatoire. Anyone familiar with Bach's chorales knows that there are a variety of harmonisations of such tunes possible within the rules, from the very simple to the very elaborate. At his most complicated, Bach could himself sail extremely close to the wind of orthodoxy, and any church organist will improvise harmonies that send a *frisson* of complicit excitement along the back row of the choir stalls and barely suppressed giggles through the line of choirboys. But these are the naughtinesses of a technically prim environment, and no doubt the fifteen-year-old Achille's peccadilloes were more or less of this order. His fellow student Paul Vidal described them as "ingenious, elegant and delightful, but totally unacademic."[8] We are surely not yet at the point of the invention of a new harmonic language. What we see is a young, intensely musical boy breaking rules that have never actually been drummed into him, and that therefore do not have the force of a *langue maternelle*, a mother tongue. He knows them because he has learned them, and because they match the music that he knows and plays. As we shall see, he can obey them and use them when it suits him, but his instinct is increasingly to stretch them, break them, and eventually abandon them.

The *tabula rasa* that was Debussy's receptive brain had been left blank in other ways than the musical. As a child in Cannes he had probably tried his hand at painting. According to his great English biographer, Edward Lockspeiser, a palette that he had kept from his childhood ended up with his first wife, Lilly Texier, after their divorce. But Lockspeiser's theory that Achille was encouraged to paint by his godfather, Achille Arosa, a well-known art collector and connoisseur who conducted a lengthy liaison with Clémentine Debussy in the 1860s, has been discredited by François Lesure, who has shown that Arosa passed out of the Debussys' life at the latest in 1868, when little Achille was five or six.[9] There is therefore no reason to suppose that the boy had any acquaintance with serious art beyond what might have been hanging on his aunt's or Mme Mauté's walls, nor that his own painting was anything other than the normal activity of an eight- or ten-year-old child. The image of Arosa, whose brother Gustave was the patron of Camille Pissarro and Paul Gauguin, introducing his little godson to the latest work of the Impressionists has sadly to be abandoned in favour of the likelihood that when he entered the Conservatoire, and probably for some time afterwards, Achille knew little or nothing about art.

He was also poorly read and generally not well informed about the world around him. For a ten-year-old from a background like his, this would not have been very surprising. Nor would it have been particularly odd if he had stayed that way, since the Conservatoire environment was culturally blinkered, academic and narrowly focused on the specific requirements of a career in music. But, from early on, he took against the rabid vocationalism of the average music student. He made friends with a handful of more broadly cultivated fellow students, but even with them he could be reserved and uncommunicative, as if wary of the facile chatter of the habitually urbane.

There is a hint of insecurity in all this, some consciousness of lacking a solid musical base in a world of automatic musicians, combined with an obstinate refusal to fall in with their habits of mind and conversation. He had gone into the Conservatoire as a pianist, almost a prodigy, but at some point he began to lose interest in a pianistic career. Up to the age of twelve he must have worked like a slave at his piano playing. How else to explain the speed of his advance to the point where, in 1874, after barely four years on the instrument, he could garner good opinions and a second prize for a performance of Chopin's F minor Piano Concerto, even if a reviewer did suggest that "youth has to be forgiven a lot."[10] Yet a mere two years later, in June 1876, Marmontel was reporting that "he isn't at all measuring up to what I hoped; careless, inexact, he could do much better."[11] His friends started noticing that this refined young player was suddenly "charging at the keyboard . . . [as if] in a rage against the instrument."[12] And though he nevertheless managed a second prize the following year, it was his last success as a pianist and the end of any thought of a solo career.

The fact is that his intelligence, much remarked by his teachers, was becoming dissatisfied with the narrow drudgery of the piano school. He was making discoveries in other, hitherto unsuspected, fields of experience. He was reading—poetry as well as prose. He was acquiring refined, unstudentlike tastes, preferring "a minuscule sandwich . . . or a small pot of macaroni to the big, filling cakes that his comrades mainly chose."[13] As he had no money, he had to count on others to pay for him on these occasions. He became an adept borrower, not quite such an eager repayer, and he developed a certain unscrupulousness in the acquisition of desirable objects. Pierné took him to meet his parents, and while they were out of the room Achille persuaded him to cut out some Meissonier reproductions from a bound set of *Le Monde illustré* for him to take home to hang on his own wall. It was as if he were in search of some pattern of existence that was the opposite in all respects of what his family home had had to offer, just as his classroom musical promiscuities seemed to be a seeking out of alternatives to the conventions of the Conservatoire.

Marmontel may have become less impressed with the boy's playing, but he never lost faith in his musical talent, and whatever his virtues as a piano teacher, he was a vigorous and effective promoter of his students' interests outside the Conservatoire. As early as 1876 he arranged for Achille to accompany a young singing student, Léontine

Mendès, in a recital in the small town of Chauny, 70 miles north-east of Paris. Then in 1879 he packed him off for the summer to the château of Chenonceau on the Loire, where the Anglo-Scottish châtelaine, Marguerite Wilson-Pelouze, needed a pianist, possibly with other chamber musicians, to provide afternoon entertainment for her guests and background music at mealtimes. Lockspeiser suggests that the sixteen-year-old Achille also had the more intimate task of playing presumably gentle piano music to relieve his hostess's insomnia far into the night, a sort of latter-day Goldberg to Mme Wilson-Pelouze's Count Keyserlingk.[14]

Whatever his exact function during these summer months, the impression of the place and its owner on the impecunious young musician must have been profound. The grandeur of Catherine de' Medici's sixteenth-century palace, extended in a series of arches across the River Cher, with its galleries and tapestries and formal gardens, had been tactfully embellished by the work of a young artist called Charles Toché, who adorned the long gallery with large-scale frescos on historical subjects and added, in the orangery, portraits of various house guests, including a nude portrait of the young cellist brother of Achille's pianist predecessor.

As a rule Mme Wilson-Pelouze seems not to have encouraged her musicians to strip off. On the contrary, she liked to dress them up in scarlet jackets and turbans with egret's plumes. Whether Achille was kitted out in this way is not known. What we do know is that Mme W.-P. was a passionate Wagnerite who had attended the first Bayreuth Festival in 1876 and, we may suppose, talked about *The Ring* and its composer in terms later described by Achille's composition teacher, Ernest Guiraud, with a certain distaste: at Bayreuth, he remarked, "you get torn to pieces if you have the imprudence to hazard the slightest criticism. Even enthusiasm is banned . . . Ecstasy alone is tolerated."[15] Mme W.-P.'s genre was ecstasy. Achille, who had at most heard the *Tannhäuser* and *Flying Dutchman* overtures and the first act of *Lohengrin*, can only have been intrigued by this kind of intemperate advocacy of a composer he had previously discussed in probably somewhat cooler terms with his harmony professor, Albert Lavignac.

François Lesure suggests that it was at this moment that he made up his mind to abandon all hope of becoming a concert pianist, and

to become a composer instead. Unfortunately, the arcane Conservatoire rules decreed that, having failed in the piano *concours*, he was
ineligible to enter a composition class. So, for the 1879–80 session, he
instead enrolled in Auguste Bazille's piano accompaniment class, and
spent much of the year subjecting the amiable Bazille to his idiosyncratic harmonisations and surprise modulations. In figured bass, for
instance, where a number code printed below the given bass line indicates the harmonies required of the keyboard player, Achille would
make colourful additions, "by way of breaking the monotony of the
harmonic progression," as a fellow student later explained. In mod-
ulating, he would change key more or less arbitrarily, without the
correct stepwise movement of the individual parts that theorists call
voice-leading. Bazille seems to have accepted that, though incorrect,
these procedures were often effective. "Good harmonist," he noted
in his report, "a bit of a fantasist, [but] with plenty of initiative and
verve."[16] And the prize jury agreed and awarded Debussy the first
prize, which meant that in the following session he would mysteri-
ously qualify for entry into a composition class in the autumn of 1880.

One inevitably wonders whether he had had twinges of composition thirst before 1879. Many years later he told Louis Laloy that his
first compositions dated back to 1876. But composers habitually get
such things wrong, not least because they tend to have reasons for
preferring one history to another. In any case nothing survives that
can reliably be dated pre-1879, and the one piece probably composed
in that year, a song called "Madrid," is more or less a crib of Gounod's "Boléro" (1871), with the same characteristic dance figure in
the piano, the same strophic form (the same music for each verse),
and harmony that is, if anything, even blander. A piano piece called
"Danse bohémienne," in a barely advanced version of the same style
plus perhaps a touch of Bizet, was probably composed early in 1880.
Then Debussy's life—and especially his creative life—was trans-
formed by two major, unrelated episodes, one of them again brought
about by Marmontel's benign intervention, the other by his own
chronic lack of funds and consequent need to generate some income
by whatever drudgery he could bring himself to perform.

That summer a certain Nadezhda von Meck, the Russian widow
of a Baltic German railway millionaire, approached the Paris Conservatoire for the services of a young pianist to make up a piano trio

for her household's entertainment at their various stopping places in France, Switzerland and Italy in the coming months. Frau von Meck's husband had died, four years before, of a heart attack brought on, it was said, by his wife's infidelity with his secretary. Thereafter she had adopted the restless, peripatetic lifestyle of the so-called "superfluous" Russian wealthy classes. She had found some kind of emotional fulfilment in her loving patronage—to call it that—of Pyotr Ilyich Tchaikovsky, whose music she came to adore to the point of nervous perturbation, but whom by her own wish she never met (she may or may not have been aware of his homosexuality). She and Tchaikovsky pursued their relationship entirely through correspondence, and from their letters we learn a good deal about the young French musician who, on Marmontel's recommendation, joined her itinerant household at Interlaken, in Switzerland, in July 1880.

On arrival, the still-seventeen-year-old Achille presented himself mendaciously as the *premier prix* of Marmontel's piano class and a composition pupil of Massenet, and told everyone that he was twenty, although, as Frau von Meck informed Tchaikovsky, "he looks sixteen." But she was impressed by his pianism, even if, she added surprisingly, he lacked sensitivity. His duties included giving piano lessons to the numerous von Meck children, accompanying the oldest daughter, Julia, a competent singer, and playing piano duets with Frau von Meck herself. For her, these were the unforgettable moments of his visit. Above all, they played arrangements of Tchaikovsky, including the Fourth Symphony, still fairly new, and dedicated to her. "I can't play it," she told its composer,

> without a fever in every fibre of my being, and for days I can't free myself from the impression. My partner didn't play it well, but he sight-read it marvellously. It's his sole, but very great, merit. He can read a score, even yours, at sight. His second, so to speak reflex, virtue is that he's entranced by your music.[17]

No doubt Achille played Tchaikovsky without the pulsating intensity that his patroness desired, while conversely telling her what she will certainly have wanted to hear, namely that he found the music ravishing. They also played the orchestral Suite in D minor, Op. 43, with its brilliant first movement fugue, of which Achille sycophantically informed his hostess that "he had never come across anything so fine among modern fugues. M. Massenet would never be able to do anything like it."[18]

From Interlaken, the caravan had proceeded across France to Arcachon, from where they soon returned to Paris before heading south once more to Nice, Geneva, Naples and finally Florence, settling there for two months until mid-November, when Achille at last decided it was time to return to the Conservatoire and take up his place in Guiraud's composition class. For a young man who had never left France, and rarely Paris, it had been a voyage of discovery. Not only had he encountered music and sights foreign to his experience, but he had run up against a culture and attitudes quite different from what he was used to within the four walls of the Conservatoire. Some Tchaikovsky he may have heard in Paris. The response to it on the part of these wealthy Russians may well have surprised him. There was Glinka, "which made the head of the household's heart beat violently,"[19] and possibly other Russian music, not mentioned in dispatches. On the other hand, when he himself announced that he was working for the Conservatoire's great prestige composition prize, the Prix de Rome, a fib presumably designed to impress his hostess, her enthusiasm will have been polite at best. "Absurd all these prizes," she wrote to Tchaikovsky, "not worth a thing."[20]

He did nevertheless compose at least one work of his own in Florence, a Piano Trio for the house trio to play. It prompted Frau von Meck to grumble to Tchaikovsky that he had never written a trio, and since he did so soon afterwards, it might be claimed that Debussy had indirectly influenced Russian music before it had had time to influence him. In itself Debussy's own trio is hardly more than a bundle of charming salon pieces, with an episodic first movement spun out to ten or eleven minutes, a pair of short intermezzo-like middle movements, and a lively if rather square-cut finale. Stylistically it belongs unequivocally to the world of French 1870s chamber music, as represented for instance by Saint-Saëns's B flat Piano Quartet of 1875, though inevitably without that work's formal sophistication. Debussy had after all so far composed nothing longer than two or three minutes, as far as anyone knows. In the circumstances, the trio was an ambitious exercise, by no means worthless in the outcome. A shame that we haven't Tchaikovsky's opinion of it, as we have of the

"Danse bohémienne," which Frau von Meck sent him: "a nice thing, but so short, with themes that lead nowhere and a ragged form that lacks unity."[21] The trio was finished too late to be copied for sending to Russia and Tchaikovsky never saw it.

Back at the Conservatoire, Debussy made a late entrance to Guiraud's composition class, and also attended César Franck's organ class, which concentrated specifically on what might be termed the random skills of the church organist, rather than keyboard and pedal technique as such. Franck taught improvisation, harmonising and transposing at sight into different keys, and his view of these matters was much what one might expect from his own music, with its rich flow of chromatic harmony and constant side-slipping from key to key—its "wearying and persistent *grisaille*," as Debussy described it years later in a review of *Les Béatitudes*.[22] Debussy's own improvisations would presumably tend to dwell on particular chord colours, and when Franck urged him to modulate, he would ask, "Why do you want me to modulate, when I'm very happy in this key?"[23] It was probably just as well that he was only auditing Franck's class rather than fully enrolled.

Meanwhile, his financial situation remained precarious, and like any modern student he was compelled to find ways of augmenting his income. In his case, the position was aggravated by a certain weakness for spending what money he had on *objets d'art*, books and knick-knacks of one kind and another, and no doubt he also took part in what Lockspeiser rather primly calls "the activities of a student's carefree life," though these activities did not as yet include playing at, or even attending, clubs such as the Chat Noir, which opened as a place of entertainment only in 1885.[24]

His solution to the problem was more sedate but at the same time more consequential. He took a part-time job as accompanist to the singing course of a certain Victorine Moreau-Sainti, a former opera singer, now widowed, who ran private sessions for what Lesure calls "jeunes femmes du monde"—young ladies of good family— and taught them a repertoire based mainly on contemporary French opera and choral music. "Already very attracted to women," Lesure remarks coolly, "Achille suddenly found himself in an aviary, and not a little drunk on it."[25] Among the feathered creatures was a beautiful young woman with a delicious high soprano voice by the name of

Marie Vasnier, the thirty-two-year-old wife of a building contractor, and the mother of their two children. Of Marie Vasnier it may be said that she was a bird of the air in need of a perch. Henri Vasnier was a decade older than her and much preoccupied with his work and intellectual interests. She was a musician of real natural talent. Achille was a young artist as yet unawakened, either sexually or, more important, creatively. The two things, together, would open floodgates.

2

Songs for Marie

For all the excitements of the summer, Debussy remained a Conservatoire student, a student now of composition, expected and expecting to work towards the supreme prize—the prize he had lied about to Mme von Meck: the Prix de Rome. He was still living in his parents' two-roomed apartment in the rue Clapeyron, behind the Gare Saint-Lazare, under constant pressure from his father to earn some money, while Victorine smothered him with maternal affection. The claustrophobia—physical and emotional—must at times have been unendurable, and no doubt grew even worse as Achille began to spend more and more time elsewhere, absences whose true cause his mother soon began to suspect: not, that is, a sudden and unexpected enthusiasm for the Conservatoire and the company of his fellow students, but that dread alternative, a woman. Her son, she seems to have learned, had befriended the Vasniers, was often at their house, and the woman in question was Henri Vasnier's much younger wife, Marie. The situation was self-perpetuating. The recriminations will have driven him away more often and for longer, only for him to return home to his mother's pleadings about "this sinister tale of adultery"[1] and his father's grumbles at his failure to turn his as yet fairly modest academic successes into hard cash.

Not that there was any question of his entering for the Prix in his first year as a composition student. Guiraud's initial response to his work, in January, was favourable but guarded: "intelligent, promises to be a good composer." By June 1881 he was "intelligent, good pupil," though a choral piece he submitted for the end-of-year assessment was dismissed by one of the examiners as "convoluted, too much modulation, bad path."[2]

What Guiraud was basing his own judgements on is a matter for speculation, but one likely candidate is a Symphony in B minor that

Debussy was writing in his first two months in the composition class, very much the sort of task that might be set in addition to the usual technical exercises—the fugues, the invertible counterpoint, the style studies, and so forth. Such of the symphony as survives, in a version for piano duet that may or may not have been the form in which it was composed, displays fluency but little or no individuality. The *Allegro* finale, which he sent to Mme von Meck that February (and which duly ended up in the Glinka Museum in Moscow), is vaguely Germanic in style, but with decorative harmonic touches that perhaps betray its Gallic descent. An *Andante cantabile*, also for piano duet and written on the same type of paper as the *Allegro*, so possibly one of the symphony movements, is more in the well-aerated keyboard manner of the older French composer Emmanuel Chabrier. Debussy may also have shown Guiraud his piano trio of the previous summer. But he probably kept to himself other things he was composing that winter, for reasons to do with their style and content that will shortly become apparent.

At some point in the late 1870s, he had started buying and reading poetry, and particularly the work of the Parnassians: Théodore Banville, Théophile Gautier and Leconte de Lisle. At what moment this essentially uneducated adolescent became obsessed with literature, as well as art, is by no means clear. It was probably in late 1878 or early 1879 that a recently arrived fellow student in Durand's class, Raymond Bonheur, came across him with a volume of Banville in his hand, and registered this as somewhat unexpected in a Conservatoire student. But it was no passing enthusiasm, for when Debussy started setting poetry to music, a year or so later, these were precisely the poets he turned to, and especially Banville, whose compact, mellifluous, exquisitely formed lyrics fitted his requirements at that moment like a glove. In the three and a half years between his enrolment as a composition student and his eventual victory in the Prix de Rome, he composed some forty songs and vocal duets, of which fourteen are settings of Banville. Of these fourteen, half are dedicated to Mme Marie Vasnier, and of the forty, no fewer than twenty-eight bear dedications to her.

Exactly in what circumstances, or how soon, Marie fixed her gaze on Mme Moreau-Sainti's brilliant young accompanist we don't know.

It was probably that way round, considering her experience and his lack of it, and she may not at first have had the field to herself. But the earliest of the dedications to her, a Banville song called "Caprice" composed by the end of 1880, already bears an inscription that, as François Lesure remarks sagely, this married woman "would have found . . . difficult to leave open on her piano."[3] "To Mme Vanier," it runs (with a misspelling of her name that it took Debussy some months of intimacy to correct), "these songs conceived to some extent in your memory can only be yours as the composer is yours." Admittedly the plural form suggests a slightly later date with several songs included, but the misspelling nevertheless keeps it no later than the early months of 1881, after which the dedications are correctly spelt. The whole dedication apart from the name has been scrubbed out, but remains legible.

At eighteen, Debussy was neither more mature nor more conventionally good-looking than the average teenager. His appearance was even mildly grotesque. He had an exceptionally high, domed forehead, which he tried to conceal by combing down his thick, crinkly black hair in a sort of curtain that gave him a curiously fifteenth-century look, like some Piero della Francesca portrait. The Vasniers' daughter Marguerite, who was eleven at the time, described him as "a large, beardless boy, with clearly defined features . . . a very interesting face; the eyes, especially, attracted your attention; you felt that here was a personality."

> I can still just recall him in the little drawing room on the fifth floor above the rue de Constantinople, where he wrote most of what he produced over a period of five years. He used to arrive most evenings and often in the afternoon as well, leaving the manuscript paper on a little table until later. He composed at the piano, a curiously shaped old Blondel. At other times he would compose walking about. He used to improvise at length, then walk up and down the room singing to himself, with his eternal cigarette in his mouth or rolling paper and tobacco in his fingers. Then when he'd found the idea, he wrote it down. He never crossed out a great deal, but he searched a long time in his head before writing anything down and was highly critical of his own work.[4]

Raymond Bonheur, a fellow student, remembered Debussy's hesitancy of speech, and his way of expressing himself "in short, incomplete phrases, in monosyllables sometimes, trying his hardest to find a word supple enough to get across the nuance of an impression or a point of view." His attitude to music was the same: "He would more readily have agreed to forge banknotes than write three bars without feeling the imperious need to do so." And from early on, according to Bonheur, he had a horror of bourgeois professionalism: "At the wedding of one of our friends, for whom we were standing as witnesses, Debussy signed the register in the usual way; then, having to say what his profession was, he thought for a moment before solemnly putting down 'gardener'."[5]

In the summer the Vasniers rented a house at Ville d'Avray, a few miles to the west of Paris, and Debussy would come out every day on the train, sometimes in order to work, sometimes to take long walks in the park at Saint-Cloud. They would play croquet, at which, according to Marguerite Vasnier, Debussy was "very good . . . but a bad loser." Then in the evening there would be music. Marie would sing and Debussy would accompany. "Sometimes, when it was raining, we played cards. Bad sport that he was, when he lost he was in a furious temper, all the more so as he needed his winnings to pay for the train which brought him to us every day. Then, to cheer him up, a packet of tobacco would be slipped under his napkin as we sat down to eat, and he would be overjoyed!"[6]

The question of whether Debussy and Marie Vasnier went to bed together, and if so how soon, has occupied his biographers, sometimes to the exclusion of the much more interesting question of her influence on his music. One is tempted to say that this was so profound, and what is more so candid, that it would be almost impossible to suppose that they did not, quite early on and as often as circumstances allowed, make love. Paul Vidal, an early Conservatoire friend who became closer to Debussy's parents, referred to Marie as his "succubus." Most of the songs are love songs of one kind and another, contain a good deal of kissing, and are—to put it no more strongly—decidedly sensuous in tone. Although any letters he may have written to her have not survived, one can read a lot into his dedications. "To Mme Vasnier," runs one (on another 1881 song, "Tragédie"), "the sole muse who has ever inspired in me anything resembling a musical sentiment (to speak only of that)." Here the entire dedication has been crossed out. Others are gushing but less explicit. After a while he gave up including messages in his dedications and confined himself, perhaps at her urging, to simply her surname, always with the discreet "Mme" at its head.

The affair itself was anything but discreet. Even without personal effusions, or the intensity of Debussy's involvement with the Vasnier household, the songs he wrote for her to sing and himself to accompany would have advertised the nature of their relationship. It was common knowledge at the Conservatoire. His mother, as we saw, guessed it and resented it. The only person who seems to have been unaware of it, unless he merely chose to ignore it, was Marie's own husband, who tolerated Debussy's almost continuous presence in his house, working, composing and, on frequent evenings, playing for Marie and later giving piano lessons to Marguerite. Not only was the young composer evidently a welcome visitor at the Vasniers', but he seems to have remained on excellent terms with Henri Vasnier himself and even later, as we shall see, to have counted on him for advice and as a shoulder to lean on. No doubt there was an element of smoke-screening in all this. Already, in his late teens, Debussy was proving not unduly scrupulous in his management of *les affaires du cœur*, partly through natural emotional and physical impulses, but partly also because the needs of his creative work were assuming an importance that overrode other considerations.

In the songs he wrote for Marie between 1880 and 1884 one can hear her voice almost as if she were in the room singing them. She was evidently a high soprano with a gift for fluid coloratura and for floating the almost accentless French language across high-lying melodies of an at times positively instrumental character. But there must also have been a great deal of sensual warmth in the voice, not only in the lower-lying lyrical passages that predominate, especially in the early bars of many of the songs, but at those moments—something of a fingerprint of the young Debussy—when the melody rises ecstatically, as it were, beyond the natural target note of the phrase then settles back down on to it. Certain expressions of this type were probably an intrinsic element of her voice, since Debussy exploits them over and over again. She must have been unusually agile for an amateur singer, and with a big, well-controlled range of two full octaves, from at least middle C sharp up to high D, over which she appears to have been able to range freely and with a measure of precision. Of course, it's possible that she handled all these difficulties poorly or in an approximate, amateurish fashion; love can be deaf as well as blind. But it's more likely that Debussy, who was becoming more and more particular about his music and the way it was executed, wrote in this way only because he could count on Marie to understand and to perform as he wished. As he wrote in his dedication of his Gautier song "Les Papillons" ("The Butterflies"): "To Madame Vasnier who alone has a voice light enough to sing songs where butterflies are involved."

Taken as a whole, the Vasnier songs enabled him to find his feet as a composer on a track parallel with but distinct from Guiraud's Conservatoire teaching and the official goal of the Prix de Rome. Not that there is a great deal in them stylistically that would have been likely to upset the severe adjudicators of the Prix, whatever they might have thought of their generally sensual tone and their tendency towards a certain musical weightlessness. To win the Prix, you had eventually to compose a big twenty- or twenty-five-minute cantata with orchestra to a set text and under exam conditions, something that might or might not suit your personal bent as an aspiring composer. As we shall see, Debussy eventually managed this, but only by suppressing his natural impulses and subduing much of his individuality. It was meanwhile through the songs, most of them short and fairly restricted in their emotional and spiritual compass, that he could begin to discover what kind of music he wanted to write and, no less crucially, how to write it.

The Banville and Leconte de Lisle poems he set in the first year or so of his association with La Vasnier are for the most part straightforward love poems that in one way or another use nature, or flowers, or the physical world as corollaries of amorous feelings or simple flirtations under the moon or stars to the sound of nightingales. Now and then a shadow may pass. In Banville's "Les Baisers" ("Kisses") there is a Heine-like conflict between the lover's caresses and his or her (unspecified) black betrayals. In "Rêverie" the shy beloved is compared unfavourably to the flowers that open readily to the amorous breath of the zephyr. But Debussy reacts to these nuances only in passing, and is mostly more interested in the general atmosphere of saturated sensuality that is typically the Gallic response to what

Ruskin called the pathetic fallacy of Nature's empathy with human passions.

The sensuality is expressed mainly in the vocal lines, and often without particular regard to the words: or, rather, with particular regard to their value as sound rather than as meaning. On the larger scale, Debussy is often cavalier with a poem's structure. He will repeat lines or whole verses for no obvious reason, or for reasons connected with the form of the song rather than that of the poem. For instance, in Banville's "Aimons-nous et dormons" ("Let us love each other and sleep") he repeats the opening theme in the middle of a sentence, thereby overriding the sense of the poem with a (possibly) preconceived musical scheme. In "Souhait" ("A Wish," also Banville), he cadences (puts a harmonic full stop) in the middle of a phrase, as if captivated by a single image, the "parfums embaumés" ("fragrant perfumes") of the roses, and forgetting what the roses are supposed, somewhat repellently, to be up to, which is shooting from the lovers' dead bodies. Now and then he seems simply to run out of text, so will repeat lines, or even have the voice carry on *la-la*-ing until the music is ready to stop. The most flagrant example of this is the Verlaine song "Pantomime," where admittedly there is a textual excuse for the fourteen bars of vocalise (song without words) that end the song, in Colombine's hearing voices, Joan of Arc-like, in her heart.

But Debussy was much more careful about formal schemes than these examples might suggest. Among the earliest poems he set are a pair of *rondels* by Leconte de Lisle, "Jane" and "La Fille aux cheveux de lin" ("The Girl with the Flaxen Hair") in each of which the opening couplet is repeated twice in the course of the poem and again at the end. Debussy duly repeats the music to these couplets, with or without minor variation (and with the single exception of the third couplet of "La Fille aux cheveux de lin"). The idea is a very Parnassian one, an antique device (the *rondel* is a medieval form) taking precedence over romantic freedom of imagery, elegance of form disciplining the free flow of emotion. His very first Banville setting, "Nuit d'étoiles" ("Starry Night"), not itself a *rondel*, turns it into one by repeating the first quatrain after the second and again after the third, each time to the same music, leaving out one of Banville's verses in order to make the form neater.

These early songs may not be profound psychological or mini-dramatic studies like the lieder of Debussy's Viennese contemporary Hugo Wolf, but they have, song after song, an exquisite beauty of vocal line that somehow matches the easy fluidity of the French language, especially in the hands of poets such as Banville and, a little later, Verlaine, who went out of their way to make music out of the pure vowels and soft consonants of their native tongue. Debussy would later make much of the idea of melodic arabesque—of the decorative and unruly vocal or instrumental lines that seem to copy the curves and swirls of Art Nouveau design. But already in the Vasnier songs the shape of a melody and the flicker of an ornament can seem far more significant than any heavier penetration into the meaning or symbolism of the words. We've seen Debussy dwell on the beauty of a single image while apparently ignoring its consequences for the poem. And in setting the metre, he makes full use of that wonderful property of French, so baffling to foreigners: its supposed indifference to verbal accent. Even a francophone Englishman can look at Debussy's "Aimons-nous et dormons," for example, and raise an eyebrow at the metric accents on the weak second syllable of "dormons," the supposedly even weaker mute "e" on the end of "reste," and the definite article "Le" in the phrase "Le soleil s'éteindrait." In Wagner's Nüremberg, such absurdities would have had Beckmesser scratching furiously at his slate. But in French they are expressive nuances that in no way seek to apply undue weight to unimportant details. They carry no emphasis. Rather, they help counteract what Debussy later referred to as "the tyranny of the barline," which can straitjacket French in a manner unproblematic in languages such as English or German, which have strong natural accents.

At some time around new year 1882 Debussy for a while turned away from Parnassus, and set Paul Verlaine's "Fantoches" ("Puppets"), a Watteauesque scene in which an array of characters from the old theatre of masks, the *commedia dell'arte*, gesticulate in the moonlight or flit through the undergrowth in search of love. Debussy must have known about Verlaine's poetry before this, just as he must have known about the poet himself from his visits to Mme Mauté, even if he never witnessed Verlaine's drunken violence towards his young wife after Rimbaud's arrival on the scene a year or so after their marriage. The discovery, such as it was, was specifically musical. Verlaine triggered a new level of imagination in Debussy's writing, something less effortlessly charming, more precise and suggestive. A decade or so later he would take "Fantoches" in hand and provide it with a completely new ending. But the original version already captures the essence of the tiny *Fêtes galantes* poem, its elusive, scurrying sophistication naughtily grafted on to the colourful, childish images of the popular theatre: hence the sliding chromatics of the main piano theme and passing figures in the vocal line, laid against fragments of what might be nursery songs, as at the moment when the doctor's daughter slips half naked through the arbour to a suspiciously merry fragment of C major.

"Fantoches" as a whole is in A minor, almost Debussy's first song in a minor key, not counting the early "Rondel chinois," whose A minor is a picturesque orientalism. More to the point is the song he wrote immediately before "Fantoches," a setting of Leconte de Lisle's "Les Elfes" in G minor, a ballad (story) song that mixes up, more garrulously, some of the elements Debussy would then refine in the Verlaine song. Then, having found a particular voice in "Fantoches," he turned back to Banville and set a trio of poems that similarly evoke the *commedia* and Watteau, all three of them, significantly, in minor keys. But these are by no means sad songs, or at least not tragic ones. Instead they evoke an antique world through the modal harmony of distant times.

Strictly speaking a mode can be any selection of notes. For instance, the five- and seven-note modes used by the gamelan orchestras of Java divide the octave in proportions that make them unplayable on Western keyboard instruments. On the other hand, the Western church modes with their enticing (if oddly classical) names—Ionian, Dorian, Phrygian, etc.—are the origin of our modern twelve-note chromatic scale, the white and black notes of the piano; you can play their music on that instrument if you want to, even if the tuning won't be exactly how it would have been when sung in the fifteenth or sixteenth century. Among these modes are some with a major character and some with a minor character. The Ionian mode is our major scale; the Dorian mode is the white notes from D to D, which sounds minor; the Phrygian is E to E, also minor, and so on. The character of each depends on the relative position of the smaller and larger intervals, the semitones and tones. But perhaps because the Ionian mode provided our modern major scale, we tend to think minor when we want to think modal; or at least that has been the tendency when modal writing has wanted to create a feeling of antiquity. So Debussy, imagining an ancient world of serenading guitarists, street players, or minuetting gallants, imagines it in the minor mode, not sadly, but perhaps with a hint of the melancholy of time past and passing.

One further qualification is necessary to all this. Old music and folk music were strictly modal, but modern composers using modes can treat them as freely as they like, mixing them with tonal elements or with other modes. With Debussy, modalism is more a way of thinking about melody and harmony than a set of rules or restrictions. Among other things, it was a means of escape from the textbook harmony of Durand's *solfège* class, itself derived from the tonal grammar of the classical German repertoire. It thus came to be seen as something specifically anti-German, in Debussy's case specifically French—which brings us back to Watteau, Banville and Debussy's somewhat Gallic version of the *commedia dell'arte*.

In "Sérénade" the first thing we hear is the plucked strings of Harlequin's guitar as he steals up below Colombine's window, only to find she has closed her shutters. The intervals of a fourth are those of the guitar's tuning (except that the real guitar also has one major third), but their effect here is to create a momentary doubt about the song's key before the singer himself strikes up. The main part of the serenader's melody is then modal, with one or two tonal asides, and with piano (alias guitar) chords that likewise mainly stick to the mode, until Colombine (the music rather than the poem tells us) peeps seductively round the closed curtain, and the harmony turns briefly, amorously tonal. The whole effect is precise and economical, like a pen-and-ink sketch, using the musical language as the sketching medium, without undue concern for its own native proprieties. "Pierrot," though fun, is less convincing, being rather crudely designed as a fantasy on the children's song "Au clair de la lune." But "Fête galante" captures all the elegance and sensual promise of Watteau's woodland glades in a slow minuet, hybrid in style like the blended modalities of "Sérénade," and which Debussy himself liked sufficiently to use, seven years later, as the basis for the minuet in his Petite Suite for piano duet.

These Banville songs from early 1882 are all, still, written for and dedicated to Marie Vasnier, and reflect what I have imagined as the particular quality of her singing. The voice floats high and light with an airy grace and joyous bursts of coloratura. Something, nevertheless, seems to have changed. Evening after evening, Marie sang Debussy's songs to his accompaniment, and one wonders whether he always played from a fully composed piano part. In the earliest songs there is a faintly generalised character about the accompaniments, as if one could just as well have served for another, allowing for changes of harmony and adjustments to the melody. Exquisitely refined though they are in the published versions, they work a similar vein of fluttering or arpeggio figures, the tonal harmony enriched with added notes of the kind that lie easily under the hands of the instinctive improviser. Debussy, one feels, could have turned out accompaniments of this kind till the cows came home. Significantly, most of the songs end more or less with the voice; there are few if any piano postludes of the individualistic type cultivated by Schumann, a pianist songwriter who did not have a Marie Vasnier as his vocal muse.

However, in "Fantoches," and then particularly in the next three Banville settings, the piano gradually takes on a more precise, considered role. In "Fantoches" it paints the shifting moonlit backcloth against which the activities of Scaramouche, Colombine and company unfold, not quite as innocently as they'd like you to think. In "Sérénade" the piano is the serenader's guitar; in "Fête galante" the piano part is in a sense the whole inspiration of the slow, stately minuet, with its classical poise but curiously ambiguous modal harmony. Finally, "Pierrot," though not one of Debussy's best songs, evolves a technique that will prove useful later. The piano part is based entirely on repetitions of the first phrase of the children's song "Au clair de la lune, mon ami Pierrot," while the voice tracks a somewhat devious course above, quoting the song phrase just once in augmentation (slowed down). Because the tune is very familiar, the composer can use what everyone knows about it with a freedom he might not risk with a tune he has made up. Accordingly, the harmony wanders about like Pierrot "drifting dreamily along the boulevard," as Banville pictures him, and with no very clear aim. The song's texture is fragmented by the montage of repetitions, left hand, right hand, both hands, with or without chords. The result is curiously provisional, but not disagreeable, because we feel at home with the material. It's a description we shall come across again with works by Debussy that cut a great deal more ice than this insignificant little song.

Debussy had meanwhile spent a second summer, 1881, with the von Meck household, and this time they were for the first two-and-a-half months based in Moscow, before proceeding to Rome and, finally, Florence by way of Vienna, Trieste and Venice. It was a trip with two nodal points that were to resonate in his subsequent life. He later told Paul Vidal that he had loathed Rome on sight (though, according to Mme von Meck's son Nikolay, "he looked back longingly on the Villa Medici" as they walked past the home of the Prix de Rome winners). But on his reaction to Russia at that time, musically and otherwise, history is virtually silent.

The year 1881 was tragic for Russia. The death of two of her greatest artists, Fyodor Dostoevsky and Modest Musorgsky, within weeks of each other in February and March had framed the assassination of the reforming Tsar Alexander II at the beginning of March. Yet it seems almost as if echoes of these unhappy events in St. Petersburg barely penetrated the walls of the von Meck household in Moscow. Music reigned as before, but Debussy later assured the music critic Pierre Lalo that Musorgsky's name had not even been mentioned.[7] Naturally there was Tchaikovsky: the Fourth Symphony once again, *Romeo and Juliet*, his opera *The Maid of Orleans*—a work that is unlikely to have roused Debussy to more than polite enthusiasm. What other Russian music he heard or played is known only circumstantially. Nikolay claimed that his mother introduced Debussy to all of the *kuchka* (the "Mighty Handful" group of composers, or "The Five"), but without specifying which of their works.[8] By the late 1880s he certainly had in his possession songs by Balakirev and Borodin, brought from Russia in 1881 or 1882, and he might conceivably have played Borodin's symphonies, four hands, with Mme von Meck. But publication of the *kuchka* was still in general patchy, not least because their completion rate was so erratic: of Musorgsky, some songs and the opera *Boris Godunov* were available; of Rimsky-Korsakov somewhat more, including songs, the symphonic poems

Sadko and *Antar*, and his first opera, *The Maid of Pskov*. The question is only of interest because Debussy later conceived a passionate admiration for, especially, Musorgsky, and was audibly influenced by Borodin and Rimsky-Korsakov. But there is no sign of these influences in his work of the early 1880s.

Instead by early 1882 he was still searching for a personal style in the setting of French lyrical poetry, while trying hard to satisfy the strait-laced requirements of his Conservatoire courses. There he had advanced along a somewhat tortuous path. In April he entered for the Prix de Rome for the first time, and though he failed to get beyond the preliminary round, his work, a setting of Anatole de Ségur's "Salut printemps" for women's voices and orchestra, drew a grudging, slightly barbed compliment from Guiraud: "Progress in some respects. Ill-balanced nature, but intelligent. Will get there, I believe," while the examiner who had grumbled about his convolutedness the previous summer now found his work "ingenious, making progress."[9] Debussy was still composing on parallel tracks. Guiraud may never have seen or even been aware of the Vasnier songs, which he would probably have regarded as frippery. For his teacher, Debussy wrote a cantata called *Daniel* on an old Prix de Rome text; a suite for piano duet, *Le Triomphe de Bacchus*, and probably an *Intermezzo* for orchestra, which he submitted for the end-of-year exam. These tasks were clearly intended to develop an ability to think and work on a larger scale, which Debussy still had some difficulty doing and which tended to distract him from the search for an individual style. The suite, for example, is boldly written, with here and there some interesting, mildly risky harmony, but it is raw and unrefined in total effect, like a poor imitation of Chabrier.

Towards the end of that summer of 1882 he again travelled to Moscow, spent September with the von Mecks at their new home outside the city, then went with them to Vienna, returning to Paris only in December. He must have had with him a copy of Verlaine's *Fêtes galantes*, since he set two of the poems—one in Russia, the other in Vienna—and it seems unlikely that such an item would have been found in the von Meck house or baggage. During the summer he had evidently been distracted from composition by almost daily visits to the Vasniers' rented house at Ville d'Avray, half an hour from Paris by train. In any case it looks as if the Verlaine songs were a prior

intention, part of the inspiration that had produced "Fantoches" and
the subsequent Banville settings, and developing some of the same
impulses as well as some new ones.

The attraction of Verlaine, one supposes, lay not only in the density and conciseness of its lyricism, not only in its sheer musicality,
but also in its lurking ambiguities, its undertow of irony and doubt.
The title "En sourdine" is essentially musical: it describes a muted
violin or a quietly humming voice, and purely as sound, the poem's
assonance has the quality of a musical instrument with its single characteristic timbre:

> Et quand, solennel, le soir
> Des chênes noirs tombera,
> Voix de notre désespoir,
> Le rossignol chantera.

But why is the nightingale "the voice of our despair"? We lie together
in the half-light created by the oak branches, and abandon ourselves
to the sensual oblivion of love. The image—though Verlaine is
unlikely to have known this when he wrote the poem in 1869—is that
of the second act of Wagner's *Tristan und Isolde*, where the lovers
on their flowery bank invoke the world of love beyond death: "Oh,
sink down, night of love, make me forget that I'm alive, take me up
into your bosom, set me free from the world." But Brangaene in her
tower intones a warning: "Habet Acht! habet Acht! Bald entweicht
die Nacht"—"Beware! Beware! Soon the night will pass." Hers is the
voice of their despair, though, alas, they ignore it.

Debussy had heard very little Wagner in performance at this stage,
and certainly not a note of *Tristan*. But to assume he was ignorant of
it would be another matter altogether. Albert Lavignac, his *solfège*
teacher, had been a keen Wagnerite; they had discussed the music
and, surely, played it. At Chenonceau, the atmosphere had been
positively Bayreuthian; Mme Wilson-Pelouze had attended the first
Bayreuth Festival in 1876 and was a co-founder of the *Revue wagnérienne*, the short-lived journal of the Parisian Wagnerites. It would
stretch credulity to imagine that a vocal score of *Tristan und Isolde*,
in print since 1860, would not have been in her possession and that
it would not have been taken down and played through, given the

presence of such an adept sight-reader as Debussy. "En sourdine" is concrete evidence that he had played or studied the score, and remembered it. The opening is so close in harmony and texture to the opening of Wagner's love duet that one could even suspect that Debussy had sensed the textual parallel and looked for a musical equivalence: the throbbing syncopations; the rich chording (Debussy's sumptuous second chord is identical to the chord on Isolde's first "Liebe," with the omission of one note); the descending quaver figure for the voice of despair, and so on. These are similarities beyond the realms of coincidence.

But even at this early stage Debussy seems not to have been at all interested in Wagner's discourse. What excited him, and stayed in his ears, was the sound and phraseology, the depth of colour, and the intensely erotic instant. It's a very French response, to adopt a crude generalisation. The German master, typically, is taking the erotic as paradigm of a philosophical concept; the Frenchman by contrast takes the erotic as an image of the beautiful, or even as an end in itself, a virtual equivalent of the feelings described. And in so doing he distils the expansive paragraphs of the opera into a series of concise musical moments, not disconnected, but not insistently consequential either, the harmony intensifying the melody, rather than all the time "leading" it towards a logical ending, towards closure. Debussy's harmonic grammar is still "correct"; it wouldn't have been marked down on technical grounds by Lavignac or Durand. But in a typological sense, it is weak: not weak-equals-inadequate, but weak-equals-secondary, as against classical harmony—of which Wagner was merely the latest exponent—which is typologically strong.

If "En sourdine" suggested *Tristan* to Debussy, the other Verlaine song he wrote while on tour with the von Mecks, "Mandoline," is essentially French in its modelling. This is another song about serenading, but now the serenaders and their "belles écouteuses"—their fair listeners—are out of Greek pastoral poetry by way of Molière, Corneille and, eventually, Watteau. The pastoral setting is an excuse for light flirtations under the trees between elegantly dressed "rustics" beneath a pink and grey moon, and the music recognises the casualness of the sensations (Verlaine's "frissons de brise") in music as deft as "En sourdine" is sultry. Elements of *Carmen* (Nietzsche's antidote to Wagner) seem to have leaked into Debussy's writing, with its dancing melody, its suggestive chromatics, and its eyelash-fluttering *la-la-la*s. The style is clean and airy, with dissonant harmony only such as a mandolinist might produce by strumming the instrument's open strings.

Debussy exploited these topics and idioms in two further Verlaine settings after returning to Paris. "Clair de lune," the opening poem of the *Fêtes galantes*, sets the agenda, with its

> . . . charming masks and bergamasks,
> playing the lute and dancing and almost
> sad behind their fanciful disguises.

Here, for the moment, the subtlety and precision of Verlaine's oxymorons escape the young composer: the melancholy revellers with their songs in the minor key about "love triumphant and the opportunistic life." Instead he comes up with a pretty but slightly wooden setting that reacts to the words rather than the poem, repeats lines, and overlooks the cycle's starting-point, the idea that these are all images from the "choice countryside" of the recipient's soul. He will do better with this poem in a later setting. In the second poem, "Pantomime," the characters of the *commedia* flit past in four brief three-line verses: Pierrot, Clitander, Cassandra, Harlequin, Colombine. But for Debussy more is still needed, so he repeats two lines of the first verse, and ends with a fourteen-bar wordless cadenza gratuitously illustrating the voices that Colombine is surprised to hear in her heart.

It's instructive to compare this song with his setting of Théophile Gautier's "Séguidille," made at about the same time. Gautier's portrait of a dancing *manola* is vivid and slightly over-coloured, as befits the dancer herself in her exaggerated costume, a permanent cigarette dangling from her mouth. Debussy expands the picture still further with a long wordless vocalise to start, and composes in effect a complete dance along the lines of Bizet's famous *seguidilla*. It's effective and fun, but not very individual. In Verlaine, he was evidently attracted by the economy and sharpness of the imagery, but hadn't yet evolved the technique to capture those qualities with any consistency in his own music. In a sense, though he set them beautifully, the Parnassians were a bad example, and so was the poet Paul Bourget, to whose verse Debussy suddenly for some reason turned in 1883.

Bourget's word-pictures are not dissimilar to Banville's, even if the verse is inferior. Nature, the setting for tragedy, betrayal or profound thought in so much nineteenth-century German song, is here mainly a place for that form of mouth-to-mouth resuscitation significantly known as French kissing. "Ah! How your mouth gave itself to my mouth more tenderly still in this great silent wood," sings the poet of "Paysage sentimental." In "Voici que le printemps," "the blackbird whistles at those who aren't loved, and for lovers, languishing and charmed, the nightingale spins out a touching song." Debussy, still thinking of Marie Vasnier (as is apparent from the range and charac-ter of the vocal writing), seems to have relished this kind of thing, and these six Bourget songs are enchanting, highly polished, immaculate lyrical outpourings, remarkable work for a student barely out of his teens. In a sense, they bring to a head his course of private study in the art of song-writing in the Romantic manner but, like his Vasnier affair, they are pleasure without prospects. In both cases, it would soon be necessary to break with the past. Luckily for Debussy, and for us, his hand was soon to be forced.

He had tried for the Prix de Rome for the first time in 1882, but had not got beyond the preliminary round, despite carefully tailoring his setting of the prescribed text—Ségur's "Salut printemps"—to the supposed conservative stylistic preferences of the judges. In 1883 he was more successful. This time the text for the qualifying stage was an excerpt from Lamartine's long poem *Invocation*, to be set for male voices and orchestra. Once again Debussy reined in any inclination he might have had to liven up these somewhat dull verses with inno-vative harmony. Guiraud had been looking at some experimental sketches he had made for a stage work based on Banville's "heroic comedy" *Diane au bois*, and had strongly advised him against risking anything of the kind in his Prix de Rome offering. Accordingly his *Invocation* is a studiously unadventurous piece of writing, and it duly took him through—admittedly only in fourth place—to the final, for which the set project was a dramatic cantata called *Le Gladiateur*, on a text supplied by one Émile Moreau.

For the final stage, the candidates were hauled off to Compiègne, fifty miles north-east of Paris, and incarcerated in the castle there for upwards of three weeks, like criminals or wild animals, while they composed their masterpieces. In the circumstances, Debussy's version of *Le Gladiateur* was a remarkable piece of work, an expertly composed piece of sub-Massenet, grandly orchestrated and forcefully written for the three solo voices that were part of the requirement. By French standards the style is perfectly modern. It belongs to that distinctive school of Gallic post-Wagnerism, the school of Lalo's *Le Roi d'Ys* (1875) or Massenet's *Hérodiade* (1881), in which superficial attributes of Wagner's music dramas—the continuous discourse, the intense chromatic harmony, the heavy orchestration—are translated into swifter-moving French melodrama with frequent relaxations of tension and plenty of full stops.

For all its polish and assurance, Debussy's *Le Gladiateur* came only second to the work of his friend Paul Vidal. It was found to display "a musical nature generous but ardent to the point of intemperance."[10] At the performance at the Institut de France on 23 June, it was praised for its originality, a quality that, it must be said, is far from evident today and was certainly not sought by its composer, who was clearly trying to avoid any tendencies that might strike the judges as unduly challenging. In any case, his second place made him a natural front-runner for the prize the following year.

The 1884 preliminary exercise was a four-part choral setting of *Le Printemps*, a poem by the co-librettist of Gounod's *Faust*, Jules Barbier. Debussy's setting was, according to François Lesure, "rather well-behaved, but not without technical errors."[11] It nevertheless squeezed him into the purdah at Compiègne, again in fourth place, and this time his prize cantata, *L'Enfant prodigue* ("The Prodigal Son"), at last won him the first prize. It seems to have been only at this point that he took full account of the fact that his victory would require him to spend a minimum of two years at the Villa Medici in Rome, far away from his beloved Marie. They tracked him down to the Pont des Arts, he recalled years later, "where I was awaiting the result of the competition, contemplating the delightful coming and going of the *bateaux-mouches* on the Seine . . . All of a sudden someone tapped me on the shoulder and said in a breathless voice, 'You've won the prize.' Believe it or not, I can assure you my heart sank! I saw clearly the tedium, the anxieties that the least official recognition fatally entails. Above all, I felt I was no longer free."[12]

L'Enfant prodigue is a good enough work to have stayed on the fringes of the repertoire to this day, though, as with *Le Gladiateur*, it would be hard for even a discriminating listener, not in the know, to identify its composer. This was certainly more or less Debussy's intention. He was by this time practised enough and well enough taught to be able to produce on demand a well-wrought score, without warts or blotches, in the idiom of the day, a work moreover by no means without inspiration, effective, colourful and even moving in its way. But it was not a music he had any desire to go on writing, and *L'Enfant prodigue* was to have no successor in his output.

3

Up at the Villa

Debussy's dread of the Villa Medici seems to have been only too justified. Having initially considered the possibility of evading capture, so to speak, by instead winning the valuable Ville de Paris Grand Prix Musical in the autumn of 1884, he bowed to the inevitable and set off for Rome with his tail between his legs in January 1885. The tail stayed put. His early letters home—that is, home to the Vasniers; letters to his parents from this time have apparently not survived— are so deep in gloom and depression, so self-pityingly negative about his surroundings, his fellow pensioners, and everything that has always made Rome a Mecca for thinking, feeling humanity that one almost suspects an ulterior motive to do with the cuckolding of the long-suffering M. Vasnier himself. For the letters we know about are all to the husband. They are the letters of a humble but determined pupil in the ways of the world. Vasnier has insisted that he take up his Prix, has urged him to make the most of his time in Rome, to absorb the lessons of the art and culture of the ancient city, and to use the opportunity to create work of his own. Debussy speaks with gratitude of the older man's advice, while countering it with his own obstinate refusal to see any virtue in "this abominable Villa" with its stiff and egotistical Prix-winners, its vast rooms "with a three-mile walk to get from one piece of furniture to another," and the "frightful" Roman climate—rain and cold in January, insufferable heat and insects in August.[1]

Anyone whose first serious absence from home has been many months long will recognise that sense of acute loneliness and alienation that Debussy describes. That it was at least partly genuine is proved by his letters to other friends with whom there was no emotional complication. Normal homesickness was compounded by his well-honed detestation of musical institutions. The Villa Medici, after all, was merely an extension into adulthood of the Conservatoire, with its hated specifications and stereotyped criteria. The students, state funded, were subject to the Academy for a minimum of two years, and were expected to produce a series of so-called *envois*, works that demonstrated their continued adherence to the fine precepts of their teachers, and would be judged accordingly. As we shall see, Debussy was to have as much difficulty with these *envois* as he had previously had with the Prix de Rome itself, and as before he would pursue his own distinct course on the side until, towards the end, the two began to converge.

He was probably not quite the total recluse that he liked to portray in his Vasnier letters. He would appear at the Director's soirées, performing duets and playing and singing his songs. No doubt there were excursions to the city, and his fellow pensioner, Paul Vidal, describes frequent poetry and play readings.[2] But his separation from Marie Vasnier undoubtedly made everything much harder. It may even be, as Lesure suggests, that he somewhat exaggerated his misery to the husband, knowing that the wife would also read his letters.[3] It does seem likely, in any case, that Vasnier's insistence on Debussy sticking it out in Rome was due to a dawning awareness of the young composer's relationship with his wife, and a hope that prolonged separation would bring it to an end. Debussy did not altogether stick it out. As early as April, or thereabouts, he made a flying return to Paris, and less than a year later, in February and March 1886, he somehow obtained a two-month leave of absence, which he again spent in Paris. We can take it that the Vasniers figured prominently in these visits, perhaps too prominently for M. Vasnier's peace of mind, since when Debussy appeared again in Paris that summer, and even, it seems, followed them to Dieppe, Marie made it clear to him that their meetings had become an embarrassment and could not in all prudence be continued. Whether Henri had at last put his foot down or Marie's own feelings had cooled is by no means certain. It might even be that Debussy's own desperation had to some extent become merely a habit, since in 1886 Marie was thirty-eight and probably no longer the eager and delectable beauty he had first encountered at Mme Moreau-Sainti's six or seven years earlier. Yet their association was still at least theoretically current when he finally gave up on Rome, and at the earliest legitimate moment, in early March 1887, returned definitively to Paris.

The emotional torments of the Villa Medici were in some degree matched by the creative ones. The *envois* preyed on his mind, and he was at first overwhelmed by the influence of his surroundings, by the chilly grandeur of the villa itself, and by the weight of artistic tradition in the city of Rome. Over everything hung the shadow of the Academy. The Director, he told Vasnier,

> raises his eyes to heaven with an ecstatic air whenever he speaks of it, and the eulogies delivered on Michelangelo–Raphael are like a reception speech. I'm pretty sure that Michelangelo would laugh if he heard all this! I may be mistaken, but it seems to me that Michelangelo is the modern pushed to the limits, he took risks to the point of madness and I think that if one followed in his tracks, it certainly wouldn't lead you straight to the Institute; it's a fact that we are too much little boys to venture along that road.[4]

All the same, he had to try to produce work that rose to the Academy's expectations, if not to the level of the Sistine Chapel ceiling. His first *envoi* was a symphonic ode for voice and orchestra called *Zuleima*, a setting of a text by Georges Boyer derived from Heine's play *Almansor*. The work caused him agonies of mind. In June he told Vasnier he was abandoning it, as being "too old and smelling too much of old string." Then, when Vasnier pressed him to persevere, he insisted he "would never be able to do the third part, it's too stupid. The second doesn't please me much either, which leaves only the first part, really not enough." Four months later, he announced that "*Zuleima* is *dead* and it certainly won't be me who revives her . . . too reminiscent of Verdi and Meyerbeer."[5] Yet he submitted some part of her—exactly how much is not known since nothing at all survives. All we know is the morose opinion of the Academy assessors:

> This pensioner, we note with regret, seems today to be preoccupied solely with creating the strange, the bizarre, the incomprehensible, the unperformable. Despite a few passages not without a certain char-

acter, the work's vocal part is interesting from the point of view neither of melody nor of declamation.[6]

His next idea was to work up his old Conservatoire sketches for *Diane au bois*. At first this seemed scarcely more promising than *Zuleima*. "One scene is done," he told Vasnier in October, but "it's not at all right and besides, I've taken on a task that may be beyond me." He now seems drawn to Wagner, whose *Lohengrin* he had probably seen, his first complete Wagner opera, in Rome soon after arriving at the Villa. But as for imitating him, "I don't need to tell you how ridiculous it would be even to try." Then a month later, "*Diane* is giving me a lot of trouble, I can't manage to find a musical phrase that gives me her physiognomy, as I would like."[7]

Sometime afterwards, during 1886, he abandoned her for good. But we know something about her music, because a certain number of drafts survive. They show that his difficulties were due not primarily to the pressures of the Academy, but on the contrary to the technical and aesthetic challenges of expanding the original, highly individual style of his most recent songs to the larger scale of what was meant as a theatre piece of some kind. In any case, it's likely that, as an *envoi*, *Diane* would have been an even greater disaster than *Zuleima*, even stranger and more incomprehensible to the academic mind.

The final *envoi* that Debussy composed at the Villa Medici (two more were to follow after his return to Paris) was a so-called "symphonic suite" for orchestra, piano and chorus (without basses), called *Printemps*, two movements only (the "suite" notwithstanding), and without text, the chorus wordless throughout, unlike in the unrelated test piece of 1884, *Le Printemps*. In this instance, the Academy assessors were never able to see the orchestral score, which Debussy told them—surely mendaciously—had been destroyed in a fire at the binder's. Had it ever existed, it probably would not have improved their opinion of the piano reduction, which is worth quoting at some length:

M. Debussy assuredly does not sin through platitude and banality; on the contrary, he has a very pronounced tendency towards the research of the strange; one recognises in him a feeling for colour and poetry whose exaggeration easily makes him forget the importance of precision in design and clarity of form. It would be desirable for him to be on guard against that vague impressionism which is one of the most dangerous enemies of truth in works of art . . . One expects and hopes for better in future from a musician as gifted as M. Debussy.[8]

Bearing in mind that the panel were not seeing an orchestral score, it looks as if they were influenced in this curiously perceptive misjudgement chiefly by the wordless choral writing, with its swirling close harmonies and its spirit of Caliban's "sometime voices" in *The Tempest*. Probably they did not recognise Debussy's source for this kind of writing, since they might not have attended Bayreuth in 1882 and heard Wagner's *Parsifal*, or studied the vocal score, published in 1883. Debussy certainly had studied that score by 1886, when he was composing *Printemps*. Even if we did not know that he had played excerpts four hands with Paul Vidal at a Villa Medici soirée in January of that year, we might well detect his enthusiasm for the music of the Flower Maidens, with its close parallel harmony and high, floating chromatic arabesques. We might also suspect the influence of Liszt in the occasional whole-tone writing and the way in which the second movement transforms the themes of the first, a perfectly respectable device that the assessors found "bizarre and incoherent," while preferring the movement in general, presumably for its catchy and rhythmic final tune. Liszt had visited the Villa that same January, and Debussy and Vidal had dined with him at least twice and played him his *Faust Symphony*, a performance that, sad to report, sent the old man to sleep.

It was thirteen years since the term "impressionist" had been applied satirically by the critic Louis Leroy to the 1874 Paris exhibition of the "Anonymous Society of Artist Painters, Sculptors, Printmakers, etc.," ever since universally known as the First Impressionist Exhibition. Leroy's alter ego, the academy artist M. Joseph Vincent, had stood in front of Monet's *Impression, Sunrise* and exclaimed: "*Impression*—I was certain of it. I was just telling myself that, since I was impressed, there had to be some impression in it . . . and what freedom, what ease of workmanship! Wallpaper in its embryonic state is more finished than that seascape." Monet's picture, of the sun rising over the harbour at Le Havre, with ships and gantries still shrouded in early-morning mist, two or three small boats gradually emerging from the half-light, and the water articulated mainly by flecks of red sun and other pink and grey reflections, is an example of what Richard R. Bretell has called rapid or performative painting. It's as if the eye has registered the complete image without waiting to focus on particular details. M. Vincent is also struck by Monet's *Boulevard des Capucines*. "There's impression, or I don't know what it means," he remarks. "Only, be so good as to tell me what those innumerable black tongue-lickings in the lower part of the picture represent." "Why, those are people walking along," Leroy has himself reply. "Then do I look like that when I'm walking along the boulevard des Capucines? Blood and thunder! So you're making fun of me at last?"[9]

Presumably the Academy panel was not suggesting that Debussy had composed his *Printemps* in a careless or "performative" manner. Their implication was that the effect of vagueness in the harmony and vocal writing was a deliberate, carefully contrived evasion of the clear outlines of classical form and harmonic grammar, just as Impressionist painting dodged the issue of precise and well-formed representation. There seems as yet to be no suggestion that the music is trying to represent spring or its attributes in a misty or approximate—"impressionistic"—way, like that of Monet's paintings. There is, though, the same sense of outrage at the overriding of those hallowed techniques and principles that, when all was said and done, the Academy existed to protect and perpetuate. Blood and thunder! So he was making fun of them at last . . .

As far as we can tell, Debussy had shown no particular interest in the Impressionists up to this time. Once, during his stay at the Villa Medici, he had burst out with "I've had enough of the Eternal City . . . I want to see some Manet and hear some Offenbach."[10] But these sound like generic terms for "French art rather than Italian." His own music had scarcely touched on the kind of outdoor subject matter favoured by Monet, Pissarro and Co., except in the conventional sense that rustling leaves or the moonlight or "the winter sky where the sun wandered among white mists" stood for fragile passion or lost love. He had recently been exploring similar themes with increasing precision and individuality in a further group of settings of poems by Verlaine (this time from his *Romances sans paroles*) whose intensity of imagery had led to a concentration of musical language very different from the somewhat gushing effusions of the *envois*.

The first two of these songs, "L'Ombre des arbres" and "Chevaux de bois" were composed in Paris in January 1885, in the weeks before he left for Rome. "L'Ombre des arbres" is another song, like "En sourdine," that seems to isolate an aspect of Wagner's musical language and use it as a microscope for the close examination of a moment in sensual time. Again the source is *Tristan und Isolde*, but in this case the music of the prelude to the first act. Wagner's opening, with its cello minor sixth, its famous dissonant chord, and its rising chromatic oboe figure, is itself notoriously incomplete, an image of unresolved and irresoluble passion, but Debussy narrows it down still further, while to some extent jumbling its elements. Thus his very first chord (without the cello lead-in) is Wagner's, up a tone and with G sharp instead of G natural, to which the G sharp descends in the next bar. Meanwhile the melody borrows the last two notes of Wagner's oboe figure, rising then descending altogether seven times in this short song. Other figures in the song also recall Wagner's prelude, without ever hinting at its discourse.

In Verlaine's poem, the idea of unsatisfiable love, resolved in death after four hours or so of the opera, is encapsulated in the three final words: "Tes espérances noyées" ("Your drowned hopes"). Debussy has evidently sought a musical idea of comparable economy and intensity, and found it in his portmanteau quotation from *Tristan*. The rest of the poem prepares this moment. At first the image does have an almost Impressionist flavour: the shadow of the trees on the mist-shrouded river dies like smoke. But then the turtle-doves moan in the treetops, like an echo of the pale traveller's "drowned hopes" (an inscription from *Cyrano de Bergerac* suggests that they see their reflections in the water and imagine themselves drowning), and the Impressionist's cool objectivity is swallowed up in the elegiac instant.

Like the earlier "En sourdine," "L'Ombre des arbres" effectively takes a sharp knife to Wagner's discourse, and slices out a single harmonic incident—a moment without past or future, endlessly relived. "Chevaux de bois" invokes a different kind of recurrence, the simple image of the fairground roundabout, with wooden horses that gallop but get nowhere in a big circle. In "L'Ombre des arbres" Debussy had neutralised Wagner's harmonic grammar; in "Chevaux de bois" he avoids grammatical harmony altogether. The song is, aptly enough, a rondo. Each time the horses come round, their "Tournez, tournez" is in a different key. But the piano chords and arpeggios follow the melody slavishly wherever it goes. They are its shadow, a melody of chords, never a harmony. The alternate verses (the episodes in the rondo form) use a slightly varied form of the same technique. But still there is no harmony, only chords.

A year later Debussy again turned to Verlaine and composed one or possibly two further songs from the *Romances sans paroles*: "Green," which is specifically dated January 1886, and "Spleen," which has no date. Verlaine called these poems "Aquarelles" (watercolours), but as before the objects painted—the fruit and flowers, the leaves and branches of "Green," the roses and ivy and holly of "Spleen"— are mere excuses for talk of love, hopeful in "Green," despairing in "Spleen." At the Villa Medici there was a visiting couple, the Hochons, friends of the Director, Ernest Hébert; and Mme Hochon, in Lesure's words, was "a pretty woman, notably in search of adventure, [who] stirred things up a good deal at the Villa."[11] It was for the Hochons that Debussy and Vidal played extracts from *Parsifal*, and Lesure is tempted to surmise that the "latest kisses" of "Green," and its "heart that beats only for you," were no longer set to music with thoughts of Mme Vasnier so much as in the presence of Mme Hochon. Not being sure of the date of "Spleen," he resists speculating that the weariness of "everything, except you, alas!" in that song has the same object. It is, certainly, a tempting thought.

"Green" is one of Debussy's most sophisticated songs to date, an intriguing mixture of the naive and the suggestive. The poet arrives "still covered with dew" but is soon resting his head on her "young breast . . . allowing it repose from the good storm," a storm that is, we may deduce, strictly non-meteorological. The harmony is a fluid blend of the modal and the chromatic—the simple and the intricate. But perhaps the most striking feature is the rhythm. Debussy picks up an ambiguity in the poem's metre, between duple and triple, and uses it to contrast the vocal line, predominantly duple, with the piano, which is more often triple (in six-eight). The smooth flow of the voice's twos against the piano's threes introduces an element of suavity into the dance-like piano figuration, and goes with the tendency of the harmony to complicate matters as the words hint at double meanings.

"Spleen" returns to the obsessive tone of "L'Ombre des arbres," reflecting the extraordinary concentration of Verlaine's poem, with its tapestry of colours and surfaces—red, black, blue, green, the varnished foliage, the shining box tree—and its clusters of internal rhymes: "toutes rouges," "tu te bouges," "du luisant buis je suis las," etc. In the music, the neurosis is expressed through the haunted repetition of the piano's opening figure, which comes seven times, usually at the same pitch. The harmony is densely chromatic, almost Hugo Wolf-like, but like the poet's spirits it fails to move, and at the end the singer's "Hélas"—detached by two slow bars from the "fors de vous" ("except you")—rings heavy against the piano's same old weary motive, resolving at last into its morose, comfortless home key of F minor.

The two remaining songs of what would initially be published in 1888 as *Ariettes* (and republished in 1903 as *Ariettes oubliées*) were composed just as he was leaving the Villa in March 1887, either in Rome or already back in Paris. Though written last, they start the cycle in its published form, as they do Verlaine's *Romances sans paroles*. "C'est l'extase," the opening song, sets the tone of suspended erotic animation that will return in "L'Ombre des arbres" and "Spleen." Debussy retains Verlaine's motto, a quotation from Charles Simon Favart:

> Le vent dans la plaine
> Suspend son haleine.

> (The wind in the plain holds its breath.)

With Verlaine, it's a case of "languorous ecstasy" and "amorous fatigue," and "all the tremors of the woods in the embrace of the breezes." The music, "slow and caressing," recreates the mood at once in a string of ninth chords, standard dissonances that would normally resolve, but that here merely subside without resolution, detumescent, descending twice in pitch and volume before twice rising against the phrase "C'est la fatigue amoureuse," a musical image at least as graphic as the words themselves.

The languor of "Il pleure dans mon coeur," played out against a fluttering semiquaver ostinato for the incessant patter of raindrops, is a different matter altogether, since—as the poet informs us in some puzzlement—it is "without love and without hate," the worst kind of heartsickness, without apparent cause. This inexplicable listlessness is beautifully caught in Debussy's floating left-hand melody, part modal, part chromatic, against which the voice duets in similar vein, later picking up and varying the original tune. The assonances of the poem take on an almost hypnotic flavour, intensified by Debussy's smooth, crotchet-by-crotchet setting, the accentless French drifting wanly across the barlines.

In these six songs, it seems that Debussy is beginning to evolve an individual language that in various respects moves against the conventional processes of classical and romantic music—the music that, in his day, formed more or less the entire substance of the concert and operatic repertoire. Revolutionary it is not. The songs are all perfectly tonal; mostly they begin and end in the one key, like any well-behaved Schubert lied, though Debussy, in these and earlier songs, for some reason favours remote keys, usually with many sharps, but occasionally many flats, as in "Green."

But he is less interested in tonal processes as such. A classical piece is like a well-told story, with a number of narrative threads, locations and characters that must all be tied up and reconciled in a coherent way. These Debussy songs are more like pictures, images drawn in notes and intensified by the repetition of brief, self-contained units, like the ninth chords in "C'est l'extase," the Wagner near-quotations in "L'Ombre des arbres," or the obsessive leitmotif in "Spleen." There is a curious sense of immobility about this music, a sense of peering into deep water. Even in more obviously mobile pieces such as "Il pleure dans mon coeur" or "Chevaux de bois" there is something either hypnotic or mechanical or circular about the motion—movement without a destination. Of course, the music does in reality proceed to a conclusion, carried along, however, not so much by harmony (as in Bach, Mozart and Wagner) as by melody and rhythm. French music, with its *ballet de cour* tradition of melody and dance, had been to some extent led astray by the challenge of Beethoven, the overpowering influence of German symphonic music in general, and now the lure of the Wagner music drama. But the melody-and-dance line could still be traced from Lully and Rameau, through Berlioz and most recently Gabriel Fauré, composers whose music, like the French language, avoided the more controlling features of German music, the strong upbeat–downbeat accentuation, the fiercely directional harmony, the dense thematic argument. Debussy was conscious of these matters and was becoming self-conscious about his own place in that particular history. The *Ariettes oubliées* were not yet a decisive step, but they were a good start for a twenty-three- or twenty-four-year-old composer fighting his way out of an academic impasse.

Just how far the *Ariettes* were affected by the particular character of Verlaine's poetry can be seen by comparing them with the more conventional settings Debussy made of other poets during his time in Rome: for instance, a further pair of beautiful romances to words by Bourget, "L'âme évaporée et souffrante" and "Les Cloches," exquisitely written pieces that could as well be by Gounod or Massenet. Debussy was clearly at a stage where he needed strong influences, and if he was unable to find them in contemporary French music, well, he would have to look elsewhere. The obvious direction in music was by way of Wagner. But though for a time overwhelmed by the beauty, especially, of *Tristan*, and though continuously fascinated by aspects of Wagner's style and subject matter, he quickly saw the danger of the intense addiction—the Wagnerolatry—to which the German master's French musician admirers were prone. On his second visit to Bayreuth in 1889, he wrote somewhat caustically to Guiraud about *The Ring*:

> What bores, these leitmotifs! What sempiternal catapults! Why didn't Wagner sup with Pluto after finishing *Tristan* and *The Mastersingers*? The *Ring*, which has pages that bowl me over, is a box of tricks. It even takes the colour out of my dear *Tristan*, and it grieves me to feel that I'm becoming detached from it.[12]

But if contemporary music offered him nothing much beyond a few slices of harmony, literature and art were another matter. At the Conservatoire he had been reading avidly and to some extent distancing himself from the company of his fellow music students. At the Villa Medici he was in touch with a Paris bookseller called Émile Baron, who regularly sent him the *Revue indépendante*, a recently reinstituted journal of literature and the arts with a strong affiliation with Symbolist writers such as Huysmans, Villiers de l'Isle-Adam and Mallarmé, and—from 1886—a close association with the *Revue wagnérienne*. Debussy's letters to Baron include remarks about recent plays and novels and requests for books, notably Huysmans's *Croquis parisiens*, the *Cantilènes* of the Symbolist poet Jean Moréas, and Félix Rabbe's translation of the complete Shelley. Presumably he read all these things, among much else. He will have learned, or guessed, the connection between symbolism and music, specifically Wagner, and noted the importance of Verlaine to the younger Moréas. Symbolism, as expounded by Moréas in *Le Figaro* in September 1886, sought to avoid the description of things and events, but to use them as a channel to feelings and ideal states. As Moréas expressed it, in his elusive way:

> In this art, scenes from nature, the actions of human beings, any concrete phenomenon, would not be presented in themselves; here they are perceptible appearances for the purpose of representing their esoteric affinities with primordial ideas.[13]

Essentially this might be taken as a somewhat roundabout definition of music, at least of programme music or the setting of words. It recalls Beethoven's famous description of his "Pastoral" Symphony: "more an expression of feeling than painting." Debussy himself had spelt this out less naively in a letter to Vasnier, probably even before his acquaintance with Baron, talking about his reasons for abandoning *Zuleima*:

> I shall always prefer something where, to some extent, the action is sacrificed to the extended expression of the feelings of the soul. It seems to me that music can make itself more human, more lived, that one can excavate and refine the means of expression.[14]

But it applies with special force to such a work as Wagner's *Tristan und Isolde*, which not only functions in that way as art, but uses it as subject matter. In *Tristan* the world is illusion, and only feeling, specifically love, is real. In Debussy's Verlaine songs something similar is in the air, albeit in a highly concentrated, even elliptical form. On one level, this is merely the Romantic idea of Nature as expressing or colluding with the sorrows and joys of love, as in so many of the earlier songs. But in fact love is not a strong presence in the *Ariettes*, treated metaphorically in "C'est l'extase," specifically denied in "Il pleure dans mon coeur" ("What! no betrayal?"), and unmentioned in "L'Ombre des arbres" or "Chevaux de bois." Even in "Spleen" the despair seems to go beyond lost love in the direction of what the Greeks called acedia and Christians call sloth, the spiritual emptiness that prevents us from seeing any point in even the most beautiful or fulfilling things. Whether one should categorise as "symbolism" a work that creates an intense, even heavy atmosphere out of commonplace objects or feelings is a question we shall confront a little later.

Back in Paris in March 1887, Debussy at twenty-four could for the first time in his life consider himself a free agent, no longer completely subject to the rules of the parental home (though he still lived there), the Conservatoire or the Villa Medici. It's true that there was still the emotional issue of Marie Vasnier, fading but not quite extinguished, and at home there remained pressures, partly financial, partly moral. To put it crudely, Achille was by no means self-supporting, even without his appreciable spending on books and knick-knacks of one kind or another. In April his father once again lost his job and was once more—or still—hoping that his talented, prize-winning son would soon turn his academic and artistic successes into compensatory hard currency. This would remain an issue between them at least until Achille left home in October 1890.

Then there was the matter of the *envois*, of which a third was still needed. The first two had given him nothing but trouble, partly because the sort of work required was not the sort he had been wanting to compose, or else not what he had been technically capable of. *Diane au bois* had clearly fallen into the latter category; he had deliberately chosen Banville's delicately sensuous account (from Ovid) of the seduction of Diana by Eros because, he told Vasnier, "it in no way recalls the poems used for *envois*, which are basically nothing but perfected cantatas." But he had failed to find a musical image for Diana herself; it would need "a beautiful coldness, not arousing any idea of passion; with Diana, love only comes much later, and is fundamentally no more than an accident."[15] There is a lot to be said for Richard Langham Smith's suggestion that in the third *envoi*, a partial setting of Dante Gabriel Rossetti's poem "The Blessed Damozel," he at last found the music for these attributes, and in so doing clinched the basis of his own mature style.[16]

At what point he decided on Rossetti is unclear. It might even have been under the influence of his seventeen-year-old brother, Alfred, who had translated Rossetti's poem "The Staff and Scrip" and had his French version published in the *Revue indépendante* in November 1887. Achille must have known about this work in advance. But both brothers probably became aware of Rossetti as a poet through Gabriel Sarrazin's French translation of "The Blessed Damozel," as "La Damoiselle élue," which came out in 1885 in his volume *Les Poètes modernes de l'Angleterre*. The Pre-Raphaelites were already known, though not yet well known, in France as painters, through book illustrations and occasional photographic reproductions. But Langham Smith is surely guessing when he suggests that Debussy "almost certainly saw" the Moxon edition of Tennyson, with its numerous Pre-Raphaelite illustrations. The composer, after all, knew no English, and would not naturally have interested himself in English poetry unless his attention was specifically drawn to the illustrations.

Langham Smith must be right, though, that Pre-Raphaelite imagery and discourse were close to Debussy's artistic needs at this moment. Though he had not yet seen *Tristan* or *Parsifal* staged when he embarked on his third *envoi*, he knew both scores well and had—presumably—warmed to their medieval settings and symbolism, whatever doubts he might have begun to harbour about their grandiloquence of scale and utterance. His experience with *Diane au bois* suggests that he was "searching for characters more detached and respectful in the face of passion, characters imbued by a dimly construed ideal of courtly love."[17] For Diana herself he had wanted "a beautiful coldness," and now here is Rossetti's Damozel, "her eyes deeper than the depth of waters stilled at even," the very image of cool but intense desire, and surrounded by symbols of purity, three lilies in her hand, seven stars in her hair, and on her dress "a white rose of Mary's gift." That curious association of sanctity, antiquity and latent sensuality so characteristic of Rossetti's Pre-Raphaelitism must have struck a chord with Debussy just when he was drawn towards the French Symbolist poets and, like them, in search of a personal and selective solution to the influence of Wagner.

La Damoiselle élue, a twenty-minute cantata for two female soloists, women's chorus and orchestra, is not at its core a Wagnerian work, though it does from time to time feel like a translation of Wagner, specifically *Parsifal*, into French. The slow root-position (keynote at the bottom) chords of the opening at once invoke some ancient church rite, and the image is enhanced when the choir enters, unaccompanied, chanting Rossetti's first stanza in block harmony, "God's choristers" to the life. But the layout of the long orchestral introduction before this entry was surely prompted by a study of the *Parsifal* prelude in the vocal score. Here, as there, a slow, quiet opening is followed, *subito*, by a highly ornate response, the two elements then repeated at a different pitch (a third higher in Wagner, a third lower in Debussy), followed by a more extended episode in six-four time. Yet the similarity is more visual than aural. It's as if Debussy had the look and feel of the *Parsifal* score in his mind, then simply mapped his own music on to it.

There are admittedly Wagnerisms elsewhere. The sharp contrast between the pure, almost too sweet diatonic music that prevails and the richer chromaticism of the brief episodes in which the Damozel indulges her yearning for her beloved to be with her in heaven is a faint echo of the shadows that pass across Wagner's score whenever Amfortas in his agony confronts the purity of the Grail. Above all the texture and pacing of Debussy's work, so unlike those of the average Gallic melodrama, suggest an acute grasp of the flavour of late Wagner. What he was perhaps unconsciously appropriating was the general rhetoric and atmosphere of an alien masterpiece that, however hard he might eventually try, he was never quite able to get out of his system.[18]

La Damoiselle élue may not itself be a masterpiece, but it was an important work for its composer, his first large-scale composition in a style that he could call his own. Some elements would even come in handy later. The archaic opening clearly foreshadows his opera, *Pelléas et Mélisande*, and the second episode is a curious anticipation of the first movement of *La Mer*. Most striking, though, are the lucid harmony—much of it modal or plain, white-note diatonic—and the beautiful, transparent orchestration, which hints at Debussy's later description of the orchestra in *Parsifal* itself, as "lit from behind." He first heard *Parsifal* in the orchestral flesh when he went to Bayreuth in July 1888, probably before *La Damoiselle élue* was complete, and certainly his own orchestration has something of precisely that quality. Harmonically the piece is notable mainly for its rejection of the advanced chromatics that were already beginning, in the 1870s and 1880s, to complicate the issue of tonality in some parts of late Wagner, Liszt and the youthful works of Richard Strauss, Mahler and others of that generation. Chromatic harmony there is, but purely as an occasional cloud on the prevailing celestial blue. In this respect *La Damoiselle élue* implies, if it doesn't wholly embody, a new kind of modernism, one that sidesteps, rather than pursues, the wretched implications of an endlessly progressive harmonic language. Not surprisingly, the academicians were distinctly cool in its praise. "The chosen text," one of them grumbled,

> is in prose and tolerably obscure; but the music adapted to it lacks neither poetry nor charm, though still affected by those fashionable systematic tendencies in expression and form with which the Academy has already had occasion to reproach the composer. Here, however, his inclinations and procedures show up more reservedly and seem, up to a point, justified by the very nature and indeterminate character of the subject.[19]

No doubt these remarks will have convinced Debussy that he was on the right track.

Musical life in Paris in the late 1880s had become all too familiar in character. Lesure quotes Chabrier grumbling about the unchanging fare: Gounod and Saint-Saëns at the Opéra, Massenet at the Opéra-Comique, Vincent d'Indy working on some masterpiece he'd been at for two years. Nothing new at the Concerts Lamoureux. "They all grow fat, and nobody rocks the boat; [Lamoureux] calmly patches up his old programmes, and the bourgeoisie come running. The time is past for serious efforts."[20] Debussy sometimes attended concerts and the opera, but had become choosey in his musical friendships. Of his Conservatoire friends, he remained close only to the older Raymond Bonheur and the younger Paul Dukas, a fellow pupil of Guiraud's

in the early 1880s, and he found a friend in the composer Ernest
Chausson, a board member of the Société Nationale de Musique
(SNM), to which Debussy was admitted as a member early in 1888.
But his most enduring new friendship of this time was with a twenty-
one-year-old Swiss journalist, novelist and musicologist by the name
of Robert Godet, a keen Wagnerite with whom Debussy coincided
at Bayreuth in 1888 and 1889, and whose subsequent career as a foreign political correspondent for *Le Temps* took him to London, then
permanently back to Switzerland. Godet and Debussy became close
early on, as their Paris exchanges show, but it was much later—with
Godet safely out of the Paris aquarium—that Debussy's letters to
him become revealing in detail about his work and attitudes, something approaching an artistic confessional to this son of a Swiss pas-
tor.[21]

In the main, however, Debussy had already had quite enough of
Paris institutional life and was soon directing his steps elsewhere. He
began to frequent various bistros and cafés: Chez Pousset, a theatrical and artistic establishment in the ninth arrondissement known
to its regulars as the "cul de bouteille" (the bottom of the barrel), a
Left Bank bistro called Chez Thommen, and the Café Vachette in the
Latin Quarter. These were variously the haunts of painters, writers,
actors and musicians of rather less regular habits and turns of mind.
At Pousset's he probably met the novelist and playwright Villiers
de l'Isle-Adam, and certainly the louche, satyr-like figure of Catulle
Mendès, a one-time associate of the Parnassians, these days an intemperate Wagnerite, and a self-appointed cult figure who would arrive
at the "petit Pousset" surrounded by "young men whom he believed
to be his disciples."[22] At the Café Vachette Debussy would have long,
probably somewhat inebriated discussions with Jean Moréas, supposedly about Schopenhauer and Goethe, but surely also about Verlaine
and Moréas's other Symbolist friends. At Thommen's he would talk
about painting and poetry far into the night with the art historian
Gabriel Mourey. And all the time he was forming connections, albeit
largely with artists of the second rank, that would bring him into contact with an alternative world of art and literature far from the orbit
of the Conservatoire, the Opéra or the Concerts Lamoureux.

It was probably at this time that he set a scene from Villiers's Symbolist play, *Axël,* music that has unfortunately never resurfaced but

is likely to have had a Wagnerian flavour, in view of the more or less overt Wagnerism of the play itself, whose hero and heroine decide that their love is too good for this world, drink poison and die ecstatically in each other's arms. Debussy paid his first visit to Bayreuth in 1888 (for *Parsifal* and *Die Meistersinger*), then went again in 1889 and saw *Tristan* for the first time. He was already well aware of the possibilities and dangers of Wagnerism as it was starting to be reflected conventionally in the harmonic language and formal continuities of the music of his French composer colleagues. But the Wagnerism of the Paris cafés was a rather different matter. Talk there will have been less about unresolved dissonance and the symphonic treatment of the leitmotif, more about the intense, saturated atmosphere that seemed to these poets, painters and theatre people to be uniquely within the reach of music, and especially *this* music, so rich in meanings and feelings beyond those of the mere words. As early as 1861 the poet Charles Baudelaire had tried to articulate this kind of response in a long article in the *Revue Européenne*, after hearing Wagner conduct excerpts from his works in Paris early in 1860, then *Tannhäuser* complete at the Opéra in March 1861. Listening to the prelude to *Lohengrin*, and before knowing its specific subject matter, he had felt "released *from the bonds of gravity*, and rediscovering in memory the extraordinary sensuality that circulates in *high places*."

> Next I involuntarily painted for myself the delicious state of a man visited by a great dream in an absolute solitude, but a solitude with *an immense horizon* and a *broadly diffuse light*; *immensity* without decor other than itself. Soon I experienced the sensation of a livelier *irradiation, of an intensity of light* that grew with such rapidity that the shades of meaning in a dictionary would not suffice to express this *constantly renewed increase in heat and whiteness*. Then I conceived plain the idea of a soul in motion in a luminous medium, of an ecstasy *formed out of sensuality and consciousness*, and hovering far above the natural world.[23]

The concept of abstraction "without décor," of fantasy released from the gravity of objects and concrete meanings, was taken up by the Symbolists and converted into verse and, no doubt, more or less airy conversation. But such things were hardly Debussy's style. In his Verlaine settings he had turned them back into music of a certain precision, and Baudelaire himself, who had died in 1867, had himself already distilled them into concise, vivid poetry in his *Fleurs du mal*, published ten years earlier, before this latest encounter with Wagner. "La Mort des amants" ("The Lovers' Death"), the first Baudelaire poem Debussy set (in December 1887), is an uncanny pre-echo of the as yet unwritten *Liebestod* in *Tristan und Isolde*. Wagner's "waves of blissful fragrance surging and rushing around" are foreshadowed in Baudelaire's "beds full of light odours" and "couches deep as tombs," on which

> Our two hearts will be two vast flaming torches
> That reflect their double light
> In our two spirits, those twin mirrors.

But the poem is brief, a sonnet; and Debussy's setting is no more than discreetly Wagnerian, mildly chromatic in harmony, but completely without the Wagnerian elevation of tone in its three minutes or so, and not once rising above the *mezzo-piano* of the final phrase, where Baudelaire's angel comes to restore "the tarnished mirrors and the dead flames."

A month or so later, however, Debussy took up a longer and more leisurely poem from *Les Fleurs du mal*, "Le Balcon" ("The Balcony"), and set it at a pace to some extent dictated by the poem's unusual form of six five-line verses, in which the last line of each verse is an exact (or, in the final verse, nearly exact) repeat of the first. From the first bar of the broad piano introduction you feel the steady, purposeful tread of an extended discourse, and suddenly Debussy's language is borrowing the long line and effusive phraseology of, for example, Wagner's *Wesendonck-Lieder* (songs he may or may not have known). "Le Balcon" may be Wagner through a French filter; the dynamic level is generally subdued, with only a couple of *forte* markings and many indications of *piano* or less; the harmony is a mix-ture of grammar *à la* Wagner and colour chording as in "Chevaux de bois." Yet with all these personal, Gallic touches, "Le Balcon" leaves an aftertaste of stylistic struggle, a sense of being not quite free from an influence that might have been better avoided. And certainly for the singer the piece is eight and a half minutes of quasi-Wagnerian intensity that can leave him or her, and the audience as well, gasping for breath at the start of what became the *Cinq poèmes de Baudelaire*, with "Le Balcon" at its head.

By the time he again turned to Baudelaire in January 1889, having composed much or all of the Petite Suite and probably tinkered with *Axël* in between, he had actually attended Bayreuth and heard *Parsifal* and *Die Meistersinger von Nürnberg* at first hand. Curiously enough, the experience seems to have helped him assimilate the Wagner sound into a discourse more recognisably his own. "Harmonie du soir" ("Evening Harmony") is a more concise poem than "Le Balcon," but with a still more schematic form in which lines two and four of each of the four verses become lines one and three of the next. This tight design, which effectively requires each line to be a self-contained unit, was evidently useful for Debussy in forcing him to concentrate on the poetic images and their musical equivalents, in a way that to some extent recalled the pool-like depths of the *Ariettes*. It probably also helped that several of Baudelaire's images are themselves musical: "the sounds and perfumes [that] turn in the evening air"; the "melancholy waltz," "the violin [that] quivers like a heart in distress." The one Wagnerian element in all this is the almost symphonic character of the piano accompaniment, which binds together the laconic series of individual poetic lines through a set of brief motives: a little triplet turn, a rising figure ending in a sighing descent (an appoggiatura, or dissonant "leaning note," that then resolves downwards), and later a tiny three-note waltz motif, presumably prompted by Baudelaire's "Valse mélancolique et langoureux vertige."

Although this piano part is perhaps over-elaborate, it contains a number of anticipations of the later Debussy, both in specific motives and in the general ability to invest tiny figures with a strong symbolic meaning. For instance, the waltz figure—quaver, dotted quaver, semiquaver—will return in the first movement of *La Mer*, and as a crucial motive in the sketches for the unfinished opera *The Fall of the House of Usher*, each time with a completely different signification. These are not quite leitmotifs in the Wagnerian sense; they don't stand for specific allusions in the poem (though they may be prompted by them) so much as for the image and atmosphere of the poem as a whole. But they do tend to saturate the texture in a Wagnerian way. Similarly the harmony ("du soir") feels as if filtered through parts of

Tristan und Isolde, absorbing its colours but not its processes. Here, as to some extent in the *Ariettes*, Debussy dwells on individual chords or chord groups that in Wagner might be simply staging posts. A feature of his method is to anchor the harmony with fixed pedal notes while the upper harmonies undergo minor adjustments that are more like ways of exploring a particular terrain than attempts to find a way out of it. Each line of the poem is a terrain in this sense, and this idea of a song divided into "rooms" is enhanced by the line repetitions, which Debussy largely honours in the vocal line, while each time varying the texture but not essentially the harmony of the accompaniment.

Within a few months he completed his cycle of five songs by composing "Le Jet d'eau" ("The Fountain") and "Recueillement" ("Meditation"). "Recueillement," a sonnet like "La Mort des amants," likewise inspired a discreetly Wagnerian setting, starting with near-quotations from *Tristan*, somewhat in the manner of "L'Ombre des arbres," but then settling into passages of intense stillness in which the chromatics seem to polarise into terrains where they lose any forward tendency in favour of harmonies that are essentially inert. Here, for the first time, he makes substantial use of whole-tone harmony—harmony that, because it lacks semitones, lacks that onward push that we associate with tonal music. Debussy found these harmonies, this time, in Wagner as well as Liszt. But in Wagner they are mere incidents; the second and third chords of *Tristan* are both whole-tone, but they don't last, whereas Debussy dwells on these colours, explores them, enjoys them for their own sake, as Liszt and the Russian *kuchka* had sometimes done. Another kind of stillness is that of the simple common chord in its root position, the chord, or triad, that ends almost every tonal work ever written. Baudelaire's wonderful images of "the dead years leaning over the balconies of heaven in outworn garments" and the sweet nightfall "trailing eastwards like a long shroud" suggest to Debussy a solemn sequence of these triads, deathly calm and almost motionless. In between, "smiling Regret rises up from the watery deep," and suddenly, briefly, we are in the world of *La Cathédrale engloutie*, the sunken cathedral of Debussy's famous prelude, rising from the ocean to the tolling of parallel piano triads.

"Le Jet d'eau" offers a more delicate and at the same time sensuous image of water, the splashing of fountains that "maintains sweetly the ecstasy in which love has this evening immersed me." This is the least Wagnerian of the five songs and in some respects the most refined. A more potent influence, it has been plausibly suggested, was Borodin's song "The Sea Princess," whose heroine lures travellers into an eternal watery orgasm to the soft clashing of whole-tone dissonances like the ones that open Debussy's song. Baudelaire's poem this time is in verse-and-refrain form, creating a kind of trance state to go with the graphic metaphors of lovemaking, the girl's senses ("âme," literally "soul") "scorched by the lightning-flash of pleasure" and soaring "swiftly and boldly towards the vast enchanted skies."

Taken as a whole, the *Cinq poèmes de Baudelaire* were a big achievement for the (in the end) twenty-seven-year-old composer. They were more ambitious than the Verlaine settings, and perhaps more uneven. They certainly covered more stylistic ground, and in the process Debussy emerged as a master who could penetrate musically the astoundingly rich and suggestive imagery of France's greatest nineteenth-century poet without his music ever seeming diminished or inadequate in this exalted company. By any standards, and with momentary exceptions, these are wonderfully beautiful songs, but they are also subtle and resonant, images of sensual consciousness that elevate the soul as well as the body, the mind as much as the heart. They prepared him for still greater projects. The only problem would be to track them down, and carry them out to his satisfaction.

4

New Rules, Old Morals

For Parisians, the great event of 1889 was the Exposition Universelle, held on and around the Champ de Mars and Les Invalides
between May and November to mark the centenary of the storming
of the Bastille and the start of the French Revolution. It was the fourth
World's Fair in the French capital since 1855, and like its predecessors
it combined a sense of confidence in the robustness of French culture
and the French nation—notwithstanding their somewhat chequered
recent history—with a vivid awareness of the world outside, which
was somehow seen as clinching Paris's status as the cultural centre
of the universe. You entered the 1889 exhibition under the world's
tallest structure, the newly built Eiffel Tower, and found yourself
suddenly in a small town of buildings and exhibits, dominated at the
far end of the central boulevard by the grand dome of the huge iron-
framed Galerie des Machines.

Such buildings, and the machinery and military weaponry they
housed, symbolised the aggressive optimism that was one aspect of
the great nineteenth-century exhibitions. But no less characteristic
were what we would now call ethnic but were at that time described
as colonial displays, which, as one reporter put it, "For the first time
[brought] vividly to the appreciation of the Frenchmen that they are
masters of lands beyond the sea."[1] This was a splendid but at best
fairly loose claim. Just as the 1867 exhibition had included Hungarian
Gypsy musicians and a pavilion of exhibits from Japan, never a French
(nor any other European) colony, so the 1889 fair had performances
by dancers and a gamelan orchestra from (not French) Java alongside a specially constructed theatre for Annamite performers from
(French) Indo-China—present-day Vietnam. The great exhibits of
the 1867 fair were a bitter memory to Frenchmen who recalled that
its show of confidence had been rapidly cancelled out by the disaster

of the Franco-Prussian War and the Commune. But to artists, 1867 had meant Japan and the detailed exploration of the range and refinement of Japanese prints, a rich source of inspiration ever since. In the same way the Annamite Theatre and Javanese dancers and gamelan orchestra attracted musicians not because they reminded them of France beyond the sea, but precisely because they did not.

Exactly when Debussy visited the exhibition is not known, but that these Asian musical and theatrical performances made a deep impression on him is clear. He recalled them later on a couple of much quoted occasions. "Remember," he wrote to Pierre Louÿs in 1895, "the Javanese music that contained every nuance, even those one can no longer name, in which tonic and dominant were no longer anything but empty ghosts for use on naughty little children."[2] And nearly twenty years after that he recalled the "embryonic opera" of the Annamites, in which "a furious little clarinet directs the emotion, a gong organizes the terror . . . and that's all! No more special theatre, no more hidden orchestra. Nothing but an instinctive need for art, needing ingenuity to satisfy; no hint of bad taste!"[3]

These were lucid memories over a quarter of a century, even if the clarinet was actually a kind of oboe, called a *song-hi*. The Annamite performance or performances that Debussy saw consisted of abbreviated scenes, partly danced and with improvised dialogue, from an epic drama about a failed attempt to assassinate the king of Duong. It was accompanied from start to finish by a small ensemble consisting of a rebec-like two-stringed fiddle, a pair of oboes, a flute, a second stringed instrument, a small gong and a pair of drums, while at the other end of the "stage" (actually a flat space surrounded by raked seating) a second drummer contributed frequent loud thwacks to mark salient moments in the action. The music, like the dialogue, was largely improvised. In its ritual way, the play was violent, so the music was sometimes violent as well, though presumably more so during the mimed action and dance than during the dialogue. A contemporary observer, Julien Tiersot, admitted that he could make neither head nor tail of the harmony that resulted from the instrumental combinations (others, less restrained, described it as a cacophony). But Debussy, we can suppose, was able to detect in this obviously expert music-making a different aesthetic, which, with his growing distaste for the academic norms of conservatoire teaching and French concert life in general, excited his interest, just as the stylised, partly perspectiveless line drawing and highly selective realism of the Japanese prints had excited the young painters of the Salon des Refusés in 1867.

In the same way, the Javanese gamelan orchestra challenged the ordinary 1880s Frenchman's conception of what constituted "music," but appealed at once to the composer of "L'Ombre des arbres" and "Harmonie du soir," who was already finding his own ways of renewing the relation between harmony, counterpoint and formal design. This was admittedly a gentler challenge. The Javanese gamelan is an orchestra of tuned gongs, metallophones (large glockenspiels and the like), plus one or more melody instrument(s), perhaps a flute, or the bowed rebab that Tiersot describes in the Paris orchestra, together with a set of hand drums, which mark the pulse. Although the music is eventually energetic, it lacks raw violence. The sonority is typically refined and translucent, an exquisite tintinnabulation of metallic sounds within a static harmonic field defined by one of two fixed modes: *slendro*, which divides the octave into five roughly equal intervals, and *pelog*, which divides it into seven. But the musical texture is extremely intricate; Debussy remarked later that "Javanese music obeys laws of counterpoint that make Palestrina seem like child's play."[4] He admired Palestrina, whose music he had heard in Rome, and he probably knew nothing about what laws, if any, governed Javanese counterpoint. But his ear told him that the gamelan music was more complex than merely a glistening surface, and his fascination for oriental music needed an intellectual justification.

Compared to the Western scales and modes, with their asymmetrical arrangement of tones and semitones, the Indonesian modes are essentially symmetrical and directionless, not unlike the six-note whole-tone scale occasionally used by Glinka and Musorgsky to create an air of mystery or signal the supernatural. On the other hand, the slight variations between this or that version of *slendro* might also remotely suggest a pentatonic scale such as the one provided by the black notes of the piano, an asymmetrical scale that also lacks semitones. Debussy's later remark about the "empty ghosts" of tonic and dominant refers specifically to the gamelan modes, which, being more or less evenly spaced, have no equivalent of the dynamic relationship between the upbeat–downbeat sense of resolution in tonal music. In a sense they are atonal, though happily not in the way later understood by Schoenberg and the Second Viennese School.

Whether or not Debussy attended the Annamite or Javanese performances before the end of June, he certainly heard Nikolay Rimsky-Korsakov conduct two concerts of Russian music at the Trocadéro, also part of the Exposition, towards the end of that month. Here he was on more familiar ground. He certainly knew music by Glinka, Borodin, Balakirev and Tchaikovsky, all of whom had pieces in Rimsky-Korsakov's programmes. He may or may not have come across Musorgsky before, but in any case Rimsky-Korsakov's performance of *Night on the Bare Mountain* will certainly have been in his own reconstructed version, which makes the music more "brilliant" but smooths out its more extreme harmonic wizardries, including its use of what Musorgsky called his "chemical" scale—none other than the whole-tone scale that Glinka had also used in his opera *Ruslan and Lyudmila*. Rimsky also conducted his own *Antar* symphony, which has its own chemical scale (the so-called octatonic scale of alternating tones and semitones), among a great many other brilliancies of harmony and orchestration; and he conducted the *Polovtsian Dances* from Borodin's *Prince Igor*, whose barbarities may well have excited a different corner of Debussy's thirst for the un-French.

To crown these exotic experiences of the World's Fair, that August of 1889 Debussy paid his second visit to Bayreuth, hearing and seeing *Tristan und Isolde* for the first time complete. Perhaps it was the vividness of the recent musical events at the Exposition that prompted his remark to Guiraud about *Tristan* on his return to Paris, that "it grieves me to feel that I'm becoming detached from it."[5] But more specifically it was probably at this moment, in the autumn of 1889, that he held the first of a number of conversations with his former composition teacher that were taken down and preserved by a younger pupil of Guiraud's, Maurice Emmanuel. Emmanuel's report is so precise and musicianly as to place its authenticity beyond question, and it sums up to the letter the aesthetic position towards which Debussy seems to have been proceeding in his recent music and which had been brought into sharp focus by the Annamites and the Javanese, and maybe even by the more unseemly of Rimsky-Korsakov's Russians.

Debussy had been arguing that *Tristan* was a direct descendant of the German classics, while for Guiraud its persistent chromaticism represented a break with tradition. No! It was symphonic, just like Beethoven. Only the voice lines were new, and in Debussy's opinion there was too much singing, too much explanation. His ideal was a music that went beyond words, and his ideal poet "a poet of things half-said."

> Two associated dreams: that's the ideal. No country, no date. No scene to be set. No pressure on the musician who seeks perfection. Music rules overbearingly in the lyric theatre. They sing too much. The music kitted out too heavily. Sing when worthwhile. Monochrome. *Grisaille.* No musical developments for the sake of "developing." All wrong! A prolonged development doesn't, can't, work with words.
>
> I dream short poems; mobile scenes. To hell with the three unities! Scenes diverse in locale and character; people not discussing; enduring life, fate, etc.

Having thus distanced himself from Wagner and the classical tradition, Debussy sat at the piano and started talking temperament, that is, the different possible tunings of the notes in the octave. Everyone knew instinctively that when you sing, or play the violin or the flute or the trombone, you vary the exact pitch of any given note according to its context. This isn't just a question of singing or playing out of tune. Your B will be fractionally sharper if the next note is the C just above than if the next note is the A below. This is the way we feel melody. But it's a terrible nuisance for keyboard players, who only have one B, whichever way the music is heading. Moreover, if you try to tune a piano by the cycle of perfect—natural—fifths, it turns out, infuriatingly, that the thirteenth fifth, which ought to come back to the starting note, will actually be appreciably sharp. (In terms of the mathematical ratios of the musical intervals, this is because 1.5^{12} is slightly more than 2^7.) In Bach's day, this inconvenient fact about Nature meant that keyboard players could not play in remote sharp or flat keys, because the tuning was all over the place, and it was to solve this problem that equal temperament—the compromise tuning demonstrated in the *Well-Tempered Clavier*—was invented.

Now Debussy (the keyboard player) is saying: away with equal temperament, back to Nature. He bandies a few numbers. In natural temperament there are eighteen different notes in the octave, thirty-six possible different keys (instead of twelve and twenty-four, respectively). "You can't fool me with temperament," he boasts. And before poor Guiraud can pick himself up from the floor, he turns to rhythm. "One suffocates in rhythms." But strictly speaking it's metre he objects to: "Simple metre, compound metre: what twaddle! . . . interminable series of the one or the other, with no attempt to vary the rhythmic figures." Then finally back to keys. Major, minor, relative major, relative minor: all humbug. Music is neither major nor minor, and the mode is whatever the composer thinks it is: preferably unstable! (Shades here of the gamelan, or possibly the Annamites.)

At this point Guiraud plays a standard textbook dissonant chord (a French sixth). "When I play this," he insists, "it has to resolve."

"I should cocoa! Why does it?"

"Well, do you find this attractive?" Guiraud plays a string of parallel triads, like the ones in Debussy's "Recueillement."

"Yes! Yes! And yes!"

Then another string, more richly textured. "How do you get out of this?"

"What you played there was very nice."

"I don't say it wasn't, but it's theoretically absurd."

"There's no such thing as theory. You just have to listen. Pleasure is the rule."

But in the end Guiraud corners him on the subject of teaching. How can you teach music without some kind of theory? And Debussy has to admit that his freedom has been won through study, and that effectively all he's arguing for is a personal approach that can't in the end be reconciled with the needs of young musicians.[6]

Quite apart from what it tells us about Debussy's own attitude to his art, the conversation is revealing about the quality of his teachers. Guiraud emerges as open-minded, tolerant, amused by his former pupil's waywardness, yet evidently respectful of his talent. The picture is somewhat different from the one Debussy liked to paint of the stiff-necked Conservatoire professors (and there is evidence that others among his teachers, notably Marmontel, and to a lesser extent Lavignac and Durand, were no less tolerant and even-handed, often in the face of a good deal of provocation). It was the institution itself that adhered to rigid procedures reinforced by its obsession with competitions and prizes.

In the autumn of 1889, Debussy was still not entirely out of the clutches of the Conservatoire in this regulatory mode. He theoretically owed them a fourth *envoi*, and to fulfil the requirement he duly embarked on a concertante piece for piano and orchestra, which, perhaps in order to avoid being ticked off for not writing a concerto like Beethoven or even Saint-Saëns, he labelled *Fantaisie*, though the work is at least as concerto-like as certain of Saint-Saëns's more speculative efforts. In fact Debussy later implicitly criticised it for its conventional way of engaging the piano and the orchestra in what he called "a slightly ridiculous struggle between these two personages."[7] It was neither performed nor published in his lifetime, and although he made some moves in both respects, one senses a lack of wholehearted conviction on his part that the music was fully worthy of him in his maturity. He was personally responsible for blocking the first partial performance in April 1890 under Vincent d'Indy, who had decided, against his wishes, to play only the first movement. He simply removed the orchestral parts from the stands after the final rehearsal. And he never submitted the work as an *envoi*.

Is it an inferior piece? The *Andante* first movement opens atmospherically with a beautiful flute and oboe theme that will also turn up in a variety of guises in the linked second and third movements, a so-called cyclic device borrowed from Liszt by way of César Franck. There is striking material elsewhere, notably in the finale, which extracts its brilliant main theme from the original woodwind melody. The form itself works well enough. It is only in the character of the discourse that Debussy's later reservations begin to make sense. As soon as the piano enters, the music becomes showy in a way essentially foreign to the Debussy of the recent songs and the *Damoiselle élue*; it becomes gestural, and to some extent stereotyped in its alternation of piano and orchestra, and in its development of material: "musical developments for the sake of 'developing'," as he had put it to Guiraud. Debussy later told Edgard Varèse that he would have liked to correct these shortcomings. But he never did, nor did he ever write anything else for piano with orchestra.

There is an intriguing aspect of the *Fantaisie* that might suggest another, more interesting reason for Debussy's subsequent rejection of it. The ethnomusicologist Richard Mueller has shown, in an impressively detailed study, that the main themes and some of the harmonies and textures are directly derived from the Javanese music that Debussy had recently been hearing. It's true, as he admits, that the pentatonic and whole-tone harmony that approximate to the gamelan modes appear, sometimes in conjunction, in earlier works of Debussy. But there is something about the raw modalities of the *Fantaisie* material that suggests a conscious attempt to reproduce some of what he had heard with such excitement in the Javanese pavilion; and Mueller argues persuasively that Debussy was aware of this rawness and may have felt that he had failed to absorb the influence sufficiently well.[8]

The argument is supported by the fact that he promptly reused a slightly modified version of the finale theme in a solo piano piece somewhat bizarrely titled *Tarentelle styrienne*, and again, almost immediately, in a setting of Verlaine's "L'Échelonnement des haies," of which more below. For a brief period, the idea was an obsession and, like most obsessions, it probably lost its charm as it faded. The *Tarentelle* was one of a number of salon pieces composed in 1890 with a view, presumably, to a quick sale to a publisher, the Choudens brothers. The pieces included a *Mazurka*, a *Valse romantique*, a *Ballade (slave)*, a *Rêverie*, and a *Marche ecossaise* (commissioned by a Scottish general), all more or less equally insignificant, to the point that, when another publisher, Fromont, planned to reissue the *Rêverie* fifteen years later, Debussy told Mme Fromont, "You're wrong to bring out *Rêverie* . . . In two words, it's bad."[9] None of these pieces contains any particular echo of Java, though the march rejoices in some mild whole-tonerie and a Scottish folk song that, for once, is not pentatonic.

The one piano work of 1890 that Choudens, though they paid good money for it, did not publish was the *Suite bergamasque*, a somewhat uneven and at times awkwardly written set of four characteristic pieces that included, nevertheless, a strikingly effective prelude, an enjoyable, breezy passepied finale, and one masterpiece, the exquisite and, as it will turn out, prophetic "Clair de lune." What is it about genius that it can suddenly, amid a slew of workaday trivia, produce a miniature of such perfection that, a century and a quarter later, it remains one of the most played, most listened to, most arranged for every other conceivable and inconceivable medium? But "Clair de lune" was not merely a find in itself, it also contained the seed of a major work on which Debussy would soon embark, and that would change the course of French music.

Meanwhile, he had been persuaded by one of his Chez Pousset acquaintances, the faun-like Catulle Mendès, to set to music an opera libretto of his called *Rodrigue et Chimène*, a tale of Spanish chivalry and honour loosely based on Corneille's *Le Cid* (recently also turned into an opera by Massenet). Mendès had apparently pulled strings with Choudens to get them to publish the *Fantaisie*, and though they did not do so, they did pay for the rights. Debussy perhaps agreed to write the opera out of a sense of obligation to Mendès, though it is just as likely that he was under pressure from his parents and nourished the simple hope that it might earn him some badly needed cash. It certainly is true that *Rodrigue et Chimène* hardly looks the kind of subject that might automatically appeal to the author of the Verlaine and Baudelaire songs, or even to a composer still nursing vestiges of a passion for Wagner. In its crude plotting and facile psychology, it more closely resembles some early Verdi libretto, without the promise of Verdi's music. Debussy would work on this unlikely project for the best part of three years, before abandoning it in favour of *Pelléas et Mélisande*.

Rodrigue and Chimène are in love and will marry, with the approval of their respective fathers but, alas, Chimène's father, the still youthful General Gormaz, insults Rodrigue's more aged father, who insists that Rodrigue avenge him. In the duel that follows, Rodrigue kills Gormaz; Chimène demands reparation from the king, but when Rodrigue appears and invites her to kill him, she cannot do so, and instead declares her undying love for him. As penance, he rides off to defend Christendom against the Moor, hoping to die or else return to her arms.

Leaving aside its fatuous motivation and generally perfunctory design, the whole spirit of the drama seems alien to Debussy's emotional and intellectual world. It's true that Spain would entice him in the future, but the Spain of hot southern evenings, street noise and guitars. Mendès's Spain is closer to that of *Il trovatore*, a medieval world of castles and heroic death, meaningless feuds, frail maidens and thumping men's choruses. Debussy could respond to the love element. The opening scene, in which Rodrigue visits Chimène in her tower at dawn, draws from him music of a sensuous beauty that to some extent anticipates Pelléas's final meeting with Mélisande— the music he would write first, just as he was abandoning *Rodrigue et Chimène* for good in 1893. He could paint the dawn light, in tones that recall the Russian music he had recently been hearing, but equally the refined harmonies of "Recueillement," and even Guiraud's parallel triads that had so roused his enthusiasm. But when it came to the rowdy choruses of Gormaz's ruffians, or the confrontations between Gormaz himself and Rodrigue's decrepit old father, or Chimène's abrupt switches between vengefulness and undying love, he could do little more than handle the conventions with the competence of the trained hand and the experienced ear. At one point he wrote to Robert Godet:

> My life is sadly feverish on account of this opera, in which everything is against me, and on which my poor little pens whose colour you liked droop in sorrow. Talking of which, I'm impatient to see you and play you the two acts I've done, as I'm afraid of having won victories over myself.[10]

He did nevertheless more or less complete the opera, in outline at least, before giving it up. A few passages are missing from the manuscript in the Pierpont Morgan Library in New York, but as these are also gaps in the page numberings, the assumption is that they were composed but for some reason removed. The draft, admittedly, is partly in sketch form, and it was never orchestrated. Like other Debussy autographs, it leaves a lot of decisions untaken, or at least unindicated: decisions about key signatures, accidentals, dynamics, tempi—details that Debussy would have filled in later. Alternative vocal lines are suggested. Robert Orledge has argued that if there had been any serious possibility of a performance, Debussy would have cleared all these matters up and completed the score.[11] But in view of his attitude to the work, the circumstances in which it was abandoned, and (as we shall see) his subsequent relationship with deadlines and promised performances, this strikes me as unlikely. The completion by Edison Denisov (on a transcript by Richard Langham Smith) is skilful and sensitive, but it reveals only a profoundly uneven piece of work in which the composer himself never subsequently expressed any interest.

In general these scores completed or begun in 1890 feel like a stylistic crossroads where the signposts have been turned round or removed. It's all very well to talk about the influence of the gamelan and the Annamite Theatre, but on the one hand it was at first fairly superficial and by no means fully assimilated, and on the other hand it merely picked up existing aspects of Debussy's style. He did not need the gamelan to teach him pentatony, the whole-tone scale or modalism. They were already part of his language. Insofar as this contact with the oriental musical mind helped release him from the toils of Wagnerism and, worse, the Conservatoire, the truth is that it did so only in part and quite gradually. The appeal of Russian music was possibly almost as great, and there are places in *Rodrigue et Chimène* where undigested Russianism is momentarily almost as much in evidence as undigested orientalism in the *Fantaisie*. Yet at the same time he was composing miniatures—potboiling or otherwise—that show no trace of any of these influences.

As in his music, so in his life: 1890 was a year of change and, in some ways, instability. It was the year in which he altered the preferred form of his Christian name from Achille to Claude-Achille; the year in which he met a certain Gabrielle Dupont, a beautiful girl of twenty-four from Normandy, with auburn hair and green eyes, with whom he would in due course form a serious liaison. In October he moved temporarily out of his parents' apartment and in with his friend the financier Étienne Dupin in the boulevard Malesherbes. Perhaps it was to Dupin that he scribbled a note: "Dear friend, forgive me, but could you lend me 20 francs until the end of the month: urgent necessity for my basic needs. I'm very ashamed at writing to you, but I'm *desperately hungry*."[12] Yet it was at this precise juncture that he made the acquaintance of the great Symbolist poet Stéphane Mallarmé. Mallarmé had been shown Debussy's Baudelaire songs, and had been so struck by them that he wanted to invite the composer to write incidental music for a stage presentation of his long poem "L'Après-midi d'un faune." In due course this performance was announced for the end of February 1891, and Debussy planned a three-part contribution: "Prélude—Interlude—Paraphrase Finale."

But whether he composed any music at this point is not known, since the performance was called off by Mallarmé a fortnight before the scheduled date, and was never rescheduled.

Gaby Dupont had arrived in Paris from her native Lisieux two or three years earlier and had taken up with a *roué* aristocrat, the Comte de Villeneuve, more or less in the role of a not particularly stylish cocotte. Exactly how and under what circumstances Debussy extracted her from Villeneuve's clutches is not recorded. Perhaps she had simply been cast adrift. She must in any case have fallen in love with him, since she effectively gave up the comfortable if emotionally empty life of a courtesan for the questionable pleasure of darning his socks and sharing (not to mention preparing) his sometimes extremely frugal meals. She would stay with him for some eight years, often under extreme provocation, as will be related in due course. And though Debussy later contracted more superficially regular liaisons, there are grounds for supposing that his association with Gaby was the closest to his heart, the most honest, for better or worse, the one that best suited his need for a helpmeet who would endure his single-minded obsession with his creative work and uncomplainingly share his bed and bohemian lifestyle.[13]

The meeting with Mallarmé opened doors of a very different kind for him, doors that would broaden his literary and artistic horizons even more than Chez Pousset or the Café Vachette had done. It secured him an entrée to Mallarmé's *jour fixe*, his Tuesdays, which since the mid-1880s had been a magnet for writers of every kind, as well as selected artists and the occasional musician. How often Debussy went is unclear, but that he went is certain. Some of the regulars he might have known already. Others were new, and would in some cases become important to him: poets such as Henri de Régnier and Pierre Louÿs, possibly Verlaine, even painters such as Whistler, Gauguin, and Odilon Redon. A few months earlier a Communard gunner-turned-publisher by the name of Edmond Bailly had opened a bookshop called La Librairie de l'art indépendant in the Chaussée d'Antin, which had also rapidly become a Mecca for literati and their hangers-on, and here Debussy was often to be found, sometimes talking books with Bailly or his other patrons, sometimes playing the piano at the rear of the shop with a new musician friend, the composer Erik Satie. It may be that it was at Bailly's that he and

Satie first met, or it might have been at the Chat Noir, an arty café-nightclub in Montmartre where Satie had been a regular pianist since 1888. Debussy, too, was a regular at the Chat Noir, though probably not one of its pianists, and its clientele, which overlapped with both Mallarmé's and Bailly's but certainly spread well beyond either of them, was one further brick in the wall of his dissociation from the mainstream of French musical life.

Perhaps Debussy's friendship with Satie was another, since of all French composers of the day, Satie was the least beholden to the establishment, the most "alternative" in the modern sense. In 1891, when they were introduced, probably by the Chat Noir writer and chansonnier Narcisse Lebeau (Vital Hocquet), Satie was just entering on his association with Sâr Péladan and the Paris Rosicrucians, and for a brief period Debussy also took a passing interest in the occult ceremonies of this curious *fin de siècle* revival. The two composers' friendship survived this phase, and it also, more surprisingly, survived the vast difference between their respective hostilities towards the official mainstream. Where Debussy's rebellion was an intensely serious quest for release from what he saw as the ossified conventions of the Conservatoire, Satie contented himself with what seemed at the time deliberately self-limiting miniatures that poked fun at serious music in general, its pretensions of scale and its affectations of title and subject matter. Exactly what Debussy thought of piano pieces such as the *Pièces froides* or the *Gnossiennes*, with their cultivated monotony and teasing repetitiveness, was never revealed. But he did later orchestrate two of the *Gymnopédies*, a service he never performed for any other composer, and he clearly enjoyed Satie's company, since Satie would regularly walk the five miles from his flat in Arcueil for lunch with Debussy in his apartment. Later he would be a witness at Debussy's first marriage, and he was one of the few friends who did not desert him when that marriage came to an abrupt end. According to René Peter, Debussy admired Satie's simplicity and serenity, but there was an element of patronage in this, a "feeling of being a benefactor [that] took his mind to some extent off his own troubles."[14]

Among the performers at the Chat Noir was a versatile singer-actor-composer by the name of Vincent Hyspa, the author of the shadowplays that were performed there, and of cabaret songs that

Satie later set to music. Debussy set precisely one poem of Hyspa's, an ironic little ballad about the Sleeping Beauty and her awakening by a knight who steals the ring from her finger, alias—one might suspect—something even more precious to her. Debussy composed "La Belle au bois dormant" that July with a straight face and a faint air of false naivety, incorporating the children's song "Nous n'irons plus au bois" ("We'll to the woods no more"), a song that apparently refers to the ban on prostitution in France in the late seventeenth century.[15] One wonders whether Debussy was aware of that connection. One other song dates, probably, from this busy but musically somewhat feckless year, a setting of Bourget's "Beau Soir." Like Debussy's other Bourget songs, "Beau Soir" is a fluid, lyrical piece of writing, beautifully laid out for the voice, stylistically unremarkable. Its most striking feature is a lovely counter-melody in the piano, somewhat upstaging the voice, and perhaps hinting at the ephemerality of life, the wave that ends in the sea as we end in the grave.

At some point late in 1890 or early in 1891, soon after meeting Gaby but before their affair began, Debussy went through an emotional crisis unlike anything he had previously experienced, the result of a broken-off love affair. He poured out his heart to Robert Godet:

> I'm still very shaken; the sadly unexpected end of that affair I told you about; banal end, with pettinesses and words that should never have been spoken, I noticed this bizarre transposition, that at the moment when such hard words fell from those lips, I heard inside me the uniquely adorable things they had said to me! and the wrong notes (real, alas!) crashing into the ones that sang inside me tore me apart, almost without my being able to understand.[16]

Who was it? The only candidate appears to be the sculptress Camille Claudel (the beautiful older sister of the playwright Paul Claudel), whom Debussy had met possibly as early as the autumn of 1890 in one or other of the Montmartre cafés they both frequented. The literature is cautious to negative on the subject, but offers no alternative. Godet, who claimed to know about the affair from Debussy's own lips, wrote later that Debussy and Auguste Rodin (with whom Camille had certainly had a lengthy relationship, working and otherwise) were for a time rivals for her affections. Camille, supposedly tone deaf, would calmly sit and listen to Debussy playing his latest pieces, or he would watch her at work, and they would talk about Degas or Hokusai. Whatever the truth of all this (and it is dismissed by Lesure),[17] Debussy remained a candid admirer of Camille's work, not least because it owed nothing to the Academy; according to Godet, he kept her *La Valse* on his mantelpiece, "and her *Petite princesse* [*Petite châtelaine*] sometimes smiled at him in his dreams."[18]

Among the pieces he may have played to Camille were the two *Arabesques* for piano that he completed, probably, early in 1891. Almost of more interest than the music of these two pieces—for all their charm—is their title. Debussy loved Schumann's *Arabeske*, and played it, it was said, exquisitely.[19] But the inspiration for his own *Arabesques* came, if anything, from his literary and artistic connections. The whole concept of the arabesque, the line that curls and spins, throwing out tendrils or folds as it goes, was an obsession of the arts of the 1880s and 1890s, under the influence partly of Japanese prints and drawings, partly of medieval decorative design of the kind imitated by the English Pre-Raphaelites and William Morris's Arts and Crafts movement. It found its way into painting and graphic design, into sculpture and architecture, into furniture and dress design. Debussy was certainly aware of this Art Nouveau long before composing his own *Arabesques*. His admiration for Degas must have been partly in response to the strength of the drawn lines that distinguish his art from that of the Impressionists in general. His love of Hokusai was essentially a love of the sweeping curve and the filigree mesh of foliage. But he might also have heard talk of arabesque as a poetic figure at Mallarmé's Tuesdays, the idea of the poetic line as an intricate web of association and suggestion weaving around an elusive reality.

The arabesques in his piano pieces of that name are decorative right-hand melodies spun out of simple motives and ornamenting essentially very plain harmonies, so that the expression is almost entirely concentrated in the melodic lines. Apart from the odd chromatic note and a single eight-bar excursion into C major, the first piece never strays from the territory of its home key, E major. The second piece, in G major, is marginally more adventurous harmonically, but even here the attention is very much focused on the treatment of the *scherzando* triplets of the main right-hand (occasionally left-hand) melody, for which the supporting chords often feel like a skeleton accompaniment kindly provided by a second instrument. It's true that this whole design has a precedent in certain piano studies of Chopin or Liszt, where the figuring represents the development of a particular finger or hand technique. But Debussy's *Arabesques* are not at all technical in that sense; in fact they are quite easy to play. The line and the motif take precedence over any question of technique.

However one analyses them, these attractive pieces are a fairly modest contribution to a movement in art that was beginning to produce major and transformative work in every visual medium. It would be good to know whether Debussy went to see Maurice Denis's designs for Verlaine's *Sagesse* poems at the Salon des Indépendants that spring and, if so, whether it influenced him in his decision to set three of these poems to music soon afterwards. It would be harder to argue that it influenced him in the matter of style. Denis's designs are an illustration of his theory about the essential flatness of the picture surface and the priority of design and pattern over realism: "Remember," he had written in 1890, "that a picture, before being a battle horse, a nude, an anecdote or whatnot, is essentially a flat surface covered with colours assembled in a certain order." Much later he added that "the arabesque and the play of strokes of colour seemed to us adequate for the expression of a picture. The picture tended to become music and a state of the soul."[20]

Music is itself, of course, already in a sense that flat surface, on which the imitation of reality is remote when not actually absent. The rolling arpeggios of "La Mer est plus belle," the first of Debussy's *Trois mélodies de Verlaine*, are as nearly a picture of the heaving ocean as music can perhaps manage. Even so, its effect has nothing much to do with its portraiture, but is bound up with the superb control of a very simple musical device, the arpeggiated (spread) chord in root position repeated many times, loud or soft, and with the sustaining pedal (never indicated by Debussy, who nearly always preferred to leave this matter to the player) ensuring maximum resonance. The variety of Verlaine's images is more or less lost in all this grandeur: the faithful nurse of the water-rail, the Virgin Mary at prayer, the pilgrims tramping on the pebbles, the drowning swimmer. The third song, "L'Échelonnement des haies" ("The procession of hedges rolls to infinity") is if anything still more oblique in its imagery, while

Debussy's setting, preoccupied with its quasi-gamelan theme (alias the flute-like bells of Verlaine's final stanza), has nothing to say about the scent of the young berries, the trees and mills, the agile colts or the ewes "as sweet as their white wool." And yet the song is irresistible. The middle song, "Le Son du cor s'afflige vers les bois" ("The sound of the horn grieves towards the woods") comes closest to attending to the complex detail of Verlaine's imagination. The poem is set as scanned recitative, so that the singer can react more readily to the always astonishing metaphors: the orphan sound dying at the foot of the hill, the wolf-soul weeping as the sun sets, the slow country-side pampering itself in the monotony of the evening. There is no way that music could sensibly respond to these things in any graphic detail, but it can leave spaces for the atmosphere to seep in, and here Debussy is, as the French say, *chez soi*—in his element.

Having got back into his Verlaine mood, he decided to make new versions of three earlier settings of his favourite poet. One of them, "Fantoches," he simply revised, composing a new, simplified ending, but making no other significant change. However, of the other two, "En sourdine" and "Clair de lune," he made completely new settings, as if acknowledging that his music had moved on from the Wagnerism of the one and (perhaps) the slightly awkward prosody of the other. The new "En sourdine" is altogether lighter textured than its predecessor, and would scarcely on its own suggest the *Tristan* references that I drew earlier, though of course they are still present in the poem. The old version was written for Marie Vasnier, with a high vocal tessitura. In the new song, the voice is set studiously low, not wanting to disturb the calm of the half-light, the profound silence beneath the high branches, and the prevailing air of detumescence. But still there is the voice of the nightingale, the "voice of our despair," and here, as if by accident, Debussy sets the words in almost exactly the same way as before, only this time avoiding the line repeat that had ended the original song with a mild touch of rhetoric.

A curious aspect of this new "En sourdine" is its complete rethinking of the poem's accentuation. It would be hard to find a better illustration of the fluidity of the French language in this respect: "Que les branches" with the downbeat accent on "que" ("which") in the first version, on "branches" in the second; "Et de ton coeur endormi" front accented on "et" ("and") and "mi" in the first version, on "coeur" and "mi" in the second; "Qui vient à tes pieds" with "qui" ("which") on an upbeat in 1882, a downbeat in 1892. It seems that none of this is incorrect or even mannered, as one or other version would almost certainly be in English or German. It conjures up Richard Strauss's later bewilderment at the variable stress in *Pelléas et Mélisande* and his wrong-headed, petulant question to Romain Rolland: "Why do the French sing differently to the way they speak?"[21] The truth is that the stress on insignificant words and syllables is a rhetorical device much used also in French conversation, and which in music can have an almost sensual effect.

The new "Clair de lune" opens with a pentatonic rhythmic figure that Mueller has shown to echo music Debussy would have heard in the Javanese pavilion. Briefly, the texture is faintly oriental, though Western harmony soon floods in, leaving only the rhythmic figure as a kind of leitmotif, a persistent glint of moonlight. The actual setting of the poem is more convincing than in the earlier version, more obviously shaped by the poem than the accompaniment, and without its gratuitous line repeats. Verlaine's poetry often presents the problem that its even scansion and regular rhyme schemes can produce a somewhat mechanical effect if set too straight, but Debussy here overrides it just enough to keep the music fluid without losing the sense of the poem's structure.

In these years of the early 1890s, you can follow the thread of Debussy's development by examining each work roughly in order of (supposed) completion. But the true picture of his musical thinking is a great deal more confused. As early as 1890, he was reported to be working on "a symphony on psychologically developed themes derived from a number of tales by [Edgar Allan] Poe, in particular *The Fall of the House of Usher*."[22] This is too plausible to have been a complete invention (in 1889, in answer to a questionnaire, Debussy had given Poe and Flaubert as his favourite prose writers). Yet nothing else is known about any such intention. Debussy certainly was prone to talk about speculative or inchoate projects, just as he was inclined to enter rather casually or opportunistically into collaborations that had little or no future. At about the time of the imaginary *Usher* project, he definitely undertook to write a symphonic commentary on a pair of short plays by Gabriel Mourey entitled *Embarquement pour ailleurs* (Embarkation for Somewhere Else), and a year or two later,

during his brief Rosicrucian moment, he agreed to compose incidental music for a play by Jules Bois called *Les Noces de Sathan* (Satan's
Wedding). Not a note of either score was ever written. Meanwhile, in
1891, he had applied to the Belgian playwright Maurice Maeterlinck
for permission to base an opera on his *La Princesse Maleine*, a play
he probably knew only by repute, but had met with a refusal because
Maeterlinck had already (vaguely) promised it to Vincent d'Indy.

He was also apt to lie about the state of genuine projects, presumably in the optimistic hope that, if necessary, he could finish them
off at short notice, though in fact (as he surely knew) his innate perfectionism always worked against him in this respect. Thus in September 1892 he told the banker and industrialist André Poniatowski,
who was trying to set up a concert of his works in New York, that
he could offer the *Fantaisie*, *La Damoiselle élue*, and a set of three
pieces called *Scènes au crépuscule* (Scenes at Twilight), which were
"almost finished, that's to say that since I've already worked out the
orchestration, it's now only a question of writing them down." Five
months later he told Poniatowski that he had "considerably reworked
the *Scènes au crépuscule*," after which nothing more was heard of the
work.[23]

It has long been supposed, without hard evidence, that the orchestral *Nocturnes* of 1897–9 were a fully realised version of the *Scènes*,
but there are strong reasons for doubting it. In 1894 Debussy wrote
to the great Belgian violinist Eugène Ysaÿe offering him a set of three
Nocturnes for violin and orchestra, an offer he repeated two years
later.[24] But Ysaÿe did not play these pieces, and they too proceeded
to vanish from the known world, except for a few pages of sketches,
which were recently worked up into a performable version of one
of the *Nocturnes* by the brilliant Debussy scholar Robert Orledge.
Whatever might be said about this particular piece of what Orledge
calls "creative musicology," it is clear that the music has little if any
connection with the orchestral *Nocturnes* of two or three years later.
As for the *Scènes au crépuscule*, all one can say is that the Régnier
poems of that name (in his *Poèmes anciens et romanesques*, published
in 1890) contain little or no imagery that might have inspired the
Nuages, *Fêtes*, and *Sirènes* of Debussy's masterpiece. There is wind
and the occasional cloud, and a final stanza that might conceivably
have suggested the wordless chorus of "Sirènes":

L'aphône parade des mimes
Par groupes impairs évolue
En masques de fards anonymes
Un rite de fable perdue.

(The voiceless parade of mimes,
in unequal groups, revolves
in anonymous painted masks,
a rite from some lost fable.)

But of the dazzling festivities of "Fêtes" there is no trace.

Altogether more plausible is the suggestion that Régnier's collection was an influence on the poems that Debussy wrote for himself to set in his *Proses lyriques*, a set of four songs that he worked on in the latter part of 1892 and the first half of 1893. Why Debussy decided to write his own texts, rather than, for example, set Régnier's or Laforgue's (another influence), is far from clear. He may have had particular imagery in mind, and certainly the images in his poems are strong, even when the connection between them is oblique to the point of obscurity (as, to tell the truth, it often is in Régnier, a huge admirer of Mallarmé). But the main clue is the freedom and sheer range of the settings, which feed on the comparative looseness of Debussy's own *vers libre*, even tending towards the poetic prose that explains his title and that he later told Pierre Louÿs he preferred for setting to music.[25] These are substantial songs, narrative in design even if the actual narratives are occasionally a little hard to discern. They may even reflect his growing interest in opera.

The form of the first song, "De rêve" ("Of dreams"), is clearly controlled by the piano, which develops and reprises its material without specific reference to the voice part, while the voice maps itself freely onto the music according to its own needs. The technique derives, perhaps, from Wagner, but is freer, recognising the essential difference between sung words and their instrumental accompaniment, which Wagner sometimes fails to do. David Grayson's neat phrase for this kind of thing is "a continuous music that has been interrupted by verse."[26] On the other hand, Debussy's meanings are mostly so opaque that the music can create its own images and its own pocket drama, from the whole-tone opening arpeggios ("The night is soft like a woman"), through the wistful second theme for "the girl who has just gone by, her head glistening in the moonlight, forever sorrowful," on by way of a grand climax at "None will any more dedicate the pride of the golden helmets, now forever tarnished," and the priceless Wagner put-down, "The Knights are dead on the road to the Grail!"

"De grève" ("Of seashores"), the second song, is more of a piece verbally, and more coherent in imagery. It is also the most visual of the four. It has Régnier's twilight and the sea, waves like silly little girls coming out of school, their frocks rustling in the wind; it has clouds "gathering on the next storm," altogether too much "for this English watercolour." The windy watery scene is unified by piano figuration that looks forward to piano pieces such as *Jardins sous la pluie* and especially *Poissons d'or*. But the words add a touch of risqué sensuality when the little waves (previously compared to little girls) "offer themselves like loving lips to [the moon's] tepid white kiss." These are different kinds of marine image from the ones to come in the orchestral *Nocturnes*, but they already anticipate the element of Impressionism in that work.

The third song, "De fleurs" ("Of flowers"), is the tragic heart of the cycle. Its central image, of the "greenhouse of sorrow" might seem to suggest Maeterlinck's poem "Serre d'ennui" in his *Serres chaudes*, recently set by Chausson, though the verse form is quite different from Maeterlinck's rhyming tetrameters. Or it might be another reminiscence of Wagner ("Im Treibhaus," one of his *Wesendonck-Lieder*), though Debussy's greenhouse is something evil, strangling the heart with too much artificial growth, where the plants in Wagner's hothouse share the poet's sense of alienation from her natural habitat. In any case Debussy's music now owes little if anything to Wagner. The solemn root-position chords that paint the heavy desolation of the greenhouse radiate an almost antique power that gradually spreads into more complex harmonies and eventually into more mobile, but still menacing figuration. This is one of Debussy's greatest songs, rendered the more powerful, as often with him, by its prevailing soft dynamic, broken only by a couple of brief *forte* explosions.

Finally "De soir" ("Of evenings") brings a certain lightening of tone, without altogether relieving the gloom that, we know, was very much the colour of Debussy's own life at this time. It is Sunday, the day, that is, when everybody else has a good time (though they ought to be in church), leaving the miserable to pray to the Virgin Mary to "have pity on the towns . . . pity on the hearts." The music is dominated by the pealing of bells, but equally by textures that recall the gamelan, a joyous tintinnabulation that, in the circumstances, has an ironic undertone, like the hum-note of a church bell.

By the time he put the finishing touches to "De soir," in September 1893, Debussy had also completed a string quartet, which he had been composing more or less in tandem with the *Proses lyriques*. Even more remarkably, he had been writing a whole scene of a new opera, *Pelléas et Mélisande*, for which he had at last received the necessary permission from Maeterlinck early in August. And he had written enough of the surviving movement of the Mallarmé "Après-midi d'un faune" project to be able to play it through to Régnier, who had thought it "as hot as a furnace."[27] Alas, what Debussy called "the ghost of old Klingsor, alias R. Wagner" had popped up in the *Pelléas* scene, and he had torn the whole thing up in a moment of anguish and "set off in search of a chemistry of more personal phrases."[28] Régnier had spoken to him about "certain words in the French language whose gilt had been tarnished through overuse by the sordid world," and he had thought to himself that "it was the same with certain chords whose sound had been cheapened by music for export—not a strikingly novel thought, unless I add that they have at the same time lost their symbolic essence."[29] This last point went to the heart of Debussy's own style, because he had for some time been investigating chords for their inherent sonority and trying to divest them of their commonplace function. He could look at his own music, and claim that he had often succeeded, but an opera was a big challenge and the temptation to fall back on conventional methods correspondingly great.

In the string quartet he had certainly avoided Wagnerism, but that was not much of a risk in chamber music. More to the point, string quartets by French composers were distinctly thin on the ground, even if you included in that category the Belgian César Franck, whose solitary quartet, in D major, had been almost his last work, composed in 1889, the year before his death. Whether or not Debussy knew that piece, its nostalgic, densely polyphonic tone hardly touched his own quartet, which borrows Franck's cyclic method of linking movements through common themes, but little else. His quartet, in

G minor, is from the first bar a sinewy, energetic work, almost as if purposely designed to ward off expectations, based on his vocal works, of a refined, perfumed exploration of string sound. The writing is articulate, with clean outlines, and carefully voiced, either with block chordings, as at the start, or with melody supported by light figuration, helped, as always with Debussy, by a preference for soft dynamics. He told Chausson that the finale had given him the most trouble, and the opening of this movement is, arguably, the only slightly laboured part of what is in the main a fine, fluent answer to a challenge he had not faced before and would not face again.[30]

5

Mallarmé and Maeterlinck

The *Proses lyriques* seem to mark a point for Debussy when different aspects of his existence come into focus. At some time during
the summer of 1892 he had at last moved permanently out of his parents' apartment and rented a small furnished flat with Gaby Dupont
in the rue de Londres. Vital Hocquet saw them often. Debussy, he
recalled in an interview, "couldn't afford to eat or clothe himself.
Lunch consisted mostly of a small bar of chocolate, such as schoolboys eat, and what was, in those days, the classic *petit pain* costing a
sou."

> Debussy adored watching games of billiards and going to the circus;
> he was particularly fond, too, of Guignol. We used to spend hours at
> the Guignol on the Champs-Élysées or at the Folies-Bergère, where
> there were often billiard matches. The room on the rue de Londres
> was a sort of panelled garret, untidily filled with a rickety table, three
> cane chairs, a sort of bed and a splendid Pleyel [piano], on loan nat-
> urally . . . In this room, where everything had to be done, Achille
> wrote masterpieces.[1]

In the year that followed he not only composed the *Proses* but also
finally worked up his sketches for the Mallarmé project into a single orchestral movement, which he called, simply, *Prélude à l'après-
midi d'un faune*. He was probably still at work on this piece when, in
May 1893, he attended the world premiere of Maeterlinck's *Pelléas
et Mélisande* at the Bouffes-Parisiens. Lugné-Poe's dimly lit, gauze-
hung production met with a frosty reception in the press, but drew
a very different response from some of Maeterlinck's fellow writers
and artists who attended the one and only performance. Mallarmé
wrote up his impressions, in his elliptical, idiosyncratic way:

These scenes, brief, supreme: everything preparatory and mechanical has been rejected, to enable to appear, drawn out, what for the spectator emerges from the performance, the essential. It seems that what is being played is a superior variation on the admirable old melodrama. Silently, almost, and abstractly, to the point that in this art, where everything becomes music in the true sense, the participation of an instrument, even a pensive violin, would do harm with its superfluity. Perhaps this tacit atmosphere inspires, in the anguish the author feels in it, that frequent need to say things twice, in order to be certain that they have been said and to guarantee them, if all else fails, the consciousness of the echo.[2]

The painter Henry Lerolle's response was more succinct: "Some very nice things, not very well played, not enough or too much décor . . . I prefer Ibsen."[3]

Debussy, who may have bought and read the play the previous year, reacted to its performance, as we saw, by impulsively setting its most dramatic scene, the lovers' final meeting by the fountain and Pelléas's murder by Golaud.[4] He could hardly be expected to agree with Mallarmé on the possible contribution of music to Maeterlinck's mysterious but in fact distinctly *un*poetic prose drama. It was Mallarmé, after all, who later that same year responded to a play-through by Debussy of the *Prélude à l'après-midi d'un faune* by admitting, "I didn't expect anything like that! This music prolongs the emotion of my poem and sets its decor more passionately than its colour."[5] But Debussy still needed to get old Klingsor out of his system. Only a few days before the Maeterlinck he had been to hear the French premiere of *Die Walküre* at the Opéra, and—what was worse—he had been playing *Ring* excerpts on the piano for a series of Wagner lectures by his *Rodrigue* nemesis, Catulle Mendès. He had been revolted by the lecturer's demonstrative manner. Mendès had talked about *Walküre*, Debussy told Chausson, "in such terms that mothers who had trustingly come with their daughters were obliged to flee the fevered words of this bad priest . . . There are aesthetic simpletons who see in this work a renewal of music and the death of the jaded old formulae. That's not my opinion, but it hardly matters."[6] His opinion, of course, was that Wagner was a great composer but a dangerous model. "The time is near," he had told Chausson only a couple of weeks earlier, "when this man will take a sweet revenge on the Parisians, and we will suffer as much, because he will be one of those fortresses the public likes to erect against every new aesthetic. And since, in all sincerity, we won't be able to call it bad, we'll just have to keep quiet."[7]

His own escape from Wagner had already been partly made good in the *Proses lyriques*, and it was pursued further, not yet in *Pelléas*, but in the Mallarmé *Prélude*. It was one thing to have isolated Wagnerian chords and phrases in songs, where the intense verbal imagery invited a disintegration of the harmonic line, quite another thing to compose a ten- or twelve-minute orchestral work, supposedly based on a narrative poem, without falling back on the old harmonic grammar that had kept music going for the past three hundred years. Admittedly Mallarmé's poem, though narrative in form, is so wrapped up in complex metaphor and arcane syntax that any attempt to turn it into programme music in the old-fashioned sense would surely have got lost in the undergrowth. Debussy later outlined his own very different aim in a letter to the music critic Henri Gauthier-Villars (Willy). The *Prélude*, he said,

> is perhaps such dream as is left at the far end of the faun's flute? More precisely, it's the poem's general impression, for if I'd followed it any closer the music would have run out of steam like a carriage-horse competing for the Grand Prix with a thoroughbred.[8]

It's as if one were to picture the faun lying in the grass with his double flute in the hot Attic sun, amid a general air of languor and sensual promise. In the distance, perhaps, are two naked girls, naiads, bathing. But the faun makes no move towards them. They are only in his mind, a complication of unrealised possibilities, a static image intensified but not extended by thought. They are, so to speak, the final freeze-frame of the poem, alongside what the composer called "the decor marvellously described in the text, together with the humanity provided by thirty-two violinists who have got up too early! The ending is the final verse prolonged: 'Couple adieu, je vais voir ce que tu devins' ('Farewell, you two, I go to see what became of you')."[9]

The famous opening flute solo picks up several key images from the poem: the flute "watering the grove with melodies," "malign Syr-

inx," and the inertia in which "everything burns in the tawny hour."
Musically, too, it sets the scene. The melody swings across the "devil's interval," the tritone, up and down, a musical symbol of immobility, since by dividing the octave exactly in half (the rest of the octave
also forming a tritone) it creates a symmetry that is essentially static.
Curiously enough this augmented fourth or diminished fifth—to
give it its correct names in tonal theory—is usually thought of as
unstable, because it asks a question without answering it. Debussy,
however, treats it as stable and inert, in line with his idea of dissonant
chords as sonorities in their own right independent of their place in
any theoretical grammar.

Meanwhile the melody decorates the interval in arabesque style,
creating an ornamental line like a rococo floral moulding. Debussy
later referred to this kind of writing as "undulating, cradle-rocking
[*berceuse*] music, abounding in curved lines."[10] Arabesque melodies
characterise the entire *Prélude*, movement and flow without direction, like light on rippling water. The idea fascinated Debussy, just
as it had fascinated painters and designers, architects and even poets,
since the discovery of Japanese prints. It was the core idea of the Art
Nouveau, but Debussy had already identified it—in his opinion—in
much earlier music, in the polyphony of Palestrina and Victoria. "It's
marvellously beautiful," he told Poniatowski, after hearing a Palestrina Mass in the church of Saint-Gervais—

> this music that is yet very strictly composed appears totally white and
> the emotion is translated not (as has since become the way) by cries,
> but by melodic arabesques, an effect, as it were, by contour and by
> the arabesques interweaving so as to produce something that seems
> unique: melodic harmonies.[11]

As it happens the arabesques in Debussy's *Prélude* don't inter-
weave, but pass from instrument to instrument, while the harmony
is provided in the conventional way by the rest of the orchestra.
This harmony, however, is for the most part extremely slow moving, sometimes more or less stationary, anchored by held or repeated
pedal notes in the bass that often contradict the movement of the inner
parts. The elaborate languor of Mallarmé's faun can almost be smelt
in this quietly sumptuous, mobile yet inert orchestral texture. And

considering that Debussy had written hardly anything previously for orchestra without voices, and had not heard the one exception (the piano *Fantaisie*), the delicacy and refinement of the scoring in the *Prélude*, for a reasonably large orchestra but without heavy brass or percussion, are simply astonishing.

The escape from Wagner, though, is by no means complete. Not so very far behind Debussy's saturated harmonies and flowing arabesques once again lies, at least in general concept, the second act love duet of *Tristan*; and in particular the start of the *Prélude* has an obvious kinship with the opening of Wagner's opera: a solo line ending on the same notorious discord, the so-called "Tristan" chord, which Wagner partially resolves in one direction, Debussy partially in another. But the differences are more striking. Though slow moving, Wagner's harmonies still push relentlessly towards closure, whereas Debussy's flow gently downstream, sometimes getting caught in side currents or running up against the bank. And Debussy's music never bullies. The dynamics in the *Prélude* seldom rise above *mezzo-piano*, and then only for brief moments of *forte* or *fortissimo* which, to tell the truth, are so only in relation to the surrounding music. With Wagner the reverse tends to be the case. With him *piano* and *pianissimo* are the relative terms. Loud is his default position; soft is Debussy's.

On 8 April 1893 *La Damoiselle élue* received its first performance, at an SNM concert in the Salle Érard, conducted by Gabriel Marie. The soloists were Julia Robert and Thérèse Roger, and the programme also included Chausson's *Poème de l'amour et de la mer* and works by Dukas and Raymond Bonheur. It was Debussy's first significant premiere since *L'Enfant prodigue* nine years earlier, and the very first of a large-scale work of his that was in any sense representative, though in truth this five-year-old score was already past history as far as his evolving style was concerned. It had, nevertheless, a mixed reception. One critic found in it "an extremity of chromaticism," another thought it "decadent, even a bit addled."[12] Some found it refined but over-long. On the other hand, it located Debussy firmly among the younger musicians who counted; it cemented his relationships with his fellow practitioners, including those with whom he shared this

particular platform, and it brought him to the attention of or into contact with important artists in other disciplines who sensed, what not every musician sensed, a new and sympathetic direction in this work so candidly linked to modern tendencies in painting and poetry.

He had known and been on good terms with Chausson for some years, but the SNM concert brought them closer. "I'm furiously bored by your absence," Debussy wrote to him a few weeks later.

I'm like a poor little footpath that everyone has abandoned for the main road, I often present myself with the melancholy illusion of going as far as your front door, and it's a sadness to think that it will not open for a long time to cheer me on my way home.[13]

Towards the end of May, he spent a few days with Chausson, Henry Lerolle, and Raymond Bonheur at Luzancy, on the River Marne, where Chausson had rented a small château for the summer. During the day they worked on their own projects; there were river excursions, and in the evening they played and discussed music. "The new Musorgskys will perhaps be there," Chausson had written, urging Debussy to "borrow whatever Russian music you can."[14] The new Musorgskys certainly included a vocal score of *Boris Godunov*, and perhaps some songs, music that was beginning to make an impact on these French composers. "How boring of you not to be here any more," Chausson wrote after Debussy had returned to Paris. "No more Russian music, no more boat trips, no more billiards."[15] For Debussy, it was a new scenario in every respect.

Ernest Chausson, though a pupil of Massenet and Franck, was a composer who belonged neither to the automatic Conservatoire set that Debussy made a point of detesting, nor to the bohemian café circuit he frequented. His world was that of the well-to-do, cultivated Parisian bourgeoisie. His father had made a fortune as a building contractor in Haussmann's redevelopment of Paris, and he himself lived well, if without ostentation, in an elegant *hôtel particulier* built by Chausson *père* on the Boulevard de Courcelles, where he and his wife Jeanne, née Escudier, entertained a circle of mainly artistic and art-loving friends, including Chausson's brothers-in-law, the painter Henry Lerolle and Arthur Fontaine, a mining engineer and civil servant increasingly concerned with employment law and social welfare. These friendships gave Debussy entrée into a social world of refined and discriminating artistic taste and musical and intellectual sophistication beyond his experience. Chausson's walls and ceilings were decorated with the work of Lerolle himself and the young Maurice Denis, and there were "Delacroix drawings, a veritable gallery of Degas pastels and drawings, canvases by Manet, Corot, Gauguin, Signac, the *Orphée* of Puvis de Chavannes, an important collection of Japanese prints and several albums of lithographs by Odilon Redon."[16] As an artist, Lerolle kept out of the limelight, but he was on dining terms with many leading painters, including Degas, Eugène Carrière (who painted him and his family), Renoir, Denis, as well as writers already known to Debussy: Mallarmé, Régnier, Valéry, Gide, and Pierre Louÿs, regulars at the Mallarmé Tuesdays. How Debussy fitted into this milieu in the question of manners can only be imagined, but his musical genius and his shared enthusiasm for Symbolist poetry and painting and oriental art in general opened many doors. Photographs of him at Luzancy show a shirt-sleeved, mildly tousled young man at the piano surrounded by admiring or at least attentive Chaussons and Lerolles. Posed as they are, these photos exude the cultured but unpretentious air of the sub-aristocratic artistic life that came, in France and elsewhere, from the new money associated with business success in the latter part of the nineteenth century.

Tousled or not, Debussy stood out in this environment by virtue of his extreme poverty. For the best part of a year after the *Damoiselle* performance Chausson helped him discreetly with gifts of money, and with an unsuccessful attempt to get him a job as assistant conductor at the casino in Royan, in return for which Debussy advised him on his opera *Le Roi Arthus*, which he had been struggling with (he called it "my battle") for the past seven years. Chausson's mother-in-law, Mme Escudier, arranged for him a series of Saturday afternoon sessions at her house, in which he played and sang Wagner to an audience of paying guests. Alas, not just the gifts and the Wagner sessions, but even the friendship, came to an abrupt end in the early spring of 1894, as a result of a marital indiscretion on Debussy's part. Though apparently settled in his life with Gaby Dupont, now in an apartment in the rue Gustave Doret, for which Chausson had provided funds, he suddenly, apparently out of the blue, announced his engagement to Thérèse Roger, his nice but not startlingly attractive

Damoiselle soprano, with whom he had just performed two of the *Proses lyriques* at an SNM concert on 17 February. He explained the situation in a letter to Lerolle:

> It's altogether uncanny, but that's how it is, and it happened as in fairy-tales! I've long had a profound affection for Mlle Roger, but it seemed to me so inadmissible that I didn't dare think about it! I beg you not to judge me harshly, I've explained my whole situation to Mme Roger, and I would want her daughter to keep her *material independence*! . . . Moreover I am *completely free*, my last little friend having gone off one morning in February to better her situation.[17]

Lerolle promptly wrote to Chausson:

> You know Debussy's getting married . . . He's in the seventh heaven. Thérèse is ravishing, young and all the rest. I had dinner with him last night after he'd played the first act of *Tristan* on the piano. And I went with him to arrange for him to play more Wagner, at 250 francs a month. He's very happy about it. He has to earn money and not live on Thérèse's.[18]

Chausson, though "stupefied" by the news, was also delighted, feeling that the marriage would settle Debussy and put his life on a more regular footing than with Gaby, who in the eyes of the Boulevard was no better than a courtesan, and was not received there.

> He's deeply in love [Chausson replied to Lerolle], and I find lovers so utterly captivating, not to say a rarity in our refined intellectual circle. This announcement is certainly going to set tongues wagging interminably . . . Personally, I'm confident about the outcome; I think it'll be a very happy marriage, precisely because it's not one that the ultimate in common sense would approve.[19]

It soon, however, became apparent that Gaby had not gone off at all, but was still installed in the Gustave Doret flat. As late as 8 March Debussy was still parroting to Chausson the prospective joys of wedlock.

I could stray into louche places! but I preserve a horror of them that will forever protect me, and I'm still young enough to be able to say that I am bringing a fully renewed soul to a new life, and I have feelings in me that have never been able to be formulated, with good reason, and which happily I have kept intact, hoping always for the moment when I shall have the intimate joy of seeing them flower.[20]

Whether or not he believed these platitudes at the time, within just over a week the engagement had been broken off. Tongues had indeed been wagging, but about Gaby, the rumours had reached Chausson, and he had written to Debussy on the 15th demanding an explanation. To call Debussy's reply of the 16th devious would be like calling Iago a naughty boy. Passing over his fiancée with an assurance that he intended to be open with her about Chausson's financial support, he insisted that "it would be impossible for me to act any differently, and I thirst for a life that is very transparent and without mysterious undercurrents," then proceeded to dun his friend for a further loan.[21] Yet he had probably already ended the engagement, which was certainly dead by the 17th. Chausson reacted in a letter to Lerolle:

Truly, the more I hear, the less I understand. At a pinch I can understand the lies, the palliatives, the subterfuges, stupid and pointless as they always are, but to lie in one's teeth, with protestation and indignation and on matters of such gravity, that defeats me.[22]

Debussy's behaviour certainly was as peculiar as it was reprehensible. Lesure suggests that he was partly motivated by the recognition that his liaison with Gaby was holding him back socially, a feeling he will have owed to his new Boulevard friendships, whether or not anything specific had been said. There was certainly outside influence of a kind. Lesure points the finger at Marguerite de Saint-Marceaux, a well-to-do sculptor's wife who had a salon into which Debussy had been introduced that winter. She was, he alleges, a matchmaker, a Mme Verdurin (who, in Proust's *À la Recherche du temps perdu*, liked to pair off the members of her "little clan"). It may be that Debussy had begun to tire of Gaby, thought she had left him, and felt genuinely disconcerted, not to say trapped, by her return. But after all they remained together for another four years after this blip. The real explanation probably lies in certain unreconciled conflicts in Debussy's own character: a strong libido, which he was inclined to mistake for lifelong devotion; a genuine desire for stability and respectability, and a degree of ruthlessness in the interests of his creative work. Genius may not openly claim special moral privileges in this sublunary world, but it will often act as if it assumed them. Behind Debussy's unsatisfactory treatment of the women in his life lay the instinctive feeling—which ordinary men usually manage to suppress—that emotional ties are a nuisance unless kept firmly in the drawer marked "when I need them."

After ripping up his first, too Wagnerian, attempt at the death of Pelléas, he lost no time in composing a replacement, which was effectively the scene as we know it. By mid-October he had finished this new version, and soon afterwards he set to work a little more systematically, starting with the first act, then leapfrogging to Act 3, which was done by August 1894, and finally mopping up Act 2, the rest of Act 4 and all of Act 5, completing the whole long opera apart from the orchestration—more than three hours of music—in August 1895. All the time he was working with Maeterlinck's text in front of him, setting it as it stood, without the intervention of a librettist. A feature of the play was its *rat-tat-tat* of short scenes, nineteen of them in all. Debussy cut out four and a number of lines from the scenes he retained. But in essence he was simply composing the play, responding to its texture and pacing rather than trying to concoct an operatic equivalent, whatever that might have been. Though he might not have known it, he was working in a specifically Russian tradition, the tradition of Dargomïzhsky's setting of Pushkin's *Stone Guest*, and Musorgsky's of Gogol's *Marriage* and Pushkin's *Boris Godunov* (but the first version of that opera, rather than the very different revised score they had been studying at Luzancy). Like *Marriage*, but unlike most of *Boris*, *Pelléas et Mélisande* is a prose play, a fact that distinguishes it also from Wagner's libretti and imposes particular constraints on the musical setting. To be more exact, it allows freedoms that are really tyrannies of a different sort and which forced Debussy into a style of vocal writing that, as it happened, answered a question of Guiraud's four years before about word-setting: "But then where is your poet?" and explained Debussy's answer: "One of things half-said . . . Music rules overbearingly in the lyric theatre. They sing too much . . ." Perhaps this, as much as the atmosphere of the plays themselves, is why he was so drawn to Maeterlinck, even though his plots are by no means without their Wagnerian aspects, however much frailer and less muscular, less decisive, his characters.

Pelléas might certainly be described as *Tristan und Isolde* without the Will and without the attendant mythology. The inhabitants of Maeterlinck's Allemonde live on a historical island if not a physical one. They have neither past nor future but merely exist in a misty dynastic but apolitical present with nominal attributes such as kingship, old age, half-brotherhood, a castle, and a famine in the land that has no known cause and no consequences. The characters seem not even to know their own environment. Golaud gets lost in his own forest; Pelléas has only once, a long time ago, entered the vaults of his own castle. Mélisande (like Parsifal) seems to know virtually nothing at all, though at least she knows her own name. In *Tristan*, King Mark seeks a political marriage with Isolde, unaware that she is already in love with the knight he has sent to bring her back. In *Pelléas* Golaud simply finds Mélisande and marries her (though King Arkel, his grandfather, had a political marriage in mind for him, but lets it go). Pelléas falls in love with Mélisande without knowing it and without, it seems, any moral scruples about the outcome.

In one sense it's a Symbolist drama characteristic of its time, full of unrelated incidents heavy with secondary meaning. For instance, Mélisande's hair tumbling from her window in the tower obviously represents her sexuality, just as the doves that fly away at the climactic moment of Pelléas's love-making with the hair clearly stand for orgasm and the loss of virginity. Yet in another sense it's nothing but an everyday story of country folk. The orgasm idea makes no sense in view of the scene of the lovers' final meeting, which is evidently their first physical encounter. So the doves were doves and the hair hair, and Golaud's worries about his wife's daughter's paternity are needless. The sick father is just a redundant character, like Pelléas's dying friend, Marcellus, who amounts to a sort of Bunbury figure concocted as an excuse for Pelléas to be always about to leave (though he never does, except in a coffin). Mélisande's death is a bourgeois misfortune to set beside the *Liebestod*, sadder perhaps, but distinctly less seismic. The play's banality of event is easy to mock, and may be why, though beautiful in its writing and penetrating in its psychology, it has not held the stage except in the form of Debussy's masterpiece.

From the start of the opera the music emphasises the strangeness and remoteness of the setting and the curious impenetrability of the characters, and glides over the banalities, either by omitting them or by investing them with gnomic significance. When, in the play, Arkel remarks, "If I were God, I would have pity on the hearts of men," it sounds like the platitude it is. When sung, at the end of the violent scene of Golaud swinging Mélisande by the hair (another possibly, if more obscurely, sexual moment), it confers a spiritual exorcism on a moment of insanity, much as Boris Godunov's "Oh God! You do not wish the death of a sinner, have mercy on the soul of the criminal Tsar Boris!" exorcises his hysteria at the end of Musorgsky's Kremlin scene, not because of the text, but because of the music.

In general Debussy's music both intensifies and elevates Maeterlinck's play, but not always exactly in the manner he had described to Guiraud: the things half said, the monochrome and *grisaille*, and the "music where the word finishes," music that emerges from the shadows. The score of *Pelléas* is initially soft and discreet, but it rides what is in due course a violent and passionate drama that eventually generates an emotional electricity at least as great as anything in Puccini or Richard Strauss. What is new is not its discretion (Debussy's term), but the means by which it achieves something a great deal more powerful, specifically through the way it sets the French text. When Musorgsky composed *Marriage*, line by line and with attention to the spoken contours of the language, he soon got bored with the flatness of the result and gave up after one act. But Gogol's play is a comedy, dispassionate and cynical. Maeterlinck's, by contrast, is tragic and emotionally violent, for all its prosaic language, which often seems designed to conceal as much as it reveals. Debussy showed that music can unlock these inhibitions without altering what is being said, and in doing this he evolved the technique for which, perhaps more than anything, his opera is famous.

He may have found some kind of model in those parts of *Boris Godunov* that survived from the original version in the edition they had on the piano at Luzancy. Musorgsky had devised a kind of flexible recitative that could move easily into arioso (a more regular, lyrical recitative) and back again, without ever settling into formal aria. There are good examples in the Chudov Monastery scene (Pimen and Grigory) and the scene of Boris's death, both in this respect essentially unaltered in the revision. The difference for Debussy was that the Russian language has a strong tonic accent, like English, whereas French is a lightly stressed language capable of inventing accents—as we saw in connection with the songs—on unimportant words and syllables. But this proved an advantage, since it permitted a much freer and above all swifter delivery of what is, after all, a longish play set verbatim with relatively few excisions, and this allowed drastic variations in the pacing of the text and corresponding variations in the density of different emotions: the reflective, the anxious, the fearful, the reproachful, the passionate, etc. There are graphic illustrations of this in the score. In the garden scene, Act 1 scene 3, where Mélisande, Geneviève and Pelléas talk calmly about the light and the sea, the tone is conversational with only minor changes of pace, whereas in Act 4 scene 4—the lovers' final meeting and Golaud's murder of Pelléas—there are indicated changes of pace every two or three bars: taking a page at random we find *librement, en retenant, plus lent, serrez, très retenu, modéré*, all within the space of fourteen bars. These kinds of change are matched by variations in the density of the orchestral accompaniment, from silent through every gradation of volume and weight and a huge variety of motion. The writing here is far from Debussy's idea of the discreet or half said, and verges almost on the Wagnerian, though with a mercurial, needlepoint quality that is decidedly French rather than German.

Both in Debussy's time and since, *Pelléas et Mélisande* has often been accused of lacking melody, to which his understandably irritated reply was that "*Pelléas* is nothing but melody," a remark that might sound dangerously close to the Wagnerian mantra of "endless melody" (*unendliche Melodie*).[23] What the accusation means, of course, is that there are no "good (vocal) tunes," in the manner of Gounod or Bizet. The orchestral part is in fact rich in what one might call melodic gestures, brief lyrical phrases that seem to break out in response to a situation or something said and that owe no specific allegiance to the vocal line. There is no trace here of Wagner's idea of motives that originate in the "musical-poetic-line," that is in the setting of the text (an idea that Wagner himself adheres to only spasmodically in any case). Debussy does use leitmotifs, but rarely in any symphonic way, and never in the vocal line. They pop up in the orchestra in relation to particular characters, more or less like what Debussy himself mocked in Wagner as their "calling cards." The vocal line, however, concerns itself only with the words, with their contour and weight of feeling.

At the back of this technique are two apparently childlike effects: note repetition and silence. Debussy's discovery of the expressive value of these two devices was of major significance, as he was well aware. After tearing up his Wagnerian false start, he wrote to Chausson:

> I've come up with something that will perhaps please you (I don't care about the rest), I've made use, quite spontaneously, of a device which appears to me rather rare, that's to say silence (don't laugh) as an expressive agent and perhaps the only way of bringing out the emotion of a phrase, for if Wagner used it, it seems to me that it was in a purely dramatic way . . .[24]

What he means, perhaps, is that Wagner's silences and near-silences, of which there are plenty in *The Ring* and elsewhere, were used mainly as special effects—the tense pauses that prepare the *Todesverkündigung* in Act 2 of *Die Walküre*, the expectant thinning of the texture at Parsifal's final-act appearance as the Black Knight—whereas for Debussy silence and repeated notes are simply the first two components of an expressive scale that shares, in somewhat enhanced form, the properties of spoken language. No doubt he slightly exaggerates this distinction. The many silences in his first scene are partly at least Mélisande's personal silences: in a sense she *is* silence. And sometimes these gaps suggest the awkwardness of talking to someone who won't speak or who answers the wrong questions. Surely that makes them dramatic effects, or at least effects of character. But if you relate these silences to the next stage in Debussy's scale, the low density of short phrases made up largely or entirely of repeated notes in more or less even values, then to the many phrases that move largely or entirely by step, you can begin to appreciate Debussy's skill in moulding the simple elements of speech into a sung language of extraordinary expressive beauty and flexibility. Even at the opera's most violent or overwrought moments—Golaud swinging Mélisande by the hair; the lovers' feverish embrace before Pelléas's murder—the vocal lines remain rooted in note repetition and step-wise motion, with isolated thrusts of upward or (less often) down-ward energy—just as in daily life, when we are angry or upset, we still mostly keep to the normal contours of speech but with explo-sions on individual words or phrases. In general, only the clinically insane talk in the jagged lines of Parsifal and Kundry in Wagner's second act or of the patently disturbed heroines of Strauss's *Salome* or Schoenberg's *Erwartung*. For all its strangeness of context, no one in *Pelléas* is in need of treatment. With odd exceptions, like the search for Golaud's ring in a cave nowhere near where it was lost, they all behave quite rationally, and if Golaud's killing of his brother falls outside that rubric, one has to admit he is provoked. A French court in 1895 would have acquitted Golaud of murder on grounds of *crime passionnel*. It might also have noted that on a previous occasion when he seemed to be contemplating murder but in a calmer spirit (after taking Pelléas down into the vaults) he had drawn back from the act. In Allemonde, in any case, there are no law courts, and Golaud is free to regret his actions by his wife's deathbed.

The other crucial aspect of *Pelléas et Mélisande*—the aspect by which most of us recognise Debussy's style even if we could never identify the reason—is its harmonic language. We have seen this developing through his songs, and in a single short orchestral mas-terpiece, over the previous ten years or so. But a three-hour opera obviously demanded a range of idiom and an overarching coherence not called for even in longer songs such as "Le Balcon" or "De rêve." Debussy had admittedly had some practice in *Rodrigue et Chimène*, and it may well have been his difficult and sometimes reluctant expe-rience with that work that helped him with the discipline needed, and achieved, in *Pelléas*. Fear of the problems involved might even have influenced him in his choice of a play in short scenes with an average length of less than ten minutes, though in the event he then made life harder for himself by the decision to link the scenes with orches-tral interludes rather than simply lowering and raising the curtain, which is presumably what happened in Lugné-Poe's production of the play. The original interludes were admittedly much shorter than the extended versions he had to compose at the last minute to cover the scene changes in the eventual first production of 1902. But the continuity was there from the start, and continuity—in a style that breaks almost every known conservatory rule of harmony without ever casting the listener adrift in a sea of modernistic complexity—is perhaps the work's greatest achievement of all.

The elements of this language are the ones we have encountered before: for the most part more or less conventional chords of tonal harmony, but treated as isolated events or colours without past or future, much like Maeterlinck's dramatis personae. These rich chords of the seventh, ninth, eleventh and thirteenth, with or without added sharps or flats, constantly suggest the tonal grammar they are culled from, but hardly ever acknowledge their parentage. When Debussy does, rarely, settle on a simple tonic chord, or even, still more rarely, an ordinary perfect cadence such as concludes almost every work in the classical repertoire, it is enough of a surprise to count as a particular gesture. For instance, Golaud's assurance to Mélisande at the start of Act 2 scene 2 that he is unhurt by his fall from his horse, or his enquiry later in the scene whether her unease was caused by Pelléas, both moments supported by unadorned perfect cadences, seems to imply some lack of subtlety in his personality, a sort of plain-man, that's-that quality remote from the complications that we the audience know lie behind both the statement and the question. He later admits, "I'm like a blind man looking for treasure on the ocean bed! . . . like a new-born baby lost in the forest," at which point the music tries, but fails, to settle on a common chord of G major. All the time one feels that home keys are never far away, even when Debussy whizzes through sequences of parallel ninth chords, in honour of his remark to Guiraud that "il faut noyer le ton" ("you have to drown the tonality"). It may be an open question which tonality. What we feel is a certain general presence, something one specifically does not feel, or should not feel, in atonal music, where the tonality is not drowned but strangled at birth.

The "field" approach, which carries the music along with surprising fluency, is especially noticeable in two particular kinds of harmony, both well established here and there in Debussy's songs, but now given specific meanings relevant to this particular story. One kind is the whole-tone scale that we came across in "Recueillement,"

where its lack of direction created a moment of rather sinister stillness appropriate to the "obscure atmosphere enveloping the town,
bringing peace to some, anxiety to others." A simple illustration of
the effect of these harmonies is at the end of the vault scene, when
Pelléas emerges on to the sunlit terrace and breathes in the smell
of the sea and the scent of the just-watered roses, and the harmony
changes from dark whole-tone to bright arpeggios of sevenths and
ninths: dissonances, at the Conservatoire, that need resolving, but
here enough of a resolution in themselves. The other kind is the
modal harmony with which the opera begins, and that creates the
once-upon-a-time flavour that goes with the story's sense of time-
less antiquity. Golaud's motive, in the fifth bar, is whole-tone on this
first appearance, so there's an early opportunity to hear how Debussy
controls the atmosphere by fluctuations of harmony, a process that,
in one way or another, runs through the entire opera. Above all, this
montage of harmonies is managed by Debussy with such brilliance
that the listener hardly has time to wonder how one thing follows
from another or whether it will be apparent when it's all over.

Pelléas et Mélisande is a masterpiece of many ambiguities. On the
face of it, it is a Symbolist work set in a dream-like environment;
yet it is a coherent love story with a beginning, a middle and an end
played out by believable, rounded characters with comprehensible
motives. It is a fairly derivative score. It plainly owes a lot to Wagner
in its broad discourse, in some of its materials and procedures, and
even in some aspects of its subject matter. There are indirect allusions to Musorgsky's *Boris Godunov*, not only in the style of word-
setting, but in various orchestral details—for instance, the oscillating
quaver and semiquaver figures that abound in the accompaniment
(as in Musorgsky's Chudov and Kremlin scenes)—and in particular
gestures, such as the flute solo that opens Debussy's second act, an
apparent reminiscence of the start of the Kremlin scene. These are
background presences, but they seldom impinge on the originality
and individuality of Debussy's opera, which have evolved through
his own earlier work and in response to ideas of his own that may
indeed have been helped along by reactions *against* Wagner and by
sketchy encounters with assorted Russians, just as Bach learned from
(and stole from) every foreign genius he could lay his hands on, and
became the great Bach. Even if his songs and Mallarmé *Prélude* had

not already done so, *Pelléas* gave notice of the great Debussy, a score of astonishing beauty and theatrical impact in itself, and a confirmation of the validity and workability of ideas that might previously have seemed not much more than the gurglings of a baby pulling the plug out of its own bath.

The question of symbolism has been well worked over in the Debussy literature. Maeterlinck's play is presumably Symbolist in the sense that it tells a story set in a strange, nowhere land about people who hardly belong to the real world. But apart from a few unexplained circumstances and impedimenta—Mélisande's personal history, the crown in the fountain, the old men asleep in the cave—it lacks the allusiveness, solipsism, and counter-intuitiveness we normally associate with true Symbolist art from Huysmans's *À rebours* to the poetry of Eliot and the paintings of Chagall and Magritte. Debussy adds the symbolic power of music, but that is a generic property shared with all music, perhaps all art. In his influential book *Debussy: Impressionism and Symbolism*, Stefan Jarocinski attempts to draw a distinction between those two troublesome -isms and to argue for the replacement of the former label with the latter in Debussy's case. There is no denying that, at the time of *Pelléas*, Debussy was much in the company of poets and writers whose work employed obscure syntax and hidden meanings to a far greater extent than Maeterlinck, and of painters such as Maurice Denis who used visual images as insignia of properties not portrayed. But this is a poor reason for a tendentious labelling of Debussy's own work. Whether *La Damoiselle élue*, the score of which was published in 1892 with a cover by Denis, is any more "Symbolist" than, say, Berlioz's *Nuits d'été* is a topic for discussion, to the point at which one might weary of the whole issue of labelling. One might simply point out the categorical error of comparing Impressionism and Symbolism at all. Symbolism is a relation of subject to meaning, while Impressionism is a relation of subject to technique. Debussy might be neither, or both at once, as Jarocinski seems to admit when he suggests that "in [Monet's] latest works (e.g. *Nymphéas*) Impressionism rejoins Symbolism."[25]

Debussy was himself well aware of the special properties of his work, without attributing to them smart pigeon-holing labels, which, like most artists, he detested. He thought of his characters as real people, and lived intensely in their company while writing. His account to Lerolle of the violent scene between Golaud and Mélisande is revealing in this respect.

> For it's there that one begins to stir up catastrophes, there that Mélisande begins to lie to Golaud and to be clear about herself, all of which demonstrates that one shouldn't be totally frank, even with little girls; I think the scene outside the cave will please you; it tries to be all the mystery of the night where, amid so much silence, a blade of grass disturbed in its sleep makes a noise that is quite disquieting; then there's the sea nearby airing its grievances to the moon, and Pelléas and Mélisande a little afraid to speak in the midst of so much mystery.[26]

"I live," he had told Pierre Louÿs a year previously, "solely in the company of Pelléas and Mélisande, who are always very accomplished young people."[27] A month later he had finished the vault scene, "full of sinister terror," he informed Lerolle, "and mysterious enough to give even the most temperate souls vertigo"; and the following scene, emerging from the vault, "full of sunshine, but sunshine bathed by our mother the sea." But the lovers themselves had

> begun by sulking and no longer wanting to come down from their tapestry, so I was obliged to play with other ideas, at which point they came and leant over me, and Mélisande, with that sweet morbid voice of hers that you know, said to me: "Drop these silly little ideas so loved by cosmopolitan audiences and stick to your dreams of my hair, you know very well that there's no love like ours."[28]

Eventually he admitted to Louÿs that "Pelléas and Mélisande are my only friends at this minute; moreover we're perhaps getting to know one another too well, and we tell each other nothing but stories whose endings we know perfectly well; but then, finishing a work is a bit like the death of someone you love, is it not? . . ."[29]

Pelléas et Mélisande was complete, apart from the orchestration, by August 1895, but it lay on the composer's desk for a good many years before reaching the stage of the Opéra-Comique in April 1902 and being published in vocal score that same year by Fromont. One problem, as Debussy foresaw, was the unconventional nature of the characters and their vocal castings. Mélisande, the only substantial female character, is hardly a typical operatic soprano, while the "tenor" part, Pelléas, is equally suitable for a high, light baritone, what the French call a "baryton Martin," and has been sung as often by baritones as by tenors. "In France," he wrote to Lerolle after finishing the score,

> whenever a woman dies in the theatre, it has to be like the "Dame aux Camélias," except that you can replace the camellias with other flowers and the "Dame" with a princess from the bazaar! People can't admit that one leaves discreetly as someone who has had enough of this planet Earth and is off to where the flowers of tranquillity grow.[30]

But then he dreaded the whole business of production and performance and the associated hullabaloo. "I hate crowds, universal suffrage and tricolore phrases!" he told Lerolle in the same letter. He had played the work, in whole or part, a number of times in private before it was accepted in principle for staging at the Opéra-Comique. Even then it was four years before the production actually happened, during which time Debussy made substantial revisions, particularly to the fourth act. The orchestration was written down—though presumably largely present in Debussy's mind—only after the work's formal acceptance in 1901.

6

Bilitis and Other Women

On 22 December 1894, a thirty-five-year-old Jewish artillery captain in the French army, Alfred Dreyfus, was convicted of the treason of communicating French military secrets to the German Embassy in Paris, and sentenced to life imprisonment and solitary confinement on Devil's Island off the coast of French Guiana. That same evening Debussy's *Prélude à l'après-midi d'un faune* had its first performance in a concert under a young Swiss conductor, Gustave Doret, in the Salle d'Harcourt. The work, which had been publicly rehearsed in the afternoon, was encored in the evening, despite the fact that the performance, by some accounts, left a good deal to be desired.

This curious coincidence of events might be taken as emblematic of the relation between French art and French political life as the nineteenth century drew to a troubled close. Debussy's *faune*, dreaming his sexual fantasies obscurely and wordily on a hot afternoon in, presumably, Attic Greece, seems unimaginably remote from the political fears and prejudices of 1890s Paris that lay behind Dreyfus's wrongful conviction. Debussy himself seems not to have been particularly interested in the Dreyfus affair, which, then and for many years afterwards, divided French opinion, French society and even French families to an extent hard to recapture today. According to his friend the writer René Peter, his instincts were on the side of the nationalist anti-Dreyfusards, but Peter admits that he failed to provoke the composer into anything approaching anger on the subject either way. Edvard Grieg's gesture of refusing to conduct in France in 1899 because of Dreyfus's reconviction that year was beyond Debussy's comprehension, and was implicitly ridiculed by him four years later in an article in *Gil Blas* that referred to Grieg as "that Scandinavian composer who was so disagreeable to France at the time of the Affair."[1] It's true that Debussy, as we shall see, was from time to time involved in theatrical projects with a definably political angle. But none of this came to fruition, while his own finished work is entirely innocent of such nuances until, near the end of his life, war created mental conditions that could even blow *L'Art pour l'art*—Art for Art's Sake—out of its still waters.

Debussy had recently formed a close friendship with a young poet by the name of Pierre Louÿs, already, at the age of twenty-three, the author of two collections of erotic verse—one entitled *Astarte* (published in the literary review, *La Conque*), and a much longer set, *Chansons de Bilitis*, which was published in book form in 1894—as well as a number of short stories. The two had met, probably, at Mallarmé's Tuesdays and at Bailly's bookshop, in 1891 or early 1892, but they became intimate only in the latter part of 1893, when they even considered sharing an apartment together. When Debussy went to Brussels in December that year to talk to Ysaÿe about his string quartet, then on to Ghent to get Maeterlinck's permission to set *Pelléas*, Louÿs went with him and, according to his own report, did most of the talking with Maeterlinck while Debussy hung back like a shy wallflower (though Debussy's own account has Maeterlinck behaving like "a young girl to whom one is presenting a future husband").[2] Three months later, at the end of the Thérèse Roger affair, Louÿs wrote to Mme de Saint-Marceaux defending Debussy's behaviour, admittedly on the somewhat fragile grounds that he could hardly be expected to send packing a mistress of two years' standing as if she were a chambermaid. "As for the rumours that have reached you about his former life," he added, "I go bail that they are monstrous calumnies . . . I know personally that Debussy is incapable of having lived the way they say."[3]

It was a brave guarantee on five or six months' friendship, and even a somewhat risky stance in the light of Louÿs's own candid attitude to sexual mores. But he and Debussy had rapidly become close, on the basis of shared tastes in art and poetry, in Symbolist theatre and literature, in the music of Wagner (absolute in Louÿs's case, guarded in Debussy's), and not least in women as the object of sensual fantasy and self-indulgence. When Louÿs took up André Gide's suggestion in 1894 that he follow him to Algeria to indulge his taste for underage girls (Gide's own preference being for boys), he invited Debussy to join him, with the encouragement of a graphic description of his sixteen-year-old mistress "who speaks French so well that, at a moment I can't specify without indecency, she let go the following affirmation: 'Tarrarraboum!! ça y est!!'," adding, "It's hot, the light is stunning, and the women are all like Bilitis, at least the little girls."[4] (Debussy declined the invitation.) Louÿs was an unashamed eroto-mane, addicted to nude photography (including of Gaby Dupont), and to literary pornography, of which the *Chansons de Bilitis* are a stylish example. But he was also genuinely erudite, a classical lin-guist and a sufficiently knowledgeable student of Greek and Roman literature to be able to fabricate plausible imitations that, at least in "translation," could for a time pass as authentic. Above all, he was—with breaks—well off, and a useful source of funds to his perennially insolvent composer friend.

Debussy had been working on a set of piano pieces that to some extent embodied the harmonic language he had perfected in *Pelléas*. There were two slow pieces—a very slow waltz and a sarabande—and a quick bravura piece based, like "La Belle au bois dormant," on the children's song "Nous n'irons plus au bois." He called them *Images*, as we know from a letter of December 1894 to Lerolle about the pieces' dedication to his daughter Yvonne.[5] But there is not much evidence in the music of any pictorial association. It was probably the first one, headed simply *Lent, mélancolique et doux*, that Debussy described to Lerolle as "a waltz for the use of people who only like such things in a good armchair."[6] The last piece, also untitled, bears the sardonic epigraph: "Some aspects of 'Nous n'irons plus au bois' because the weather is unbearable." The middle piece is labelled "In the tempo of a 'Sarabande', that is, with a grave and slow elegance, even a bit old-portrait, souvenir of the Louvre, etc." It was the only one of the three to be published in Debussy's lifetime; it was printed by *Le Grand journal du lundi* in February 1896, and it then reappeared in 1901, slightly revised, as the central panel of the cycle *Pour le piano*.

As a pianist, Debussy must have known his instrument inside out, and as a keen improviser, he must have explored its unique properties of sound production, sound combination, and resonance as a musical recreation. But these *Images oubliées* (*Forgotten Images*), as they were called when they were at last published as a set in 1977, are gener-ally vague about such questions beyond the actual notes and basic indications of touch and phrasing. Above all, pedal markings are completely absent, even though some details cannot be performed as written without the sustaining pedal. This is an issue that will raise its head especially in connection with Debussy's great piano works of the 1900s, but it's worth mentioning here—since it relates to his harmonic idiom of the 1890s—that these slow sequences of sevenths, ninths and elevenths, and the strings of parallel sixth chords and triads, all demand refined pedalling to avoid a total fog of dissonant harmony while achieving what Marguerite Long called the "intense *legato*" of Debussy's own playing.[7] In this respect the first two *Images* are to some extent versions of each other. They explore the same or very similar chords. The third piece is crisper and brighter, like some Couperin harpsichord piece for the modern age. At one point the keyboard imitates "harps pretending to be peacocks spreading their tails, or the peacocks imitate the harps (as you like it!) and the sky again becomes favourable to bright clothing." But this is little more than a study for a later piece whose sky is duller and whose clothing is tighter, *Jardins sous la pluie*, the last of the *Estampes* of 1902. It's easy to see why the pernickety Debussy preferred not to publish the outer two *Images*, though he announced all three on publishing the sarabande. He knew he could do them better. The sarabande was, almost, done.

Work on these somewhat inchoate pieces, as well as on the violin nocturnes for Ysaÿe, seems to have been interrupted spasmodically by a project for a collaboration with Louÿs on a Christmas opera called *Cendrelune*, about a little girl who longs to wander in the forest but is kept locked up by her stepmother, until one day she is enticed away by a group of enchanted girls who tell her she is the daughter of the Dame Verte (the Green Lady) and that she will be able to find her mother if she goes of her own free will. A pair of Catholic saints tries to prevent Cendrelune from yielding to the temptation of the pagan greenery, but all in vain. Debussy was quite drawn to this hotchpotch, but Louÿs, after various modifications, turned against it. "One might make a book of it," he wrote, perhaps worried by the absence of male characters, "but to put it on the stage in 1895, *there is no way*." "Write *Cendrelune* yourself," he suggested a week or two later.[8] He himself had other proposals. There was a ballet called *Daphnis et Khloé*, and a ballet or pantomime based on Louÿs's novel *Aphrodite* (some elements of which might have been problematic even for the Parisian stage). Somewhat later Debussy himself (or, as he put it, "that little neurasthenic Mélisande") had the idea of a symphonic suite based on Louÿs's story *Les Aventures du roi Pausole*. So far as anyone knows, not one of these projects resulted in a note of music, even though Debussy pestered Louÿs about *Cendrelune* and claimed at least once to be working on *Daphnis*.[9]

A setting of Louÿs's partial (and very free) translation of Rossetti's *Willowwood* was slightly, but only slightly, more fortunate. In October 1896, Debussy wrote to Ysaÿe refusing him permission to perform excerpts from *Pelléas*, and offering instead "a thing I've done on a poem of D. G. Rossetti: *La Saulaie*. Note that this is very important and written according to my latest experiments in musical chemistry."[10] In fact at this stage Debussy had probably not so much as uncorked a single chemical, but three years later *La Saulaie* was again in hand, and this time, in the winter of 1900, a few sketches were made. As usual with Debussy, they are mere outlines, fragmentary, hard to read, and ambiguously notated, which has not prevented the resourceful Professor Orledge from producing a performable, genuinely beautiful if not chemically all that Debussyan score of the "entire" twelve-minute cantata. Only one work of Louÿs's, his *Chansons de Bilitis*, produced anything substantial from Debussy's own hand, and this inspired two works, a short cycle of three songs, and a somewhat slender, but finished, score of incidental music for a *tableaux vivants* presentation of another twelve of the poems.

The *Trois Chansons de Bilitis* was the first vocal work he had seriously embarked on since completing *Pelléas*, and the songs are closely allied to that opera in a number of ways. In particular the writing for voice is almost entirely close set, with much note repetition and stepwise motion, frequent implied silences and an almost complete absence of melisma (more than one note to the syllable). As usual with Debussy, the prevailing dynamic level is soft or very soft, so that the few moments of *mezzo-forte* or louder—none in the first song, a couple in the second, one in the third—draw attention to themselves, and invite interpretation. The girl of the poems, supposedly a young lesbian courtesan on the island of Cyprus in the time of Sappho (seventh–sixth century BC), recounts a series of brief episodes in her life, mostly of an intimate, sometimes overtly sexual character, involving men, women and even children. In the very first poem, under the cheery subheading "Bucoliques en Pamphylie," she climbs naked into a tree and masturbates against a high branch. When he first published the collection, in 1894, Louÿs passed the poems off as prose translations from authentic Greek originals, supposedly found inscribed on the walls of a tomb in Cyprus, but as with most fakes, it is hard subsequently to believe that experts were genuinely taken in. The poems are so obviously the product of a voyeuristic male fantasy on the decadent fringe of 1890s Art Nouveau. Fortunately, this has little bearing on their quality, and even less on their musical potential, which Debussy was able to show was considerable.

Perhaps pointedly, he selected three poems from the first of Louÿs's three parts, in which, in her native Pamphylia, Bilitis is loved by men. In the first song, "La Flûte de Pan" (in Louÿs simply "La Flûte," but Debussy was still in the grip of his *faune*), he gives her a syrinx, a reed pipe, which they play in turns, one of Louÿs's more discreet metaphors for the sexual act. ("My mother will never believe," the poem ends, "that I stayed so long looking for my lost girdle.") The song itself is a masterpiece of antique simplicity. The singer chants softly within a range no greater than would be required to recite the poem with a moderate degree of emotion, while the piano oscillates between plain triadic chords coloured by gentle dissonances of the usual Debussyan kind, and modest filigree patterns with the occasional flourish, evidently meant as flute music. The whole effect is rather like the soundtrack of a *Nouvelle Vague* film: cool and matter of fact about an extremely delicate sensual experience, told without excess or insistence, but with a quiet intensity that verges on the private.

In the second song, Mallarmé's flute is replaced by Maeterlinck's hair, "La Chevelure." In fact, the poem, which was added later by Louÿs and sent to Debussy when as yet unpublished, reads like a conscious plagiarism of the tower scene in *Pelléas*. He tells her that he dreamed he had her hair round his neck and over his chest, that they were forever locked together, mouth to mouth, etc., etc. Debussy's setting is more restrained than the opera scene, though it does rise to the cycle's only *fortissimo*, at the image of their members becoming "so intermingled that I became you" and "you entered into me like my dream." But the real tone of the song is set by the surreal colouring of the figures that represent her hair, floating and waving across the "screen," to harmonies that express the curious mixture of intensity and inconsequentiality we associate with dreams. Here, as before, Debussy achieves a daring simplicity of musical effect: an almost comatose quality of vocal narrative against gently nagging ostinato repetitions in the accompaniment.

Finally, in "Le Tombeau des Naïades," we witness the death of heterosexual love, though this is not apparent from the song, which concentrates on the Schubertian image of the winter ice as a sign of the end of a particular affair. In the book, the poem is the last in the first part, before Bilitis takes ship to Mytilene and discovers herself as a lover of women. Debussy captures the poem's haunting picture of the girl walking slowly through the frosted landscape, her hair glistening with icicles, the whole image encapsulated in the rolling semiquaver figures in the piano right hand, and the melancholy thumb melodies, right hand and left hand. These middle voices are, literally, a Debussy fingerprint; they are important in "La Chevelure" as well. As for the general style of the three songs, it's perhaps worth noting that Debussy had just been orchestrating two of his friend Erik Satie's *Gymnopédies*, and may have been infected with the studied emotional neutrality of Satie's repetitiousness. The *Chansons de Bilitis* are far from neutral, but by feeding that base idea back into the intensely experienced but untheatrical sensuality of Louÿs's prose poems, they achieve something new and individual, a kind of concentrated motion that constantly suggests cinematic parallels, whether the *Nouvelle Vague* of Truffaut or the surrealism of Buñuel or Robbe-Grillet.

Soon after completing the *Bilitis* songs, Debussy performed them, with an unnamed singer, at a soirée given by a certain Mlle Worms de Romilly, after which "an old Argentinian gentleman who had for some time been containing himself with difficulty . . . marched up and down the room, shouting, 'No, no, that's not music! How do people come to write stuff like that?'"

We were all transfixed with embarrassment. I took him by the hand and led him up to Debussy, whom I introduced to him so as to put an end to his imprecations. Debussy was enchanted. He smiled and shook his hand and afterwards he would often ask me for news of this charming gentleman; and he would add, in his slightly nasal voice: "I like that man, I should be delighted to see him again."[11]

The first public performance of the songs was given by the young Blanche Marot in March 1900, who later reported that Debussy had called on her mother and enquired:

"Tell me, Madame, your daughter is not yet twenty? Good. It's very important, because if she understands the second song, 'La Cheve-lure', she won't sing it in the right way: she mustn't grasp the true brazenness of Bilitis's language." . . . My mother set Debussy's anxi-eties at rest and everything went splendidly.[12]

Roger Nichols, the editor of *Debussy Remembered*, elsewhere casts doubt on this story, pointing out that Blanche was already the mis-tress of Debussy's publisher Georges Hartmann, a fact of which the composer must have been aware.

A solution to the problem could be that Debussy went to see her mother some time before the performance and that she and Hartmann formed their liaison some time in the interim. But for our understand-ing of Debussy's mentality, the crucial point is that she was obviously able to sing the song *as though* not understanding it (otherwise he would surely have cancelled the concert).[13]

The issue is one of "knowingness," as opposed to the native, unself-conscious sensuality of Louÿs's poems and Debussy's songs. "There is, therefore, no requirement," Nichols adds, "to label the songs 'for virgins only'."

The *Chansons de Bilitis* are almost the only solid product of the two years following the completion of *Pelléas et Mélisande*, and strictly speaking only the first two songs, since "Le Tombeau des Naïades" was not composed till the spring of 1898. Debussy had spent so much time, or at least mental energy, on abortive plans such as the various Louÿs projects, as well as all sorts of other theatrical schemes, some of them—like the idea for an opera on Verlaine's verse comedy *Les uns et les autres*—never actually begun, others, like René Peter's *Tragédie de la mort* and Mme Jean-Louis Forain's Rosicrucian pantomime *Le Chevalier d'or*, at least tinkered with if not seriously worked on, that his focus on new conceptions of his own seems to have been severely undermined.[14] But there were personal and circumstantial reasons as well. There was *Pelléas* still lying on his desk, unperformed and with no immediate prospect of performance. He had little money and had often to go cap in hand to friends to whom he was already in debt. He resumed the Wagner sessions that had been curtailed as a result of the Thérèse Roger affair, no longer *chez* Mme Escudier, but now in the salon of a certain Mme Godard-Decrais. He took on the direction of a family choir started in 1894 by Arthur Fontaine's brother Lucien, and was still directing it four years later when he composed for it beautiful four-part settings of a pair of poems ("Dieu! Qu'il a fait bon regarder!" and "Yver, vous n'estes qu'un villain") by the fifteenth-century Duke of Orleans.[15] He took the occasional pupil, including Mlle Worms de Romilly, who sang in the choir and persuaded him to give her singing and, more believably, piano lessons. But over and above all these distractions, his love life once again, early in 1897, threatened to come between him and the calm contemplation he desperately needed for his creative work.

The affair with Gaby had survived the Thérèse engagement, and there had been other dangerous episodes, such as when Debussy had convinced himself that he was in love with Catherine Stevens, the pretty daughter of the Belgian painter Alfred Stevens, and had proposed to her sometime early in 1896. "He gave me proof," she told René Peter, "of such *disinterested* love during the worst moments of a family crisis, he whom people have called 'grasping', and he was so intelligent and he played me *Pelléas*, which he was working on. I would have married him, despite everything that was being said about him at the time . . . if I hadn't met Henry!"[16]

Towards the end of that same year there had been another fling of some kind, possibly with Alice Peter, the estranged wife of René's brother. Then, at some point in January 1897, Gaby had found a letter in his pocket that, as he wrote to Louÿs, "left no doubt about the development, even somewhat advanced, of a love affair with all the most romantic details needed to move the hardest of hearts."

Thereupon! . . . drama . . . tears . . . a real revolver and the *Petit Journal* to tell the tale . . . Ah! my dear fellow, I would have needed you to be there to help me recognise myself in that bad literature. All this is barbarous, pointless, and changes absolutely nothing; you can't erase a mouth's kisses or a body's caresses with an india rubber. That would be a nice invention, a Rubber to rub out Adultery.[17]

Somehow it was all patched up without such help, and Gaby was probably still around when, just over a year later, Debussy met a couturier's model by the name of Rosalie Texier, an attractive, elegant blonde from a bourgeois background in the Yonne. Lilly Texier came on the scene just when, at the age of 35, he was in search, not of sexual adventure, but of some kind of stability that he could regard as permanent. "I've been very unhappy since you left," he wrote to Louÿs (who had gone to Cairo),

unhappy in the most passionate sense, and have wept a great deal, since that simple act, in which all humanity meets, was the one thing that remained for me in so much anguish . . . What's more, I've never been able to get anything done whenever things have happened in my life; I think that's what makes for the superiority of memory: you can draw valuable emotions from it, but people who weep while writing masterpieces are incorrigible humbugs.[18]

Perhaps all the same he needed to feel passionately attached to the stable object. Peter's later reminiscence that at this time, "imperceptibly, the preoccupation with women was relegated to a secondary tier in his mind"[19] has to be moderated in the light of his eventually overwhelming physical passion for Lilly, which nevertheless did not preclude at least one infidelity that nearly brought the relationship to an end, and which, after four years of marriage, faded as quickly as it had blossomed, with results even more drastic than in the Gaby case. One might suggest that, as for other great artists, Debussy's work was always paramount but that it created a parallel need for emotional and sexual expression, a sort of reassurance on the human level. Creative work demands dullness in life outside, but life outside is not always willing to stay dull. Hence Debussy's penetrating remark about the superiority of memory, through which creativity can be fed by excitement without being blocked by it.

Another remark of Peter's, that Lilly "was remote from the dreamer Bilitis whose songs Claude was then singing," is beyond denial.[20] One wouldn't imagine this daughter of a railway telegraph manager in the provincial town of Montereau who, according to Marcel Dietschy, "prepared tea surpassingly well," echoing Bilitis's "I enjoy life only when naked. My lover, take me as I am . . . Take me as my mother made me in a night of love long past."[21] But Debussy could accommodate both types. A year after marrying Lilly in October 1899 he agreed to write incidental music for a stage performance of a selection of the *Bilitis* poems, consisting of readings illustrated by *tableaux vivants*, and accompanied by what Louÿs modestly described as "eight pages of violins, silences and brassy chords that give what one might call 'an impression of art' at the Variétés."[22] Debussy's eventual music for the private performance at the premises of *Le Journal* on 7 February 1901 was hardly more substantial than Louÿs's prediction—not more than ten minutes of music as interludes accompanying the *tableaux* for a mere eleven or twelve poems. But since the composer was probably playing the celesta (with a pair of flutes and a pair of harps), he will have participated in the preparations as well as the performance itself, which included enough nudity and "erotic contact between women" to provoke a threat of legal action by a certain Senator Béranger, a threat Louÿs seems simply to have ignored. As for Debussy's music, it has silences but no violins and no brassy chords. All is refined and delicately sensuous, a fragmentary afternoon of another *faune*. Unfortunately the celesta part disappeared, perhaps into Debussy's pocket, and has had to be reconstructed for modern performances.[23]

For the past seven or eight years, Debussy had had on his desk, or in his mind, or at least in his letters, a conception of an orchestral suite of an essentially nocturnal character, a conception that may or may not have remained broadly the same throughout those years, even if the actual notes on paper—such as they were—altered over time.

There is actually no hard evidence that he ever composed a note of the *Scènes au crepuscule*, which he told André Poniatowski in September 1892 were "practically finished" and five months later had been "well reworked."[24] As for the *Nocturnes* for violin and orchestra that he described in some detail to Ysaÿe in September 1894 and reminded him about two years later, there were, as we saw, enough sketches for a speculative performing version to be made, but no resemblance in them to any of the three *Nocturnes* that Debussy eventually completed at the end of 1899. This doesn't mean, though, that there was never a connection. During 1897 and 1898 Debussy kept up a running commentary with Georges Hartmann, his new publisher, about progress on the *Nocturnes*. Finally, in June 1898, he declared them finished, but then three weeks later, typically, modified the announcement: "As I told you, I've finished the *Nocturnes*, but the orchestration isn't yet done, which shouldn't hold things up too long . . ."[25] Alas, the delay turned into a worry. "You will hear and possess the three *Nocturnes*," he assured Hartmann in September, adding that "the three of them have given me more grief than the five acts of *Pelléas*."[26] But at the New Year he was still sitting on them, and finally in April he admitted that the first piece was not good enough and he was starting it all over again. Worse, perhaps, was to follow. On 3 July 1899 he wrote again to his long-suffering publisher: "You ask me what I'm doing! . . . I can scarcely do more than tell you what I *shall* be doing . . . I shall finish *La Saulaie*, then three other *Nocturnes* and the *Nuits blanches*."[27]

Three "other" ("autres") *Nocturnes*, meaning that he had discarded all three of the originals? This is hard to believe, since less than three months later he was again announcing their completion, if not happily. "If I haven't handed the *Nocturnes* over for engraving," he now told Hartmann, "it's because of my terrible mania [fussiness], of which I am moreover the first victim; so I was leaving them for a while and working on *La Saulaie*, another nightmare."[28] Not till January 1900 did he finally hand the *Nocturnes* over for performance and publication.

Poor Hartmann! Already bankrupted once (in 1891) and forbidden to reincorporate as a publisher, he had nevertheless done so under the name Eugène Fromont, and had bought the *Prélude à l'après-midi d'un faune* in October 1894, before it had even been performed. Now he was embroiled with that work's composer at his most evasive. The

Nocturnes might have clinched their relationship; in fact it was to be his epitaph, since just over three months after finally receiving the manuscript he died suddenly at the age of fifty-six. He saw the score but may well have been unsure of its effect, so strange and original must it have seemed to eyes and ears used to the appearance and sound of the music of Massenet or Saint-Saëns.

Whether or not any musical connection existed between the different stages, it seems likely that there was a persistent background idea that survived from first to last. The word "scenes" in connection with "twilight" in the original title is a visual, not a theatrical, trope, and when he first wrote to Ysaÿe he described the violin and orchestra piece he was writing as "a research into the various arrangements that a single colour can yield, like for example what, in painting, would be a study in grey."[29] As for the eventual title, *Nocturnes*, this clearly has nothing to do with the piano music of Chopin or Fauré, but is a borrowing from the American painter James McNeill Whistler, whose own *Nocturnes*—a title he himself took from music—are studies in particular named colours: blue and silver, black and gold, blue and green, etc., and who had also painted a portrait (of his mother) called *Arrangement in Grey and Black* (No. 1). These are all figurative paintings, not abstracts, but the artist seems at least to want us to believe that the subject matter is merely a peg on which to hang the colour scheme, since he usually places the subject after the colours in the title.

Debussy's own titles are precise but generic: *Nuages* ("Clouds"), *Fêtes* ("Festivities") and *Sirènes* ("Sirens"). The clouds idea looks as if it might be the study in grey he mentioned to Ysaÿe, except that the first piece was the one he discarded, so either the order was changed or *Nuages* as we have it was based on the same general idea as before but recomposed. These are not quite his first instrumental pieces based on visual images, but they are the first for orchestra—apart from *Printemps*, with its wordless chorus and lost or never executed orchestration—and the first in which the visual idea is worked into the bones of the music, rather than being merely a picturesque programme, as in "En bateau" in the Petite Suite or "Clair de lune" in the *Suite bergamasque*. It was *Printemps* that had prompted the deathless insult "vague impressionism" from the Conservatoire assessors, and these *Nocturnes* have, in their turn, been taken as a prime example of

Debussy's Impressionism by an age that did not see it as an insult. The original application of the term had, of course, nothing to do with the techniques of the Impressionist painters, everything to do with the effect of their work on the viewer. Monet's *Impression, Sunrise* and his *Boulevard des Capucines* gave a vague idea of the subjects, as long as you were willing to accept that the black splodges on the water were boats (what else could they be?) and that what M. Vincent called the "innumerable black tongue-lickings" at the near end of the boulevard were people. In the same way, Debussy's *Nocturnes* are "impressionistic" because they sound blurred at the edges, just as the paintings look rather blurred. You don't expect to identify objects in quite the way you do with a picture; after all, this is music. But somehow you feel the same way about Debussy as you do about Monet, and the descriptive term puts that feeling into words.

It is easy to make fun of this kind of thing, but as so often with Vox Pop there is a truth lurking in the pigeonholes. From a technical point of view Debussy is about as far from Monet or Pissarro or Sisley as it would be possible to get. The idea behind so-called Impressionist painting was to capture the image very quickly, painting typically in the open air in the presence of the subject, and the techniques involved related to physical matters such as the changing light and the drying speed of paint. Such issues have no meaning to a composer, working indoors in a medium that is not, like the painter's canvas, the eventual object, but only a set of instructions for its production (that is, performance). This is an essentially meticulous, partly abstract process involving the thinking through of an aural idea that may or may not have been prompted—still in the composer's mind—by a picture or a story or even a concept, like the one behind Liszt's *From the Cradle to the Grave* or Strauss's *Ein Heldenleben*. As composers go, Debussy was generally slow and painstaking, not because he couldn't write quickly, but because he wouldn't compromise with the smallest detail. With Monet, one supposes, compromise was avoided by preserving only what was deemed satisfactory. As a "quick" painter, you could in theory cover many canvases in a single day (save for the considerable cost of canvas and paint, a problem composers are largely spared), and you could discard or paint over most or all of them. The idea of a composer writing, say, half a dozen symphonic movements in a day, then binning five of them, is absurd, surely, even to those who have never thought what might be involved in composing and writing out five minutes of music for a large orchestra.

So where shall we find the truth? Debussy, as we've seen many times, was in revolt against the musical establishment, with its rule-books and its thou-shalts and thou-shalt-nots, and he had been spending most of his social time in the company of outcasts from other academies: Symbolists, Impressionists, café artists and performers, theatre people of a more or less alternative kind. Since his student days he had taken an enthusiastic interest in art and theatre, more than in new music, which he would have agreed with Chabrier was self-satisfied and stick-in-the-mud. Then in the mid-1890s he found himself accepted, even lionised, by a circle that, while bourgeois in its lifestyle, was artistically open and progressive. Chausson and Lerolle were that comparative rarity, artists with money. In their houses, and that of their brother-in-law Arthur Fontaine, you were surrounded by paintings and murals and drawings by all the new artists, and you met the artists themselves and perhaps discussed their work. There was a saturation of artistic talk, a sharing of tastes and distastes, a continuous contact with the maker and the made and, surely, a swapping of notes about aims and processes.

Take drawing, for instance. At the Académie des Beaux-Arts the ability to draw well was still regarded as a *sine qua non* for a properly equipped artist. But drawing implies outlines, whereas in Monet's and Pissarro's pictures form was defined not by drawn lines but by areas of colour. In a famous essay on Impressionism, the poet and critic Jules Laforgue traced the preoccupation with drawing to the idea that our sense of form is derived from our sense of touch, and has no direct connection with the eye.[30] A musician who is likewise eager to break down academic prejudices might suggest a parallel with form defined by harmony or, worse, presented as a set of schemata to which a properly trained composer is expected to adhere. Of course, this isn't really a very good parallel. Drawing is a fundamental discipline that only needs to know its place. Harmony and sonata form might seem to be advanced, if ossified, studies that only academy students bother with. Singing might be closer to drawing as a basic requirement, but singing and melody were certainly not on Debussy's hate list. For him it looks as if the example of Impressionism breaking the primary rules of draughtsmanship was suggestive as a general model for the

diffusion of boundaries. But there was also a sense that, in blurring
the detail of the subject and concentrating it into a set of motifs, the
painters were making discoveries about its soul that were obscured in
the more painstakingly accurate Academy landscapes. And this was a
terrain on which the composer could meet them as an equal. Wassily
Kandinsky, a painter with musical credentials, numbered Debussy
among the modern composers who "reproduce *spiritual* impressions
which they often borrow from nature and transform into spiritual
images of a purely musical form."[31] But in implying that this was a
property unavailable to visual art, he was being too modest. This is
exactly what (apart from the kind of form) one finds in the greatest
work of Monet, Cézanne, Gauguin, and Kandinsky himself, and it
is this shared "interior content" (Kandinsky again) that justifies the
shared terminology at a level somewhat deeper than the mere blurring of objects and textures.

Exactly why Debussy's drifting chords and fragmentary melodies
in *Nuages* suggest clouds moving slowly across a sky of melancholy
grey with occasional breaks is a question in perceptual psychology
that is beyond my competence. Not many listeners would dispute that
they do, though it can be argued that the trigger word is needed for the
ear to hit the right image (as opposed, say, to water flowing past water
lilies, or even the hallucinations of a troubled mind). To call this piece
Fêtes would be patently absurd; to include it as a movement in a symphonic work called *La Mer*, much less so. But the choice of subject is
itself significant. Clouds not only drift; like water they imperceptibly
change shape, so that the skyscape is not like a landscape seen from
a moving train, which changes only because of the changed perspective. Debussy's chord sequences seem to flow into one another, and
although this is obviously an illusion (not least because precise repetition is an aspect of musical form), it's the illusion that counts.

More even than most orchestral works, *Nuages* is formed as much
as anything by its scoring. The orchestra is not blended but layered, a
feature of clouds more than water or, perhaps, hallucinations, though
the opening chord sequence, for clarinets and bassoons, has often
been identified with a sequence in Musorgsky's "The busy, noisy day
is over," the third song in his *Sunless* cycle, where the poet is "inhal-
ing the poison of passionate spring dreams." There are other reasons
for accepting this influence. In the summer of 1898 while at work on

the *Nocturnes*, Debussy wrote two songs towards an intended cycle of five called *Nuits blanches*, to *vers libre* poems of his own, songs that resemble *Sunless* so closely in general texture and atmosphere as to virtually rule out coincidence.[32] In *Nuages* the chords outline the main theme, but their scoring is almost always discriminatory: woodwind for the rather severe, open-textured version that starts the work off, divided strings for the altogether more sumptuous extended version that follows. Wind and strings hardly ever play these sequences together. In the same way, the lapidary cor anglais theme (bar 5, etc.) is never played by a stringed instrument. It hangs in the texture like some motionless object, always the same and always at the same pitch. To identify this motif with some actual conceivable object in the sky (a hovering kestrel, a drone, a flying saucer) would be infantile. It's at this point that Kandinsky's idea of interior content comes into play.

Nuages is motion without change, surface change without existential change. Things drift but do not mingle. "Plus ça change," the French say, "plus c'est la même chose"; the more it changes, the more it's the same. This is a profoundly French, un-Germanic, un-British sentiment. All progress is apparent, not real. Just when we think we've moved on, we look up, and there is the same cor anglais theme in the same place, unaltered. Even when what seems to be a real change takes place and flute and harp play a much brighter, more hopeful theme in a pentatonic F sharp major, the cor anglais quickly reminds us that hope—like despair—is an illusion of temporality. By now Debussy's harmonic language has developed to the point where chords no longer carry implications, but generate colours prismatically and in a series of fluctuating patterns. The beauty of this music lies not in dramatic development or the strong contrasting of themes, but in the refined juxtaposition of colours, melodic, harmonic and instrumental. Debussy's ear for chord voicing—the exact placing of each note in terms of register, balance and timbre—was equalled in his lifetime only perhaps by Wagner, whose orchestration (in *Parsifal*) Debussy once memorably described as "seeming to be lit from behind," though he had also on an earlier occasion dismissed Wagner's scoring as "a kind of multi-coloured cement, almost uniformly spread, in which [M. Croche] told me he could no longer distinguish the sound of a violin from that of a trombone."[33] His own palette is unique, but a Russian influence might be detected in the desire to separate rather than blend the orchestral sonorities, a preference that goes back to Glinka and survives in Rimsky-Korsakov and to some extent in Tchaikovsky.

This separation is still more apparent in the brilliant second nocturne, *Fêtes*. It is even visible, and perhaps even more Russian. For much of the time the orchestra is laid out in blocks, or choruses, clearly grouped on the page, which has an antiphonal appearance not unlike certain Tchaikovsky scores, for instance, the Fourth Symphony, a work Debussy knew well. The clear spacing is the source of the music's transparency, and perhaps also of that sense of illumination, of lights moving from hand to hand, which Debussy implied in a description to a lawyer friend, Paul Poujaud: "a memory," he called it, "of popular festivities in the Bois de Boulogne in the old days, lit and invaded by the crowd."[34] The festivities evidently included dancing, of a somewhat bucolic variety. The programme note for the first performance, probably by Debussy, referred to

the movement, the dancing rhythm of the atmosphere with abrupt flashes of light, together with the intervention of a procession (a dazzling and chimerical vision) passing through the celebration, mingling with it: but the event remains intact, and there is still the festival and its mélange of music, of luminous dust participating in a total rhythm.[35]

There is in this account a fusion of visual inspiration and something more generalised and abstract. The visual parallel might be with a canvas such as Camille Pissarro's *Boulevard Montmartre at Night*, painted at more or less the same time (1897). Very obviously done at speed, the painting is a partially abstracted vision of Paris metropolitan life on a wet evening, with a procession of carriage lights down the boulevard, and a chaos of restaurant and hotel lights down either side, the whole thing executed with swift brush-strokes and a deliberate approximation of detail. There is no question of approximation in Debussy's wonderfully calculated orchestration, and instead the sense of an imprecise, flickering image comes from music's natural tendency to generalise, so that the festivities might be what Debussy tells us they are, or they might be Pissarro's, or they might be any one of a number of other possibilities.

A clue to this lies in Debussy's title, which denotes a concept rather than a specific event or locale. In subsequent works he would sometimes be precise (*La Soirée dans Grenade*, *Les Collines d'Anacapri*), sometimes conceptual (*Mouvement*, *Voiles*). In odd cases he would change from one to the other. The first movement of *La Mer* was originally "Mer belle aux îles Sanguinaires," but ended up as "De l'aube à midi sur la mer." But whatever the title, there is always—because music is the way it is—a leaning inwards beyond the implications of a particular event or place or person. Just as festivities leave a certain platonic impression on our mental retina, aside from the specifics of the event itself, so music seems able to go directly to that retina without passing through the event, which may be attached to it afterwards as a kind of excuse or explanation. We know what the *Symphonie fantastique* is about, but we wouldn't know if Berlioz hadn't told us, though we might sense the presence of something beyond the mere notes. The Russian art historian Vladimir Stasov considered that all music was programme music, and he had explanations for the "Eroica" Symphony and even for Schumann's Piano Quintet, neither of which had the remotest authority from the composer. In his view, the finale of the "Eroica" was itself a "fête," "a *crowd* of people, a popular festival, in which diverse groups of people succeed one another: now ordinary people, now soldiers, now women, now children—and all against the background of some rural landscape."[36] Nothing in this description clashes with Debussy's *Fêtes*, not even the soldiers, whom he represents with "a trio of muted trumpets [that] correspond to the memory of the music of the Republican Guard sounding the retreat."[37]

At the time, *Fêtes* probably seemed an odd sort of middle panel for the triptych, and certainly *Sirènes* was an unusual finale, not least because (like *Printemps*) it required a female chorus singing without text. Probably Debussy did not think of the *Nocturnes* as inseparable, since when Camille Chevillard conducted the first performance in December 1900 he left *Sirénes* out, presumably because of difficulties with the female chorus; and as we've seen in the cases of the *Fantaisie* and *Pelléas*, Debussy was inclined to be awkward about the excerpting of works he thought of as integrated.[38] All the same, *Sirènes* does balance *Nuages* in some ways. Between them, they provide a framing character of the unworldly, music that is slow moving, mysteri-

ous and above all intangible, offset by the brilliantly lit festivities of
the centrepiece. In other ways, these outer movements could hardly
be more different. Where *Nuages* presents a fairly straightforward
musical simulacrum of natural phenomena in terms of clearly defined
instrumental blocks, *Sirènes* is complicated by a hidden human narrative, not specified by the composer or the music, but implied by the
title.

In Greek mythology the Sirens are a pair (or more) of winged
maidens whose song is of such irresistible beauty that it lures mari-
ners to shipwreck on the rocks. Odysseus, their most famous target,
had himself roped to the mast of his ship in order to hear the song
without being enticed to his death. Debussy's sirens are of course the
female choir, and if one imagines what a siren song might be like, the
chances are one will be in the same mental parish as Debussy, even
if one has never heard *Sirènes*. There are precedents. For instance, in
Rimsky-Korsakov's *Sadko*, first performed in St. Petersburg in January 1898, the hero is lured (not fatally) to the ocean depths by a wordless chorus of sea-maidens that would not be wholly out of place in
Debussy's score. In the final act of Wagner's *Götterdämmerung* the
Rhinemaidens extend their lament for the gold in a wordless string
of *Weia-la-la*s. This is not to imply anything unduly derivative about
Debussy's siren song; nevertheless the mere presence of a wordless
female chorus in the finale of an orchestral work of this kind is perhaps more original than the actual music he gives them to sing.

Debussy regarded *Sirènes* as a work about the sea, and the siren
song is plainly heard as an emanation of the windy-watery music
played by the orchestra, to the point where it is sometimes hard to
distinguish the one from the other. The interior of this orchestral
writing is more complex and varied than in either of the other nocturnes; in certain respects it looks forward tentatively to the intrica-
cies of *La Mer* and even his Diaghilev ballet, *Jeux*. But once again the
appearance of the music on the page reveals a layering similar to that
in *Nuages*, if more fluid and with more sharing of material, as befits
the action of wind on water. Occasionally the layering makes for a
visual effect that already, amazingly, hints at the Stravinsky of *The
Rite of Spring*, the only thing, perhaps, the two works have in common. Also sometimes visible on the page, even to the non-musician,
is the unusual degree of repetition of two-bar phrases, conceivably

a weakness, or possibly a deliberate factor in the hypnotic quality of the siren song.

What sets *Sirènes* firmly apart from its two companions is the character of its melodic lines. In *Nuages* melodies are fragmentary; texture is all. *Fêtes* is a (somewhat erratic) tarantella made up of fast dance tunes and brass fanfares. But *Sirènes* is all about ornamented melody, arabesque and what Nectoux calls *fouetté*, the "whipped" flourishes that start in the clarinet in bar 1 and decorate the texture throughout.[39] These flourishes set up regular patterns against the slow weave of the melodies, which sometimes take on a positively oriental colour, because of this or that interval or this or that arabesque pattern. One recalls that the curling arabesque line was an aspect of the Art Nouveau that it derived from (among other things) Japanese prints. Whether this makes *Sirènes* an example of musical Art Nouveau, as Nectoux suggests, is a question that takes us straight back to the whole issue of equivalences that I discussed in relation to *Nuages* and Impressionism. A Beardsley drawing or a Shekhtel balustrade reveals its debt to the East in a direct imitation or indirect derivation from a visual model, but all a composer can do is translate this mimicry into a metaphor of line, a line that strictly speaking doesn't exist. Needless to add, if line is a legitimate description of melody, it can be found in every composer of the nineteenth century and before (Debussy heard it in Victoria and Palestrina). So the musical Art Nouveau turns out to be an extremely Vieil Art.

Diverse as they are, these three pieces make up a beautiful and highly original triptych. As with the *Prélude à l'après-midi d'un faune*, and bearing in mind that Debussy had not yet orchestrated, let alone heard, *Pelléas*, his refinement of orchestral touch in three such different contexts is little short of astonishing. The voicing and balancing of chords in *Nuages*, the deftness and athleticism of *Fêtes*, and the idiomatic instrumental detailing of *Sirènes*, show a range of mastery in a skill that remains elusive for some composers even after years of experience. And Debussy's scoring is never merely functional, never simply a question of transferring to the orchestra music conceived at or for the piano. In every case, for instance, the contrast and layering of wind and strings is vital for the articulation of the form, just as the contrasting and sequencing of colour are the main formative elements in an Impressionist painting.

No less significant is the way he uses his harmonic language as part of an overarching design, while mostly avoiding its traditional, textbook procedures. His method actually varies from piece to piece. In *Nuages* certain chords are effectively motivic; though often dissonant, they no longer remotely call for resolution, but provide a colour motif for the piece as a whole. In *Sirènes* the harmony is mainly underpinned by tonic–dominant pedals: for instance, F sharp and C sharp in the key of F sharp major in which the piece begins, then moving, more or less arbitrarily, to A plus E in A major at bar 5, and C plus G in C major at bar 8, and so on. These open fifths give stability and depth to the decorative polyphonies of the upper parts, like the deep ocean waters below the turbulent surface. In *Fêtes* open fifths are a motif, often in rapid parallel sequences, with or without the missing third. All three pieces show that Debussy was not in rebellion against tonality, only against the rules by which it supposedly worked. There is always a key just round the corner, even if it never quite arrives, which is probably one reason why, though it disturbed academic musicians, his music never seems to have created serious problems for audiences.

7

Lilly Versus the Piano

In the autumn of 1899, just as Debussy was finishing the *Nocturnes*, his domestic life took a new and superficially encouraging turn. He married Lilly Texier. He was so poor that they were unable to pay a priest and had to marry at the *mairie*; in order to afford a wedding breakfast, he had to give a piano lesson to his Fontaine pupil, Mlle Worms de Romilly, on the morning of the ceremony, and their honeymoon after it was a visit to the zoo at the Jardin des Plantes.[1] His letters to Lilly in the months leading up to their nuptials are evidence of an almost overpowering commitment, both emotional and sexual, to this pretty but intellectually rather ordinary young woman. Or perhaps what they indicate is a desperate need for the emotional security that he optimistically imagined would come with the sexual attraction he patently felt for her. One wonders what she can have thought of the gushing intimacy of these letters, so extravagant that the editor of the original French (1980) edition of his letters preferred to leave them all out. She must certainly have doubted their complete sincerity after returning to Paris unannounced one day in May 1899 and finding her Claude in bed with another woman, identity unknown. Briefly she walked out on him, then responded to his remorseful pleadings and avowals, if anything even more extravagant than before. He seems to have calculated correctly that she would respond to effusions of the "I yearn for the blush of your red lips" variety that he would never have stooped to set to music, always for him the mistress whose character and judgement he respected above those of any mere mortal woman.

It looks, all the same, as if Lilly may temporarily have shut the door on this more demanding lover. After finishing the *Nocturnes* in December 1899 Debussy composed practically nothing for the best part of a year, nothing except the fragmentary music for the *Bilitis tableaux vivants*, composed the following winter. He was probably toying with ideas for piano pieces that began to take shape early in 1901, and there was the small matter of preparing a proper piano-vocal score of *Pelléas et Mélisande* with a view to a possible production in the 1900–1901 season. Two years before, the then new director of the Opéra-Comique, Albert Carré, had issued a vague promise to programme the opera, after struggling up to the composer's fifth-floor apartment in the rue Cardinet with the theatre's conductor, André Messager, and hearing him play it through. But for that to become a practical reality, it was necessary to produce materials that would be of use to other performers. On one level this will have been a routine task, since the music was fully composed and Debussy had given private performances on the piano on a number of occasions. But the need to produce a piano part that other people could play may well have confronted him with precise issues of keyboard texture and colouring in contexts with a visual or theatrical dimension beyond that of a song accompaniment. More generally, it may have given him a taste for keyboard composition on a scale that, for one reason or another, he had seldom previously attempted. But, if so, that certainly was not the only prompting that, in the next two or three years, turned him decisively towards the piano as a vehicle for his most advanced musical ideas.

For one thing, he was certainly acutely conscious of an existing repertoire of French piano music that to some extent avoided the—in his opinion—tedious conventionality of so much of his countrymen's symphonic and operatic work. He was a particular admirer of Chabrier, whose piano works had a vividness and individuality very different from the kind of well-organised *écriture* that was taught at the Conservatoire (where as a matter of fact he had never studied). Chabrier had written for the piano with instinctive bravura, incorporating popular and pictorial elements, and rule-breaking harmonic procedures; there was a colouristic and rhythmic brilliance to his pianism and an absence of head-in-hands self-communing that surely appealed to Debussy, though he never remarked on it. Chabrier had died in 1894. But in March 1898 Debussy had attended a concert given by Marthe Dron and the Catalan pianist Ricardo Viñes that included a pair of piano duos entitled *Sites auriculaires* by a Conservatoire pupil of Fauré's by the name of Maurice Ravel. Debussy had been so impressed by one of the pieces, *Habanera*, that he had borrowed the manuscript from the young composer. No doubt he was aware of the music's debt to a piece by Chabrier with the same title; it even has an ostinato pedal C sharp picked up from Chabrier's *Habanera* (where it is written D flat). But harmonically Ravel's piece is more daring than Chabrier's, as if the image of exotic Spain had inspired a specifically colouristic approach to chord design.

How long Debussy kept Ravel's manuscript is not recorded, but within three years he had composed a two-piano habanera of his own, which he called *Lindaraja*, after the courtyard garden of that name in the Alhambra, Granada. It was his first, but by no means last, keyboard homage to Spain, a country he barely visited (he had seen a picture of the Court of the Lindaraja in a magazine).[2] Nor would it be his last piece of modest plagiarism of Ravel. *Lindaraja* is almost twice as long as Ravel's *Habanera*, but harmonically more discreet and pianistically less colourful. Debussy would soon do better than this in the Hispanic field, while still retaining memories of the borrowed manuscript.

Something else happened in Paris in 1900 that might have influenced him to write for the piano. The Exposition Universelle of that year was in many ways as grand as its 1889 predecessor. It gave birth to the Grand Palais and the Petit Palais; it was a major showcase for Art Nouveau in general, and for a whole gallery of improbable scientific and technological concepts, including talking films, diesel engines, various applications of electricity, and Russian dolls. As in 1889, it had a colonial section that enabled French visitors to congratulate themselves on their superior culture and their noble, disinterested efforts at civilising the rest of the world, especially the parts colonised by them. Debussy was not the kind of liberal thinker who might be shocked by such condescension, whether or not he would exactly have condoned it. As before, his interest was purely musical, and here he was by no means disposed to regard the "colonial" performances *de haut en bas*. Though there is no certain evidence that he heard the Javanese gamelan that was again on display, it would be hard to imagine that he did not. As for circumstantial evidence, there is a good deal of this in the music he composed in the next two or three years.

Roy Howat, in his superb *Art of French Piano Music*, argues plausibly that Debussy's return to piano music early in 1901 was precisely because the recent experience of the gamelan had reminded him that the percussive nature of his own instrument was as much a matter of refined, precisely articulated sonorities as it was of the rich, blended textures of the romantic keyboard.[3] His first essay of this kind, after finishing the *Bilitis* music, was a pair of toccata-like pieces—a *Prélude* and a *Toccata* so called—which he combined with a slightly revised version of the *Sarabande* from his otherwise unpublished set of *Images* of 1894, and published under the baldly functional title *Pour le piano*, as if deliberately hinting that this might be music conceived for some other instrument or instruments, then recast "for the piano."

Whether or not that instrument might have been a refined percussion orchestra like the gamelan is an open question. The clipped, *non legato* opening of the *Prélude* and the bravura "touch" music of the *Toccata* might suggest some such equivalence. But, leaving aside the Debussyan modal and whole-tone harmony, the parallel chord sequences and long sustained bass pedal notes, the music both looks and sounds more like something out of a Couperin *ordre* or a Rameau harpsichord suite, or even a Bach partita. Admittedly, influence is a slippery beast. How many composers, after hearing a Wagner opera, go home and start writing like Wagner, or planning an opera about gods and dwarves? They are at least as likely to do the opposite and write a comedy of manners for chamber forces, or go off at some tangent or other, directed by some remote association entirely private to themselves. Just occasionally, when influence takes the form of mimicry, we can cheerfully spot the connection. But these are not the most interesting cases.

Debussy completed *Pour le piano* in April 1901, and that same month, a married man with responsibilities, he finally yielded to the calls of Mammon and took a job as music critic for the twice-monthly arts magazine *La Revue blanche*. The hoped-for production of *Pelléas* that season had not materialised, and he perhaps felt momentarily at a loose end in his creative work. But he had no intention, as he told readers of his first column at the start of April, of acting as a common or garden reviewer.

> You will find here sincere impressions, honestly felt, rather than criticism, which is too often brilliant variations on the theme of "you were

wrong because you didn't do as I would," or else "you have talent, I have none, and that cannot go on any longer" . . . I shall talk very little about works established either by popular success or by tradition. Once and for all: Meyerbeer, Thalberg, Reyer—they are men of genius, but that otherwise is of no importance.[4]

He was as good as his word, but only for a short time. Between April and December he wrote a total of nine columns, then resigned, claiming "overwork and nervous strain."[5] *Pelléas* was now firmly timetabled and in need of orchestrating. The gamekeeper had to return to poaching.

The *Revue blanche* at that time, in the closing years of its relatively short life, was or had recently been associated with a number of the most prominent figures on the anti-establishment wing of the arts, many of them, including André Gide and Henri de Régnier, personal friends of Debussy. Insofar as it had a specifically political tendency, it was anarchist. Its managing editor, Félix Fénéon, had been arrested and briefly imprisoned in 1894 on suspicion of involvement in the bombing of the Foyot restaurant, and when the Dreyfus affair erupted soon afterwards, the *Revue* sided firmly with the Dreyfusards. But to call Debussy an anarchist in this sense, as Richard Langham Smith does in his invaluable English edition of the composer's articles, is a shade far-fetched. On Dreyfus, he seems to have been neutral or to have blown with the wind, and in general, politically, he could best be described as disengaged. Intellectually, though, he was antinomian to the point of perversity. For reasons of artistic self-identification, he fought ceaseless battles with the fashionable tendencies of the day, refusing on principle to accept even the most normal or uncontroversial *idées reçues*. To some extent this was no more than a willingness to be rude about composers and conductors whose genius or talent he didn't at bottom deny. Sometimes when reviewing new works by minor locals, he seems to have been curiously incapable of distinguishing gold from pinchbeck, but what music critic, however brilliant, was ever good at this? Schumann, for instance, was not. Hanslick, Ernest Newman, Andrew Porter were not. But Schumann (like Newman and Porter) saw it as his duty as a critic to keep himself informed and to describe and assess what he heard as sensitively and dependably as he could. Debussy was interested only in defining his own position in relation to what he was reviewing, with the result that his criticisms have a curiously lopsided feeling, something idiosyncratic that in the end relates to nothing except his own creative consciousness.

Thus, a symphony by Georges Witkowski sparks off a diatribe on the uselessness of the symphony since Beethoven. A group of Schubert songs are "bits of faded ribbon, flowers forever dried, and photographs of the departed." Beethoven's sonatas are "very badly written for the piano." The main aim of Massenet's operas is "to find documents to serve as a history of the female soul . . . [His] harmonies are like arms, the melodies like the napes of necks. We bend over women's foreheads in order to find out at all costs what is going on behind." "What I like best is a few notes on an Egyptian shepherd's flute: he is part of the landscape, and hears harmonies unknown to your treatises." For some reason, but perhaps with the Impressionist painters in the back of his mind, he calls for a music of the open air, which "would play in the free air and soar joyfully over the tops of the trees . . . Perhaps we would find there a way of obliterating those petty obsessions with over-precise form and tonality that encumber music so maladroitly." On the other hand, his composer's percipience gave him insight into the genius of Musorgsky's *Nursery* songs, three of which he had heard sung by Marie Olénine at a concert of the SNM in March.[6] Meanwhile, he completely ignored several concerts that professional critics would have regarded as unmissable.

In order to justify such omissions and purvey such thoughts with a certain degree of impunity, he invented the figure of Monsieur Croche, a latter-day version of Valéry's Monsieur Teste, a crotchety (though a "croche" is a quaver in French), embittered, wizened old cynic who has seen and heard everything, describes himself as an "antidilettante," and makes purposely provocative remarks such as: "To see the day dawn is more valuable than to hear the 'Pastoral' Symphony. What's the use of your almost incomprehensible art?" He rings the composer's doorbell one evening, for no apparent reason, and walks or is invited in. "At once he aroused my curiosity," Debussy tells us disingenuously, "with his particular vision of music. He would talk about an orchestral score as if it were a painting, hardly ever using technical terms." Debussy then makes the classic mistake of insulting his readership's musical perceptions, but by putting the

insult into M. Croche's mouth he can claim innocence. He even has
the old brute insult him.

> As I argued that I had witnessed and even taken part in very wor-
> thy enthusiasms, he replied, "You are quite mistaken, and if you did
> show so much enthusiasm it was with the secret thought that one day
> they would do you the same honour! So bear in mind that a truthful
> impression of beauty should induce nothing but silence."[7]

M. Croche is of course simply a *reductio ad absurdum* of Debussy's
own attitudes, which still reflect his student rebellions against everything the Conservatoire held dear. Obviously he regards the Prix de
Rome as ridiculous. Predictably he makes fun of the Opéra, and in
particular lays into Saint-Saëns and his latest opera, *Les Barbares*. He
attacks narrow musical specialists, those who by implication know
only music. "For me, to specialise is by as much to limit one's universe . . . I know all the music there is, and all I've retained is the special pride of being protected against any kind of surprise. Two bars
give me the key to any symphony or any other musical anecdote."[8]
This is essentially Chabrier's complaint about the tedious repetitiousness of Paris musical life, coloured by Debussy's own preference for
the company of non-musicians. The trouble is that M. Croche offers
no solutions to the problems he identifies. All he seems to be saying, in the end, is that musical life is a waste of time and the sooner
we're shot of it the better. And Debussy, as devil's advocate, reduces
himself to the weak protestations of the ordinary punter who buys
his tickets at the box office when he can afford them and expects to
be allowed to enjoy himself. Taken as a whole, these early reviews
are entertainingly, enjoyably perverse, but they change nothing.
As a later composer, Hugh Wood, has memorably written, "'The
composer speaks'—as great a moment as 'Groucho sings'. Similar,
too, in other ways: you hope that this is not what he does best."[9] In
Debussy's case, we can safely say that it was not.

Debussy's final article for the *Revue blanche* appeared at the beginning of December 1901, and within a few weeks he was in the thick of

preparations for *Pelléas et Mélisande* at the Opéra-Comique. Rehearsals with the singers began in mid-January, but even before that a quar-
rel had blown up between him and Maeterlinck over the casting of the
role of Mélisande. At the end of December the Scottish soprano Mary
Garden, recently the star of Gustave Charpentier's *Louise*, had been
announced for the part, which Maeterlinck claimed had been promised to his mistress, Georgette Leblanc, a more dramatic soprano who
had sung Carmen. By the end of January, Debussy was claiming to
friends that Maeterlinck was "in the bag," but if so he refused, like the
proverbial cat, to stay there. In February the composer had to endure
tribunals at the Société des Auteurs together with Maeterlinck. While
it seems to have been officially accepted that Debussy was within his
rights to cast the opera as he wished, Maeterlinck remained on a war
footing almost until the premiere. On 14 April, with the performance
imminent (though not yet finally scheduled), he published a letter in
Le Figaro disclaiming any association with the opera and wishing it
"a prompt and resounding failure."[10] Worse, he plotted physical violence. Leblanc herself describes an occasion when her lover, brandishing a walking stick, announced that he was off to give Debussy "a
few whacks to teach him some manners." She goes on:

> I waited in a state of anguish, certain there was going to be trouble. I
> couldn't visualise Debussy, with his tragic features, taking correction
> kindly! At every instant I looked down the deserted street to watch for
> Maeterlinck's return. At last he appeared at the top of the rise, wav-
> ing his stick at the sky with comical gestures. His report was pitiful.
> While still barely in the drawing room, he had threatened Debussy,
> who had calmly sat down in an armchair, while Mme Debussy rushed
> distraught to her husband with a bottle of salts. She had begged the
> poet to leave, and, to tell the truth, there was nothing else he could do.
> Maeterlinck liked musicians no more than he liked music, and he went
> on repeating: "They're all mentally sick, these musicians!"[11]

For Debussy, the Maeterlinck affair was merely a sideshow amid
the stresses and strains of rehearsing *Pelléas*, music of a completely
unfamiliar character both for the orchestra and for the cast, who, a
fortnight before the premiere, were still singing their music as if it
were normal opera, that is "at the tops of their voices."[12] Then with

only a fortnight to go before the pencilled-in premiere in mid-April, the conductor André Messager suddenly started asking for extra interlude music to cover the changes of scene: initially between the scenes of Act 2, then for the Act 1 changes, and finally for the change between the second and third scenes of Act 4. Altogether, Debussy had to write almost 150 bars of new orchestral music in time, as it turned out, for the delayed premiere on 30 April. As Orledge points out, Debussy could compose fast when he had to, but without the time to be as meticulous as usual, and above all without the opportunity to prevaricate about the likely completion date, the result inevitably lacked the stylistic precision of the rest of the opera. Writing at speed, he tends to lapse into a refined Wagnerism; he himself drew a young composer friend Gustave Samazeuilh's attention to a certain flavour of *Parsifal* in the Act 4 interlude, which he had supposedly written in one night just before the dress rehearsal.[13] But though designed to solve a problem ad hoc, the interludes improve the opera's pacing and formal balance even when it is staged, as most often now, with a single set and no drop curtain. The occasional performance omitting them tends to emphasise the brevity and multiplicity of the scenes, as against the continuity of the whole.

For various reasons the open dress rehearsal on the 28th was occasionally disrupted by laughter and some cat-calling, provoked especially by Yniold's scene with Golaud (his scene with the sheep was cut), and by Mary Garden's Scottish accent, which drew forth a good deal of mimicry from those audience members who could be relied on to see nothing absurd in Siegfried's "Das ist kein Mann" or Werther's detailed description of his own grave as he dies of a self-inflicted bullet wound. The premiere on the 30th, however, went off smoothly and without any disturbance, and was even a great success. Debussy had evidently managed to impose a certain restraint on the operatic singers, to judge by one reviewer's comment on the "sober declamation where not a word was lost and the orchestra was used with the utmost discretion."[14] Garden's accent seems to have faded into insignificance beside her musical artistry and strong dramatic presence. And though the press was mixed, as it nearly always is where radical art is concerned, there was enough support for Debussy to take a whole paragraph of his "Reply to the Critics" in *Le Figaro* listing those he wanted to exclude from the strictures and satires that followed.[15] "Accusations," Roger Nichols reports of the reviews, "were largely of formlessness (no arias), melodic and rhythmic monotony (no dances), lack of noise (sparing use of trombones) and unintelligible harmonic progressions (few perfect cadences)."[16]

The truth is that *Pelléas* was so unlike anything ever previously staged at the Opéra-Comique or, for that matter, at the Opéra, that it would have been astonishing if press reaction in general had been anything but bemused or hostile. Audiences are different in this respect from critics, being used to enjoying things that strike them as beautiful, without worrying how they are made or how they might best be described. *Pelléas* had an important precedent in Musorgsky's *Boris Godunov*, a profoundly radical masterpiece detested by the St. Petersburg critics in 1874 but so successful with audiences that it remained in the Maryinsky repertoire until Musorgsky died in 1881. It is perhaps no surprise that Debussy loved *Boris* and considered it an important influence on his own opera, though at this time he knew it only from the vocal score. *Pelléas*, too, was successful enough to be frequently revived, both in France and abroad, and it established its composer, more or less overnight, as one of the most important and influential figures in French music.

Earlier that same April a concert had taken place in Paris that was to have a profound effect on Debussy, though he was probably not present, being intensely involved with the *Pelléas* rehearsals. Ricardo Viñes, the young Catalan pianist of the *Sites auriculaires*, gave another Ravel premiere, this time of a solo piece with the Lisztian title *Jeux d'eau*. Debussy was already a friend and admirer of Viñes, who had given the first performance of his *Pour le piano* three months earlier. So even if unable to attend the Ravel premiere, he might already have known the work, which Viñes had previously performed privately, or he might have first encountered it when it was published later in the year.

Jeux d'eau is not a big piece (it lasts five minutes or so), nor is it a theatrical bravura study in the manner of Liszt, although its technical difficulties are on the Lisztian scale, and its graphic portrayal of the play of water in an artificial fountain was surely inspired by the Master's *Jeux d'eaux à la villa d'Este*. Ravel completely escapes from the idea of the romantic showpiece, and concentrates instead on the image of the fountain as a mechanical construct, controlled indeed by a highly complex algorithm, but in no sense expressive of human fantasy or aspiration. The effect is achieved mainly by exploiting the glittering, more resonant upper register of the piano with, at the same time, both the soft (*una corda*) pedal and the sustaining pedal in play. The upper registers of the piano are in any case undamped—that is, reverberate freely whether or not the sustaining pedal is depressed. But they ring still more when the lower registers are undamped, and it is Ravel's exploration of this aspect of piano acoustics that gives *Jeux d'eau* its unusual fascination.

However, there is another quite different yet in a strange way related feature of the piece that will certainly have intrigued Debussy. The lettering on the title page suggests an Art Nouveau derivation from some kind of oriental script, and the music itself is very obviously a reminiscence of the gamelan, which Ravel will already have heard aged fourteen at the 1889 Exhibition, and no doubt again in 1900. At the start, the right-hand arpeggios hint at a pentatonic (black-note) scale, and although the music quickly diverges into all kinds of more or less chromatic variants, the pentatonic motive returns several times, both in the form of arpeggios and as melody, for instance at bar 19. The black-note figures ring out more than the chromatically altered ones, because the notes are all on the same harmonic spectrum, and this means that the degree of reverberation constantly fluctuates, like sunlight reflecting off water droplets. Of course, the resonances also vary in an ordinary piece of tonal music: in fact, it's partly because the notes of the tonic triad are the lowest notes on the spectrum that they create a sense of closure. But Ravel exploits this property outside the region of strict tonality, allowing the colours and shades to flicker in and out, until the final page, where the music settles on a pentatonic version of an E major chord (with added C sharp and D sharp), pedalled "jusqu'à la fin" ("to the end").

Debussy's *Pour le piano* predates *Jeux d'eau* and reflects different keyboard interests, more technical and abstract, less graphic. But according to Lesure he had for some time had in mind a series of piano pieces that he intended to call *Images*, in which some graphic element would presumably come into play.[17] There is no evidence that any of this got composed before the actual signing of a contract with a new publisher, Jacques Durand, for two sets of solo *Images* and a set for two pianos or orchestra in July 1903. Instead he completed that same month a quite different set, which he called *Estampes* (*Prints*) and which Durand published three months later.

Since the *Pelléas* premiere, and its revival six months later, which also took up a good deal of his time, Debussy had toyed with other theatrical projects. A plan to turn *As You Like It* into an opera with a libretto by Paul-Jean Toulet never got as far as music paper, though it generated some lively scenic ideas. Debussy had spent a few days in London in July 1902, and had come home in a Shakespearean mood after seeing (though certainly not understanding) Forbes Robertson as Hamlet. But Toulet had gone off to Indo-China at the end of the year, had come back an opium addict, and that was that. Debussy's ideas for the scenario show that he had an idiosyncratic vision of Shakespearean comedy that sheds some light on his other choice of topic this same year, Edgar Allan Poe's farcical tale *The Devil in the Belfry*. He wanted, for instance, to introduce an offstage chorus to provide a commentary to the wrestling match in Shakespeare's first act; he wanted the character of the clown, Touchstone, made more of; and he wanted the final scene, the betrothal of Rosalind and Orlando, stylised into a masque, strictly choreographed and "mixed in with songs, but in the antique manner, that is, forming part of the action."[18]

This project was soon abandoned, but the Poe idea was the prelude to what was to become a lifelong obsession with the American writer, whose work, then as now, was far more highly regarded in France than in either the United States or Britain, and had been lovingly translated by two of her greatest poets, Baudelaire and Mallarmé. French writers of the Mallarmé generation found in Poe an echo of their own preoccupation with the fantasies and psychological terrors left uncared for by the materialism of the modern world. For them, in a word, he was a father figure of Symbolism. Debussy seems already to have tangled with one of his most disturbing tales, *The Fall of the House of Usher*, and would do so again. But *The Devil in the Belfry* is more of a satire on fantasy, in which, in the Dutch village of Vondervotteimittis, the devil decides to upset the ordered lives of the good villagers by making the midday clock strike thirteen. Debussy produced a scenario that shows that he planned to turn this humble nonsense into a wild ensemble piece, with dancing and choruses and a devil who whistles throughout. A few pages of sketches survive, and

Debussy was still thinking about the work in 1908, when he included it in a contract with the New York Metropolitan Opera, and possibly even still in 1911, when the Opéra-Comique announced it, along with *Usher*, for its coming season. But the actual music made no progress after 1903, unless one counts the one-minute *Morceau de concours* that Debussy knocked up out of the sketches as his contribution to an identification competition run by the journal *Musica* towards the end of 1904.

In fact he had made no progress with anything of any substance since the completion of the *Nocturnes* at the end of 1899. *Pour le piano* had been only partly new, and there had been a commission for a saxophone piece ("that aquatic instrument," as Debussy called it)[19] from the president of the Boston Orchestral Club, Elise Hall. But in the main he was drifting, marking time, waiting for *Pelléas* and waiting, probably, to find out what could conceivably productively follow that epoch-making work.

Then at the start of 1903 he again found himself employed as a music critic, this time by the literary journal *Gil Blas*. This was a more intense commitment than his *Revue blanche* column of two years earlier. For the same reason, it lasted a mere six months, but involved far more and more frequent writing and even some travel. His first piece took him to Brussels to review (very favourably) d'Indy's opera *L'Étranger*; then in late April he paid a second visit to London in order to write about Wagner's *Ring* conducted (marvellously, he said) by Hans Richter. Mostly, though, he was caught up with the usual Paris music, its occasional triumphs and frequent irritations. There are the same old obsessions, the same prejudices as well as some new ones. In only his second article he launches into an extended and only half-ironic defence of the barrel organ, as the basis for another diatribe about open-air music, but declines to discuss Berlioz's *Damnation de Faust*, a work—the reader is left to deduce—that he dislikes. Another bête noire is Gluck, whom he consistently compares unfavourably with Rameau, thereby reviving a famous eighteenth-century controversy in a new form. Gluck is partly to blame for Wagner and Berlioz ("always the favourite musician of those who knew little about music"[20]). Debussy loves Weber, loathes Mendelssohn and Grieg ("Scandinavian one might be, one is nonetheless human"),[21] admires Richard Strauss in spite of himself, and is warm in his praise of Franck's Symphony and Rimsky-Korsakov's *Antar*.

Behind all this is a certain incipient nationalism, a feeling (not unnoticed even now by visitors to France) that French is best—French delicacy, French precision, French restraint—even if "one may regret that French music has, for too long, followed paths that treacherously distance it from that clarity of expression, that precision and compactness of form, particular and significant qualities peculiar to French genius."[22] And the villains? The usual suspects: the Opéra, the Conservatoire, the Prix de Rome, the concert repertoire in general (too many operatic excerpts). But as before Debussy is better at identifying shortcomings than at suggesting remedies, with one striking exception. Reviewing Chevillard's concert performance of *Das Rheingold* on Good Friday, he expresses regret at the whole idea of performing Wagner in this way.

> You will object that there's magic in the orchestra. But if one is a Wagnerian, is that enough? I shall dare timidly to propose film as a means of animation; we have seen in a recent play at the Ambigu how powerfully it could increase the emotion. We should be of our time, and we have no right to deprive Wagner of the expressive ingenuity of this invention, of which the "Music Halls" make such marvellous use, in an infinitely less lofty cause.[23]

Not until the 1940s was film used in this way for Wagner, either in concert or on stage. And although, as Debussy admits, the idea wasn't strictly his own, it was typical of his eclectic approach to the arts that he picked it up on the streets and, in his mind, transferred it to the art he knew best.

There was one other eclectic element about Debussy's music column, namely that *Gil Blas* had decided—perhaps fearing his expertise—to employ a second music critic, in the attractive and not over-specialised form of the popular novelist Colette. Week by week the two columns were printed side by side, and Colette, though by no means musically unversed (after all, her husband was the prominent music critic Henri Gauthier-Villars, alias Willy), treated hers partly as an outlet for social comment, gossip and an occasional flurry of bitching. She was good at playing the poor little audience member. For instance, in praising Gabriel Pierné's *Concertstück* for harp and orchestra (which Debussy also liked), she added that "between ourselves, I never know whether it is just a nice tickle I get from harp concertos or whether they make me want to go *pipi*."[24] When Strauss conducted in Paris at the end of March, she went into paroxysms of distaste.

> No! Even if Debussy attacks me—or, worse, replies with a spiteful silence—I do not like that music! . . . I cannot accustom myself to this man, who chooses an aggressive tumult barbed with piercing piccolos for a sticky romance—a hedgehog garlanded with forget-me-nots! . . . Richard Strauss [also] conducted a "love scene" from his opera *Feuersnot*. Once again my ears went *bʒi-bʒi*! That a love scene? My God, if I went into such tumultuous ecstasies I'd be afraid of what my neighbours downstairs might say![25]

History is silent on whether or not Debussy attacked her for such remarks, though his own reaction was somewhat different. Over *Feuersnot*, he agreed that "one episode that raised orchestral torrents seemed ferocious for a love scene," but conceded that "they were probably justified by the drama." He rather liked *Aus Italien* (which was Colette's garlanded hedgehog), was carried along by *Ein Heldenleben*, and concluded that Strauss was "a great figure [with] the frank and decisive appeal of those great explorers who walk among savage tribes with a smile on their lips."[26] Between the two of them, it must be said, a by no means entirely misleading picture of Strauss and his music emerges.

Debussy's final *Gil Blas* column appeared at the end of June in the form of what he somewhat prematurely called "The Balance Sheet of Music in 1903." Much of it was about opera, or to be exact the Opéra and the Opéra-Comique. But it included two deathless remarks of a more general and revealing character. "To conclude," he urged, "let us stay in France. Let us wish people there to like music a little less, only so as to like it a little better." "Those devoted to Art," he had written a few paragraphs before, "[are] unshakeably in love with her, and on the other hand, one will never know to what extent music is a woman, which perhaps explains the frequent chastity of men of genius."[27]

⚬⚬⚬

In the case of this particular genius, Art had returned unexpectedly, like Lilly three years earlier, and caught him in flagrante delicto with a news sheet. Early in August he wrote to Louÿs from Lilly's parental home in the Yonne that he had just composed a piano piece called *La Soirée dans Grenade*, and had also been working on the Saxophone Rhapsody that was his belated, and somewhat reluctant, answer to the Boston commission of 1901.[28] *La Soirée dans Grenade* is the second of the three *Estampes*, so he had perhaps already written the first piece, *Pagodes*, and must have added the third, *Jardins sous la pluie*, well before the end of August, since by mid-September he was returning corrected proofs of the whole set to Durand and making suggestions for the cover design. On the same day that he sent back the proofs, he told Durand that he was working on his new orchestral piece, *La Mer*, which may or may not have delighted the publisher, who had a signed contract for three sets of *Images* still on his desk, its ink barely dry. Truly, the floodgates had burst open. "I've been doing a lot of work for you," Debussy had written coyly at the start of August, "and my music is perhaps worth more than my literature."[29]

Debussy scholars have tended to be guarded about whether this sudden rush of piano music had or had not been inspired by Ravel's *Jeux d'eau*. On the face of it, it seems improbable. Why should Debussy, a newly famous composer entering his forties, allow himself to be led by the nose by a young whipper-snapper barely out of his Conservatoire short trousers? Rivalry would be absurd, not least because, however brilliant the Ravel, Debussy, with half a dozen or more masterpieces behind him, had no need to feel upstaged by one five-minute piece. And yet *Pagodes* responds to *Jeux d'eau* in so many ways that the connection is hard to deny, especially if you then turn to *Soirée dans Grenade* and consider its debt to Ravel's *Habanera*. The simple explanation is that Debussy was intrigued by Ravel's music and wanted to adapt its underlying concepts to certain ideas of his own, in a spirit more of cooperation than of rivalry. It's as if, in hearing it or, more likely, trying it out, he thought: yes, excellent, but what if, instead . . . ? For *Pagodes* is not just a kind of oriental clone of *Jeux d'eau*. It does certain things in a specifically Debussyan way; and *Soirée dans Grenade* might use Ravel as a starting-point, but is soon exploring a somewhat different musical terrain. "If this music isn't exactly what they hear in Granada," he remarked to Louÿs, "well, so much the worse for Granada."[30]

The first thing one might notice about *Pagodes* is the marking below the first bar: "2 Ped," exactly the same as at the start of *Jeux d'eau*. Both pieces start *pianissimo*, with the soft and sustaining pedals both depressed, suggesting a very refined touch with the upper registers of the instrument creating a delicate harmonic aura around the melody. But such markings are a rarity with Debussy, who, as we saw, generally preferred to leave pedalling to the performer, in view of the great differences between instruments, hall acoustics and atmospheric conditions. In *Pour le piano*, for instance, there is not a single pedal indication. *Pagodes*, much more than *Jeux d'eau*, is built round unchanging harmonies that can be pedalled without unwanted clashes. Ravel's piece starts with a simple pentatonic melody, but the left hand clouds the issue and soon creates complexities of light and shade that require extremely subtle half-pedalling—light touches on the sustaining pedal—to avoid harmonic chaos by limiting bass reverberation. *Pagodes* is more about harmonic "fields," of the kind already identified in earlier works, including *Pelléas*, but especially a feature of gamelan music. *Jeux d'eau* may be gamelan-like in its texture and sonority, but *Pagodes* comes as close to imitating gamelan music as would seem possible without completely abandoning the aesthetic and intellectual world of Western music.

This difference already comes out in the titles. *Jeux d'eau* is a description, an image translated into sound, with an epigraph, from Henri de Régnier, that backs this up: "Dieu fluvial riant de l'eau qui le chatouille" ("The river god laughing at the water that tickles him"). *Pagodes* is obviously not graphic in this sense, but is more like a key-word, directing our gaze towards the lands where pagodas raise their upturned eaves. The intention is suitably vague, because pagodas are not characteristic of Java, so have no topographical connection with the gamelan. But Debussy may also have had a structural principle in mind, because pagodas are layered towers, and *Pagodes*, too, is composed in layers, both vertical and horizontal.

The vertical layers are the various strands of melody starting with the pentatonic melody in the right hand at bar 3, accompanied first by offbeat chords, then by a left-hand counter-melody plus chords. These elements grow in complexity, but never really interact; like a peal of bells, they form strands that resonate each other but remain essentially separate. The horizontal layering is more hybrid, because for the piece to make sense within its five minutes or so duration it needs a narrative element. It has, therefore, a kind of rondo form, with brief episodes of a more chromatic, less stable harmony, that lead eventually to a rhetorical climax of a distinctly Western character. But within this conventional-looking design, the music is a series of distinct units, linked by family resemblance but not really developing or evolving except through more and more elaborate ornament. Compared to *Jeux d'eau*, *Pagodes* perhaps leaves a somewhat primitive impression. But it has consequences in Debussy's music that are anything but primitive.

There are hints of this already in *La Soirée dans Grenade* ("Evening-time in Granada"). The only, slightly embarrassing, snag with this beautiful piece is that it is so obviously a parody (in the original, neutral sense) of Ravel's *Habanera*—a better piece than the Ravel, no doubt, but shamelessly derivative of it. The borrowings are flagrant: the repeated C sharps, less persistent in Debussy but essentially the same figure; the sultry triplet chords at bar 23 (from Ravel, bar 9, etc.); the dotted left-hand figures at bar 33 (from Ravel, bar 14, also on F sharp), and in general the habanera rhythm and detailing. It's true that Ravel's piece is little more than a sketch, a montage of a few style features bound together by a persistent ostinato pitch and rhythm. If it had been found among Debussy's papers and in his hand, it would probably have been accepted without much question as a preliminary draft for *La Soirée dans Grenade*. Instead, Debussy must consciously or unconsciously have thought: excellent, but a lot more can be done with that material. This piece is the result.

It may be that the montage idea was what initially appealed to him. Ravel, a native of the Basque country (but on the French side), seems to have thought of Spain as a set of picture postcards, a slideshow of characteristic scenes or fragmentary impressions: a hot sultry day, a girl in a mantilla, a man driving a donkey up a hill, a boy tuning a guitar, a general flavour of *mañana*. Why it should have been Spain that inspired this particular approach (rather than, say, Turkey or Morocco) is something of a mystery; perhaps it was its proximity and relative familiarity, combined precisely with those other exotic aspects, the Moorish, the African. But the first composers to think of Spain in this travel-poster way were Russian: notably Glinka, and Rimsky-Korsakov, a composer admired, and occasionally imitated, by both Ravel and Debussy. Glinka's *Souvenir d'une nuit d'été à Madrid* ("Memory of a Summer Night in Madrid") might have been a specific precedent for Debussy, though he probably didn't know it. He almost certainly *had* heard Rimsky-Korsakov conduct his *Capriccio espagnol* at the 1889 Exhibition, and perhaps the fourteen-year-old Ravel had as well.

La Soirée dans Grenade is a street scene: atmosphere with passersby. The C sharp ostinato at the start hangs expectantly in the air, and soon a distant voice intones one of those laments, all triplets and augmented seconds, that announce deep Spain as surely as the "Song of the Volga Boatmen" announces antique Russia. This in turn is interrupted by a strummed guitar phrase, and so it goes on. At first the events alternate, then briefly they combine, at which point Debussy adds a third stave in order to clarify the various layers of the texture. Towards the end a fragment of flamenco is spliced in, different from its context in both rhythm and tempo, and then on the final page the various episodes reappear in a more rapid montage of fading incident, leaving first the lament, then the ostinato, more restful because the harmony is now resolved on to the F sharp major that Debussy decides, on the basis of earlier unresolved dissonances, to treat as the home key.

The ancestry of *Jardins sous la pluie* ("Gardens in the Rain"), unlike that of the other two *Estampes*, lies in Debussy's own music. The content, like the title, of the third of his 1894 set of *Images*, "Some aspects of 'Nous n'irons plus au bois' because the weather is unbearable," had been obviously provisional. Bad weather now suggested a recast and more tightly composed piece based partly on that song, but more especially on another children's ditty, "Dodo, l'enfant do" (a lullaby of the "Rock-a-bye baby" variety), a phrase from which is played by the left hand at the outset. Various stories were told of Debussy refusing to come in out of the rain while sketching this piece, but nobody seems to have had any theory about the connection between the children's songs and wet weather. The alleged reason in the poem for not going to the woods was that the laurels had been cut, though as usual with nursery rhymes the subtexts proliferate and logic goes out of the window (where it may or may not be raining).[31]

Debussy of course chose these tunes, not for their texts, but for their value as melody; their simplicity of line was useful to him as a framework for a variety of watery figurations. There is, if you like, rain a-plenty here, though it may be harder to detect the gardens under it. But at bottom, *Jardins sous la pluie* is an abstract keyboard study in the melodic articulation of right-hand arpeggios. Debussy, like Schumann, was fond of left-hand melodies in the middle of the texture, and this piece is a prime example. "Nous n'irons plus au bois," however, comes only high in the right hand until near the end, when it twice rings out *fortissimo* in the left hand, but in treble register.

It was also presumably important for him that the tunes were well known; anybody French would recognise them at once (foreigners perhaps less so). They are, in effect, inset images, and in this respect they work like "Au clair de la lune" in the song "Pierrot," or the slices of musical life in *La Soirée dans Grenade*, breaking into the natural discourse of the piece, usually in a strange key, so that the inset quality is doubly underlined. But whereas the *Soirée* is made up almost entirely of such images, in the form of montage, *Jardins sous la pluie* is carried along for most of its length by sheer bravura, and the layering, such as it is, is little more than the outlining of familiar tunes by the figuration itself. To this extent, it is not essentially different from any worthwhile nineteenth-century piano study, where the tedium of exercise is lightened by an unexpected richness of hidden melody.

How much weight should we give at this point to Debussy's choice of the title *Estampes* for these three pieces? To compare them to Japanese prints as such would clearly be hopelessly laboured, even if *Pagodes* and *Jardins sous la pluie* are the kind of subject matter we might not be surprised to find in such prints. After all, the music barely represents these subjects in any case; and, as Paul Roberts has pointed out, Spanish flamenco is not a subject much treated by Japanese artists. What I think Debussy was trying to do was associate himself with a tendency in the visual arts with which he sympathised and which he felt himself to be in some sense adapting to the medium of sound. The changing colours and perspectives in *La Soirée dans*

Grenade, the concentrated tone-colour motives in *Pagodes*, the flickering waters of *Jardins sous la pluie*: above all, perhaps the sense that, in pursuing these subjects in these ways, he was creating a new kind of music that disrupted the old grammar and the old routines, just as the Impressionist painters were replacing the figurative grammar of the Académie des Beaux-Arts. The comparison is interesting and useful, as long as it is not pressed too far. Two of the main qualities of these pieces, their simultaneities and discontinuities, have no real equivalent in the visual arts, being aspects of our experience of time. Maybe they suggest an experience of space, just as painting can imply the passage of time, but only as metaphor.

8

Taking to the Water

For Jacques Durand it may have been bad news that, just when Debussy had contracted to write a whole series of piano and orchestral *Images*, it turned out that he was starting a quite different orchestral work about the sea. But Durand could see only half the picture. Either that summer or very soon afterwards Debussy seems also to have been hatching a completely new set of piano pieces under the title *Suite bergamasque*.

Exactly what was going on is still by no means entirely clear. Long ago he had written the suite of pieces that is today universally famous under that title, but it had never been published and was still lying idle, along with other short pieces, in his bottom drawer. Meanwhile he had the idea for a set of three more substantial pieces that seemed to justify a title of that kind. One of them, *L'Isle joyeuse*, was connected in his mind with Watteau's painting *L'Embarquement pour Cythère* and perhaps from there with Verlaine and the "charmant masques et bergamasques" of "Clair de lune." Another was actually called *Masques*. A third piece, dividing these two allegros, was another sarabande. As early as June 1903, Viñes noted in his journal that Debussy had played him a piece called *L'Isle joyeuse*, presumably an early version of the piece we know; and the following January he played him all three pieces, again presumably versions of the intended *Suite bergamasque* pieces. How it came about that in 1905 Fromont printed the *Suite bergamasque* we now know—a completely different work that seems to have no particular call on that title—is a commercial mystery: in other words, no mystery at all. Fromont wanted to bring out some marketable piano music and Debussy, albeit under protest, needed cash. The Viñes pieces stayed separate, and to this day we don't know absolutely for certain the identity of the sarabande, or even that the music Viñes heard was the music we know under the other two titles. Only the one title, *L'Isle joyeuse*, is certain; the music not.

How much does all of this matter, beyond the resistible entertainment of watching musicologists count the angels on the points of each others' needles? The answer is that if it were to lead to the identification of the sarabande it could release musical information about the other two pieces. Roy Howat, himself a brilliant pianist as well as a leading scholar, came to the conclusion that the missing piece was in fact a perfectly well-known work called *D'un cahier d'esquisses* ("From a book of sketches"), which was published in *Paris illustré* in February 1904. This was no idle speculation. The piece is indeed a sarabande of sorts—that is, a slow dance in triple time with an accent on the second beat of the three. Admittedly it is mostly barred in six-eight time, but it could quite reasonably be rebarred in three. It has significant thematic connections with both *Masques* and *L'Isle joyeuse*. Its sixth bar picks up a rocking minor-third figure from *Masques*, while *L'Isle joyeuse* begins pointedly on the keynote of the sarabande (D flat rewritten as C sharp) and clearly develops rhythmic and melodic ideas from the sarabande material as a whole.

Nobody knows precisely why Debussy decided after all to publish these three pieces separately. He may have become dissatisfied with them as a balanced set, but that can hardly have been for lack of integration between the three, which is a lot greater than between the three *Estampes* or, for that matter, the three pieces in his next set, the first book of *Images*. The fact that he allowed *D'un cahier d'esquisses* to come out in an illustrated magazine suggests, according to Howat, an intention to publicise the forthcoming triptych, rather than any doubts about the piece itself or the suite to which, on this interpretation, it belonged. Unfortunately Debussy then for some, no doubt financial, reason sold the piece to the Brussels branch of Schott & Co., so that when he struck a deal with Durand later that spring only *Masques* and *L'Isle joyeuse* remained available for him to publish. Debussy then proceeded to rewrite both pieces; Durand brought them out separately in the autumn, and by then the whole *Fêtes galantes* connection had leaked away into a new cycle of Verlaine songs under that title, also published by Durand in September.

None of this, of course, prevents the three pieces from being played in sequence, as a coherent set, and when done in this way they convince absolutely. Debussy had been working on his three-movement symphonic piece *La Mer* since the previous autumn and was clearly thinking in longer spans than usual. Thus *Masques*, the natural first piece of the suite and a dazzling, bravura dance in its own right, at the same time sets up thematic and stylistic links with the other two pieces that might not be noticed in separate performance but are unmistakable in sequence. For instance, its prominent open fifths, perhaps suggested by fiddle music, are immediately picked up by *D'un cahier d'esquisses* alongside the rocking minor-third figure (B flat–D flat), first heard at bar 22 of *Masques* and echoed in the first two bars of *D'un cahier d'esquisses* at the same pitch. There is instantly a sense of reflection on things heard. The sarabande also takes issue, so to speak, with the cross-rhythms, the so-called hemiolas of three against two, that energise *Masques* from its first bar but which the sarabande turns over very slowly, like some strange object picked up on the beach. Out of this process there then emerges a rising theme that anyone familiar with *L'Isle joyeuse* will recognise as a preliminary version of its spectacular second subject, slow sarabande transmogrified into lilting barcarolle. *L'Isle joyeuse* also has its own version of the rocking thirds figure, major rather than minor, and rhythmically reversed, but still a clearly audible reference.

This is not quite cyclic writing in the Liszt or Franck sense. There is no laborious reworking of the same old material, merely a succession of hints, combined with an effortless consistency of harmonic and rhythmic style. In all three pieces Debussy handles his resources with a virtuosity that seems to belie the essential novelty of the language. *Masques*, in a clear A major, nevertheless has little truck with tonality in any textbook sense; instead it speeds through different regions of harmony, sometimes uncomplicatedly diatonic, sometimes pentatonic, sometimes whole-tone, sometimes chromatic. For much of the time the music is anchored by ostinato and tonic pedals—held or repeated notes that are the roots ("keynotes") of the chords in question, allowing for the fact that Debussy uses all kinds of chords, whether traditionally consonant or dissonant, as if they were consonant: tonal music without process, but highly refined, a peasant dance for masked courtiers in smocks. As usual with him, the predominant dynamic is *pianissimo*, rising steeply here and there to *fortissimo*, and without much in between.

In *Masques* the continuity is rhythmic, that of a fast dance with a lot of repetition. *D'un cahier d'esquisses*, very slow and *"sans rigueur,"* reveals the essential discontinuity of Debussy's harmony. Like the *Soirée dans Grenade*, and as its title suggests, it has the character of a montage of unused fragments left over from other work. The first page presents no fewer than five basic ideas, one after the other and without formal linkage; and though there is some show of development on the second page, the montage principle returns and survives to the end. On its own, the piece remains somewhat baffling, which is probably why it has been relatively little played. But as part of the triptych it acts as a meaningful pause, bound together in itself by the sarabande rhythms, and linking *Masques* to *L'Isle joyeuse* by the motivic allusions I've mentioned. It seems to enshrine an unanswered question (the title itself is actually preceded by an ellipsis, as if something before it has gone missing). But if so, an answer is immediately forthcoming.

Of all Debussy's piano pieces before the *Études*, *L'Isle joyeuse* is the most confident and self-assured, the most superbly extrovert. Perhaps it describes an island, but above all it describes a feeling about an island, and that feeling is certainly one of exuberance and delight. Were the exuberance and delight Debussy's own, or were they virtual, imagined, in the spirit of his remark to Louÿs that "people who weep while writing masterpieces are incorrigible humbugs"?[1]

Sometime in 1903 he had met Emma Bardac, the wife of a well-to-do banker and the mother of an aspiring composer, Raoul Bardac, who for the past four years had been an informal pupil of his. Emma was an attractive, well-kept forty-year-old, intelligent and cultivated, and Debussy was slowly beginning to weary of his sexy but intellectually limited model wife. Unlike Lilly, Emma was a good amateur musician, a singer, and a former lover of Gabriel Fauré, whose great Verlaine cycle, *La Bonne chanson*, she seems to have inspired back in the early 1890s. Photographs of Emma reveal a tiny, smart, somewhat bourgeois lady in expensive hats. But in such matters appearances are often deceptive, and she evidently had no qualms about making herself available, for the second time, to one of France's leading composers.

They were probably lovers by the early months of 1904. That April they went away together for a few days to the Vallée de Chevreuse, beyond Versailles in the Île de France, and by June they surely knew in their hearts, if not in so many words, that his marriage to Lilly was at an end. He was finding excuses to get her out of the house, or to be out of it himself. At the end of June he told his new friend, the music critic Louis Laloy, that they were shortly off to Lilly's parents in the country. But in fact only Lilly went, on 15 July, seen off at the station by her husband and his crocodile tears. "Don't believe," he wrote to her the next day,

> that I felt very joyful helping you drily into the carriage. It was even hard! Only, for reasons I'll tell you later, it was necessary . . . I have next to find new things, or it will be my downfall; I've been uneasy for some time at turning in the same circle of ideas, [and] it seems to me that I've found a new track, which is why I daren't let it go, whatever the cost.[2]

Lilly's reply is lost, but it must have expressed puzzlement and some measure of self-abasement, to judge from Debussy's next letter.

> No, little Lily-Lilo, you're not stupid . . . You're a very spoilt little girl who won't allow one to discuss one's wilfulness and one's caprice. As for me, I have the grave fault of not explaining myself enough . . . Do you see! my poor darling, an artist is, all in all, a detestable, inward-facing man and perhaps also a deplorable husband? Besides, if you turn it round, a perfect husband will often make a pitiful artist . . . It's a vicious circle. Will you tell me that, in that case, one shouldn't marry?[3]

Several letters and a flying visit to the Yonne later, he at last came clean, at least by his standards. "I have the very clear conviction," he said,

> after these days spent far from you, when I've for the first time been able to reflect on our life coolly, that even while loving you so much, I had never made you happy in the way I should . . . And I also recalled those trying moments when you demanded that *I give you your liberty*.[4]

"We're no longer children," he went on. "Let's try to extract our-selves from this episode, without noise and without involving other people." A very grown-up sentiment. But alas it was crushed by a juvenile lie. The letter was sent from Dieppe and claimed that its author was on his way to London with the painter Jacques-Émil Blanche, whereas he was in fact returning to Jersey, where he had arrived with Emma at the end of July and put up at the Grand Hotel in St. Helier. There he was, on his "joyous isle," for several days, before moving to the mainland seaside at Pourville, just west of Dieppe. Here he could contemplate his new life, in the charming person of Mme Emma Bardac and in the abstract form of his other main work-in-progress, *La Mer*.

As we know, Jersey was not in fact Debussy's original "Isle joy-euse," since the title, if not the music, had been attached to a work of some kind for more than a year.[5] But Debussy certainly revised the piece, possibly even recomposed it, during these weeks with Emma, and perhaps for once it really does report on feelings as, or soon after, they were being felt. Quite apart from its brilliance as keyboard music, it has a kind of structural energy and range not to be found in any previous single movement of his, not even in *Fêtes*, but which we shall find again, still more thrillingly, in all three movements of *La Mer*. The energy is already contained, waiting to be released, in the single trilled C sharp that starts the piece off, for some reason all the more exciting when it follows the final D flat chord of *D'un cahier d'esquisses*. Then comes the dancing main theme, "light and rhythmed," cleverly expanding the trill into a melody, which adds a B to the trilled notes, then gradually spreads upwards through a scale that approximates to the old Lydian mode, with a sharp fourth, but also occasionally a flattened seventh. One might almost hear this whole first subject as a glorified variation on the trill, anchored for most of the time by rhythmic ostinatos in the left hand. The one (brief) intruder is the "thirds" motive from the two preceding pieces. Then suddenly the passionately expressive second subject bursts on the scene, still in Lydian A major, but lyrical where the first theme was puckish. This is the theme adumbrated in *D'un cahier d'esquisses*. Debussy next, rather uncharacteristically, supplies a true develop-ment section, harmonically vagrant as in a classical sonata, followed by a compressed recapitulation and a coda based on the opening trill music, rounding the seven-minute piece off, rather untypically, with several flourishes and a loud bang.

L'Isle joyeuse is a moderately bravura, rather than a toweringly virtuoso, piece of piano writing. Yet Debussy, having only just composed it, complained to Durand about its difficulties. Still in Dieppe, he had received the printed copy and approved it. "But, Lord!" he exclaimed. "How hard it is to play . . . this piece seems to me to combine all the different forms of piano attack, for it combines force with grace . . . if I dare say so."[6] Not only technically, but also aesthetically, the description goes to the heart of this masterpiece. Unlike the *Estampes*, it is neither descriptive imagery (*Soirée dans Grenade*, *Jardins sous la pluie*) nor the focused exploration of a single idea (*Pagodes*), but a sonata movement in all but name, complete with working of contrasted themes, a certain measure of tonal contrast, and a decisive ending. In some ways it is less radical than those pieces or than the *Images* that were to follow. It represents the maturing of the radical. But the truly radical had plenty more up its sleeve.

Joyful these Jersey days may have been, but they had their shadows. Four years later, Debussy scribbled a note, perhaps to himself, perhaps to his divorce lawyer, about the Lilly episode:

> Constant dissimulation—sought only a slightly better *situation*— anyway it was a mistake and took its vengeance by imposing a daily tyranny on my thoughts, my relationships—material proof in my output of these last four years.[7]

The couple returned to Paris from Dieppe on about 12 October, and on the 13th poor Lilly took a revolver and shot herself in the stomach. Pierre Louÿs, whose own marriage had perhaps been a factor in precipitating Debussy's, went to see her in hospital.

> The bullet [Louÿs informed his brother] went through her stomach twice and hasn't been retrieved. However, the operation went well, and the poor thing seems out of danger, but she's still broke and

homeless. The husband left with a Jewess of forty-something, Mme S. Bardac. I think you know Bardac . . . Quite accustomed to his wife's escapades, he smiles in response to any request for news: "She's simply having a good time with the latest musician à la mode, but I'm the one with the money, so she'll be back. Nice race."[8]

Lilly's attempted suicide was widely reported, and there were even subsequent false stories that she had tried to kill herself a second time. So once again Debussy was faced with the opprobrium of a society at ease with adultery but unable to reconcile itself to (or perhaps too ready to enjoy) the marital failures of the famous and their sometimes tragic consequences. Once again many of his friends turned against him, and when on 6 November his *Danses sacré et profane* for harp and strings had their first performance at the Concerts Colonne, the critics either absented themselves or took the opportunity to twist the knife in the composer's chest, even if they liked his music. "I did everything I could to dislike the piece," one critic informed his readers. "It wasn't possible . . . An invincible attraction . . . tantalising whole-tone scales." And Fauré, Mme Bardac's previous musician *à la mode*, wrote in *Le Figaro* that "one finds there once again in profusion the same harmonic singularities, sometimes curious and seductive, sometimes merely disagreeable."[9]

These charming but harmless harp dances were an ironic comment on the painful events on which they set their seal. They had been commissioned a year earlier by Gustave Lyon, director of the instrument makers Pleyel and Wolff, for a harp of his own invention, a fully chromatic, cross-strung instrument that was intended to cope better than the standard pedal harp with the complicated demands of modern music. Debussy's work, completed in May 1904, was a promotional exercise; but it fell flat, partly because his music—harmonically quite straightforward—was playable and just as effective on the pedal harp, so made no particular case for the chromatic instrument, and partly because the music itself, however attractive, was hardly calculated to set the doves fluttering in the musical dovecots. When Ravel composed his *Introduction and Allegro* the following year to a commission by the Érard firm for their pedal harp, the result was in every way more spectacular and persuasive. Debussy's pieces are lightweight, but the instrument was heavy, and yet less powerful than its rival.

Today the chromatic harp still has its enthusiasts, but orchestral players play the pedal harp, even when they play Debussy's dances.

Soon after finishing these pieces, he had composed two more sets of songs, one a setting of Charles d'Orléans and the seventeenth-century poet and dramatist Tristan (François) l'Hermite, the other a new series of *Fêtes galantes* to poems by Verlaine. No wonder, one might think, that *La Mer* was hanging fire, despite the optimistic predictions of the previous autumn. The *Trois Chansons de France*—as Debussy called the Orléans–l'Hermite set—are admittedly very short, not much more than five minutes for the three songs, but they have an intensity that belies their brevity. The two Orléans settings are both rondels, in which the first line (or two) is repeated at the end of each subsequent verse, a device that Debussy respects musically, as he had in the rondels by Leconte de Lisle many years before; but a feature of both songs is that, Schumann-like, they are composed essentially as piano pieces with the voice, so to speak, "reciting" the poem discreetly above while the piano proceeds on its way. In the second rondel, "Pour ce que Plaisance est morte" there are echoes in the piano writing of the "sketches" on which *D'un cahier d'esquisses* is supposedly based, just as in the central Tristan l'Hermite song, "Auprès de cette grotte sombre," the image of the flow of water engaged in a struggle with the pebbles generates a dark, crab-like ostinato figure that looks forward to the footprint motive in *Des pas sur la neige* in the first book of *Préludes*. If one wants to argue Debussy as a Symbolist, this tiny, concentrated song would be a good place to start. The sleeping, dreaming pool, with its bright red flowers and dangling rushes and memories of the demigod Narcissus, is like a deep dark womb into which we are ineluctably drawn, with Debussy's nagging, swelling motive urging us on and down.

Symbolist elements intrude also in the second book of *Fêtes galantes*, though here they are more overt, less oblique. The supposedly innocent girls in "Les ingénus" probably put on their loose skirts and unbuttoned collars knowing that the wind would reveal more than was proper; and Debussy's wind motive, soft and suggestive in its persistent whole-tone harmonies, has a definite glint in its eye. The second song, "Le Faune," about a terracotta faun laughing on the bowling-green and "no doubt foretelling a bad outcome to these serene moments," must have had a special significance for the com-

poser, since he wrote its opening "flute-like" flourish on a postcard
to Emma on 19 June. The erotic link with Mallarmé's faun hardly
needs pointing out. But the song itself, with its unbroken, tabor-like
piano ostinato, is one of Debussy's least interesting. On an altogether
higher plane is the final song, "Colloque sentimental," in which two
ghosts wander round a park disagreeing about the significance of their
former love. In Verlaine's *Fêtes galantes* series this is the final poem,
immediately preceded by "En sourdine," with its nightingale, "the
voice of our despair." In the poem itself the despair comes as a kind of
Heine-esque surprise, but "Colloque sentimental" might be its explanation, and Debussy duly quotes extensively from the earlier song in
this later one. "Do you always see my soul in your dreams?—No!"
"Ah! the beautiful days of unspeakable happiness when our mouths
joined!—It's possible." "How blue the sky and great the hope!—
Hope has fled, defeated, towards the black sky." Whether or not the
complex emotional texture of Debussy's song needs "En sourdine"
to make complete sense of it is an interesting question. But even as it
stands it is one of his most darkly moving compositions.

All this time *La Mer* had been brewing. It was almost a year since
he had written to Colonne tentatively offering him "some orchestral
pieces" he was working on, and to Durand a fortnight later listing
the titles of the three movements: "Mer belle aux îles sanguinaires,"
"Jeux de vagues," and "Le vent fait danser la Mer."[10] But thereafter
the trail goes dead until July 1904, when he writes to Lilly from Paris
expressing the (no doubt hypocritical) hope that "*La Mer* will be so
kind as to release me so as to be with you by the 15th August," though
by the end of the month it's "this 'Mer' that so disturbs me" that is
keeping him in the capital.[11]

Of course, these were evasions, but all the same it was probably
true that *La Mer* was giving him trouble. A glance at the eventual
score reveals an intricacy of texture and a thematic complexity well in
advance of anything he had previously attempted for orchestra, and
at the same time he was battling with a concept that was pictorial only
up to a point, and beyond that distinctly abstract and imaginary. His
personal relationship with the sea was not at all like that of Turner
or Monet, for whom the sea in all its moods was one crucial aspect of
their thinking about light and movement. Writing to André Messager
from the Yonne in the early stages of composition, he explained that

"I was promised for the fine career of a sailor, and only the chances of existence made me branch off. I've nevertheless preserved a sincere passion for Her [the sea]." But he added:

> You'll tell me that the ocean doesn't exactly wash the hillsides of Burgundy . . . ! And that this could well turn out like some studio landscape! But I have countless memories; that's better, to my mind, than a reality whose charm generally weighs too heavily on one's thoughts.[12]

Perhaps predictably, the sea was at its kindest for him in Jersey with Emma. He told Durand that it "has been very good for me, and showed me all her dresses. I'm still quite giddy with it."[13] He always loved the sea as an object of contemplation, in its changing colours and moods. The sea at Dieppe, he wrote many years later, "is as blue as a waltz [presumably "The Blue Danube"]; grey as an unusable sheet of metal; most often: green as the absinthe the old captain does without. All the same it's beautiful, more beautiful than *La Mer* of a certain C.D." But he came to dislike resorts like Pourville, with their ugly holidaymakers ("thieves for sure"), crowded beaches and shabby hotels. He did not—could not—swim, and seldom if ever so much as dipped his toes or even exposed any more of his body than would normally have been acceptable in a Paris boulevard. Above all he relished the calm of the ocean (even, perhaps, when it was not calm), and the fact that it was "always in the same place."[14]

None of these images seems reflected in "*La Mer* of a certain C.D.," except perhaps the many dresses. The original title of the first movement ("Beautiful sea at the Sanguinary Isles") looks like an inspiration in itself, before the music appeared, to deny its sense of placid Mediterranean radiance. The assumption that Debussy pinched the title from a short story of 1893 by Camille Bellaigue has been disputed, but chiefly on the grounds that the story has hardly any bearing on the music (apart from a brief description of the sea, it mainly has to do with the travellers' experiences on the three islands), and that the story's magazine publication was too remote in time for Debussy to have remembered it. But beautiful names may stick, and then be abandoned for want of real connection, or simply to avoid what might begin to look like a facile association. Debussy's eventual title for his first movement, *De l'aube à midi sur la mer* ("From dawn to midday on the sea") already expresses the unsuitability of the original, and the music does so decisively. The middle movement, by contrast, kept its first title, *Jeux de vagues* ("Wave games"); but the third movement also changed, from a dance to a conversation: *Dialogue du vent et de la mer* ("Dialogue of the wind and the sea"). In all three movements, the static vision of the "Mer belle" is replaced by images of motion, turbulence and fluidity. At one point, while still at Pourville in September 1904, he told Durand that "I would have liked to complete *La Mer* here, but I shall still have to finish off the orchestration, which is tumultuous and varied like the . . . sea!"[15] So tumultuous, in fact, that it took him another six months to finish.

Of all Debussy's greatest works, *La Mer* is the one that shows most clearly the benefits of his inflexibly meticulous, hyper-perfectionist approach to composition. In February 1905, excusing himself this time to Lilly for not visiting her at an agreed time, he claimed that he had spent the whole day orchestrating one page of the score: a pretext, perhaps, but a believable one. Lilly had sent him a heartbreaking letter imploring him to visit her in order to discuss their divorce rather than involving lawyers, and insisting that "whatever they may say or do to you, you have no better defender than the one you once loved (Lily or Lilo), the two!" She uses the polite "vous" throughout, but only, she explains, because "I no longer dare *tutoyer* you, not out of irony, but solely because it's the normal thing in our situation. Please believe for always in the sincerity of my affection."[16] As Debussy later admitted, such pleadings did not leave him entirely cold. But they could not (whatever he also claimed) penetrate his work.

The importance of the orchestration in *La Mer* becomes immediately apparent from close listening. In the first movement especially, the whole form—the shape of what one hears—is articulated by it. It's as if Debussy set sail, as one might, without a clear itinerary in mind, and allowed the conditions, the wind and waves, the sun and rain, to dictate his course. On the sea there is a certain monotony of context, a sameness or relatedness, quite unlike the varied character of a journey by rail or road; and Debussy is able to use this idea as a unifying factor while presenting his material as a sequence of more or less consequential events. At first each event is defined by its instrumental colour, as was also the case with *Nuages*. In essence, motives are not shared: a seagull is not a fish or a wave, though they all depend on the water. This is not babyish pictorialism. The music works, precisely, as a chain, with occasional repetition but no formal, structural recapitulations; these aesthetically clinching elements will come later in the work. Meanwhile the first movement proceeds, through the musical spray, in the manner of a journey, until (at about halfway, though of course this isn't apparent as one listens) there is a pause and a sudden, dramatic change of colour, in the form of a rhetorical theme for divided cellos (Debussy requires sixteen of them). This is the start of a slow build-up to the movement's coda, where, for the literal minded, the midday sun suddenly emerges and irradiates the entire watery scene.[17]

No wonder Debussy changed his title. This is not at all music you could put in a frame; it is too active and protean. It has at least a dozen important themes, some fragmentary, some decorative, some lyrical, some ceremonious, all linked by a sort of musical DNA, but differentiated by the astonishing diversity and refinement of Debussy's orchestration. On the DNA side, some features pop up like the family nose. Most of the themes have triplet figures prominent, or sometimes triplets squashed into a Scotch snap,[18] as in the very first oboe and clarinet motive, which also introduces a semitone rise and fall—a sort of aquatic sigh—that will infect several of the later themes. Some motives remain fragmentary, single figures attached to variants of themselves; others are extended into arabesques that nevertheless depend on multiple repetition. By the end of the movement one is conscious of having travelled in a coherent but progressive way; but as for the destination, that remains to be seen.

The second movement, though scherzo-like in general character, is more static in its sense of place. We are, let's say, in mid-ocean, and the play of waves is to some extent a play of ideas already glimpsed in passing. Debussy establishes the position harmonically. The first movement ends brilliantly in D flat major (having started far away in B minor); the second opens in C sharp (that is, D flat) minor, but with a disturbing element of F sharp minor in the first chords. The D flat–C sharp linkage is exactly as between *D'un cahier d'esquisses* and *L'Isle joyeuse*, but here more sombre and unstable. As before Debussy tends to define his motives instrumentally. For instance, the main cor anglais theme (apparently a descendant of that instrument's theme in *Nuages*) is only ever played by woodwind, usually oboe or cor anglais. Later, however, there is some fusion and a growing sense of culmination in the sharing and extension of ideas. The second theme (violins), whose DNA goes all the way back to the flickering semitones of the initial oboe theme of the first movement, is later recapitulated by flutes and oboes, and throws off a long-drawn string counter-melody leading to a genuine climax, before the waves die down and the music fades out quietly in E major.

The "dialogue" of the finale turns out to be to a large extent a conversation between themes already heard. Debussy refrained from calling *La Mer* a symphony, no doubt all too aware of the expectations that would arouse. Instead he compromised with "symphonic sketches," though that in turn carries implications—of some kind of improvisatory freedom—that might be no less misleading. His structures and linkages may be of a new kind, but they are far from casual. All the same, his third movement reminds us that the French symphonic tradition (Berlioz, Franck, Saint-Saëns, etc.) was cyclic, with themes transmogrified from movement to movement. This leaps to the ear with the trumpet theme a minute or so into the finale, a brightened-up version of the horn theme in the first movement introduction, while the increasingly dominant second subject is the culmination of the sighing triplet and Scotch snap motifs from the previous movements. Eventually the sea falls calm, and this theme sounds out over the waters, like the cry of a sea bird, in the first movement's D flat major, leading finally—after further wind-blown dialogue with the trumpet theme—to a coda based on that movement's "midday" coda, at which point we recognise that the aesthetics of musical form have triumphed over the logic of imagery and anecdote.

Leaving aside all these colourful details, the brilliance of *La Mer* lies especially in its mastery of continuity and balanced form without any recourse to textbook procedures. Impressionist sea paintings like Monet's *Storm, off the Coast of Belle-Île* or Whistler's *Arrangement in Blue and Silver: The Great Sea* are organised partly, of course, by a deliberate limitation of motive, but within that by a big colour variation within a narrow range of tones. Essentially, Debussy does the same in *La Mer*. The subject is self-limiting and, like the two paintings, devoid of human interest (apart from a barely perceptible ship on Whistler's distant horizon). Like them, it depends on brush-strokes to suggest the texture of wind and water, brush-strokes that combine to create the whole image, while remaining distinct as contributory detail. The differences are obviously generic. Music, since it operates by the clock, can create motion of a kind, where a picture can suggest it only metaphorically. But in the end it cannot, unlike Whistler's watercolour, prove to us that its subject matter is what the title says it is. One hostile critic, reviewing the first performance on 15 October 1905, satirised Debussy as "dedicated to the writing down of the impalpable. He makes of the impalpable a sonority."[19] Another, by no means hostile, critic found that

> for the first time, listening to a picturesque work by Debussy, I have the impression of being, not at all in front of nature, but in front of a reproduction of nature: a marvellously refined, ingenious and industrious reproduction, perhaps too much so; but a reproduction all the same . . . I don't hear, I don't see, I don't smell the sea.[20]

Since this particular critic, Pierre Lalo of *Le Temps*, had written very sympathetically about *Pelléas et Mélisande*, Debussy saw fit to respond.

> I love the sea; I have listened to it with the passionate respect one owes it. If I've transcribed badly what it dictated to me, that's no concern of yours or mine. And you'll allow that all ears don't hear in the same way. In the end you love and defend traditions that no longer exist for me, or at least that only exist as representatives of an epoch, in which they weren't all as beautiful or as worthwhile as one might care to say, and the dust of the Past isn't always respectable.[21]

He thus moved his ground from a defence of his imagery to a defence of his music, about which Lalo had remarked that "the lack of development and logic that existed in his previous works, and which went by unnoticed, here becomes visible." In effect, Debussy is insisting that whether or not we can see, hear or smell the sea in *La Mer* is of no great importance; what matters is that we feel the coherence and abstract beauty of his music inspired by it. Perhaps, *mutatis mutandis*, Whistler and Monet might have said the same about their paintings.

He had at last completed *La Mer*, after so many distractions, in early March 1905. There had been the usual phantom completions, and the inevitable interruptions for more or less fruitless theatre projects, of which only two fragments of music for a production of *King Lear* by André Antoine ever saw the light. The disasters of his private life (at least as seen from the vantage point of the Paris press) had fanned the flames of artistic notoriety arising out of the success of *Pelléas*. All of a sudden he was a public figure. Even the behaviour of his admirers became the object of scrutiny. The Symbolist poet Jean Lorrain satirised what he called the "Pelléastres" in *Le Journal*:

> Thanks to these gentlemen and these ladies, M. Claude Debussy became the head of a new religion, and there was, in the Salle Favart at each performance of *Pelléas*, a sanctuary atmosphere. They now came only with solemn brows, winks of complicity and knowing glances. After the preludes heard in a religious silence, there were the greetings of initiates in the corridors, fingers on lips, strange handshakes hastily exchanged in the half-light of boxes, crucified expressions and faraway looks.[22]

As for Emma, it was widely supposed that Debussy was pursuing her for her money, though, as we saw, her disposable finances were in fact her husband's. There was question of an inheritance from a rich uncle, but Lesure has suggested that she had no particular reason in 1904 to expect anything from that direction, and in any case the uncle was still very much alive, and died only in 1907.[23] They were, nevertheless, well enough off to be able, in October 1905, to take an apartment in the Avenue du Bois de Boulogne (now the Avenue Foch, one of the smartest addresses in Paris). Debussy had just signed an exclusive contract with Durand, and though his own divorce from Lilly, which finally came through in early August, was expensive for him as the guilty party, Emma had managed to divorce her husband (in May) on the basis of shared responsibility, because of his misdemeanours with assorted actresses and call-girls, which will have secured her some alimony. Through all these trials and tribulations she was expecting a baby, and at the end of October she gave birth to a little girl, Claude-Emma, quickly and thereafter known as Chouchou.

Fatherhood intrigued Debussy, and his letters henceforth contain frequent colourful references to his clever and personable daughter. It did not, however, help his finances, any more than the expensive address guaranteed the funds to maintain it. He never again moved house, but his finances soon reverted to their original state.

After finishing *La Mer* in March he had had to turn his attention to preparing various of his earlier piano pieces, including *Pour le piano* and the old (but newly titled) *Suite bergamasque* for publication by Fromont. With most of the older pieces—the *Rêverie*, the *Mazurka*, etc.—this was pure commerce. But he thought well enough of the suite to revise it, especially "Clair de lune," work that might have partly served as preparation for the new piano pieces that he had contracted to write for Durand in July 1903 before even starting *La Mer*. He now wrote to Durand once again listing the titles of the first three of these solo piano *Images* and the three for piano duo. Then, unable to face the concluding confrontations of his divorce proceedings, he fled in late July with Emma to Eastbourne, on the south coast of England, and put up grandly in the Grand Hotel. "The sea," he informed Durand, "stretches out with a very British propriety. In the foreground a combed and pomaded lawn on which important little imperialist Englishmen disport themselves."

> But what a place for working . . . ! no noise, no pianos apart from delicious mechanical pianos, no musicians talking painting or painters talking music . . . All in all a nice place for cultivating one's egoism. Besides, up to now I've only seen one pauper, and even he was comfortable. It's not possible—they must hide the poor away during the season.[24]

"I think," he added, "that I'll be able to send you some music next week." But as usual the week stretched out like the sea, and three weeks later he was still writing to his long-suffering publisher excusing his delay in sending the pieces. He had corrected the proofs of the piano duo arrangement of *La Mer*. But he had, he explained, finally decided that he didn't like the first *Image*, *Reflets dans l'eau*, and had made up his mind to write a completely new piece with the same title, but "based on new ideas and according to the most recent discoveries of harmonic chemistry."[25] At last, after another ten days, he sent the three *Images*, blaming the further delay on an attack of facial neuralgia caused, apparently, by the cool sea breezes. But he was proud of the music. "Without false vanity," he told Durand, "I think these three pieces will hold their own and take their place in the piano literature . . . (as Chevillard would say) to the left of Schumann or to the right of Chopin . . . as you like it."[26]

The original *Reflets dans l'eau* ("Reflections in the water") was presumably one of the two pieces that Debussy had already played to Viñes in December 1901 (the other was *Mouvement*). If so, it is hardly surprising that he came to feel, in 1905, that it would no longer do. In between had come Ravel's *Jeux d'eau*; and although Debussy's new *Reflets* have rather little in common with Ravel's *Jeux* in specifically musical terms, they certainly bear the imprint of the possibilities not only of "harmonic chemistry" (an old phrase of Debussy's) but also of keyboard sonority and imagery that Ravel's piece had unlocked.

Not the least striking thing about *Reflets dans l'eau* is that, composed only a few months after the completion of *La Mer*, it presents such a startlingly different musical image of water. There, all was movement and flecks of colour, flying spray, wind and a sense of travel. Here, the waters are at first still and silent (how else would they give back reflections?); Debussy called the opening "a little circle in water, with a little pebble falling into it."[27] The pebble distorts and fragments the reflections, and the music gradually explores the resulting colours and shapes, peering more and more deeply into the spreading ripples of the dark pool, like Narcissus in "Auprès de cette grotte sombre." Debussy's musical image for this mobile stillness is a softly resonant series of D flat major harmonies in chords ranging up and down the keyboard, some consonant, some dissonant, but at first without chromatic notes, then gradually complicating the sound with chromatics and increasingly brilliant arpeggio flourishes, as if the pool had suddenly developed a cascade or two, before slowly subsiding into a stillness even more profound than the one with which it began. What is truly astonishing about this wonderful music is that Debussy presumably composed it without a piano at his disposal; at least he told Durand there were none, and one can hardly imagine that, even with his newfound affluence, he had a room with a grand piano in it. Yet the voicing and delicacy of the chords and the treatment of resonance and pedallings (implied but, as usual with him, never indicated) are of a precision seldom to be found even in keyboard music where voicing and resonance obey textbook procedures that Debussy had by now abandoned.

Is *Reflets dans l'eau* really about reflections in a dark pool, or is the water a metaphor for something in the human psyche? Is it just a pool, like the pools in Monet's garden at Giverny, or is it a symbol of emotional or sexual perturbation, or a mother fixation, or general goings-on in the unconscious? If it comes to that, are Monet's water lilies just water lilies, or are they "a vision of the secret, inner communication of things, a sense for the way flower and cloud, earth and sky, are bound together by sublime affinities"?[28] The answer is, presumably, that Debussy's music and Monet's paintings can be all or any of these things, according to the preferences of the listener or viewer. It's certainly true that *Reflets dans l'eau* rises very briefly to a *fortissimo* climax that is hard to explain in terms of pools or cascades or anything less spectacular in watery terms than a flash flood, though it is easy enough to explain in terms of the music itself, whose harmonic and textural build-up positively cries out for some such release. One of the problems about the silly argument between Impressionism and Symbolism where Debussy is concerned ("useful terms of abuse," he called them) is precisely the neither-or-both syndrome, as we saw in the discussion of *La Damoiselle élue* in Chapter 5. All one can say with confidence is that, like the Impressionist painters and the Symbolist poets (among others), Debussy achieved his greatest work by discarding traditional grammars and trusting his own formal and aesthetic instincts.

At least the title of *Reflets dans l'eau* obviously goes with the music. The title of the second *Image*, *Hommage à Rameau*, might almost strike one as ironic. In his *Gil Blas* articles Debussy had made no bones about his admiration for the eighteenth-century French composer Jean-Philippe Rameau, and his corresponding dislike of the German-born Gluck. It was a preference based only partly on nationalist prejudice, but partly also on what he saw as shared musical values: French elegance and lightness and a feeling for the subtle rhythms of the French language, as against Gluck's "affectation of German profundity" and his "need to emphasise everything by thumping the table or to explain breathlessly, as if to say, 'You are a collection of particular idiots who understand nothing.'"[29] But one can play Debussy's homage, or listen to it many times, without detecting any hint of the French eighteenth century in any shape or form. There is no trace of pastiche, in the sense of Ravel's *Tombeau de Couperin*. The pianist is directed to play "in the style of a Sarabande, but without strictness [*sans rigueur*]," and it's true that the music is in a slow triple time with an occasional sarabande stress on the second beat. But this is a purely technical point. The music has no flavour of the dance, the barring is irregular, and the phrasing often contradicts any conceivable dance pulse.

None of this, needless to say, is intended as negative criticism of Debussy's piece, which is beyond question one of his finest. Like *Reflets dans l'eau* it works through a process of gradual intensification and elaboration from a simple, in this case unison, beginning. But there is no image; the idea is entirely musical. After the chant-like opening melody, again dominated by rocking thirds like the ones that linked the three pieces of the *L'Isle joyeuse* set, Debussy progressively intensifies the procession of chords and harmonies to a level of subtlety and richness even he has not achieved before. The music is in effect a study in soft, transparent, plangent sonorities, sometimes sequences of triads using the full spread of the hands, sometimes complex dissonances that seem to emerge from these triads and, so to speak, interrogate them. There are two or three loud climaxes, bracing the structure; but for the most part the chords, voiced with incredible care and precision, need to be quiet and attentively pedalled for their resonances to shine through. The whole piece is a vindication of Debussy's argument (with Guiraud) for a criterion of beauty in harmonic design independent of rules or theory. Yet behind these seemingly arbitrary chordings is a masterly feeling for the architecture of very slow music, achieved, amazingly, without the help of harmonic conventions that guided Beethoven in his great slow movements or Wagner in his *mauvais* (as Rossini thought, but Debussy did not) *quarts d'heure*.

Mouvement, by contrast, reverts to bravura pianism in the manner of *Pour le piano*, but with many refinements. The particular subtlety lies in the hidden melodies, which float across the right-hand arpeggios, triple *piano*, but with stress marks on the melody notes and the instruction: "All the notes marked with the __ sign [to be] sonorous, without hardness, the rest very light but without dryness." The difficulty of coordinating this network of requirements, at high speed and without breaking the rhythm, can probably be imagined, even by those for whom the piano and all its ways are an impenetrable mystery. *Mouvement* is not, on the face of it, one of Debussy's most musically interesting pieces, but in performance, with the right delicacy, the right distinctions of touch, and, once again, discriminating control of the sustaining pedal, it can make a brilliant conclusion to this first book of so-called *Images*.

Do they, as a set, justify the generic title? Not if one insists that an image is something exclusively visual. But there is such a thing as a verbal image, which amounts to a metaphor, a representation of one thing by another; so why not a musical image, for instance, representing movement (in general) by music that reduces movement to a series of rapid elemental figures articulated by melody? *Hommage à Rameau* perhaps escapes even this piece of special pleading. One of Debussy's most completely self-contained pieces, it superbly defies classification.

9

Images in Name as Well as Fact

D ebussy had lost friends over Thérèse Roger, and he lost more over Lilly. It was not so much that old friends broke with him explicitly or lectured him on his behaviour. Rather, they simply faded out. With some, it was a question of choice between the divorcees. Raymond Bonheur and René Peter stayed friends with Lilly and no longer communicated with Debussy, and the same was true, at least for a time, of Robert Godet, although in point of fact he and Debussy had not corresponded for two years at the time of the split. The Fontaines, whom he had seen less since his marriage to Lilly, vanished finally from his radar. With a few, the break was temporary. With Pierre Louÿs, though, it was decisive. Their respective marriages in 1899 had, it's true, weakened the intensity of their relationship, but Debussy's second marriage, to the Jewish Emma, was too much for the anti-Semitic Louÿs. Ironically, what was apparently Louÿs's final letter to Debussy, in June 1904, seems to have regretted the cooling of their friendship; yet Debussy's reply was their last communication.

The vacuum created by the loss of old friends was gradually filled, was already being filled, by new ones. Most important, as well as perhaps most surprising, was his friendship with the music journalist Louis Laloy, who had written a sympathetic article on *Pelléas et Mélisande* in the *Revue musicale* of November 1902 that attracted Debussy's attention and inspired him to invite Laloy to call on him. A few weeks later Laloy toiled up to the composer's fifth-floor apartment in the Rue Cardinet "like an explorer in an unknown country." But Debussy was not the wild beast he seems to have expected. He put Laloy at his ease at once:

First, because of his sinuous countenance, which reminded me of the courteous calm of the Far East, and above all because I felt in him a

certain wariness, very like mine, of offending the stranger by taking
anything for granted about his comprehension. He spoke in a clear
bass voice, in short phrases in which, at a stroke and without ever
searching for his words, he would suddenly produce some marvellous image.[1]

Laloy was himself an orientalist, interested especially in the music
of the Far East. But he also shared Debussy's love of the eighteenth-
century French *clavecinistes*, especially Rameau and Couperin. He
had studied under Vincent d'Indy at the Schola Cantorum, an institution founded in 1896 as a repository for the teaching of music on
the basis of Gregorian chant and fifteenth- and sixteenth-century
polyphony. To cap all this erudition of the exotic and the antique,
Laloy had written his doctoral thesis on the Greek musical theorist
Aristoxenus. But his polymathy did not stop at music. He was also
a graduate of the Paris École Normale Supérieure, one of the four
French ENSs that creamed off the best university undergraduates to
become top scientists, administrators and thinkers. "He was," Lesure
remarks drily, "the only academic we shall ever encounter in the
entourage of the composer, who had a certain mistrust of people who
were 'too well informed'."[2]

Laloy's first service to Debussy, early in 1903, had been as intermediary in the award to him of the Légion d'honneur, engineered by the
proprietor of the *Revue musicale*, Jules Combarieu, an admirer of *Pelléas* and, no doubt more conveniently, younger brother of President
Émile Loubet's cabinet secretary. Debussy accepted this unlooked-
for accolade with an attitude that he described, somewhat obscurely,
as "well designed to discourage the best goodwill."[3] But he was more
openly grateful for Laloy's behaviour towards him after the break
with Lilly. Laloy had written to him in April 1905 with what he called
"a clear-sighted sympathy that forbade itself to trample on life without a care." The composer replied:

I've seen such desertions around me! Enough to be sickened forever
by anything that bears the name of humanity. However (telepathy
being certainly no child's play) I had long had the desire to write to
you, telling myself that you could not be like the others, resting my
certainty on the memory of past conversations in which we exchanged

a little more than just words . . . I won't tell you what I've been through. It's ugly, tragic, and sometimes ironical, like the *Roman chez la portière*. In the end I've suffered a great deal in my morale. Was I having to pay some forgotten debt to life? I don't know, but I've often had to smile so that nobody suspected I was about to weep.[4]

Laloy had been out of town when the news broke and became common gossip. But "having no direct information," he later wrote, "I refused to pronounce."

It's so agreeable to judge one's neighbour severely that few deny themselves the pleasure. They have fun pitying the victim, blaming the betrayer, exaggerating the sorrows of the one and the crimes of the other, and throwing oil on the fire. As it seemed that Debussy must have been rescued by this event from material cares, they crudely accused him of having acted in a calculating manner, and of having sold himself.[5]

Obviously Laloy was more interested in Debussy's music than in his behaviour, a position he shared with the composer himself, who was still finding it hard to understand what people thought he had done wrong. ("It seems I'm not allowed to divorce like everyone else," he had complained to Durand, another friend with a professional loyalty to Debussy's music.[6]) Nevertheless the friendship with Laloy was genuine and became close. They would often dine together and even—an arresting image—play bridge (the recently invented auction variety, one hopes).

Laloy had left the *Revue musicale* early in 1905 and started a new journal, the *Mercure musical*, to which he was naturally hoping to get Debussy to contribute. But the composer wriggled. At first it was his divorce; then it was the title, *Mercure*, which he decided would become the butt of vulgar jokes about remedies for syphilis. In due course he offered a new series of "Entretiens avec M. Croche," "a man I spent a lot of time with in the past, let's hope I can find him again." But M. Croche did not reappear, and a few months later Debussy finally wrote him and his interlocutor out of the *Mercure* script, with complimentary remarks about Laloy's own study on *Pelléas*, and rude remarks about the other contributors, whom he found "sinister [and] above all terribly well informed; I really don't see what this poor M. Croche could manage among so many bold specialists." Instead he wrote his obituary:

> M. Croche, anti-dilettante, rightly sickened by the musical customs of the day, has gently snuffed himself out amid general indifference. It is requested that there be neither flowers nor wreaths, and above all no music.[7]

And Debussy never did contribute to the *Mercure musical*.

The reality was that he was struggling with the composition of a new set of *Images* for two pianos. The solo piano set had run into difficulties at Eastbourne in August. Now, in September, he was turning to the next component of his original contract with Durand. At that time, in July 1903, he had listed the duo pieces as *Ibéria*, *Gigue triste* and *Rondes*; but by May 1905, this had changed, *Rondes* had disappeared and been replaced, rather hesitantly, by *Valse*.[8] As it turned out this was the sole mention of any such piece, and by the time Debussy next named the final part of his original trilogy, it was once again *Rondes*, though whether out of uncertainty about its content or merely about the aptness of this or that title we shall probably never know. In *Rondes de printemps*, to give the piece its eventual name, there is some triple-time music, but it is not very waltz-like. Most likely, it was the dance idea that lodged itself in Debussy's mind from the start, while the exact type of the dance and character of the music took time to take shape.

No less mysterious is the fact that he initially thought of these as two-piano pieces (though the possibility of an orchestral version was already mooted in the 1903 contract). The *Image* concept had been born at the piano, and, to judge from the first solo book, was tied up with the exploration of particular harmonic and textural colourings peculiar to that instrument, with its special resonances and integrated sonorities. Yet from the start the two-piano *Images* (of which there were to have been six in all, though only three were named) seem to have taken on a more complex type of discourse, more symphonic at least in the sense of a varied procession of thematic materials, if not in the sense of what Debussy called "a robust symphony that marches on all fours."[9] It's hard to imagine the music of *Ibéria*, especially, as ever having been thought of purely in keyboard terms. Nor indeed is there any indication in the contract of the three-movement form in which that particular *Image* ended up. Its closest ancestor in Debussy's work is, it's true, a keyboard piece, also about Spain, *La Soirée dans Grenade*. But for *Ibéria* that piece was no more than the starting-point for an almost cinematic stretch of musical footage, a twenty-minute travelogue that depends for its effect on the multiple layering of different colours and the rapid intercutting of quasi-visual images and slices of musical life. The other two *Images* will make somewhat different, less specifically visual use of comparable techniques, with the help of fragmented quotations from popular tunes.

Debussy was surely thinking of these orchestral *Images* when he wrote to Gabriel Mourey early in 1909 about "la maladie du retard . . . et ce curieux besoin de ne jamais finir" ("the sickness of delay . . . and this curious need to never finish").[10] "I'm now going to finish the two-piano *Images* as quickly as possible," he assured Durand at the end of September 1905. Early the following July it was "if the ironic hazard of things doesn't come and mess up my papers, I think I shall finish *Ibéria* next week, and the other two later this month." But a month later, he still had "three different ways of finishing *Ibéria*; should I toss a coin or look for a fourth?"[11] And so it went on. After several more such half-promises, *Ibéria* was eventually completed on Christmas Day 1908, and *Rondes de printemps*, in short score at least, a few days later, though Debussy went on tinkering with it for several months thereafter. As for *Gigues*, now plural but no longer *triste* except about not being written, it hung fire for almost a further four years, promised and repromised, while Debussy became caught up with other things, most of which remained forever *tristes* for much the same reason.

As usual the distractions were largely due to Debussy's unrequited obsession with the theatre. At first it was the *King Lear* music, which lingered in his mind long after the Antoine production of December 1904 for which it had originally been intended, but was never got down on paper beyond two exiguous episodes, a tiny fanfare, and a slightly more substantial movement called "Le Sommeil de Lear," which Orledge locates to the scene in Act 4 of the play where Lear sleeps in the French camp.[12]

Then in April 1906 he received a visit from a young writer and amateur musician by the name of Victor Segalen, who was hoping to interest him in an opera on the life of the Buddha. Segalen was a marine doctor by profession who had travelled widely in Oceania, but had also recently spent several weeks in the Sri Lankan capital, Colombo. In Tahiti he had made a study of Polynesian music, and their conversations on this topic seem to have reawakened Debussy's dormant enthusiasm for this or that music of the Far East, and were probably what led him at least to affect an interest in the Buddha subject, *Siddhartha*, though he soon realised, as he told Segalen frankly, that "in its current form, I don't know of any music capable of reaching into this abyss! It could scarcely do more than underline certain gestures or make certain settings more precise: in the end, an illustration, much more than a perfect union with the text and the alarming immobility of the central character."[13]

Instead he suggested that Segalen might consider writing a libretto on the Orpheus myth, which had formed the basis of his recent novel, *Dans un monde sonore*. Segalen duly obliged. But Debussy, when confronted with a detailed draft, reacted in much the same way as before. The text was "more literary than lyrical," like "whole pages of Chateaubriand, V. Hugo, Flaubert that are said to be bursting with lyricism, but which, in my opinion, contain no music whatever." "No doubt," he added soothingly, "a few hours together will sort it all out."[14] But they never did; and Laloy considered that Debussy always knew that the Segalen projects were abortive but liked Segalen too much to say so, "and wasted a lot of time discussing an *Orpheus* text, endlessly corrected and redone."[15]

Meanwhile Debussy had been placed in an embarrassing position vis-à-vis Segalen by an announcement of 15 June 1907 in *Le Courrier musical*, to the effect that "M. Gabriel Mourey is finishing the libretto of a lyric drama, *L'Histoire de Tristan*, for which M. Claude Debussy has agreed to write the music."[16] The report, it seemed, was perfectly true. Mourey—last heard of in connection with *L'Embarquement pour ailleurs* in 1891—had presented him with an outline for a libretto based on Joseph Bédier's *Roman de Tristan*, and Debussy, who had been enthralled by Bédier's deeply researched novel when it first came out in 1900, and had thought then of turning it into an opera, had promptly accepted. Alas, the Mourey project foundered on the same sort of reef as *La Princesse Maleine* had done. Bédier had already licensed the work to his cousin Louis Artus, a *boulevardier* playwright with whom Debussy had no wish to collaborate, but who was unwilling to give up his priority. So a Debussy *Tristan* went the way of all but one of his other theatre projects to date, to be swiftly followed by a series of other Mourey proposals, all but one of which he rejected more or less out of hand.

Apart from a single *Tristan* theme in a letter to Durand, none of these projects produced a note of music, but merely used up precious time and creative energy. One other operatic scheme that began seriously to obsess him in 1908, without any literary intermediary, was one that he had almost certainly had in mind before but had never seriously addressed, Poe's tale *The Fall of the House of Usher*. He had done nothing to his previous Poe opera, *The Devil in the Belfry*, for the best part of five years, unless one counts his enigmatic remark to Durand in July 1906 that "for the *Devil* I think I've found a quite new way of having the voices move around, with the added merit of being simple."[17] Yet in July 1908 he made a formal agreement with Giulio Gatti-Casazza, the newly appointed director of the New York Metropolitan Opera, to give the Met priority in his two Poe operas, as well as, still more speculatively, in subsequent operas including *The Legend of Tristan*, in return for an immediate advance of 2,000 francs. With the cheque in his pocket, Debussy is supposed then to have told Gatti-Casazza, "It's bad business you're doing, and I even have some remorse in taking these few dollars, as I think I shall never succeed in finishing any of these works. I write solely for myself, and other people's impatience doesn't concern me."[18]

Nevertheless, *The Fall of the House of Usher* did genuinely preoccupy him, on and off, for the rest of his life, and it generated far more material, in however confused a form, than any of his other operatic projects apart from *Pelléas* and *Rodrigue et Chimène*. It undermined his concentration on more achievable works. In June 1908, at a time when *Ibéria* was still incomplete, he admitted to Durand:

These last few days I've been working a lot on *The Fall of the House of Usher* . . . it's an excellent way of steadying the nerves against all kinds of terror; all the same, there are moments when I lose all sense of the things around me; and if Roderick Usher's sister were to walk into the room, I wouldn't be all that surprised.[19]

Then, a month later:

I've been meaning to write to you these last few days, but the heir to the Usher family has hardly left me a moment's peace . . . I commit a dozen rudenesses every hour, and the external world almost ceases to exist for me.[20]

And another year on, with *Ibéria* and *Rondes de printemps* in Durand's hands but with *Gigues* languishing:

Choisnel [Durand's chief copy editor] conveyed to me your wish to have the next part of the *Images* . . . I have to confess that I've recently left them a bit to one side, in favour of Edgar Allan Poe. I've got so much to do on that that you'll forgive me, won't you?[21]

He had truly become a victim of his own *maladie du retard*, and was in some danger of losing the impulse of the *Images* altogether. He did eventually complete *Gigues*, but it was not without an effort of will that, it might be argued, is not altogether disguised in the finished work.

Not everything in this period was "rotting away in the factories of Nothingness," as Debussy had on one occasion described his state of mind to Durand, quoting Laforgue.[22] He had completed the Saxophone Rhapsody and composed a brilliant little suite of piano pieces inspired, initially, by the birth of Chouchou, though well outside even the mental compass of the not quite three-year-old child that she was when he finished it in the summer of 1908. The real birth piece in *Children's Corner*, as he called the suite (using the English form for all its titles, perhaps because Chouchou's governess was English), was *Serenade of the Doll*, written in March 1906 and imagined, clearly, in the presence of the five-month-old little girl and her actual doll. The other five pieces were added a couple of years later, and the whole suite was dedicated to "my dear little Chouchou, with the tender excuses of her Father for what follows."

Children's Corner is sometimes very easy to play, sometimes less so.

But mostly it has the virtue of sounding harder than it is, which of all instrumental qualities is probably the one that pleases show-off children best. Thus the first piece, *Doctor Gradus ad Parnassum*, though a gentle parody of Muzio Clementi's progressive piano tutor *Gradus ad Parnassum*, lies so well under the fingers that it hardly works as a study at all, despite crossing hands and singing inner voices. When Durand asked how fast it should go, Debussy replied that it was "a sort of hygienic and progressive gymnastics; best to play it every morning before breakfast, beginning *moderato* and ending *animé*."[23] Serious study, he perhaps wanted it thought, was not quite his cup of tea. In *Jimbo's Lullaby* we encounter our old friend from *Jardins sous la pluie*, the nursery song "Dodo, l'enfant do," as a melody, as a clashing chord of its two main notes, and as a galumphing five-finger exercise in whole tones. The *Serenade* is correspondingly delicate, with inner and hidden voices like the ones in *Doctor Gradus ad Parnassum*, which, as there, make for a neat effect that sounds tricky but is not too hard to play, whereas *The Snow Is Dancing*, more Clementi-like in its offset left-hand/right-hand semiquaver figurings, is genuinely awkward if only because of the constant variation in the figures, as the snowflakes swirl around in the wind. At one point the English nursery song, "Ding-dong Bell" materialises unexpectedly out of the mist. *The Little Shepherd*, simplest and sweetest of the six pieces, seems to derive some of its ideas, especially the *plus mouvementé* dotted rhythm, from Rimsky-Korsakov's *Sheherazade*, which Debussy had liked in the 1890s, then turned against after hearing it in 1906 ("more bazaar than oriental," he told Raoul Bardac[24]). Finally the *Golliwog's Cakewalk*, still perhaps Debussy's most famous piece, with its snappy ragtime rhythms and snide little parody of the opening of Wagner's *Tristan*, marked "*avec une grande émotion*," just in case we miss the point (which no child, and not all music students, would get in any case).

Debussy was a great admirer of Musorgsky's song cycle *The Nursery*, which he will have known in Rimsky-Korsakov's expanded and edited version of 1882. He adored the clarity and simplicity with which Musorgsky integrated his music and his subject matter; he loved the way the Russian composer handled his materials empirically, without troubling himself with textbook procedures or established forms, everything "made up of small successive touches, bound together by a mysterious linkage and by a gift of luminous clairvoyance." "Sometimes too," he had added in the same *Revue blanche* article of April 1901, "Musorgsky conveys a sense of shuddering, restless shadow that envelops and grips the heart to the point of anguish." Musorgsky had a "Doll's Lullaby" to compare with Debussy's *Serenade* (though the Russian title simply means "With Dolly"), which seemed to him to have been "divined word by word, thanks to a prodigious power of assimilation, that gift for imagining landscapes of fairy intimacy so special to childish minds."[25] Whether or not Debussy himself quite managed the degree of pure, unselfconscious identification with childhood that he attributed to Musorgsky, he did beautifully map his more sophisticated manner on to the image of a better-behaved childhood such as might have been observed in a drawing room of the Avenue du Bois de Boulogne in 1908.

Like Musorgsky, he often seemed to be feeling his way stylistically, testing every chord and chord sequence, every rhythm, every colour for their precise effect, since he too had abandoned the rule books that, in moments of failing inspiration, guaranteed coherence, if not interest. It was the real cause of his *maladie du retard*, his slowness to complete and his reluctance to hand over. But was it truly such a *maladie*? In terms of artistic method, he knew perfectly well, it was his greatest virtue. "You have facility," he had written to Raoul, "and are certainly gifted, but you will never sufficiently distrust the path that your ideas make you take."

> This sometimes means that you end up with something disjointed and at the same time rushed, which gives the disconcerting impression that you have wanted to finish at all costs . . . Have patience! It's a major virtue . . . Gather impressions—Don't hurry to write them down. Because Music has this over Painting, that it can centralise variations of colour and light in a single dimension. This is a truth very poorly observed, for all its simplicity . . . Even from time to time forget all other music . . .[26]

Was he thinking of particular composers? Of Richard Strauss, for instance, whose *Salome* he had joked about to Durand after studying the score but before hearing it ("*Salome*, or the lack of cordiality between all the chords"[27]), though just before attending a perfor-

Debussy as a young man
in the early 1880s

Antoine Marmontel, Debussy's first
piano teacher at the Conservatoire

Ernest Guiraud, Debussy's first
composition teacher

Marie Vasnier, after a portrait by Paul Baudry

At Luzancy (seated) with Jeanne Chausson, Ernest Chausson
and Raymond Bonheur, 1893

At the piano at Luzancy, with Bonheur and the Chaussons, 1893

Gaby Dupont

Pierre Louÿs

The day after the première of *Pelléas et Mélisande*, May 1902

Jacques Durand, Debussy's principal publisher

Lilly Debussy in Paul Dukas's library at Eragny, 1902

With Louis Laloy (left), *c.* 1905

With his wife Emma, *c.* 1913

With his fox terrier, Boy, and collie, Xanto, 1907

With Erik Satie in 1910, taken by Igor Stravinsky

Chouchou, *c.* 1912

On the beach with Chouchou, Houlgate, 1911

At Saint-Jean-de-Luz, summer 1917

mance in May 1907 he told Gabriel Astruc, with only mild sarcasm, that "it seems to me difficult to have anything but enthusiasm for this work, which was 'at once' a masterpiece."[28] Or of Ravel, whose latest piano work, the brilliant five-movement *Miroirs*, Viñes had played to him and Emma three weeks before his letter to Raoul. Or even of Rimsky-Korsakov, or Vincent d'Indy, whose *Jour d'été à la montagne* he had just heard in a Concert Colonne, and described to Raoul as "a bit of d'Indy from the backside of the Cévennes."

> As I'm not exactly well informed about the atmosphere of that region, I can hardly say anything about it. He seemed to me to overuse the bassoon, and one was astonished to hear a piano; I thought pianos were only found on Swiss mountains.[29]

It hardly needs a depth psychologist to see that these various jests about the star novelties of the day barely conceal a certain unease, even insecurity, in their presence. A year later he would take issue with Laloy over his laudatory review of Ravel's *Histoires naturelles* in the *S.I.M.* (Société Internationale de Musique) journal, "astonished," he said, "to read there that a man of your taste deliberately sacrifices the pure and instinctive masterpiece that is [Musorgsky's] *Nursery* to the self-conscious Americanism of M. Ravel's *Histoires naturelles*. For all its undeniable expertise, it can only be 'displaced' music. Leave that to the *valet de chambre*, [Michel-Dimitri] Calvocoressi."[30] But he was broadly enthusiastic about Serge Diaghilev's Paris concerts of Russian music that May. "They are admirable," he told Astruc, who was promoting the series, "a shade nepotistic in the programming, and some odd omissions from the ones labelled 'historic'. But it's very good to have played the second act of *Boris*."[31]

It wasn't, however, only the music of other composers that came between Debussy and his own work. Family life also imposed sacrifices. These included trips to the seaside, no longer to the romantic shore of Jersey 1904, but to the holiday resort of Puy, one of the Dieppe beaches, where they put up in August 1906 in a hotel run by a sinister Italian "who does his own shopping, brings back the most doubtful food substances, messes up the fish and the meat, and is patently an assassin."[32] "The beach," he told Laloy, "is absurd, the hotel the last word in discomfort, and the English the sort who render any *entente cordiale* impossible." Photographs of Debussy with Chouchou on the sands at Pourville and Houlgate in later years say more than words can about his stoical tolerance of the double-edged seaside ritual: suited, waistcoated and boatered, he stands like a well-dressed attendant, ready to carry his little daughter's bucket and spade, but not quite equal to the fun and games they offer. For his own work, he goes on, "I've at last got a 75-centimetre table for writing things that have without fail to revolutionise the world. You'll tell me that there's the Sea . . . ! Unfortunately it's a bit like a 'tub' that empties out! The coasts feel too close, and I can't manage to rediscover my emotion of last year faced with the Ocean."[33] "Can you work by the sea?" he asked Segalen. "I can work pretty well anywhere." "You're very lucky!"[34]

The following summer it was Pourville again, and this time for two whole months, while a faulty boiler in the Paris house was being repaired. So for once Debussy was forced to work by the sea, despite another horrible hotel, inedible food, stomach upsets, and the usual army of uncordial Englishmen. It was probably during these months that he somehow got *Ibéria* and, less certainly, *Rondes de printemps* into something close to their final form. But he must also have worked on a very different but similarly titled work, his second book of *Images* for solo piano, which he was able to present to Durand in its finished state at the end of September 1907. The perfection of this work, achieved under frequently hostile conditions and without his usual equivocations and prevarications, is in startling contrast with the erratic progress and in some ways uneven outcome of the orchestral set. Of course, the orchestral composition is in many ways the more complex. The concentration and unified character of the piano pieces was more in the direct line of Debussy's recent work. But if one wants to consider what he meant about revolutionising the world at a 75-centimetre table, it's necessary to take account of both these brilliant sets of contrasted pieces.

The three pieces in the second book of *Images* all have titles referring to things seen or visible, but in each case the reference is somewhat oblique. *Cloches à travers les feuilles* ("Bells through the leaves") relates a visual impression, the leaves, to an aural one, since one doesn't watch bells through foliage, but might hear them through it. Even so, the suggestion is slightly odd. To what extent would foliage affect the sound of the bells? The question is naive, and misses Debussy's point, which is surely a transference between the different senses: bell sounds converted into the rustle of leaves, leaves thought of as an image of the intricate polyphony of pealing bells. Laloy is supposed to have inspired this idea with a description of the tolling of bells on All Souls' Day in the Jura, "passing from village to village, through the yellowing forests in the silence of the evening."[35] But Debussy might equally have stored up his own memories of English bell peals, a very different phenomenon from anything to be heard, then or now, in France, and one that sets up its own complex associations with nature and the outdoors.

English change-ringing, with peals of six, eight or up to twelve bells, is a unique kind of music that is at once static and highly mobile: static, because the content of each round never changes, each bell being rung exactly once; mobile, because the order of the bells changes all the time, creating a complex network of interior patterns within the unvarying harmony. Nobody—and certainly no musician—who has ever listened to change-ringing of this type will be unaware of the contrast between the fixed reverberation—Tennyson's continuous "mellow lin-lan-lone of evening bells"—and the subtle rhythm of the interior changes, mathematically determined, but deeply affecting aesthetically. Debussy might well have sensed a parallel with the gamelan music that he still revered: there was the same kind of interior polyphony (genuine with the gamelan, merely implied in the case of the bells) within the same kind of static harmony. There was the same tintinnabulation, the same "molten golden-notes," that he must have known from his beloved Edgar Allan Poe's poem "The Bells."

Cloches à travers les feuilles is, consciously or unconsciously, his version of this intriguing and complex idea. Take the opening page (plus one bar: so, the first eight bars). With the exception of two C naturals in bar six, the entire passage is derived from a single whole-tone scale, a completely static harmony but with an intricate filigree of layered interior motion, laid out on three staves for clarity, mainly scales (as in the early and final stages of ringing a peal), similar and contrary motion, but with much rhythmic variety and extremely refined articulation, which Debussy, when he sent the music to Durand, made a point of asking the engraver to respect. At bar 9 the harmonic colour changes abruptly, and it does so again at bar 13, switching to a new colour altogether, in a soft left-hand ostinato that Debussy wants "very even, like an iridescent vapour." These changes are not unlike the changes of angle or focus with fixed cameras in a film about nocturnal animals. Debussy seems to be peering into the innards of his harmonies and sonorities, trying not to disturb them, then after a few minutes moving quietly on to the next. He doesn't ignore the needs of music as a temporal structure. "But I'm more and more convinced," he told Durand, "that Music is not, in its essence, something that can flow along in rigorous traditional forms. It's a matter of colours and rhythmicised time."[36] So he makes a textural climax, "a little animated and brighter," with sharper dynamic and rhythmic contrasts and more brilliant figuration, but still unchanging harmonically for five full bars (24–8), then another four (33–6), before the piece dies away triple *piano* in a variant of the opening material.

For the pianist, the difficulty of this incomparably subtle music lies, first, in observing the complexities of Debussy's instructions on dynamics and articulation, and, secondly, in pedalling, without over-pedalling, music so dependent on resonance, for which Debussy gives no instructions at all. Paul Roberts has explained the importance of pedalling in the first two bars, a "simple" five-finger exercise, down and up, with the top note held, the bottom note accented (slightly lengthened), and the intervening notes semi-staccato.[37] Should all five notes resonate, with the sustaining pedal held down; or is it a question of half-pedalling—with the dampers almost touching the strings—giving a delicate blurring of each note but avoiding the Turneresque fog that passes for Impressionism with certain pianists who may remain nameless? Too much pedal obliterates the all-important sense of touch; too little leaves a dryness that cannot have been Debussy's intention. This problem is if anything still more acute in the next *Image*.

One of the many intriguing questions about *Et la lune descend sur le temple qui fut* ("And the moon goes down over the temple of old") is whether Debussy had any music in his head when he thought of the title. For a long time it was accepted that the title, with its oriental flavour, came from the orientalist Laloy, the dedicatee of the piece. But it already figures on the contract Debussy signed with Durand in 1903, before he knew Laloy well. More to the point, as the eventual music hardly seems to represent anything specific about the title beyond its generally mysterious atmosphere, one might suppose that Debussy came up with one he liked the sound of, then wrote the music he wanted to write, possibly changed the title, then reinstated the original, as is proved by an otherwise incomprehensible remark to Durand in the letter accompanying the *Images*. Was it just the sound, the metre of the title, "a faultless alexandrine," as he joked to Durand?[38] Or was it the imagined scene, a Japanese print to be set to music, in the way that the third *Image*, *Poissons d'or*, is a lacquered bowl set to music?

Whatever it represents, *Et la lune descend sur le temple qui fut* is one of the most perfectly imagined and executed of all Debussy's piano pieces. In a sense it establishes its own sound world with a single chord, an open fifth (E–B) with a hanging dissonant whole tone (A) attached to the upper note like a limpet, repeated more softly, in the manner of an echo, then with the same chord attached to each note of the ensuing melody as a particular colour: a colour, not a harmony. In fact the colour varies slightly. At one point, for the sake of fluency, the whole tone becomes a semitone, and on the last two chords of the opening phrase the open fifth contracts to an augmented fourth, as if questioning the previous chords. Debussy's judgement here is incredibly refined. Play this phrase with the last two chords the same as the others and it will sound flat and closed, leading nowhere. Play it, as Cécile Ousset does in her recording, with the final chord contracted to a perfect fourth, and it sounds banal. In the second phrase the chords gradually evaporate, leaving the unison B, with or without whatever resonance the player chooses to allow to survive through the sustaining pedal.

To describe this music and what follows—the parallel triads, the two-part counterpoints of vaguely oriental melody, the different variants of the opening chord sequence—is easy enough. To explain its unique, haunting beauty and its formal perfection is another matter. The sequence of apparently unconnected events is like an irregular series of lines of poetry in a half-understood language. But just as verse is bound together, however informally, by metre and rhyme schemes, so Debussy's piece is linked by its procession of balanced phrases, its alternating reprises, and crucially by the note B, which is the top note of the first and last chords, begins or ends most of the intervening phrases (either as a single pitch or as a chord), and is left hanging on its own at the very end, probably without the reverberation of the previous bar, though as usual Debussy is silent on the issue of pedalling. His own description of Musorgsky's *Nursery* as "made up of small successive touches, bound together by a mysterious linkage and by a gift of luminous clairvoyance" could just as well have been prompted by *Et la lune descend*. His other remark, about the "sense of shuddering, restless shadow that envelops and grips the heart to the point of anguish," might overplay the element of emotion in this restrained, enigmatic *Image*. But context is all-important, and it's precisely the restraint that empowers Debussy's discreet *expressif* markings, and gives his single *très expressif* (bar 32) the force of a minor explosion.

The final *Image*, *Poissons d'or* ("Goldfish" or perhaps, in view of the supposed inspiration, "Golden Fish"), is altogether more specific in its imagery, almost a return to normality after the mysterious excursion to the temple of the setting moon. Debussy owned an exquisite Japanese lacquered panel depicting two goldfish—one light, one dark—swimming in a stylised river overhung by a golden-leafed willow, against a black sky. (The panel can now be seen in the Musée Debussy at his first home in Saint-Germain-en-Laye.) This panel may or may not have been the direct inspiration for *Poissons d'or*, but the music suggests it was. Somehow, partly through the angle of the fish to each other, partly through the slope and implied flow of the water, the anonymous artist has achieved an extraordinary sense of swirling motion, an icon of realism in an essentially stylised context. Debussy converts all this, *con bravura*, into a musical image of flowing water and pirouetting fish. The smooth, rippling waters of the opening are soon invaded by all kinds of fishy activity: darting, plunging, "capricious and supple," almost as if the composer had sat down at the piano and improvised a variety of musical representations of the panel before his eyes. One or two details might indeed appear capricious on the part of the composer; at one point, the fish seem to pause while the pianist throws in two or three fragments of blues ("expressive and without strictness") a year or so before Debussy could possibly have known about that genre; then they laugh and go back to their pirouetting.

One can talk about some Debussy in this programmatic way. But, as ever, in turning such images into music, he is concerned exclusively with musical values. Though formally free (after early hints at a rondo), *Poissons d'or* is immaculately designed and balanced, with just enough of a climax generated, so to speak, by the incessant motion of the figuration, and a firm tonal framework (F sharp major) within which the chromatic fish can cavort without muddying the waters too much. As usual with Debussy, the default dynamic is *piano* dying on the final pages to *pianissimo* then triple *piano* at the end. Refinement and clarity are required of the player throughout; clumsy virtuosity has no place in this music. Whether or not Debussy specifically intended these three pieces to be played as a set, they make perfect sense that way, and were in fact done complete by Ricardo Viñes when he premiered them in February 1908: the bells, the leaves, the moonlit temple, the river, the fish—a series of panels from an imaginary gallery of symbolic images, with every degree of subtle colouring, texture and motion, concluding with the most brilliant and the most delicate.

Debussy might have boasted to Durand that the second set of piano *Images* was written "with the skill born of habit." In fact he made this remark about the orchestral *Images*, and not as a boast but as a confession. Writing from Pourville that August (1907) a slightly more guarded version of his usual promise to finish the work soon, he told his publisher that there had remained "a lot of places that bothered me . . . it was well written, but with that skill born of habit that one has so much difficulty conquering and which is so tedious."[39] What these bothersome places were we have no means of knowing, but one might guess that they had to do with linkage, continuity and how to end. The question of montage arises also in the keyboard pieces, because of Debussy's technique of the static moment connected to the next by an instantaneous switch of angle or texture, with or without the shared notes that provided the logic for composers such as Schubert or Bruckner who cultivated modulation to remote keys. In the orchestral pieces, however, the issue of changing colour is more acute, because of the many different timbres involved, added to which *Ibéria*, especially, has a specifically cinematic kind of form with graphic effects of montage.

The other problem may have been the orchestration of what, as we saw, had started life as music for two pianos. *Rondes de printemps,* he explained to Durand, was "*immatérielle*" (probably best translated as "insubstantial") and not to be handled like an ordinary symphony. As for *Ibéria*, here an old rivalry would soon rear its head. Debussy certainly knew Ravel's *Alborada del gracioso,* as yet a piano work only, and he may or may not have known that his younger colleague had been working on an opera about Spain, *L'Heure espagnole.* There had been a rather too obvious similarity between *La Soirée dans Grenade* and Ravel's *Habanera,* and there would soon be another near-collision, with Ravel's *Rapsodie espagnole,* not composed—initially as a two-piano work—until October 1907, but then rapidly orchestrated, and premiered at a Colonne concert in March 1908, several months before Debussy completed *Ibéria.* Both composers' Spanish music depends to a significant extent on style clichés, particular dance rhythms, flamenco idioms of melody and ornamentation, and also images of rural Spain and its people. Avoiding each other's take on these matters was plainly no trivial matter in the small world of Parisian music.

As it happens, the first movement of *Ibéria* is closer to a less threatening model, the *Fandango* finale of Rimsky-Korsakov's *Capriccio espagnol,* which Debussy had first heard at the Trocadéro concerts in 1889, conducted by Rimsky himself. Debussy's own fandango first movement is more complex, with subtleties of rhythm and metre presumably intended as a response to the displaced accents of the Andalusian dance, with its on- and offbeat stamping and clapping. One wonders, equally, whether he had yet encountered those parts of Albéniz's *Iberia* piano collection that were being published in Paris in 1906 and 1907.[40] But his own approach, notwithstanding the music's supposed origin as a work for two pianos, is so quintessentially, meticulously orchestral in its detailing as to distance itself, not only from other people's piano music, but from his own. Instead of the self-contained, whole-cloth quality of the keyboard *Images,* *Ibéria* feels composed in a linear, almost anecdotal fashion, its music passed from hand to hand like the baton in a relay race, *Par les rues et par les chemins* ("Through the streets and byways"), as Debussy in fact called the piece. Halfway through, horns and trumpets announce what amounts to a rival dance in the rhythm of a tarantella, with brilliant fanfares, and a brief expressive climax (violas and cellos) where the composer seems to step aside from the physical dance and reflect on its emotional undercurrents, after which the music reverts to the original fandango.

In the same way the second movement, *Parfums de la nuit* ("Perfumes of the night"), mingles observation and passion, but inextricably, so that the nocturnal atmosphere, its rustlings and chirrupings and distant fragments of melody—including the daytime melody of the first movement—become images of the emotions they arouse, those intangible feelings of love, sensuality and regret that seem inseparable from hot southern nights. We are back in the world of *La Soirée dans Grenade*, with the same habanera rhythm, but less in the thick of things, less actively engaged. We stand in the gardens and simply listen to—and smell—the intensity of the darkness, just as we previously listened to the bells through the leaves, the one sense—or two—turned into music, and back again.

From this experience we wake up to the morning of a feast day (*Le Matin d'un jour de fête*), by way of a transition that brings into play Debussy's montage technique, the dying night intercut with the dawning day. But the day itself is also a montage, of singers and guitarists, a solitary violinist, the laughter of schoolboys and the braying of donkeys. The whole piece is spectacularly scored and makes a brilliant finish to *Ibéria* as a three-movement suite in its own right. Musically, though, it feels riskily lightweight, with a flavour of the travel poster or the tour guide, and a disconcertingly abrupt ending that might suggest that Debussy was having difficulty extending his snapshot material into a fully fledged narrative. As a whole *Ibéria* lives by the beauty of its colourings and the vividness of its atmosphere, rather than by the accumulated structural power of *La Mer* or the intense focus of the piano *Images*. But at least it adds up to a substantial concert work with a beginning, a middle and an end, all beguilingly imagined and heard. The exact role of the other two *Images* was to prove much harder to define.

Debussy's description of *Rondes de printemps* as "*immatérielle*," feather-light in texture and content, located it as far as possible from the symphonic and operatic traditions of the day as represented by, say, Mahler or Strauss, or in France by Franck or, recently, Dukas, whose *Ariane et Barbe-bleue* Debussy had found beautiful but somewhat implacable when he attended its dress rehearsal in May 1907. If anything, *Rondes de printemps* has the opposite fault of being insubstantial in the negative sense, another possible but unintended meaning of *immatérielle*. Ideas flow past, exquisitely but a touch short-windedly, a quality highlighted by the tendency to play each phrase twice; and the now familiar children's songs—"Dodo, l'enfant do" and "Nous n'irons plus aux bois"—seem to come out of the blue, like old standbys in adversity. Admittedly they fit the image of the piece. "*Vive le Mai*," runs the epigraph at the head of the score, invoking the Tuscan spring festival of the Maggiolata, "*bienvenu soit le Mai, avec son gonfalon sauvage*" ("Long live May, welcome, May, with its wild streaming pennant").[41] Debussy's spring rounds are another of his 1908 tributes to childhood. Ideally they might provide the scherzo for a larger but more conventionally formed work. But their position in the whole set of orchestral *Images* has always raised questions.

"These poor *Images*," as Debussy called them after handing over *Ibéria* and *Rondes de printemps* to Durand, were never published as a set, even when eventually completed with *Gigues*, only as three separate works. When Debussy conducted the complete premiere, in January 1913, he played them in the order *Gigues—Ibéria—Rondes de printemps*, and this order has tended to stick, on the comparatively rare occasions when all five movements have been played, even though the elusive *Rondes de printemps* makes a less than ideal finale, not least because its own actual ending is somewhat contrived. André Caplet, who worked with Debussy on the orchestration of *Gigues*, conducted the *Images* after the composer's death in the order *Rondes de printemps—Gigues—Ibéria*, which has the virtue of ending with the strongest music. But the problem is ultimately intractable, and lies with the fact that the concept changed from a book of pieces to a multi-movement concert work, without sufficient corresponding change to the contents.

Debussy began work on *Gigues* a few days after handing the other two over, but it would be almost four years before he finished the seven-minute work. At the start he was suffering rectal pains, apparently caused by haemorrhoids and severe enough to be treated with "morphine, cocaine, and other nice drugs," as he grumbled to Durand a month later.[42] But during that same period, as we shall see, he was writing works that belong with his most perfect, so the problems with *Gigues* can't reliably be blamed on illness. They were inherent in the idea of adding an English *image* to the Spanish and French ones already completed, or rather in the character of that addition. According to Lockspeiser this derived from a song by Charles Bordes, a setting of Verlaine's poem "Streets" called "Dansons la gigue," based on the tune of the Northumbrian folk song "The Keel Row."[43] Since Debussy certainly knew Bordes, a former fellow pupil of Franck's and one of the co-founders of the Schola cantorum, Lockspeiser's is as good an explanation as any of Debussy's appropriation of that tune, though there is no particular evidence that he knew Bordes's piece (composed in 1890), and "The Keel Row" was a pretty well-known song. In any case, Debussy was taken with it and used it to the point of saturation in *Gigues*.

The result is intriguing: sometimes successful, sometimes less so. For the most part, Debussy uses only the first line of the tune ("As I came thro' Sandgate"), sharpening the fourth and flattening the seventh, as in *L'Isle joyeuse*, so that the effect is curiously melancholy, especially in conjunction with an achingly beautiful oboe solo that hints at the spirit, if not the music, of Wagner's cor anglais in the final act of *Tristan*: a *gigue triste*, indeed. But when the music speeds up, the incessant, bouncy dotted rhythms of the folk tune begin to sound slightly crude. Lockspeiser, who greatly admired *Gigues*, found these effects "subtly ironic," but it's hard to believe that Debussy was setting out to make fun of his material, any more than one feels that way about his treatment of "Nous n'irons plus aux bois," where the issue is more a mildly sentimental version of *nostalgie de la boue*. The truth is, surely, that Debussy does many lovely and some clever things with this actually very fine folk melody, but in the end expects too much of it, both melodically and rhythmically. It's striking that he uses the answering title phrase, "O weel may the keel row," only on a single page late in the piece, almost as an afterthought.

I've expressed reservations about these *Images*. Yet all the time when one listens to them one is listening to authentic Debussy, everything heard and balanced to a degree of refinement beyond the reach of almost any other composer, and with breathtaking moments that remind one that a genius is a genius even in his difficult times. A page of *Gigues* is worth a hundred pages of—well, I leave the name to be filled in by the reader, in the spirit of the late lamented M. Croche.

IO

A Crumbling House and a Sunken Cathedral

On consecutive days in January 1908 two momentous things happened to Debussy. On the 19th he conducted an orchestra in concert for the first time in his life, and on the 20th he married Emma Bardac. No doubt it was Emma who dragged him to the registry office in order to regularise their domestic situation. She, like Gaby Dupont before her, must have suffered from the pursed lips and raised eyebrows of the people one met—or who walked past one—at concerts or theatres or art galleries, and she had the added concern of a young daughter who needed to be legitimised, in an age when illegitimacy still counted against the mother as well as the child. If Debussy had died she would have had no claim on his intellectual property. His rich mistress when they met, she would have ended up as his impoverished common-law widow, and poor, clever Chouchou could have been cast out, ostracised, socially abandoned—or so Emma probably feared.

The conducting debut was similarly a marriage of convenience. Edouard Colonne had programmed *La Mer* for the 12th—his first attempt at the piece—in the full expectation, one imagines, that it would be just another item in his repertoire. Then the unthinkable happened at rehearsal: his own orchestra proved unable to play the work, and he was forced to withdraw it from the programme. Instead he invited Debussy to step up to the rostrum at the Châtelet on the following two Sundays and somehow manage, from the depths of what he himself called his "candid inexperience," something that had proved beyond the orchestra's experienced and usually competent founder. Curiously enough, the orchestra seems to have responded well, and Debussy, though shaking in his shoes, had the gratifying sensation, as he told Segalen, of "feeling truly at the heart of [my] own music . . . When it 'sounds' properly, you seem yourself to become

an instrument in the total sonority, unleashed on the sole authority
of gestures from the little baton."[1] The audience evidently shared his
delight and roared their approval. "For a length of time impossible to
tell," Willy wrote,

> there were howls of wild enthusiasm, the clatter of colliding palms,
> demented cries of encore. Debussy traversed the forest of desks ten
> times to return to the prompt box to show his warm gratitude; the
> occasional whistle, violent and energetic as a station-master's signal
> to a departing train, would start up the triumphal procession all over
> again, reviving the zeal of tired biceps and smarting hands. To satisfy
> these delirious melomanes, the conqueror had to be brought back one
> last time from the staircase he was descending, already in his overcoat
> and the bowler hat, which, in our modern costume, fulfils the role of
> the laurel wreath of old.[2]

This was his debut by chance, but it was not inconsistent with his
actual plans. He was already booked to conduct in London a fortnight
later, and in Rome and Milan in April, or so he had informed Durand.
In the event, the Italian dates fell through, but he duly conducted *La
Mer* and the *Prélude à l'après-midi d'un faune* at the Queen's Hall on
1 February. Victor Segalen, who was in London at the time, sent his
wife a revealing account of the composer in rehearsal. Debussy had
grumbled at having to conduct on only a single rehearsal, and Henry
Wood, whose orchestra it was, had arranged for extra sectionals in
a side hall. In the morning, Debussy rehearsed the brass, the woodwind and the percussion.

> At first it was pitiful, for all their goodwill. It was "the sea in bits,"
> according to Mme Debussy, who I was with. One had the painful
> sensation of grimly chewing over all the composer's ways of con-
> structing sound. Then little by little it came together. On the rostrum,
> Debussy never changed, very much in charge, very cool, not noisy.
> No need to tell you what a marvellous harmony lesson it was. Wood
> had got me a full score and I didn't miss a note. But the impression of
> the morning remained, perforce, tantalising, incomplete, like show-
> ing the fragments of a sumptuous mosaic piece by piece . . . Then at
> 2 back to work, this time with the strings: much more finish, more

nuances; not far off satisfactory. Debussy brightened up. He confided to me that these English, "the minute a Javanese or black conductor arrives, make enormous efforts to please him, and would rather drop dead on the spot—truly, on the spot—than not manage it." Well, they didn't drop dead, and they did manage.[3]

Not surprisingly, Debussy was invited back a year later, in February 1909, when he conducted the same orchestra in the same hall, this time in the *Nocturnes* and the *Après-midi d'un faune*. On this occasion, Wood had prepared the orchestra in advance, and that may have been the cause of a curious incident during the second nocturne, *Fêtes*, when Debussy got in a muddle over a tempo change, rapped the lectern with his baton for a restart, rapped a second time, and then (Wood recalled), "the most extraordinary thing happened. *The orchestra refused to stop*. It really was an amazing situation. Here was a famous composer directing a work of his own and, having got into difficulties, was asking the orchestra to stop, and was being met with refusal." Debussy, Wood thought, "quite candidly, was not a good conductor, even of his own works." But the audience, who must have realised that something had happened, "because it was so evident that he had tried to stop the orchestra," did something very English, and "recorded their appreciation to such an extent that he was compelled to repeat the movement."[4]

To do him justice, Debussy scarcely regarded himself as a conductor, and accepted conducting dates mainly because, as ever, he needed the money, but perhaps also because he was tired of hearing his music mangled by conductors who were unwilling or unable to adapt to the new aesthetic that his mature works represented. There had reportedly been a symbolic confrontation with Chevillard at a rehearsal for the first complete performance of the *Nocturnes* back in October 1901. Hearing a faint voice from the back of the auditorium, Chevillard had stopped the orchestra and waited: "Je voudrais cela plus flou.—Plus vite?—Non, plus flou.—Plus lent?—Plus flou.—Je ne sais pas ce que vous voulez dire. Reprenons, messieurs!" ("I'd like that more indefinite."—"Faster?"—"No, more indefinite."—"Slower?"—"More indefinite"—"I don't know what you mean. On we go, gentlemen!").[5] On various other occasions, Debussy was rude about Chevillard, about Colonne, even about Pierné, his old comrade at the Conservatoire and the Villa Medici, who conducted the first performance of *Ibéria* in February 1910. "The hyper-Spanish rhythm of the first movement," he grumbled to André Caplet, "became 'rive-gauche' under our young 'Capellmeister's' intelligent direction, and *Les Parfums de la nuit* crept out prudently from under a bolster, no doubt so as not to upset anyone." But after a rehearsal for the repeat performance a week later, things had improved, and Pierné and his orchestra had "consented to having fewer feet and a few more wings."[6]

It was undoubtedly hard for Debussy to emerge from his compositional world into the glare of public performance without some sense of being misunderstood and misrepresented. Ever since June 1908 he had been preoccupied with *The Fall of the House of Usher*, to the extent, as he had admitted to Durand, of sometimes losing his sense of the real world. Of all his theatrical projects, this was the one that most clearly exemplified his understanding of the word "*flou*," and his preference for wings over feet. He even for a time put it about that his two works based on Poe, for which he had just signed a contract with the Metropolitan Opera House, would not be operas, supposedly "because I do not want to write anything which in any way resembles *Pelléas*," but perhaps also because he was starting to have doubts as to how the mystery and intangibility of the *Usher* tale, in particular, could possibly survive the all-too-physical, all-too-tangible practicalities of the operatic stage. A year or so later he was describing the House of Usher to Caplet as "not exactly the house one would choose for calming one's nerves, quite the contrary . . . One develops there the singular dottiness of listening to the dialogue of the stones; of expecting houses to fall down as a natural, even obligatory, phenomenon."[7] These are the remarks of an obsessive, more than a clear-headed, creative mind. And so it would prove.

Exactly how much of *Usher* Debussy composed in the three and a half years up to his writing to Caplet in December 1911 that "I'm not managing to finish the two little Poe dramas" is far from clear. "It all seems to me as dreary as a vault," he told Caplet on that occasion. "For every one bar that is almost free, there are twenty that suffocate under the weight of a deaf tradition whose flabby and hypocritical influence I admit, in spite of all my efforts."[8] He had certainly drafted two different versions of the libretto, and had made a handful of musical sketches, including eighteen bars of what he told Emma would perhaps form the work's prelude. But this was precious little to show for the intensity of his involvement, hardly anything to match the picture he painted to Durand of "going to sleep with [Roderick Usher and *The Devil in the Belfry*], and waking to the sombre melancholy of the one, or the mocking laughter of the other!"[9] He had in fact, as we saw, long since abandoned the comic opera, while the sinister *Fall of the House of Usher* had been and continued to be pushed aside by other work, by the orchestral *Images*, by a ballet commission from Diaghilev, by a big new set of piano pieces that he composed in the latter part of 1909, and by a complicated and demanding theatre commission from Gabriele D'Annunzio at the end of 1910, among other, smaller projects.

However, there was more to this failure than met the cataloguing eye. There were generic difficulties in turning Poe's tale into a stage drama, but there were also problems connected with Debussy's own work, the clue to which was his insistence that his *Usher* would be a totally different kind of opera from *Pelléas*. He suggested to an interviewer in Budapest in December 1910 that "one cannot find a more complete contrast than between Poe and Maeterlinck," and "I believe that it should be the aim of every artist to depart as far as possible from the nature and subject of his success."[10] Plainly, he was deceiving himself. "How," Andrew Porter once asked, "could an opera set in an ancient castle where the air seems stifling, where the action passes into subterranean vaults, where a pale, mysterious maiden suffers, fail to recall *Pelléas* in subject or atmosphere?"[11] Maeterlinck's own enthusiasm for Poe is well documented. And the fact that Debussy felt it necessary to deny this obvious resemblance lends further support to the idea that *Usher* was for him more an obsession, perhaps to some extent a psychological retreat, than a practical creative project.

As for the generic difficulties, they hinge on the character of the tale itself and especially on the way it is told. The story is a first-person narrative with no more than a few phrases of reported speech, strong on atmosphere and situation, low on incident. At its core are the narrator's former school friend Roderick Usher, the last in the line of the Usher family, still young but pale, sickly and neurasthenic, the product of constant inbreeding, and his cataleptic twin sister, Madeline, a mere ghostly presence early in the story, who supposedly dies in the course of it and, in typical Poe fashion, is buried alive in a vault beneath the house by Roderick and the narrator, only to extract herself noisily and bloodily from the tomb, drag herself up the castle stairway, and collapse on top of her fragile brother, killing them both. The one other vital character is the house itself, a symbol of the Usher family and an embodiment of its history and fate. "I know not how it was," the narrator confides at the start, "but, with the first glimpse of the building, a sense of insufferable gloom pervaded my spirit."

> I looked upon the scene before me—upon the mere house, and the simple landscape features of the domain—upon the bleak walls— upon the vacant eye-like windows—upon a few rank sedges—and upon a few white trunks of decayed trees—with an utter depression of soul which I can compare to no earthly sensation more properly than to the after-dream of the reveller upon opium—the bitter lapse into everyday life—the hideous dropping off of the veil.

The house is a continual reflection of everything about Roderick and his sister. Its dark angles and strange echoes are the dark angles and strange echoes of their consciousness. Its remote, unlit passageways are the uncharted regions of their minds. And when they collapse and disintegrate at the end of the story, the house likewise—and otherwise inexplicably—collapses and disintegrates as well.

For the stage it seemed necessary to flesh out this tale in a variety of ways. The narrator, an ill-defined but essential character, had more or less to be invented from scratch, and what, in Poe, is a predestined, unmotivated descent into oblivion had to be provided with a more immediate causal logic—or so Debussy, who compiled all three versions of the libretto, evidently thought. To that end, he created from the merest hint in the story a malign family doctor, in love with Madeline (according to Roderick), but who, on finding her apparently dead one night at the foot of the stairs, himself buries her in one of the household vaults. Roderick believes the doctor to desire his death too, presumably with some idea of seizing the family property. The doctor, on the other hand, alleges an incestuous passion for his sister on Roderick's part ("that isn't the way one loves a sister"), and he urges the inconvenient friend to leave, "before this sombre maniac creates one further victim . . ."

None of these motivations exist in Poe, and to some extent they coarsen the texture of his story by rendering it more concrete, more matter-of-fact, where everything in Poe hangs on the inevitable doom of tainted blood and the unhealthy air of inbreeding. Debussy may even have had this in mind when he complained to Caplet about the "weight of deaf tradition": convention forever getting in the way of imagination. For whatever reason, he found it hard to get the music down on paper in any continuous form. In June 1909 he presented his wife with a page of music, eighteen bars, "which will perhaps be the prelude to *The Fall of the House of Usher*," and a fortnight later he told Durand that he had "almost finished a long monologue for this poor Roderick. It's sad enough to make the stones weep . . . for truly it's a question of the influence that stones have on the morale of neurasthenics"[12] ("Old stones," Roderick sings, "pallid stones, what have you made of me?") But how much of the monologue he actually composed at that time is very uncertain. He was working with his second libretto draft, in which Roderick's lengthy, barely coherent outburst against his fate and that of his adored sister comes in the first scene, before the arrival of the friend, and so may have blocked progress with the actual narrative. Debussy subsequently transferred the monologue to the second scene, after the arrival of the friend and his disturbing conversation with the doctor. But that was a good deal later, possibly as late as 1916.

As for 1909 and 1910, very little music survives to provide an image of the style he was looking for early on to portray the menace and solitude of Poe's Usher or the irrational terrors of its owner. His sketch for Emma suggests the bleak melancholy of the house itself through whole-tone harmonies that seem to hang in the air like the "pestilent and mystic vapour" the narrator imagines rising out of the black tarn where he reins in his horse. But in general Debussy's sketches, where they exist, are often so vague about crucial details such as sharps and flats that the precise harmony is partly a matter of guesswork. "It all feels like toil," he wrote to Godet at the end of 1911, "and the seams show! The farther I go, the more I have a horror of that *studied* disorder which is nothing but aural illusion. Or like the bizarre or amusing harmonies that are mere social jests . . . How much has first to be found, then suppressed, in order to arrive at the naked flesh of emotion . . . Yet pure instinct ought to warn us that the stuffs, the colours, are mere illusory façades."[13] This might almost be Roderick Usher himself talking.

On the very day in June 1909 that he gave Emma the eighteen-bar manuscript, they attended a performance by Diaghilev's Russian company of Rimsky-Korsakov's opera *The Maid of Pskov* (alias *Ivan the Terrible*), together with a short ballet called *Le Festin*, a more or less vacuous *divertissement* danced by Karsavina, Nijinsky et al., to a typical Russian salad of music by Tchaikovsky, Glinka, Musorgsky and Co. This seems to have been Debussy's first experience of the brilliant Russian dancers who had been setting Paris alight for the previous three weeks, and it can't be said that he was overwhelmed by it. He could admire Chaliapin as Ivan the Terrible, as he had admired him as Boris Godunov the previous year. But as for the ballet, he told the impresario Gabriel Astruc, "I've probably lost all sense of this kind of display since it bored me stiff. All the same, what an odd way of dressing people! It seems to me that we've got better at the Folies-Bergère."[14]

It was true that, for a musician, this first Paris season of the Ballets Russes (not so-called until their second) was a disappointment. The dancers, the choreography, the stage and costume designs, *pace* Debussy, were by general agreement unforgettable, but the music was nothing but the same old Russian stuff, colourful and amusing in its way, but without any of the freshness or novelty of the visual spectacle. The one substantial new (at least to Paris) ballet score, Nikolay Cherepnin's *Le Pavillon d'Armide*, drew from Laloy the damning observation that "the only extenuating circumstance one could think of in favour of such insignificant music is that after five minutes one no longer hears it." Diaghilev was stung into action. By the end of the season, in mid-June, he had commissioned Ravel, and tried and failed to commission Fauré and Reynaldo Hahn. By mid-July he, Debussy and Laloy had met and planned an eighteenth-century ballet, eventually to be called *Masques et bergamasques*, for which Laloy was to write the scenario. For some reason Debussy, who had never successfully collaborated with anyone on a theatre piece, proceeded to write the scenario himself, placating Laloy with the (very) distant possibility—which had presumably been discussed between them—of an operatic setting of the *Oresteia*. The ballet text, which was actually printed and published in June 1910, is a complicated piece of sub-*commedia dell'arte* mixed with sub-Beaumarchais. But by that time Diaghilev had found the ballet composer, himself Russian, whose music would supersede the Russian salads: the twenty-seven-year-old Igor Stravinsky. Debussy never started composing *Masques et bergamasques*; and, unsurprisingly, nothing more was ever heard of the *Oresteia*.

Amid all these theatrical failures, he turned to his own instrument for solace, perhaps partly stimulated by a pair of bread-and-butter commissions: a tiny follow-up to the *Golliwog's Cakewalk* called "The Little Nigar" [*sic*], written for Théodore Lack's "elementary piano method," and a slightly more substantial piece, "Hommage à Haydn," composed in May 1909 for a Haydn centenary issue of the *S.I.M.* monthly bulletin, and based, by way of an arcane, Boy-Scout code, on the letters of Haydn's name. ("It'll disappear in a puff of smoke," he told the journal's director, Jules Écorcheville.[15]) Then, within the space of a couple of months, from early December 1909 to early February 1910, he composed the brilliant series of twelve piano pieces that became book one of the *Préludes*.

Just as with the *Images*, it seems that in contact with the piano Debussy could write freely, exploring the implications of his unique idiom in a completely uninhibited way, but that when it was a matter of composing for a more "impersonal" medium and on a larger scale—for orchestra, with or without voices, or for the stage—he was forced to think in a more linear, syntactical, perhaps objective manner that raised issues of procedure he was increasingly reluctant to confront. When he had talked to Caplet about the twenty bars suffocated by tradition, he may well have meant the sort of music that, in every eighteenth- and nineteenth-century composer you could name, bore the structure along from one distinctive gesture to the next, that made sense of works that might otherwise disintegrate under the sheer weight of irrepressible, disconnected inventiveness: the musical details that information theorists describe with the charming term "redundant." It may go against the grain to think of anything in, say, Mozart or Schubert or even Brahms as redundant. But, purely in the sense that a lot of what happens in their music is predictable, the redundant is an important, if humble, part of their language. It looks as if, at least where the House of Usher was concerned, Claude Debussy—the lifelong enemy of rules—was now in rebellion against redundancy.

All but three of the *Préludes* are dated, and for all but one of those nine the implication is that they were each composed in a single day. The undated exceptions include two of the biggest pieces: *Ce qu'a vu le vent d'Ouest* and *La Cathédrale engloutie*, which would explain why they took longer to write, if not why Debussy failed to date them. As for the generic title of the set as a whole, its superficial models are obviously Bach's "48" and Chopin's twenty-four preludes. But whereas the factor of twelve in those sets is related to the succession of keys (all twenty-four twice in Bach's case), Debussy has no such pattern. He does maintain what amounts to a fictional abstractness by titling his preludes only at the end of each piece, though since the imagery is generally at least as specific as in the actual *Images* it's hard to take seriously the idea that he was wanting the player to ignore the title until having played the piece. The real model for this kind of writing is Liszt, who often gave programmatic titles to pieces ostensibly in abstract genres, but who also, in his *Années de pèlerinage*, mixed quite easy pieces with pieces in a more bravura manner, as Debussy does here. One other Lisztian feature of Debussy's preludes is that several of the titles, though graphic in appearance, come from literary sources, several of them familiar from earlier works of his. "Le Vent dans la plaine," for instance, is a quotation from the eighteenth-century playwright Charles Simon Favart which Debussy had already used as epigraph to his Verlaine song "C'est l'extase"; "Les sons et les parfums tournent dans l'air du soir" is a line from Baudelaire's "Harmonie du soir"; "La Fille aux cheveux de lin" is the title of a poem by Leconte de Lisle set by Debussy almost thirty years earlier.

Although these titles are literary, Debussy's interest in them is mainly not. His wind in the plain doesn't hold its breath, as Favart's does in the next line, and his flaxen-haired girl is not, like Leconte de Lisle's, an object of sensual fantasy. The Baudelaire quotation hints at something that has inspired Debussy before, the synaesthetic linking of the senses, in this case sound and scent, and here perhaps he does respond marginally to the poem beyond his chosen line, in the shape of Baudelaire's next line, "Valse mélancolique et langoureux vertige," which seems to prompt the slow, sometimes disrupted waltz of Debussy's prelude. But on the whole the titles are instant triggers from the visual to the musical. The first prelude, *Danseuses de Delphes*, was inspired—Debussy told an English admirer—by the beautiful column of that name exhibited on the landing of the grand staircase of the Louvre, a plaster copy of a stone original recently excavated by the French archaeologist Théophile Homolle at Delphi. Perhaps the sculpture was rotated so that the three female figures appeared in succession, or perhaps one could walk round it. There is certainly some feeling in the prelude of a slow circling, as of stately dancers with linked arms. But the real miracle of this piece is its harmonic concentration, the alternation of music made of soft dissonance and music made of plain triads in irrational but perfectly poised sequence. If, as the autograph suggests, the piece was written in a single day (7 December 1909), one might picture Debussy at the piano—literally or metaphorically—carefully testing each chord, each sequence, listening to the spacing and balance, the resonances, the dynamic shadings, the effect of the two pedals (not indicated, as usual). At first glance, this is not difficult music to play, but to play it well, with attention to every nuance, every painstaking detail, is a serious exercise in mental and physical control. Hearing Debussy play it, his English friend reported, "was like hearing a poet reciting some of his own delicate lyrics. He had a soft, deep touch which evoked full, rich, many-shaded sonorities . . . I have never heard more beautiful pianoforte playing."[16]

By comparison, the second prelude, *Voiles*, is a curiously doctrinaire piece, a pair of entirely whole-tone episodes framing a pentatonic middle section that could almost be a remnant of the gamelan music of *Pagodes*. The title might mean "Sails," or it might mean "Veils" (like the ones shed by Salome in Strauss's opera or deployed with coloured lighting by the American dancer Loïe Fuller). But the music has a sinister edge, provided by the bass ostinato B flats and the curious floating metre, that seems to contradict both meanings. The B flats are an echo of *Danseuses de Delphes*, which is in that key, and they continue into *Le Vent dans la plaine*, supporting the windy sextuplets that blow on and off throughout the prelude. Once again the challenge of this tricky piece of mild virtuosity is to play it softly enough, "as lightly as possible," Debussy indicates, and in fact the only markings above *piano* are the sudden *forte*s halfway through, violent gusts that, like real wind, blow your hat off, subside at once just long enough for you to retrieve it, then blow it off again. The effect is stunning, but hard to control.

With the fourth prelude, *Les Sons et les parfums tournent dans l'air du soir* ("The sounds and perfumes turn in the evening air"), we are back with the supreme refinement of *Danseuses de Delphes*, except that here it is the intangible, not the sculptural, that rotates in the air, and this has an impact on Debussy's harmony and, no less intriguingly, his form that takes us into new realms bordering, perhaps, on the regions he was trying to imagine for *The Fall of the House of Usher*. Time and again the music is disorientated by the chromatic chord sequences (starting in bar 3) that effectively liquidate the harmony, and with it any clear, simple sense of form: magical sounds and scents that teach the brain new logics. The form breaks down into a kind of montage of brief images, at first apparently incoherent, then reconstructed through repetition and the forming of new connections. It again reminds one of Debussy's remark about the twenty suffocated bars. In this prelude there is not a single bar remotely stifled by tradition, convention or any other concept imposed from outside. Risks are taken, assessed, listened to. At the piano he could bring this off; he was in his element. In other media he could not, yet, quite make it work, at least to his own satisfaction.

Impressionism or Symbolism? In this music the question is once again exposed as meaningless. The sounds are sounds and the perfumes are absent. Without the title, we could have no conception of the subject matter of the fourth prelude. *Voiles*, with its blurring whole tones—especially in the final bars, where Debussy supplies a rare pedal marking that ensures a wash of harmony—could loosely be compared to any one of the countless Impressionist seascapes with sailing boats (Paul Roberts opts for Whistler and Degas), though the sinister undertow of low B flats suggests a more mysterious agenda while failing to identify it.[17] The fifth prelude, *Les Collines d'Anacapri* ("The Hills of Anacapri"), might or might not be an impression of that part of the island of Capri, which Debussy probably never visited.[18] One theory, offered guardedly by no less an authority than

Roy Howat in the Foreword to the Collected Edition, is that the piece was inspired by the label on a bottle of Anacapri wine (presumably with a picture of the landscape). It includes bells, two popular songs, a tarantella and, unexpectedly, a habanera, and has the vividness and colouristic brilliance of a Derain or Matisse painting of the sea-side village of Collioure.[19] In complete contrast, *Des pas sur la neige* ("Footprints on the snow") is an intensely concentrated piece domi-nated by a single two-note, snap-rhythm motif, an image as haunting and relentless as the *tap-tap* of Blind Pew's stick in *Treasure Island.* "This rhythm," Debussy instructs, "must have the sonorous value of the depths of a sad, frozen landscape"—another piece of implied synaesthesia that can, perhaps, be felt rather than explained. But here, as at times in *Pelléas et Mélisande* (notably the grotto and dungeon scenes), the symbolic idea is unmistakable. The figure stands for some obsessive fear or other; fragments of lyrical melody, "expressive and sorrowful," overlay it like a lament, but cannot allay it. Music, as Debussy had told Durand, "is a matter of colours and rhythmicised time,"[20] and in *Des pas sur la neige* the idea of time being stretched out and probed for its hidden content is almost palpable. In a sense, the music gets nowhere; it is a time capsule in which we experience extension, then step out, like the soldier in Stravinsky's *L'Histoire du soldat,* exactly as and where we were when we stepped in, but with knowledge that was not previously ours.

In different ways these first six preludes show Debussy deploying a method of assembly that reflects the harmonic revolution his music has been quietly carrying through ever since the early Verlaine songs. Uninterested in the old grammar, but fascinated by the structure and variability of its elements, he shines a torch on them, examines them from different angles, rotates them, repeats them, arranges them in arbitrary-seeming ways, like pictures hung—but tastefully, scrupu-lously hung—in a gallery. There is about all this an empirical, anti-doctrinal genius, a refusal to be bullied by history or its debris, that is without precedent in Western music since Monteverdi. It perhaps explains why he fussed so much over the detail of his work, ignoring contracts and schedules and promises; everything depended on his own sensibility, and he could not—would not—fall back on tradi-tional best practice to help him over awkward joins or moments of failing inspiration.

Now and then he would make an ironic comment on his own idio-syncratic way of working. In the ninth prelude, *La Sérénade inter-rompue* ("The Interrupted Serenade"), a guitarist solemnly tunes up, practises a few Spanish twiddles, then launches into a keening song on two notes, only for the girl to slam her shutters closed (in a differ-ent key). Nothing daunted, the guitarist strikes up again, somewhat more enterprisingly, but is again interrupted, this time by another, distant singer and by the early morning music, *Le Matin d'un jour de fête*, from *Ibéria* (a reference that would have been lost on anyone looking over Debussy's shoulder in January 1910 as *Ibéria* was not performed until February).[21] The guitarist resumes, crossly at first, but then wanders off, mildly disgruntled.

At other times, Debussy could graft his method on to the narra-tive styles of Romantic music. *Ce qu'a vu le vent d'Ouest* ("What the West Wind saw"), prelude no. 7, is a more or less candid parody of Liszt, especially *Orage*, in the first set of *Années de pèlerinage*, with which Paul Roberts has found clear thematic connections. But Rob-erts also points out that Debussy's prelude, though frightening in its violence and virtuosity, is devoid of the pathos in Liszt's parallel between the wild elements and human suffering. "Debussy's West Wind," he notes, "never sees the valley of despair experienced by Liszt's Obermann."[22] The clue to this lies in Debussy's own actual source, a story by Hans Christian Andersen called *The Garden of Eden*, in which a prince wandering in the forest comes across an old lady roasting a stag who turns out to be the mother of the four winds. Each wind comes home and tells what he has seen that day. When the West Wind appears, he turns out to be no gentle zephyr but a wild man in a slouch hat brandishing a mahogany club. He comes, he says, "from the wildernesses of the forest, where the thorny lianas make a fence from one tree to the next, where the water snake lies in the wet growth and human beings seem not to be wanted."

> I looked at the deep river, where it was dashing down from the rocks and turning into spray to carry the rainbow. I saw the wild buffalo try to swim the river, but the stream hurried him down with it. Drifting with a flock of wild ducks which flew up in the air when they came to the waterfall; but the buffalo had to go down it. I liked that, and I blew such a gale that the oldest trees sailed off and turned to chips . . . I

turned somersaults over the savannahs, I patted the wild horses and shook down cocoanuts. Yes, yes, I've plenty of stories to tell, but one mustn't tell everything one knows.[23]

The diametrical opposite to this spectacular piece is the next prelude, *La Fille aux cheveux de lin*, which is both technically and stylistically the simplest piece in the book. Apart from the title, as we saw, Leconte de Lisle's poem (one of his "Chansons écossaises") is largely irrelevant to the tender, unstrained lyricism of Debussy's prelude, which more than anything recalls the Schumann of *Träumerei*, even if some of its chord parallels belong, in their uninsistent way, to a later vocabulary than his. This pretty Scottish lass tells no story, is without coquetry, does not pose. She is Annie Laurie without the promise. Or, in Debussy's own book, she is sister to the little shepherd in *Children's Corner*, where he was "very sweet and delicately expressive," she is "very calm and sweetly expressive." But where the shepherd dances as well as piping, his flaxen-haired sister only sings, and where he cadences brightly, with textbook perfect cadences, her endings are yieldingly plagal, like amens.

Two preludes later, in *La Cathédrale engloutie* ("The Sunken Cathedral"), we are back with the bells, not now of Anacapri, but of the ancient Breton city of Ys, which, according to legend, sank into the sea but will rise out of it again when the city of Paris is engulfed. It is also said that, on calm days on the Britanny coast, you can hear the bells of the cathedral of Ys ringing out from beneath the waves. Debussy may have come across this legend in detail in the opera *Le Roi d'Ys* by Édouard Lalo, a composer he admired, or he may have read about it in Ernest Renan's *Souvenirs d'enfance et de jeunesse*. But he ignored the elaborate tale of the origins of the city and the circumstances of its inundation. The prelude starts with the bells, heard softly through "une brume doucement sonore" ("a gently sonorous mist"), but soon we hear also the sounds of the cathedral organ, distantly at first, swelling in volume as the city rises from the sea, then finally contracting as it sinks back beneath the waves.

In concept, the piece could hardly be more basic, but its effect, oddly enough, depends on certain advanced aspects of Debussy's style. For instance, though coloured for much of its length by big, full-handed chords, it contains very little harmony in the conventional sense. The chords are mainly parallel triads, as if Captain Nemo were seated at the underwater organ with all the stops out and doubling the melody with rigid hands. The bells likewise start as parallel chords, but with open fifths, which lends them a colour similar to that at the start of *Les Collines d'Anacapri*, but fuller because the chords are sounded rather than merely an effect of pedalling. Later the bells are enriched by dissonance, like real bells with their rogue overtones. At bottom, the whole prelude is a majestic study in the synaesthesia of water and reverberation, the swell of the ocean as seen and heard, the boom of waves on rock, and the hidden mysteries of the sea itself.

After these solemnities, the last two preludes are lighter character sketches. *La Danse de Puck* is a deft portrait of Shakespeare's "merry wanderer of the night," perhaps inspired, as Howat suggests, by Arthur Rackham's illustration of Puck as a naughty little boy with a sparkler, though Debussy had himself described the character more vividly, some years earlier in connection with Weber's *Oberon*, as "equally adept at suddenly descending to the ground as in vanishing into space with a flap of his wings,"[24] an image that suggests Ravel's more dangerous and brilliant *Scarbo*, the final movement of *Gaspard de la nuit*. Debussy's piece opens with seventeen straight bars of highly ornamented melodic arabesque, unaccompanied, then continues, mainly, as a series of accompanied variants on this idea. *Minstrels*, the final prelude of the twelve, reflects from a slightly different angle the circus and music-hall obsessions of French art in the late nineteenth and early twentieth centuries: the clown as counter-image of the self-absorption of Romanticism, with a certain tinge of Baudelaire's *nostalgie de la boue*. The piece is a skilful montage of musical tricks, like a song-and-dance routine by a cabaret artiste or the blacked-up clowns that Debussy is supposed to have watched performing outside his hotel in Eastbourne in 1905. As with his other montage pieces, and no doubt like the clowns, Debussy binds everything together by repetition and skilful timing. The art of the entertainer, he seems to tell us, is brevity and surprise, and *Minstrels* is a perfect throwaway ending to this wonderfully varied procession of musical landscapes, portraits and vignettes.

Did Debussy intend the *Préludes* to be performed as a cycle? He certainly never did so himself, and there is no outside evidence that he thought of them in that way, rather than as a book of pieces from which to select. The first time any of them were played in public was in May 1910, the month of their publication, when the composer himself played *Danseuses de Delphes*, *Voiles*, *La Cathédrale engloutie*, and *La Danse de Puck* in an S.I.M. concert; and subsequent performances in his lifetime seem all to have been of groups or individual preludes. However, as lovers of late Bach know, performance practice and the abstract process of composition can be very different things, and there is good internal evidence that Debussy worked out the first book of *Préludes* as a continuum while never supposing they would be played that way. For a start the pattern of contrasts is telling: *Ce qu'a vu le vent d'Ouest* preceded by the very still *Des pas sur la neige* and followed by the gentle *La Fille aux cheveux de lin*; the grandiose *Cathédrale engloutie* framed by the comedy of *La Sérénade interrompue* and *La Danse de Puck*; *Minstrels* as a *coup de grâce* comparable to Beethoven's Op. 135 or the Rossinian coda to his hyper-serious Op. 95 Quartet. Then there is the matter of key sequence: *Danseuses de Delphes* in B flat followed by *Voiles* with a B flat bass pedal; *Le Vent dans la plaine* on, if not in, B flat; *Les Sons et les parfums* hitting B flat ostentatiously in its first bar; then later *Ce qu'a vu le vent d'Ouest* in F sharp minor followed by *La Fille aux cheveux de lin* in G flat (the same note) major, and *La Sérénade interrompue* with G flat prominent in *its* first bar. These connections might be a matter of compositional accident (the exact order of composition being sometimes unknown), or they might not. In any case all they suggest is that Debussy had internal integration in mind, but not necessarily that he saw it as desirable in performance.

Somehow, while engrossed in this project, he also managed to produce an eight-minute piece for clarinet and piano, optimistically titled First Rhapsody for B flat clarinet and piano, as a test piece for the Conservatoire exams that had so tormented him in his own time as a student. At the age of forty-seven he might still preserve his Crochelike distaste for the rules and processes of Conservatoire life, but he no longer breathed fire at the mere mention of them. Early in 1909 he had even accepted Fauré's invitation to become a member of the institution's governing Council, and, presumably as a consequence, soon found himself in the unaccustomed role of jury member, initially for the female voice trials, next for woodwind, and in November for piano. His Clarinet Rhapsody is an attractive but well-behaved piece that gives the instrument a few necessary flourishes, but is mainly lyrical in tone and typically on the soft side of *mezzo-forte* in dynamics. Its test is as much of musicianship as of virtuosity, and when in July 1910 Debussy sat on the jury for the clarinet exam (for which he had also composed the sight-reading test) he noted that "one of the participants, Vandercruyssen, played [the rhapsody] by heart and like a great musician. The others were tidy and mediocre."[25]

When he was composing with the intensity of this particular midwinter, Debussy cannot have been the easiest of living companions, and at some point early in 1910 matters between him and Emma threatened to come to a head. "My life," he wrote to Durand at the end of March, "is still in the same sad mess," and three months later:

> Those around me insist on not understanding that I have never been able to live in the reality of things and people, from which comes this invincible need to escape into myself, into experiences that seem inexplicable because I reveal there a person nobody knows, and which is perhaps the best of me! Besides, an artist is by definition someone accustomed to dreaming and who lives among phantoms . . . How can they want this same person to be able to conduct himself in daily life in strict observance of traditions, laws, and other obstacles placed in his way by a cowardly and hypocritical world? In the end I live in memory and regret, a sad pair of companions! But they are more faithful than joy and happiness.[26]

Plainly there had been scenes, and at some point Emma consulted a divorce lawyer. "I'm still hesitating," she wrote. "I'm waiting . . . It will cost me so much to separate from this man who makes me suffer so inexpressibly—alas, I shall never lack reasons."[27] Her health suffered as much as her morale, and their finances were increasingly precarious. Her alimony together with the modest bequest from her uncle covered their rent and not much more, and though Debussy's retainer from Durand kept them from starvation, his working methods were hardly such as might augment it enough to fund their bourgeois lifestyle. No wonder he tended to exaggerate progress on works such as *Le Diable dans le beffroi* and *L'Histoire de Tristan*; they were a useful source of cash advances, which he knew would never be called in. Somehow the couple kept afloat, buoyed up, perhaps, by

Chouchou, who puts in ever more frequent appearances in the composer's letters, as a sort of child muse, and a handy way of deflecting the heavy mood of reality. His letters to Emma, meanwhile, suggest that his affection for her never seriously wavered. It was just that his work meant even more to him, and that was a cross for her to bear.

The mood of suppressed anger is curiously reflected in the first of a group of three settings of the fifteenth-century gangster poet François Villon that Debussy made in May 1910. "False beauty that costs me so dear," the poet rages. "Coarse behaviour, hypocritical tenderness," and so on with unremitting fury for four long verses, each one ending with the same piteous complaint, "Sans empirer, ung povre secourir"—"to succour a poor man, without ruining him." Of course, the boot was on the other foot in the Debussy household, but the pen as usual was in the hand of the husband. In all three songs, the *Trois Ballades de François Villon*, the poet's brilliant verse brings the best out of the composer, and these are not only some of his most dazzling songs, but they are also among his cleverest and most subtly intellectual. Not only does he pick up many technical nuances in the poems, but he also refers the songs to his own recent music, including the *Préludes*.

The "Ballad of Villon to his beloved" ("Faulse beauté, qui tant me couste cher") starts with an acrostic, the first letter of each line spelling out, first, the poet's own name—François—and then the name of the wretched girl—Marthe—whose "perfidious charm is the death of a poor heart." Debussy's answer to this is to refer, consciously or unconsciously, to his own *Des pas sur la neige*, with its trudging snap rhythm and its air of sorrowful reproach. The figure dominates the piano part, while the words are set in free *Pelléas* recitative, but always carefully responding to (without rigidly respecting) the poetic metre. In the same way, the accompaniment includes reprises not matched to the verse form, except for the last line of each verse, which is set always—with minor variants—to the same music. Thus Debussy echoes something of the formality of the poem, but also its vigorous, half-suppressed rage.

The other two songs present a complete contrast. The second, "Ballad composed by Villon at his mother's request to pray to Our Lady," emerges from the same world as *La Fille aux cheveux de lin* with a simple, tender unaccompanied melody, but quickly goes religious, with open modal harmonies and parallel chords in the archaic manner of *Pelléas* or the first *Bilitis* song, but without the sensuality. Here, too, each verse ends with a line of refrain: "En ceste foy je vueil vivre et mourir" ("In this faith I would live and die"), which Debussy treats like an Amen, with a plagal cadence as in the prelude, interrupted the first two times, then resolved the third time, an effect of extraordinarily touching simplicity.

Finally the "Ballad of the Women of Paris" is a sparkling catalogue song, like Leporello's list of Don Giovanni's conquests, or Hugo Wolf's "Ich hab' in Penna." The Florentine and Venetian girls may talk nicely; Lombards, Romans, Neapolitans may make good conversation; but for repartee and backchat, for a good sharp tongue, the Parisiennes are in a class of their own. The song whizzes along from one idea to the next, somewhat in the manner of *La Sérénade interrompue*, each group neatly characterised ("Have I included enough places?" Villon asks at one point), but always, in the end, "Il n'est bon bec que de Paris" to the same music, yet another refrain ending to formalise the total effect. Was this a compliment to Emma or a warning to her? The awful truth is that her Claude probably wasn't even thinking of her.

At about the same time, or possibly somewhat later, he put together a second cycle of three songs on ancient texts, *Le Promenoir des deux amants*, using an existing song, "Auprès de cette grotte sombre" from the *Trois Chansons de France*, as launching pad for two more settings of the same poet, Tristan l'Hermite. Oddly enough the old song was the original of the footprint motive in *Des pas sur la neige* that Debussy had just revisited in his first Villon ballade. The new settings are both short, elegant but somewhat inconsequential love songs, ballads in the romantic sense but updated in harmonic style. Here Debussy does seem to have been thinking of Emma, since he dedicated the cycle to her, thereby hopefully identifying the "two lovers" of the title.

There is more substance, though, in the unlikely-sounding shape of an isolated piano piece he composed probably towards the end of 1910. *La plus que lente* ("The Slower than Slow") is a *valse triste*, a slow dance that inevitably packs a gently ironic punch, but is beautiful and affecting in its way. Though of prelude length, it would presumably have been out of place among the pieces collected under that title, lacking the objective character that seems to bind the actual preludes into a set. Debussy marked it *"con morbidezza,"* a piece of hyperbole that forbids what might otherwise seem a natural enough assumption—that the piece was written in memory of his father, who died in October 1910.

II

Theatres of the Body and the Mind

One hopes that Debussy's parents had eventually managed to be proud of their son's fame and distinction—the Légion d'honneur, the seat on the Conseil Supérieur, the prominence of his (and their) name on the Paris billboards—even if they found it hard to understand why these accolades never seemed to convert into the kind of affluence that most parents hope for—not entirely disinterestedly—for their offspring. Whatever they thought, at the time, of his divorce and eventual remarriage, they had drawn closer thereafter. And whatever the Avenue du Bois de Boulogne did to his finances, it did no harm to his outward respectability. Manuel and Victorine Debussy had moved into an apartment nearby, and a late photograph of them with their son suggests the warmth and mutuality of a suburban homecoming.

Debussy was sincerely distressed by his father's death. "Although we practically never had an idea in common," he wrote to Caplet, "it's a loss I feel more deeply each passing day. He had a sort of admiration for *L'Enfant prodigue*, and the Chicago success [of *Pelléas* a week after he died] would certainly have enhanced that beyond all measure; one can, without irony, regret that he never could have that simple pleasure."[1] The "without irony" tells us, of course, that Manuel Debussy would never have been capable of understanding *Pelléas* itself or its continued success. But, like most of us, he understood fame and would have been happy to refer that understanding back to his genuine liking for his son's, after all by no means wholly conventional, earlier work.

Manuel would also have been impressed with a pair of agreements that Claude struck that autumn, the first a month before his death but when he was already desperately ill, the second six weeks after it. At the end of September 1910 the composer signed a contract with the

Canadian dancer Maud Allan to provide by the end of February 1911 the music for an Egyptian ballet of her devising called *Isis*, for which he would receive the impressive sum of 20,000 francs plus a fee of 50 francs per performance. Then on 9 December he signed another contract, this time with Gabriel Astruc, to supply by early April the incidental music for a monumental drama about St. Sebastian by the Italian playwright and literary adventurer Gabriele D'Annunzio, in return for a further 20,000 francs. Manuel might not have noticed or been troubled by the absurdity of his painstaking, unpunctual composer son undertaking to produce twenty or thirty minutes of dance music and an hour or so of theatre music for chorus and large orchestra within the space of about six months. But Claude, as we have seen, could be as devious about deadlines as he was meticulous about his work, and there is good evidence that he never had any serious intention of fulfilling his contract with Maud Allan to the letter. D'Annunzio's initial approach at the end of November found him in Vienna, where he was conducting the Konzert-Verein orchestra in a programme of his own music, and in reporting to Emma about the concert and about his reply to D'Annunzio he added casually, "I mustn't forget Miss Maud Allan," as if that is precisely what he would have liked to do.[2] It was true that by that time the work had changed its title, and presumably its subject matter, though not its locale. It was now *Khamma*; but "as we're nevertheless staying in Egypt," he wrote to the impresario Joseph Schurmann, "it's much the same to me."[3]

Maud Allan was a new kind of fish in Debussy's aquarium. He had had dealings with women of doubtful reputation, had certainly slept with them and had even, in the opinion of some of his former friends, married one. But he had never written music for one; nor had he come across anyone who had elevated the louche and the seductive into something at least approaching high art. Maud was a dancer in the spirit of Loïe Fuller and Isadora Duncan—not, that is, a trained ballerina, but a free movement artist who performed solo in a partly improvised fashion, using the whole body as a vehicle for emotional expression. But there was more to her than pure expression. Her work was strongly angled towards the sensual, and tended to favour subjects of a sexually suggestive kind, such as Botticelli's *Primavera* and, most famously, what she called *The Vision of Salome*, in which she danced the seven veils in an exiguous, mostly transparent costume of her own design clutching a gruesomely realistic head of John the Baptist; but she was also a good musician, a trained pianist, and an intelligent woman who saw her work, not just as staged flirtation, but as the visual realisation of an idea. It was in the nature of the time, and as it happened of her own background, that she attracted scandalous gossip. Her brother, Theodore Durrant, had been hanged at San Quentin prison in 1898 for the murder and necrophilia of two young women, and no doubt in people's minds her dancing was the sort of thing you might expect of someone with a brother like that. It was also rumoured that she was lesbian. It was a combination of horrors that sent a shiver down the collective spine of the middle-class audiences who nevertheless flocked to her shows.

Probably *Khamma* and *Isis* were the same plot with the title changed. It had been extracted by Maud Allan herself, in collaboration with an admirer, the English writer William Leonard Courtney, from an Egyptian story found on a stele in a Theban temple by the Rosetta Stone decipherer, Jean-François Champollion, and retold by Gaston Maspéro in his *Contes populaires de l'Égypte ancienne*. It concerns a young dancer who is instructed by the high priest to dance before the statue of the god Amun-Ra in order to secure deliverance from the hordes besieging the city. She performs three dances, and when, at the conclusion of the third dance, the statue moves its arms and turns the palms of its hands towards the dancer, she launches into a fourth, more ecstatic dance, at the end of which she falls dead. Needless to say, and despite the need for a corps de ballet of worshippers and a supporting male mime for the priest, all this was really no more than a pretext for Allan to display her talent for sinuous, improvised movement to suitably exotic music. But she had reckoned without Debussy's dilatoriness, and his instinctive obstinacy when faced with anything in the nature of an ultimatum. She was also careless over contractual details. She had omitted to include in the agreement any mention of the work's duration, so that when Debussy finally, in January 1912, got round to producing a piano score lasting twenty minutes, she was in no position to grumble that she had expected forty, nor that she had wanted six or seven dances when he had given her only four. Bully as she might, he flatly refused to extend his score by a single bar, and when she tried to lecture him on the effect of his music, he exploded to Durand about the "detestable Maud Allan."

> Your reply to her is perfectly proper; but I shall allow myself to insist on the vulgarity of this madam. It's unacceptable for her to form judgements on things she knows nothing about, and to express them in terms that would hardly do for a bootmaker who had misunderstood an order. My philosophical bent is probably not strong enough, for I confess to being profoundly sick of this debate . . . Why, here is somebody who provides a plot so flat that a black man could do better. I find a way all the same, helped by I don't know what providence, to write some music. And here comes this madam giving me lessons in aesthetics, going on about her taste and that of the English—which is a bit much. It's again enough to make you weep, or better still: give her a good smack! All right, but without going to that extreme, one could perhaps at least give her a lesson in manners.[4]

But although he was rude about the dancer-librettist and claimed to hate the subject matter of her "wretched little Anglo-Egyptian ballet," he took composing the score perfectly seriously and never for a moment lapsed into the kind of routine snake-charmer's music that the subject might have seemed to invite. In fact, *Khamma* is surprisingly unremitting in its harmonic strangeness, from the sinister chromatic rumblings of the opening with its distant trumpet fanfares "that savour of riot and conflagration and send a cold shiver down your back,"[5] through the chilly whole-tone solemnities of the high priest's prayer to Amun-Ra, and on into the three dances that Khamma reluctantly offers, like the sacrificial victim in Stravinsky's exactly contemporary *Rite of Spring*, knowing perhaps that it will cost her her life. The first dance is another of Debussy's slow sarabandes, much varied in rhythmic texture but constant in tempo, and punctuated at one point by the distant fanfares of the opening. The second dance is quicker, more volatile, "light and fearful" the composer indicates. The third is again slow, and the most overtly sensuous of the three, as if the dancer were straining all her physical resources to draw a response from the stone god. Only in the spontaneous fourth dance,

Khamma's dance of triumph, does the music develop a strong forward impulse, and the frenzy hardly lasts long enough or achieves enough abandon to explain the death of a healthy young girl.

At this point one can almost sympathise with Maud Allan's regret at the ballet's brevity. One can picture her (if she had ever danced the work, which she never did), exotically costumed, moving and gesturing with great improvisatory freedom, then coming too suddenly and literally to a dead end, and having to lie still for several minutes while the corps de ballet pirouetted round her and the high priest pronounced a blessing over her. But this is the inevitable fate of the solo dancer who aspires to something loftier than the variety turn of Pavlova's dying swan or Allan's own *Vision of Salome*. Debussy's score is not his greatest, neither as rich in ideas as *Le Martyre de Saint Sébastien*, nor as brilliantly achieved as *Jeux*, but it is a well-organised, intriguing miniature drama, intensely personal in its harmonic idiom, and lacking only the radiant beauty of his very finest work. Orledge detects the influence of Stravinsky in the unusually abrasive harmonies; by the time Debussy composed *Khamma* he had heard *Petrushka*, and it's true that analytically the chord structures are now and then similar, though Debussy's subtle sound perspective, his way of distancing elements of the harmony behind or beyond other elements, together with the extreme refinement of his detailing, produces a totally different effect from Stravinsky's habitually bold, forward textures.[6] Orledge, a great admirer of *Khamma*, is probably right that it would have had a better fate if Durand had ever published an orchestral score. The reason he didn't, presumably, is that Debussy himself orchestrated only a few bars at the start, then handed the finished piano score to Charles Koechlin, a composition pupil of Fauré, who duly orchestrated the rest. The result is stylish and effective, but it naturally handles the music respectfully rather than creatively. There are no discoveries, as in Debussy's own orchestral scores, only colourings in.

If Maud Allan's business-like, slightly controlling tone was distasteful to Debussy from the outset, D'Annunzio knew how to chat up a touchy composer as if he were the one person in the world worth knowing and working with. His first, unsolicited letter of November 1910 is almost like a proposal of marriage.

One faraway day, on the hill of Settignano that is the birthplace of that most melodious of Tuscan sculptors, Gabriel Mourey spoke to me of you and of *Tristan* in accents profound. I knew you and loved you already. I frequented a little Florentine group in which a number of serious artists made a cult of your work and were excited by your "reform." Then as now I suffered from the inability to write the music for my tragedies. And I dreamt of the possibility of meeting you. That summer, while I was planning a long-meditated *Mystery*, a lady friend was in the habit of singing me the most beautiful of your songs, with that interior voice so necessary for you. At times my dawning work trembled at it. But I dared not hope for you . . . Do you love my poetry?[7]

It would be pleasant to report that these heart-warming sentiments were wholly sincere, though in fact Debussy was D'Annunzio's third choice, after failed approaches to Jean Roger-Ducasse and Henry Février. But in any case he was probably seduced at least as much by the financial aspect of the collaboration as by the poet's honeyed phrases. From Budapest, where he was playing immediately after his Vienna concert, he responded to D'Annunzio in kind. "How could it be possible for me not to love your poetry, just as the thought of working with you puts me, in advance, into some kind of fever?"[8] But he told Emma that "this business doesn't tell me anything worthwhile," and there is more than a trace of irony in his reply to another "terrible and charming" missive from D'Annunzio in January, "in which one can hear the triumphant reverberations of a march towards glory. And now all music seems pointless to me beside the endlessly renewed splendour of your imagination. Which is why it's not without a certain terror that I see the moment approaching when I shall decidedly have to start writing . . ."[9]

The triumphant reverberations of D'Annunzio's *Le Martyre de Saint Sébastien* echoed to an enormous, wordy five-act drama that, when performed with Debussy's music, lasted the best part of five hours. The music was an essential part of the concept, and the composer himself figured in a lengthy prologue spoken before the curtain by the Nuncius (Messenger, or Announcer), in language akin to that of the author's correspondence. It speaks of Claude Debussy,

who sounds fresh as the new
leaves under the latest shower
in an orchard of the Île-de-France,
where the almondless almond trees
light up the surrounding grass
in a Saint Germain grove
which remembers Gabrielle
and the faun king, and their love . . .

and so on for many lines. The play itself is mainly in blank verse, but includes more formal, rhyming sections that look as if intended for musical setting, though not all were set by Debussy. What he did write amounts in time to about a fifth of the drama, nearly an hour of music, composed in less than three months, an unprecedented rate for him, considering the size of the forces involved and the complexity of the whole project, with text arriving erratically and out of order. It necessitated, he told one correspondent, "writing music without stopping and with the regularity of a machine for manufacturing hats."[10]

D'Annunzio's actual title for his play was *Le Mystère de Saint Sébastien*, and it added a number of uncanonical details to what was known about the saint's life. The (more or less) historical Sebastian had joined the Roman army in about AD 283 as a cover for his Christianity, became a captain of archers, made many secret converts but was eventually exposed and ordered by the Emperor Diocletian to be tied to a post and shot by his own archers. D'Annunzio's long first act (or "mansion," as he rather obscurely termed his acts) is dominated by the torture of a pair of Christian twins, Marc and Marcellien, observed by Sebastian, who subsequently converts the twins' parents and sisters and a procession of other pagans, and in the process inevitably reveals his own Christianity. In the second act, Sebastian breaks into the magic chamber of the seven planetary sorceresses. In the third he confronts Diocletian in the altar room of the many "false gods"; in the fourth he is tied to a pole, while his archers plead with him to renounce his faith so that they will not be forced to kill him, but to no avail, and in the short final act the Soul of Sebastian is received into Paradise, in the garden of light and beatitude.

No doubt as for many of the artists who have painted the beautiful Sebastian naked and pierced with arrows, the sexual and sado-masochistic aspects of the subject were a major attraction for D'Annunzio, a noted poetic decadent and poseur who liked to extend the extravagances of his writing into the way he lived his life. Deeply in debt, he had abandoned his Florentine villa early in 1910, arrived in Paris in time to attend the Ballets Russes productions of *Scheherazade* and *Cléopatra*, and been fascinated by the performances of Ida Rubinstein in these two works. Ida, like Maud, was not a fully trained dancer; she depended for her effectiveness on stage on her slender, willowy physique, beauty of movement, and an intense presence, helped, from time to time, by her willingness to appear with next to nothing on. It's possible that the idea for a Sebastian spectacular was hers; it was the initial production of a company she herself formed after breaking with Diaghilev at the end of the 1910 season, and it offered her a part that both precisely suited her somewhat androgynous beauty and fed her ambition to take on speaking as well as dancing roles.

The pagan elements in D'Annunzio's treatment may well also have appealed to her, with her memories of Cleopatra and the Sultana Zobeïda in *Scheherazade*. But the handling was his contribution alone: the blurring of the division between the pagan and the Christian, the image of Sebastian as an Adonis, a Greek god led astray, as Diocletian seems to argue, or as a Roman officer almost too much loved by his men. The author shares their regret that this beautiful young man should renounce the sensual pleasures of the world for a painful death and the questionable joys of an afterlife without sin, and for the agnostic, beauty-loving Debussy, these ambiguities were surely a stimulus. They colour, for instance, the exquisite song of the Virgin Erigone in the second act, with its magical, serpentine polyphony of flutes and high soprano, and the rich chordings of the Syrian women's lament for (as they suppose) "the beautiful Adonis" in the third act. They even colour the more churchy elements, such as the Prelude, with its *Cathédrale engloutie* parallel chords, rendered more mysterious by their curiously irrational sequence of minor and major, not governed, as in the piano piece, by the obvious shape of a melodic top line.

Debussy's *Saint Sébastien* score is hardly a unified piece of work. How could it be, consisting as it does of eighteen separate movements, some purely orchestral, some vocal or choral, some in the form of melodrama (speech over music), often separated by long stretches of heavily metaphorical poetic declamation? Instead its varied character might suggest a new set of preludes, a succession of images controlled, however, by a text and a single narrative line. Even within sections there is something of the same kind of montage. The solemn prelude, an unbroken sequence of tonic triads for woodwind followed by a haunting oboe melody in Dorian E flat minor, runs directly into the strange unaccompanied duet of the twin brothers, tied—as Sebastian will be—to posts, facing one another, a sadistic tableau with obvious sexual—not to say homosexual and incestuous—overtones, which Debussy seems to abet by casting them both as contraltos singing in unison or close harmony. The oboe melody comes back in the next chorus ("Sébastien, tu es le témoin"), but a good forty minutes later and probably long forgotten by the audience. Finally, in this more than hour-long first act, Sebastian dances on the burning lilies, to music of an urgent refinement somewhat in the manner of *Le Vent dans la plaine*, but with a barely definable elevation that seems to echo the saint's "Je danse plus haut que la flamme, sept fois plus haut" ("I'm dancing higher than the flame, seven times higher").

Often in this marvellous but uneven score one is conscious of Debussy's familiar style taking on new colourings in response to the overheated strangeness of D'Annunzio's conception, in which early Christianity is—perhaps rightly—depicted as no less remote and cabbalistic in its way than the seven planetary sorceresses in their magic chamber. The Virgin Erigone sings a beautiful floating arabesque; Sebastian dances, and is mourned, to dissonant but finely designed harmonies that take to a new pitch Debussy's preoccupation with the voicing and balancing of individual chords. Simple parallel chords like the ones that open the work crop up a number of times, often in mysterious sequences that suggest a secret and alien church. Some of these new colourings come from his work on *The Fall of the House of Usher*, and perhaps, in his haste, he even used material intended for the opera, but there are also less interesting patches. The persistent slow music occasionally drags its heels, and the choral final act, in Paradise, has that slight flatness that often afflicts the music of Heaven by composers who have no particular desire to go there. It has been suggested that the weaker moments are the work of André

Caplet, who certainly orchestrated substantial parts of the score under Debussy's guidance, as is confirmed by a precise memoir of Jacques Durand. But Durand says nothing about Caplet writing any music, only about his having filled in spaces in Debussy's marked-up open score—a more or less mechanical process for a trained musician, and one easily checked by the composer. As Lesure insists, the character of the actual orchestration—its radiance and transparency—is plainly Debussy's own achievement.[11]

D'Annunzio's play, with Debussy's music, was performed for the first time on 22 May 1911 at the Théâtre du Châtelet, with Ida Rubinstein as Sebastian, choreography by Mikhail Fokine and designs by Lev Bakst. Caplet conducted. All kinds of problems attended Armand Bour's staging, especially to do with the difficulty of coordinating the music with the action in the scenes with chorus, a situation aggravated by Bakst's insistence on spreading the chorus round the stage as part of his colour scheme. Then, a week before the performance, the Archbishop of Paris gave the show unintentional publicity by pronouncing anathema on it and threatening Catholics who attended with excommunication, a fairly reliable way, one would think, of ensuring that they would turn up in droves. In the end the long evening, which continued into the small hours, was a tolerably ramshackle affair. Ida as ever moved beautifully, showed off her wonderful legs to great effect, but spoke an impenetrable French "through her nose," and rolling her *r*'s "as if she had a mouthful of pebbles."[12] Louis Laloy, who adored and admired D'Annunzio personally, considered that "he has never had any sense of the theatre."

Carried away by his own lyricising and erudition, he constantly immobilises his characters for speeches of which every one is a monologue, often very beautiful to read, interminable on the stage. The dress rehearsal had begun at 8.30. At two in the morning we emerged on to the Place du Châtelet with not a cab on the horizon. We were weighed down with oratory, suffocated by the torrent of words like Saint Sebastian under the flowers, and still more irritated by our impatience finally to hear the music, through those scenes where the dialogue kept on when one supposed everything had been said, words like a blown-up balloon passed all the time from hand to hand; and when at last the orchestra or chorus raised their harmonious voices,

our immense relief was sullied by the fatigue that left us insufficient
strength to be equal to so much emotion. I understood the profound
sense of this music much better from the score, and the following year
in concert. But then, what a revelation![13]

Three weeks after the D'Annunzio premiere, on 13 June, Debussy
attended the first performance of the new Diaghilev ballet, Stravinsky's *Petrushka*, also at the Châtelet, and like many in the audience
that night was stunned by the work's mastery and originality, and
perhaps also, with D'Annunzio still big in his ears, by its economy
of means. He had also been at the first night, the previous June, of
Stravinsky's *Firebird*. But this was something different. His supposed
reply when the young Russian asked him what he thought of *The
Firebird*—"what do you expect, one has to start with something"—
may or may not be apocryphal, but he certainly told Stravinsky, "You
will go farther than *Petrushka*, that's certain, but you can already be
proud of what that work represents." He was particularly struck by
the scoring. "I don't know many things," he said, "as good as what
you call: 'Le Tour de Passe-Passe' ['The Conjuring Trick', by which
the Magician brings his three puppets to life]; there is in it a sort of
sound magic, the mysterious transformation of mechanical souls who
become human by a magic spell, of which you so far seem to me to
be the sole inventor."[14] He imagined Stravinsky living with his characters in the way he had been living with the Usher family; and he
must have talked about the work a good deal at home, because a few
months later the seven-year-old Chouchou had "composed a fantasy
on *Petrushka* to make tigers roar."[15] But he had nothing to say about
the dancing, not even about Nijinsky, whose Petrushka was to remain
one of his greatest roles.

Debussy himself may have had enough of the theatre for a while.
Though he was nominally at work on *Usher*, and still more nominally
on *The Devil in the Belfry*, there is scant evidence of even fragmentary progress on either of them. By the end of the year he was claiming to be bored by them both. He may have tinkered with *Khamma*
but probably composed little of substance before December. He was
still trying to complete *Gigues*, and by October was in a position to

send Durand the four-hand reduction but not yet the orchestral score, which he took another whole year to complete. But there were the usual interruptions. In June, a month after *Saint Sébastien*, he went to Turin to conduct his *Après-midi d'un faune* and *Ibéria* and endured the humiliation of completely failing to manage the Scala orchestra and having to hand the baton to the young Vittorio Gui, who rehearsed the programme efficiently, then handed the baton back to him for the concert. "At bottom," he grumbled to Durand, without mentioning the more painful details, "the music of Claude Debussy means nothing to them, and at the first opportunity they'll go back to their Puccini, Verdi, and whatever else in the language of *si*."[16] Then suddenly he was ill: "temperature, overwork, nervous stress, and forbidden to do anything for at least a month."[17] So off they went to the seaside, this time to Houlgate, near Deauville, where he hoped—presumably against doctors' orders—to work on the Poe operas, but in fact managed hardly anything apart from picking at the orchestration of his Clarinet Rhapsody. As before he liked the sea but not the holiday-makers, and when not holding Chouchou's bucket and spade he spent much of his time, as he told Caplet, reading cheap novels and the *Chronicles of the Crusades* of Jean de Joinville.

> "And the children [he reported, quoting *Pelléas*] go down to the beach to bathe" . . . and some of them are even quite nice. But my God! Their mummies and daddies are hideous to contemplate! It's really hard to compare the children and the parents without coming to a disagreeable conclusion about the virtue of at least one of the parties. After all, might there not be more mystery than one supposes in making a child?—As Horatio said to Hamlet.[18]

Finally, for 1911, he accepted an invitation to go to Boston for what looked like being a well-designed and musically strong *Pelléas*, conducted by Caplet. But at this point Emma, herself in indifferent health, put her foot down. Like many self-centred people, Debussy disliked confrontations, preferring to go his own way quietly and avoid the accusing gaze; he took it for granted that "people [*l'on*] would help me with all possible tenderness." But "to detail for you all my arguments, my daily battles, was going to be so painful for me that I've put off writing to you for as long as I could! The worst of it is that I've got lost in all this, and have forgotten that calm egoism that is such an admirable strength, and that one knows so well how to use. In the end I'm extremely demoralised."[19]

It was at this low point, however, that he set to work on what would in due course become a second book of piano *Préludes*. They came less quickly than the first book, were themselves interrupted by other commissions, and are mostly undated. But at least two of them, *Brouillards* and *Feuilles mortes*, the first two in the eventual book of twelve, seem to have existed in draft by Christmas 1911, and there were probably more by the spring, since no other music is known to have been written by him in the early months of 1912 after *Khamma* in January. At that point a series of theatrical projects once again intervened, and the piano pieces were probably put to one side until the autumn, and the volume completed only in the early part of 1913.

The first partial interruption came in March from the poet Charles Morice, an old acquaintance from the Mallarmé Tuesdays, in the form of a project for a ballet to be danced to settings of poems by Verlaine under the sinister title *Crimen amoris* ("Crime of love"). Exactly what this was about is uncertain, because Morice's scenario has not survived; but Orledge speculates that it was at least partly based on the poem of that name in Verlaine's *Jadis et naguère*, in which the most beautiful of the fallen angels, a boy of sixteen, rebels against the diabolical goings-on in the silk and gold palace of Ecbatane and sets fire to it, killing himself and all his fellow devils and returning the land to "the clement God who will guard us from evil." Debussy was intrigued by this idea and contributed some detailed suggestions for the staging that seem to prove he had every intention of composing the music. There was even a contract, dated May, and André Messager expressed interest in programming the work at the Opéra. But for some reason Debussy turned against the Morice scenario, recruited Laloy to supply an alternative version under the new-old title, *Fêtes galantes*, and eventually (in 1914 or 1915) sketched a page or two of music before abandoning the whole thing, as he abandoned every other sung theatrical project with a libretto not devised by himself.[20]

In this same March of 1912, rehearsals began in Monte Carlo for the Ballets Russes staging of *L'Après-midi d'un faune* with choreography by Nijinsky. Debussy must have given his permission for this somewhat improbable adaptation, but he seems not to have been involved in it in any way, did not advise on (or object to) the treatment of his music, and in fact attended no rehearsal before the dress rehearsal on 28 May, having been constantly told by Nijinsky, "It's too soon, come tomorrow."

> I refrain from describing my terror when, at the dress rehearsal, I observed the nymphs and faun moving round the stage like marionettes, or rather, like cardboard figurines, always presenting themselves side on, with hard, angular gestures stylised in an archaic and grotesque fashion. Can you imagine the relationship between an undulating, cradle-rocking music abounding in curved lines, and a stage action in which the characters move like the figures on old Greek or Etruscan vases, without grace or suppleness, as if their schematic gestures were regulated by pure geometry?[21]

Nijinsky had in fact probably been inspired by Egyptian vases, but he had also, with Diaghilev, visited the eurhythmicist Émile Jaques-Dalcroze at his school in Hellerau (Dresden) and had tried to adapt Dalcrozian rhythmic exercises to the needs of a stage choreography, more in the character of gesture than that of actual rhythm—hence the at the time widely held view that the movement of the dance contradicted that of the music, even though the whole point of Dalcroze was to match each gesture to the music. But Debussy was slow to express himself publicly on the subject because by the time he saw the ballet, or very soon afterwards, he was engaged in discussions with Diaghilev and Nijinsky about a new ballet commission, which, no doubt mainly for financial reasons, he was reluctant to put at risk.

This new idea was a disguised version of a sexual fantasy that Nijinsky later attributed to Diaghilev. "*Jeux*," he wrote in his diary,

> is the life of which Diaghilev dreamed. He wanted to have two boys as lovers. He often told me so but I refused. Diaghilev wanted to make love to two boys at the same time, and wanted these boys to make love to him. In the ballet the two girls represent the two boys and the young man is Diaghilev. I changed the characters, as love between three men could not be represented on the stage. I wanted people to

feel as disgusted with the idea of evil love as I did, but I could not finish the ballet. Debussy did not like the subject either, but he was paid 10,000 gold francs for this ballet and therefore had to finish it.[22]

In the ballet, the *Jeux* ("Games") were played out on or near a tennis court, but they were not exactly tennis. When the curtain went up, a tennis ball would bounce on to the stage and a young man in tennis kit would leap across brandishing a racket. But then two young girls would appear, the young man would emerge from the shrubbery, and there would follow a series of flirtations, between the young man and the girls in turn, then between all three together, culminating in a triple kiss of a disturbingly ecstatic intensity, at which point a tennis ball would again bounce on to the stage like a passing policeman, and the "players" would flee. The original idea—Diaghilev's or Nijinsky's—was for the ballet to end with an aeroplane crash-landing on the stage, but it looks as if the composer objected to this modish concept and was allowed to suppress it.[23]

Debussy was presumably as yet unaware of these details when, on 18 June, he contracted with Diaghilev to compose the music, but he certainly knew that he would be on his mettle to compete with other Ballets Russes commissions of the hour. On the 9th they had all attended the premiere of Ravel's brilliant *Daphnis et Chloë*, a substantial, hour-long ballet much concerned with flirtation and abduction. The next day Debussy had been at Laloy's house to hear Stravinsky play the completed parts of his new ballet about a primitive fertility sacrifice, *The Rite of Spring*, and been bowled over by it.[24] "I still preserve the memory," he told Stravinsky five months later, "of the performance of your *Rite of Spring* at Laloy's . . . It haunts me like a beautiful nightmare and I try in vain to retrieve the terrifying impression it made."[25] Clearly his own ballet would not have much in common with Stravinsky's, perhaps slightly more with Ravel's. Above all it had to be written almost as speedily as *Le Martyre de Saint Sébastien* had been. Diaghilev wanted a complete piano score by the end of August and the orchestral score by the end of March 1913.

Quite apart from the plot, such as it was, Nijinsky had new ideas about the actual dancing. Diaghilev conveyed to Debussy his view of the work as pure dance:

Scherzo—waltz—a lot of *point* work for all *three*. Big secret—because up to now *never* has a man danced on points. He would be the first to do it, and I think it would be very elegant. He envisages dance from start to finish of the ballet, as in the *Spectre de la Rose*. He says he will try to have all three of them perform the same kind of dancing so as to unify them as much as possible. So that's the general style, which as you see will have nothing in common with the ideas he expressed in the *Faune*.[26]

Debussy must have read this letter carefully, since his score reflects most of its indications closely. His *Jeux* is, precisely, a scherzo-waltz, and it cultivates the lightness and elegance that Diaghilev emphasised in his remarks about dancing on point. Having completed the piano score, and as he contemplated the orchestration, he told Caplet that "I'll have to find an orchestra 'without feet' for this music. But don't suppose that I'm thinking of an orchestra made up exclusively of amputees! No! I'm thinking of that orchestral colour that seems lit from behind and of which there are such marvellous examples in *Parsifal*!"[27] It would mean concentrated work to achieve the necessary refinement and precision, and there would be no seaside that year for Chouchou. Now nearly seven, she had written a song, Debussy told Durand, announcing that "the Sea is cross at not having had a visit from Mr. and Mrs. Debussy and their charming little daughter."

I used up a great deal of eloquence persuading her that this year the Sea has gone out so far that they despair of ever finding it again! That didn't go down at all well, and there are times when it's very delicate being a father.[28]

Delicate, too, being a ballet composer. His orchestra without feet announces itself so softly in the opening bars of *Jeux* that one wonders how much of it was audible as the curtain rose on that first night of the first ballet season in the new Théâtre des Champs-Élysées, 15 May 1913.[29] Not until bar 70, some time after the curtain has risen on "an empty park" (in Bakst's atmospheric setting a densely tree-lined London square), does the dynamic level rise momentarily above *piano*, in honour of the bouncing tennis ball, and for the rest of the twenty-minute score *forte* markings of any category remain the exception and usually of brief duration until the closing pages, where (as in Act 4 of *Pelléas*) the repressed passion explodes in a series of (comparatively) violent outbursts. Debussy's prevailing technique, which would so impress avant-garde composers half a century later, is to distribute tiny gestures round the orchestra like fragments of overheard conversation or like simulacra of the unspoken, barely expressed, only half-recognised passions that fleetingly develop between the three dancers. Every detail is touched in with a fine brush. Snatches of decorative arabesque melody flit from instrument to instrument; the exquisitely complex dissonances of *Le Martyre de Saint Sébastien* acquire here a transparency and airiness like the brush-strokes in an Impressionist watercolour. This is the *Parsifal* effect in practice. Debussy was perhaps thinking of the way the solo oboe floats on a wave of string triplets in the Good Friday Music, or the soft orchestration for full woodwind in the Grail scene of the first act, or in general Wagner's method of scoring for full orchestra at quiet dynamics, an effect he had first explored, less translucently, in the second act of *Tristan*. But Debussy's textures are not in themselves Wagnerian, any more than his debt to Wagner in other respects, brilliantly analysed by Robin Holloway, results here in a Wagnerian kind of music, as it did to some extent in the hastily composed interludes of *Pelléas et Mélisande*.[30]

The music's needlepoint sensuality comes, of course, from the subject matter, while being inherently, profoundly Debussyan in itself. Its delicious suggestiveness is that of the early songs and the *Après-midi d'un faune*, albeit expressed in a more sophisticated language. But the fact that this atmosphere impresses so strongly through the music is due to something else that Diaghilev referred to in his letter, Nijinsky's attempt at unifying the work through a conformity of dancing style (as opposed, presumably, to the differences between male and female ballet conventions). The music, though scattered in its elements and texture, is bound together by an overriding rhythmic impulse. Even though the rhythmic components are themselves diverse, they swing along together on a shared conveyor belt, and while the melodies are in a constant state of flux, they evolve from one another as in a stream of consciousness, stray thoughts connected by personality more than logic. In this, *Jeux* might be seen as a more abstract continuation of *La Mer*, a score whose tone was set by the pictorial subject, but whose coherence depended on subtle internal linkages worked at a purely musical level. *Jeux* may, as Holloway insists, be about sexual pleasure, but since Diaghilev it has flourished, when it has, in the concert hall, where subject matter is more provisional, and the music is enjoyed for its innate beauty and coherence, like any symphonic work.

However much Debussy may have been prompted in the kind of music he wrote by Diaghilev's account of Nijinsky's ideas, Nijinsky himself seems not to have fulfilled them. By all accounts the staging and choreography were heavy-handed, worked out literally on the hoof, and largely unresponsive to the music's delicacy and refinement. There were absurdities that provoked laughter. Nijinsky had never played tennis, though he had watched it, and his sole concessions to anything related to that particular game seem to have been the dancers' modern, white costumes and the "tennis" ball, which was in fact more the size of a football. The movement, for this flickering, feather-light score, was again Dalcrozian, not fluid but posed, and again inspired (according to one reviewer) by the figures on Greek vases.[31] The real problem for Nijinsky, and in the end for *Jeux* itself, was that he was simultaneously preparing his production of *The Rite of Spring*, which would have its turbulent premiere on the corresponding subscription Thursday two weeks later. Because *The Rite* was a complex piece involving a large corps de ballet and a revolutionary score, while *Jeux* had only soloists, it was the Stravinsky that claimed most of Nijinsky's attention. Tamara Karsavina, one of the two female dancers, described the difficulty of working with a choreographer who was also dancing the male role, and who could not or would not explain his intentions clearly:

> As I had to keep my head screwed on one side, both hands curled in as one maimed from birth, it would have helped me to know what it was for . . . Unaided by understanding, I had to learn by heart the sequence of movements and once asked, "What comes after . . ."— "You should have known by now, I won't tell you." "Then I will give up my part."[32]

How much worse it must have been for the other ballerina, Lyudmila Shollar, who took over from Nijinsky's pregnant sister, Bronislava, at short notice.

As for the composer, he was tactful to those involved, but did not hold back either in print or in private. On the day of the premiere, *Le Matin* printed an open letter from him containing a double-edged account of the ballet and a sharp satire of Nijinsky himself as "a gentleman very good at arithmetic." Later he unburdened himself in detail to Robert Godet:

> This man adds up demisemiquavers with his feet, does the proof with his arms, then, suddenly struck with hemiplegia, gives the music a dirty look as it goes by. It seems this is called the "stylisation of gesture" . . . It's horrible! It's even Dalcrozian, for I consider Monsieur Dalcroze one of music's worst enemies! And can you imagine what ravages his method can cause in the soul of this young savage that is Nijinsky?[33]

Between completing the short score of *Jeux* in September 1912 and the first performance in May, Debussy not only composed the remaining preludes for his second volume but delivered them to Durand, who published them in April 1913. At the last minute there was some equivocation about what to include. There was a piece called "Tomai des éléphants," based analphabetically on Kipling's "Toomai of the Elephants" (in the *Jungle Book*), which Debussy persisted with but then decided was "impossible as a prelude," and had to compose a last-minute substitute—probably the penultimate prelude in the eventual set, *Les Tierces alternées*. What happened to "Tomai," who couldn't become a proper elephant handler until he had seen the elephants dance, is unknown, but he may possibly have found himself, in a different guise, in the "Pas de l'éléphant" of Debussy's next ballet, *La Boîte à joujoux*.[34]

In subject matter, and to some extent in musical character, the preludes of book two map quite neatly on to those of book one. Occasionally the similarities are disturbing: for instance, *Bruyères* ("Heathlands") in book two starts uncomfortably like a re-run of *La Fille aux cheveux de lin*, but soon diverges, both musically and technically; *Général Lavine—eccentric* (about the American clown, Edward Lavine) has moments of sounding like a second-hand *Min-*

strels, but varies the music-hall imagery and exaggerates the montage so entertainingly that it would be rank pedantry to object. There is a certain recurrence of imagery. *Brouillards* ("Mists") might recall *Voiles*, though certainly not musically: its left-hand triads and right-hand bravura are worlds away from the steady whole-tonerie of the earlier piece. *Feuilles mortes* ("Dead Leaves") could be a sad Baude-lairean epitaph to the *Sons et parfums* of book one: the same slow triple time, the same saturated chromatic harmony, the same transfer-ence of Nature into music. *La Puerta del Vino* (one of the gates of the Alhambra, which Debussy saw on a postcard) matches the *Sérénade interrompue*, with similar violent contrasts, there of montage, here of dynamics. *Canope* (a funerary urn from the ancient Egyptian city of that name) resonates as an image with *Danseuses de Delphes*, but could hardly be less like it musically, with its solemn tread of parallel triads, and stifled fragments of chromatic plainchant. A closer prec-edent for this profoundly mysterious piece is the chord parallels that open *Le Martyre de Saint Sébastien*: the same solemn, stately tread, and something of the same tendency to suggest strangeness by break-ing the natural sequence of these essentially very plain, uncompli-cated chords.[35]

Taken as a whole the second book breathes a different air from the first. *La Cathédrale engloutie* notwithstanding, consecutive triads play a bigger part in the later set, often in that disjunct character that seems to have been a discovery of *Le Martyre*. At times there is more than a hint of *Petrushka* about these parallels: compare *Brouillards* and the opening of the fourth tableau of Stravinsky's ballet, or the start of *Général Lavine* with Petrushka's music in the second tableau. Sometimes the similarities are more noticeable with the four-hand piano version of the ballet, which Debussy had in his possession by Easter 1912, a gift from the composer, to judge by Debussy's letter of 13 April: "Thanks to you, I have spent an exquisite Easter holi-day in the company of Petrushka, the terrible Moor and the delicious Ballerina."[36] In general the tendency of the second book to combine or juxtapose different keys (bitonality) might have been prompted by the Stravinsky not only of *Petrushka* but also of the first part of *The Rite of Spring*, which Debussy had heard its composer play in June 1912. But the bravura of *Les Fées sont d'exquises danseuses* ("The Fairies are Exquisite Dancers") or the last two preludes, *Les Tierces alternées* ("Alternating thirds") and *Feux d'artifice* ("Fireworks") has a purely Debussyan lightness of touch, however Stravinskyan some of their figuration and harmony might look on the page. The French composer could somehow capture the mercurial grace of the Arthur Rackham illustrations that inspired *Les Fées sont d'exquises danseuses* and the eighth prelude, *Ondine*, without lapsing into the somewhat arch fayness of the original drawings. On the other hand, he was equal to the heavier, more picaresque comedy of Dickens, an author he adored. *Hommage à S. Pickwick Esq. P.P.M.P.C.* is like a multi-frame picture postcard from London, starting with "God Save the King" (Union Jack T-shirt) and proceeding through what might be a series of street scenes culminating in a whistled tune straight out of the mouth of Sam Weller. The British national anthem is balanced at the very end of the book by a distant fragment of the "Marseillaise" breaking in on the fireworks of 14 July.

In one other respect, the appearance of the preludes (as opposed to their sound) might have been prompted by the young Russian, though we have already noted something like it in Debussy's much earlier *Nocturnes*. Beginning with *Petrushka*, Stravinsky's orchestral scores are often layered, in a way that forms visible strips on the page, each strip being a continuing figure or texture in that particular section of the orchestra. In a solo piano work, of course, such layering is less obvious. Nevertheless, the preludes in book two have something of the same appearance. As in the second book of *Images* but not at all in the first book of *Preludes*, Debussy sets the music out on three staves for at least part of every piece, whether or not the music's complexity seems to require it. Often this layout has the effect of isolating a middle voice, with accompanying chords or figures handed from right hand to left around it. In particular it undermines the automatic association between the upper and lower staves and the right and left hands. In pieces like the seventh prelude, *La Terrasse des audiences du clair de lune*, the music spans an immense range, greater at first sight than two hands could manage. But the three-stave layout not only identifies the separate layers of the music, it also helps explain how they can be performed by a normal human being not blessed with three arms.

The mysterious title of this seventh prelude, one of Debussy's most fascinating piano works, calls for explanation, not least because in every book on Debussy that discusses the title, including the relevant volume of the *Oeuvres complètes*, it is explained wrongly. Debussy is said to have picked up the title from an article by the historian René Puaux in the Paris newspaper *Le Temps*, "describing the coronation festivities of George V as Emperor of India" (the great Durbar of December 1911). The text is usually quoted. It refers to "la salle de la victoire, la salle du plaisir, les jardins des sultanes, la terrasse des audiences du clair de lune, le couloir des reines." Curiously enough this list of features is quoted correctly, and it is indeed from an article by Puaux. But it has nothing to do with the Durbar or with George V. It figures in the issue of *Le Temps* for 10 August 1912, and is a beautiful account of a visit Puaux made to the abandoned city of Amber, near Jaipur, some hundred and fifty miles from Delhi.

Debussy clearly read this article and was struck by the particular phrase he chose for his title. But it is hard to believe that there was not, behind that choice, a response to the whole description. Puaux relates his approach to the deserted palaces, not like the prince in *The Sleeping Beauty*, cutting his way through hedges of wild brambles, but like a normal visitor arriving at a well-maintained but completely uninhabited city "by way of a broad, paved ramp, into the imposing interior courtyard, which must, it seems, have been crowded only yesterday with chariots, elephants, ostlers, mahouts."

> And yet silence has reigned here for two centuries. The young Hindu functionary they have given me as a guide must have understood my desire to explore like the prince in the fairy-tale. He follows me without a word, and once he has taken off his shoes at the foot of the stairway of the Diwan-i'Am [the Hall of Public Audience], I no longer even hear him walking behind me. When we cross some room richer in decor than the others and whose former purpose I should like to know, I turn to him and, in an undertone, very simply, without architectural nomenclature, without a profusion of dates or details, he tells me: the hall of victory, the hall of pleasure, the gardens of the sultans, the terrace of the moonlight audiences, the corridor of the queens.

After contemplating the interior courtyard of the women's quarter "where twelve young maharanis lent themselves each day to the whim of their master," Puaux reflects:

There remains, of these creatures of love, only what was impersonal: the white and black marble water channel in the middle of their great summer salon, the screens of perforated marble in the corridors reserved for their access to the terraces in the cool evening hours, and the pavilion of Sohag Mandir from which, hidden from the gaze, they could attend the solemn audiences in the Diwan i'Khas, the Hall of Private Audience.[37]

Might there have been some remote connection in Debussy's mind between Puaux arriving at the deserted city and Poe's narrator arriving at the House of Usher? The two destinations have one thing only in common, but it is a big thing: they are actually or spiritually abandoned places, shipwrecks of history. Both narrators find their imagination exercised by the scene before their eyes.

What was it [Poe asks] that so unnerved me in the contemplation of the House of Usher? It was a mystery all insoluble; nor could I grapple with the shadowy fancies that crowded upon me as I pondered. I was forced to fall back upon the unsatisfactory conclusion, that while, beyond doubt, there *are* combinations of very simple natural objects which have the power of thus affecting us, still the analysis of this power lies among considerations beyond our depth.

What use [asks Puaux] would more precise information have, since it is my imagination that has to bring this silence to life? What use the extracts from learned works by [James] Fergusson, since my memory will only retain, as with every impression of life, that which has left the profoundest impression on my eyes and my heart?

There is no obvious sense in which Debussy's piece represents Puaux's Amber, in the way *La Cathédrale engloutie* represents the legend of Ys. It might, though, be regarded as a response to the activity of the imagination in the face of the beautiful but inexplicable relics of history. At first the eye sees and the ear hears only debris, musical fragments, at least seven apparently unrelated "objects" in the first fourteen bars. Then gradually some kind of picture materialises, with a distinct shape, yet no clear connection with the fragments that preceded it. At the end, the visitor turns away, picking up a fragment or two, souvenirs, as he leaves, moved by what he has seen, but still in truth mystified as to what precisely it was.

Of all Debussy's piano pieces, this is one of the most original in form. Jann Pasler has shown how the seemingly unrelated elements are linked by carefully planned voice leadings, by the way in which the melodic line of one will spill into the line of the next, or the way in which apparently random repeated bars serve a pivotal function between superficially disparate types of music.[38] The technique is a kind of montage, but with a carefully devised hidden flow. In an uncomprehending performance, it barely hangs together. But Pasler has demonstrated how a grasp of the linkages can make sense of the continuities. Every detail is arresting, and to claim that anything is irrelevant or unconnected is merely to admit a failure to penetrate the mystery. It is precisely the enigma of great art that we know it is great even when we cannot put our finger on what distinguishes it from the trivial. About *La Terrasse des audiences du clair de lune* there is no hint of the trivial, but what it adds up to is as difficult to know as the phenomenon it purports to describe.

12

War in Black and White

A t the age of fifty, Debussy had achieved success as a composer. His music was in the repertoire of the Ballets Russes and the main Paris orchestras, he was in demand to conduct it both there and abroad, and on 23 August 1912, the day after his fiftieth birthday, he completed the initial draft of his major new Diaghilev commission. His music was argued over, and sometimes abused, in the press (probably the best an innovative composer could hope for), and was admired and imitated by younger composers. He even bore an official stamp. He had the Légion d'honneur, was on the Council of the Conservatoire and a regular juror for its competitions. His performances did not, it's true, provoke riots, unlike that of the real pacemakers, the Stravinskys (*Rite of Spring*, 29 May 1913), or the Schoenbergs, Bergs and Weberns (the Vienna *Skandalkonzert*, 31 March 1913). It was strange but not threatening, dissonant but not noisy: it wouldn't remotely have fitted his own witty description of *The Rite of Spring* as "savage music with all modern conveniences."[1] Instead it seemed to have struck a perfect balance between the novel and the familiar, like the best modern domestic architecture, which borrowed vernacular styles to create a sense of the new without completely disrupting the old.

Out of the public gaze, however, all was far from well. For some time Debussy had been in fragile health, ever since having to cancel concerts in Manchester and Edinburgh in March 1909 as a result of what he referred to as "almost daily haemorrhages." He frequently complained of nervous exhaustion and, quite apart from the effects of overwork, the incessant worrying over detail and the pressure of unmeetable deadlines, he did not live a healthy life. He smoked and, perhaps, drank to excess, and he took almost no exercise.[2] To what extent these troubles were early signs of the rectal cancer that eventually killed him has been a matter of dispute. Lesure and others have routinely assumed so, but Debussy's most recent biographer, Eric Jensen, discussed the question with a cancer specialist and concluded that the cancer "would have had to spread at an astonishingly slow rate for Debussy to have continued a normal life [as he more or less did] until 1915." On the other hand, Jensen mentions "substantial bleeding" as an early indication of rectal cancer, which might seem to lend significance to the "almost daily haemorrhages" of 1909.[3]

Emma's health also was up and down; she too had been ill in England, and there were frequent relapses. It's tempting here to look for psychological factors, if not actual malingering. Emma did not like her husband's absences, and seems not to have been above exaggerating the illness and misery they brought down on her. Eventually, in July 1913, her doctor "strongly advised" a season at Vichy for the waters, and, in Debussy's opinion, she was making the most of this highly inconvenient and expensive prognosis. "With a nature as impressionable as hers," he wrote to Durand,

> you will guess what this can leave behind in terms of heavy moments and thoughts unspoken by either of us. It's intolerable and disobliging. To do battle with oneself alone is nothing! But to do battle "en famille" becomes odious! Add to that the domestic demands of a former luxury, which she finds it hard to understand has now become impossible to sustain.[4]

Emma had put a stop to his Boston trip in 1911, and when, at the end of 1913, he went to Russia for two weeks, she evidently let him know in advance what unhappiness it would cause her. A string of telegrams from him along the way expressed, surely, her distress more than his, even though he certainly was not himself one of nature's travellers, except of course in the mind.

Everything was made harder by their financial troubles, which, despite the fat advances from Maud Allan and Gabriele D'Annunzio, had gone steadily from bad to worse. Sometimes the shortage took extravagant forms. At one point in January 1912 Debussy asked Laloy if he knew anyone who could lend him 20,000 francs, the equivalent of his entire contract with D'Annunzio. At about the same time he borrowed 5,000 francs from Henry Russell, the director of the Boston Opera, whom he had been forced by Emma to let down, a debt he was never able to repay and had eventually to renounce. He continually took advances from Durand, sometimes against works that had little or no chance of ever seeing the light of day. His nominal debt to his publisher simply grew and grew, until on the day he died it amounted, according to Lesure, to 66,000 francs. To his eternal credit, Durand seems never to have made trouble over this money, trusting—no doubt rightly—that it would be repaid many times over by Debussy's music. During his lifetime, however, the composer repaid him only with his (admittedly expensive) loyalty.

It was presumably to help with the exchequer (though also, he told Godet, "to try to rediscover the values that arbitrary judgements and capricious interpretations have falsified"[5]) that, towards the end of 1912, he once again took up reviewing, this time for the monthly *S.I.M.* journal. Since his *Gil Blas* days he had published the occasional article and a number of interviews, but had not had a regular column. He now wrote in every issue of the journal from November 1912 to May 1913 (except, for some reason, April), then again from November to March the following season. As before, he reviewed erratically, picking up some events but not others, and in the main using his column to grind his favourite axes, which were by and large the same ones as before. Of M. Croche there is now no sign, until in the *Annales politiques et littéraires* of May 1913 Debussy used a short note on the Wagner centenary to refer back to the old dragon's passing. The late M. Croche, he remembers, "was in the habit of calling the tetralogy [*The Ring*] 'The A to Z of the gods'. An irreverent enough formula, but one that can nevertheless serve to emphasise that, if the Wagnerian art no longer exerts the same influence on French music, it will still be necessary to consult this admirable directory for a long time to come."[6]

The note encapsulates his continuing obsessions, with Wagner on the one hand, and with old French music on the other. "Why," he asks the readers of the *S.I.M.* journal, "are we so indifferent to our great Rameau? To Destouches, virtually unknown? To Couperin, the most poetic of our harpsichordists, whose tender melancholy is like some adorable echo from the mysterious depths of those landscapes where Watteau's characters grow sad."[7] He proposes the formation of a Rameau Society, but then, two months later, satirises the whole fuss about "precursors." "According to the latest cosmogonical researches," he observes with mock earnestness, "it seems certain that the monkey was the precursor of mankind . . . The profession of precursor has followed a development parallel to that of music, that's to say that the more music has been made, the more precursors there have been. If any epoch lacked them, the next epoch invented them."[8] Essentially this is a jibe at the teaching of old methods as if past composers had ever consciously applied them. For instance, the crisis in French dramatic music as he sees it is due to the fact that "it has wrongly interpreted the Wagnerian ideal and has tried to extract from it a formula that doesn't suit our race. Wagner was not a good teacher of French."[9] And even his beloved Palestrina, whose music he had studied before writing the choral last act of *Le Martyre de Saint Sébastien*, has to be superseded, one feels, because of his music's role in the teaching of counterpoint. So "Javanese music observes a counterpoint next to which that of Palestrina is mere child's play."[10] In every case, he is talking about music he loves while deploring the use to which it has been put, and perhaps he is also reassuring himself that his own meticulous re-creation of musical language has not simply been a waste of time. "The century of aeroplanes," he insists, no doubt with half a thought for the Futurists Pratella and Russolo, "has a right to its own music."[11]

In June 1912, Debussy had attended a ceremony inaugurating a commemorative plaque to Stéphane Mallarmé on his old house in the rue de Rome. Then a few months later, early in 1913, a complete edition of the master's verse had been published by the Éditions de la *Nouvelle Revue Française*. One might reasonably suppose that it was this concatenation of events that prompted Debussy to set some of Mallarmé's poetry to music, something he had done only once before, in the early song "Apparition" of 1884.[12] Or had he somehow heard on the Paris grapevine of a similar project of Ravel's and decided to compete, or even pre-empt? In March 1913 Ravel had visited Stravinsky in Clarens to work on their joint contribution to Musorgsky's unfinished opera *Khovanshchina*, which Diaghilev was presenting in his

Paris season that year. Stravinsky had shown Ravel his recently completed *Three Japanese Lyrics*, with their faint echoes of Schoenberg's *Pierrot Lunaire*, which Stravinsky had heard in Berlin in December, and Ravel seems to have decided there and then to compose a cycle of three Mallarmé songs accompanied by the same little band as Stravinsky's (two flutes, two clarinets, string quartet and piano), with a view to a Paris concert that would include the two works and the Schoenberg and would "stir up a row." The curious aspect of this coincidence—if coincidence it were—is that, out of the large repertoire of possibilities, Debussy chose to set two of the same poems as Ravel, "Soupir" and "Placet futile," even though neither poem contains anything particularly suggestive of music, apart from a metaphorical shepherd's flute in the penultimate line of "Placet futile."

Debussy completed his set of three songs with piano, ending with "Autre éventail de Mademoiselle Mallarmé," in July, and handed them over to Durand, who at once pointed out that the poems were in copyright and he would have to get permission for the songs' publication from the poet's son-in-law, Edmond Bonniot. Bonniot, however, had already granted this permission to Ravel, and refused Debussy. "This business of the Mallarmé family and Ravel is not very amusing," Debussy grumbled to Durand, "and anyway isn't it strange that Ravel chose exactly the same poems as I did? It's a case of autosuggestion worth communicating to the Academy of Medicine."[13] But in the end it was thanks to Ravel's intervention (or so he claimed) that Bonniot finally agreed to the publication of both sets.

The two composers' settings have in fact relatively little in common, even allowing for the very different accompaniment. At times the differences are even stark. Both cycles begin with "Soupir" ("A Sigh"), but while Ravel imagines this as a generalised autumnal rustle of string harmonics, Debussy leaves the first and third lines of the poem completely unaccompanied and introduces any kind of external imagery only for the "blanc jet d'eau," the white fountain of water, in line 5. In "Placet futile" ("Futile Petition") the textures are less distinct, but almost every decision about prosody and metre differs, and sometimes there are such opposite choices that one almost suspects collusion. For instance, the first word of "Placet futile," the invocatory "Princesse," is set each time by Ravel as a rising minor sixth, by Debussy as a falling minor (later major) sixth; the futile petition itself, "Nommez nous" ("Name us"), three times reiterated, is set by Ravel always as a falling figure, by Debussy always rising. For Ravel, the poet's insistence that he is neither her "bearded lapdog, nor her sweetmeat, nor her rouge, nor her fragile plaything" is a word in her ear, soft and insinuating; for Debussy it is a moment of irritation, a wave of the arm, a gesture of impatience.

These poems of Mallarmé are unlike anything Debussy had ever set before. In Baudelaire and Verlaine the metaphors might be elaborate and fanciful, but the sense was nearly always clear. Maeterlinck, for all his characters' curious habitat and often odd behaviour, seldom strayed beyond the syntax and vocabulary of the suburban drawing room. If Villon and Charles d'Orléans were occasionally more opaque, theirs was merely the opacity of the antique. Mallarmé, however, in his exploration of the interface between sense and sound, will often enter a poetic world in which surface meaning is provisional, a network of double entendres, intimations, verbal patterns and grammatical ambiguities that challenge the reader, and *a fortiori* the composer, to extract (or impose) a single thread of interpretation, or simply to report with absolute certainty exactly what is being said. Many of his successors in these respects wrote in English: Eliot, Joyce, Gertrude Stein and others. But their writing is generally more allusive, more acquisitive, less pure—as Mallarmé would probably have said—than his, and hence, up to a point, easier to understand.

The three Mallarmé poems set by Debussy are modest examples of the genre: lyrics, one might say, viewed in a Symbolist prism, and Debussy responds to them accordingly. He sets them, that is, as scattered lyrics, but not in any particular sense as avant-garde poetry calling for a linguistic upheaval. More than usual with him, "Soupir" is a montage of keyboard gestures, more or less prompted by the text line by line, while the voice rides the words in a flexible, expressive, lyrical style, as if it were the most normal thing in the world to follow the subject ("My soul") with a network of indirect object clauses, and make the verb ("Rises") wait three whole lines before clinching the sense of the image. But Debussy is not so naive as that description might suggest. The silences in the piano part are indeed waiting for the verb, which—when it comes—sets off the fountain as if it had thrown a switch. Now the music knows what the soul is doing, it can help it, with a "jet d'eau" figure that "sighs towards the Azure" in octaves like the ones in the Baudelaire song of that name.

Mallarmé's "Placet futile" is more lucid in its syntax if not always in its expression. The poem is a pastiche of an eighteenth-century sonnet, and its images are neoclassical: Hebe (the cup-bearer of the gods), Sèvres vases, the bearded lapdog already mentioned, the shepherd of the princess's smiles that the poet hopes to become, and Debussy matches all this with a gentle, subtly witty pastiche of his own, modal, faintly rustic, coloured by simple chord parallels, formally transparent like the poem itself. Finally, the most ambiguous and harmonically refined of the three songs, "Éventail" ("A Fan"), is a setting of one of a pair of poems supposedly inspired by fans belonging to Mallarmé's daughter, Geneviève; the poem's title is "Autre éventail (de Mademoiselle Mallarmé)." I say "supposedly" because the imagery is by no means devoid of erotic nuance: the space that "quivers like a big kiss," the "fierce paradise" that "flows from the corner of your mouth," etc. Admittedly it is the fan speaking, not the father, but in any case Debussy responds to these strong thoughts with harmony that at times verges on the atonal, while on the other hand much else in the song is a linear montage of figures responding, presumably, to the capricious flickings and wavings of the fan itself, "au pur délice, sans chemin" ("purely by whim, without a goal").

Apart from a single *pièce d'occasion*, these songs are the last Debussy composed, and they stand somewhat apart from his most recent works for voice, the settings of Villon and Tristan l'Hermite, and the pseudo-medievalisms of D'Annunzio. Compared with his last setting of modern French verse, "Colloque sentimental" in the second book of *Fêtes galantes* (1904), they might even seem trivial, though they make up in refinement for what they lack in weight. Above all, they are almost Debussy's most modern-sounding music. They could not be more remote in style from the recent Stravinsky that he knew, but they surely reflect his general experience of the up-to-date in *Petrushka* and *The Rite of Spring*, rather than Schoenberg, whom he knew only by repute. When, a year or two later, he suggested to Godet that Stravinsky was "leaning dangerously in the Schoenberg direction," he was probably thinking of the *Japanese Lyrics* and *The King of the Stars* (which was dedicated to him). But by his own confession, he had never heard any Schoenberg, had tried to read one of his string quartets in score, but had not managed it. It was merely a certain consciousness of the way things were going that prompted the thought, and that was beginning, to an extent, to invade his own music.[14]

Meanwhile, with *Jeux* over and done with (literally so in the case of Nijinsky's production, which was never revived), Debussy was soon involved with other theatre projects. The Laloy version of *Crimen amoris*, now known as *Fêtes galantes*, was still theoretically on the table, though somewhere towards the back of it, where in fact it stayed, apart from a page or two of sketches, until firmly abandoned in favour of *The Fall of the House of Usher* in 1915. Mourey's *Tristan* project had long since fallen by the wayside, but he had remained a fertile source of other suggestions, one of which, a stage version of the myth of Psyche, was still in the air in 1913. Mourey had wanted Debussy to compose incidental music as long ago as 1909, but he had resisted. "Imagine what genius would be needed," he said to Mourey, "to rejuvenate this old myth, already so exploited that it seems to me that Cupid's wing feathers have all been pulled out by it."[15] He did nevertheless agree to compose a piece for solo flute called *La Flûte de Pan*, to be played in the wings as the god Pan lies dying on the stage. The task proved harder than he might have expected. Having obviously supposed that writing a short single-line piece would be the work of a day or so, he had to admit to Mourey towards the end of November that "I haven't yet finished, and to tell the truth it's simply a matter of finishing what, as everyone knows, is the very devil."[16] He did get it done, though, and the piece was duly included, as intended, in a performance of Mourey's play at the house of the car manufacturer Louis Mors in December 1913.

Syrinx, as the piece was renamed when published in 1927 (presumably to avoid confusion with the first of the *Chansons de Bilitis*), is an immaculate realisation of Debussy's ideas about arabesque. The decorative line remains melodic throughout, avoiding bravura and implied counterpoint almost entirely. Nor does it make much use of the flute's upper register. Like the flute solo in the *Prélude à l'après-midi d'un faune*, it leans constantly towards the instrument's lower octave, with its husky, erotic colouring and, like that work, it makes suggestive play with chromatic lines in which flats (or sharps) and naturals alternate: for instance at the start, B flat followed by A natural, B natural, then A flat, a kind of sinuous curve that breathes sensuality. In its context, and as the only music heard all evening, *Syrinx* must have created an atmosphere out of all proportion to its scale. Its subsequent history as an exam piece and the subject of analytical papers (not to mention as blueprint for a seemingly endless succession of solo flute pieces at festivals of modern music) is one of the less amiable consequences of Debussy's adoption as a hero of the post-war French musical avant-garde.

Much of Debussy's time since *Jeux* had in fact been taken up with a theatre piece of a very different kind, a "ballet for children" called *La Boîte à joujoux* ("The Toybox"), based on a children's illustrated book of that name by André Hellé. Hellé had contacted the composer with the ballet idea back in February, and Debussy, with little Chouchou constantly in his mind and under his gaze, had immediately pricked up his ears. After signing a contract with Durand in July, he entered into the work's spirit more wholeheartedly than he had ever done before with a proposal from outside. He told his publisher that he was "snatching secrets from Chouchou's old dolls, and learning to play the drum, with *La Boîte à joujoux* in mind," and he wrote to Hellé enthusing about his designs ("Do I have to send them back? Despite my regret at doing so!"[17]). By 7 August he had almost finished the first tableau, or so he told Hellé, and on the 11th he wrote to Durand that he was "constantly in *La Boîte à joujoux*." "I've tried," he assured Durand a little later, "to be clear and even 'amusing', without pose, and without needless acrobatics."[18] By the end of October the piano score was complete, and all that remained, apart from the orchestration, was to decide who would perform it: whether it would be puppets, as Debussy initially preferred, or children, as Hellé wanted, or common-or-garden ballet dancers, as eventually happened when the work had its belated premiere, almost two years after Debussy's death, at the Théâtre Lyrique du Vaudeville in Paris.

Anyone who has seen Hellé's colourful and witty illustrations, especially of animals and various toy characters and objects— soldiers, dolls, ships, windmills, etc.—will have some feeling of what Debussy was aiming at when he complained to Hellé that "my music doesn't have the charming simplicity of outline that your drawings have."[19] To an interviewer he called the simplicity "enfantine," which means "childish" but without the English term's pejorative undertones. And he gave a sketch of the plot that catches the mood.

A cardboard soldier falls in love with a doll; he tries to reveal it to her; but the pretty girl deceives him with a polichinelle. The soldier finds out and horrible things result: a fight between wooden soldiers and polichinelles. To cut a long story short, the pretty doll's admirer is badly wounded in the battle. The doll looks after him and . . . it all ends happily.[20]

Originally there were three tableaux: "The Toyshop," "The Battlefield," "Sheep Farm for Sale" (some editions divide the third tableau, making a fourth: "Happy Ever After—Epilogue"). In the first we meet various toys, including an elephant who dances to what Debussy calls "an old Hindu chant that to this day serves to tame elephants. It is built on the scale of 'five o'clock in the morning', so has to be in five-four time";[21] also an English soldier, who marches about to the tune of Debussy's piano piece, "The Little Nigar." The pretty doll dances a waltz (somewhat in the genre of the ballerina's waltzes in *Petrushka*), drops a flower at the cardboard soldier's feet, but then goes off with the polichinelle. At the start of Tableau II the doll and the polichinelle are canoodling, but soon a platoon of toy soldiers marches in to the Soldiers' Chorus from Gounod's *Faust*, followed by a band of polichinelles, and there is a battle, at the end of which the soldier, still with the flower, lies wounded, and is tended to by the pretty doll. Tableau III is introduced by a fragment of the nursery rhyme, "Il était une bergère," and the curtain rises on a dilapidated sheep farm with a for-sale board; the soldier has his arm in a sling, the pretty doll buys two sheep off a passing shepherd and two geese off a goose-girl, and suddenly, to the strains of Mendelssohn's Wedding March, the scene changes and we are twenty years on, soldier and doll have been fruitful, have multiplied, grown fat, and bought a comfortable chalet, and the polichinelle is the local policeman. But alas all games come to an end, and in the Epilogue the toys are all back in their box and, as the curtain falls, the cardboard soldier pokes his head out and salutes.

In *Jeux* the action, though apparently trivial, was integrated, and invited a continuous, non-episodic kind of music. *La Boîte à joujoux* is obviously a very different affair: an anecdotal story ballet in the tradition of *Giselle* or *Coppelia*, written for children (to enjoy, if not perform), but to some degree tongue in cheek, scattered with more or less ironic quotations that would fly well over most children's heads. There are admittedly also folk songs, nursery rhymes, a fragment of our old friend "Dodo, l'enfant do" and a handful of leitmotifs—a fanfare for the soldier, a graceful waltz theme for the doll, a menacing, discordant theme for the polichinelle—that children will recognise instantly. Here and there are faint reminders of *Petrushka*, not only in the three central characters (compare Petrushka, the Ballerina and the Moor), but in the type, if not the style, of music Debussy attaches to them. Yet, as a whole, the music is as French as Hellé's drawings, colourful, witty and stylish, concise, never exaggerated, absurd but never vulgar. It hardly adds up to one of Debussy's greatest works, but it certainly deserves more performance than it gets, and the only sad thing about it is that, as with *Le Martyre de Saint Sébastien* and *Khamma*, he orchestrated only part of it himself—an extremely small part in this case—and the rest was scored, very skilfully, after his death by the long-suffering Caplet.

One other theatre project reared its head towards the end of 1913 but soon sank under the weight of outside events. This was a ballet called *Le Palais du silence*, which was commissioned by the director of the Alhambra Theatre in London, André Charlot, as part of one of those curious mixed Edwardian revues that combined popular music-hall turns with more serious semi-classical items. This particular revue was aptly titled *Not Likely!*

The Palace of Silence is in Formosa, where Prince Hong-Lo, dumb from birth, has imposed silence on his entire realm, the penalty for speaking being death. Unfortunately for him (and her), he has fallen in love with a captive princess turned slave-girl, No-Ja-Li, who, not surprisingly, is less than entirely happy at the restriction on speech, while Hong-Lo is inhibited by his affliction from declaring himself. Somehow this impasse is resolved and the scenario, by Georges de Feure, ends happily. But Debussy never managed to compose more than a few brief stretches of the supposedly twenty-minute score. In November he merrily signed a contract that gave him a desperately needed 10,000 francs on signature and promised a further 10,000 on delivery and 5,000 on first performance. But in December he was travelling to Russia on a two-week conducting tour; there were other conducting trips, to Rome and Amsterdam, in February, and though he seems to have worked on the score a certain amount during January, by April (with the performance scheduled for early May) it had become apparent that the deadline could not be met. Instead he gave Charlot his early *Printemps*, one of his Rome *envois*, orchestrated by Henri Busser. And when Charlot returned to the idea of what was now called *No-Ja-Li* in October 1914, Debussy declined to have anything to do with it, "until the fate of France is decided, since she can neither laugh nor cry while so many of our men are heroically getting themselves smashed up."[22]

Robert Orledge is no doubt right that the oriental setting, complete with masks and gamelan orchestra, was in theory right up Debussy's street. But in practice it looks as if he may have struggled to escape from the conventional musical ping-pong of parallel fourths and pentatonic melodies, in the manner of *Pagodes*. In any case this kind of orientalism was less *à la mode* in 1913 than it had been in the 1880s when, again according to Orledge, the scenario was probably written, or even in 1903, when *Pagodes* was. As usual with Debussy's aborted theatre projects, one senses a lack of real engagement, an initial willingness exposed by his infallible artistic instinct.[23]

Russia was by far the most distant land that he ever visited, and on this, his third trip, he went under something of a cloud created by his own equivocations. He had been invited separately by the conductors Alexander Ziloti and Serge Koussevitzky, each of whom had his own orchestra; he had agreed to appear for Ziloti, but then for some reason stood him up in favour of Koussevitzky. Ziloti himself was in no doubt as to Debussy's motive. "Since he 'sells himself' like a street girl on the Nevsky Prospect," he grumbled to Stravinsky (of all people), "and has gone where they gave him the most money, forgetting that I have played all his new things, and Koussevitzky none of them, then there's nothing more to be said."[24] To Debussy himself he had been not much less direct.

> I must admit that your decision has dealt a huge blow to my morale and it's one of the biggest disillusions of my artistic life. First you promised to come to me, then you refused for lack of time to make

such a long voyage, then you made the same promise to Koussevitzky, then, knowing this would upset me, you refused to come at all so as not to "offend" either of us, and then you have definitely accepted Koussevitzky, while proposing to come to me afterwards (!!!). So, you have decided, after first giving me your word, to hand the great honour of your visit to Koussevitzky, and leave the "offence" to me. It's not good when any particular person doesn't keep his word, but when it's done by a musician like you, it's "lèse-genius": you've forgotten that if *noblesse oblige*, all the more does *génie oblige*.[25]

It was true that it was mainly because of the money that Debussy went to Russia at all, and perhaps if Ziloti had had sight of his bank statements or his begging letters he might have been slightly less censorious about his motives. But it was also true that Debussy could be as pragmatic in his professional dealings as he had sometimes been with the women in his life. On the other hand, his treatment of working musicians seems to have been exemplary, and the concerts were an unmitigated triumph with both orchestra and audiences. He conducted two enormous (identical) programmes of his own music, one in St. Petersburg on 10 December, one in Moscow on the 13th, and after the Moscow concert the players wrote him a moving, plainly sincere (not "official") thank you:

> Illustrious Maître, we have long been impatiently awaiting the moment when you would come and conduct your works, we have long anticipated the joy we would experience exploring with you the captivating charm of everything you have created, and our expectations have not been disappointed . . . We have lived with you through days that will never leave our memory, and that will remain with us as a festival, as a radiation of light that will forever illuminate our musical careers.[26]

Somewhat less appreciative of his Russian trip was his wife, Emma, who—to judge by his replies—wrote to him in a bitterly resentful tone, accusing him of neglecting her in favour of his music, of not loving her, of deserting her, etc., etc. It is not clear that she ever enquired about Russia or the Russians, nor did he vouchsafe much of that kind of information. "Your letter," he wrote from St. Petersburg after his concert there, "gave me so much misery that I've waited till now to reply."

> What mean, unjust words . . . How can you think such things? And must it be that suffering makes you so far forget the love of your poor Claude? I know very well that, in this sad episode, you can't find anything that even remotely resembles a consolation! All the same, you know perfectly well why I've made this trip. Once again, I beseech you not to twist reality in an angry way, perfectly justified it's true, but whose effect goes far beyond what you suppose.[27]

She had written (we know, because he quotes it back at her): "I don't know how I will manage not to go on resenting your music," to which he replied:

> First, as between you and music, if there's anyone who could be jealous, it's music! And if I continue to make it and love it, it's because I'm indebted to it—this music that you treat so badly—for having got to know you, love you, and so forth![28]

The "so forth" wrote more sweetly, and Debussy replied in kind. "It's very sad to be deprived for so many days of seeing your pretty little Chouchou face, of hearing your songs, your outbursts of laughter, and lastly all that noise that sometimes makes you an unbearable little person, but most often a charming one." And he added, "Be nice to your poor little Maman; do everything you can to stop her getting too upset."[29]

For various reasons 1914 would be a frustratingly unproductive year for Debussy. Early on there were the abortive theatre projects, *Fêtes galantes*—still theoretically alive though soon abandoned—and *No-Ja-Li*, which he effectively gave up in April, supposedly telling Charles Koechlin, "You compose it and I'll sign it." There were concerts: in Rome and Amsterdam, Brussels, London, and of course Paris. His health was poor, and he was in low spirits. His mother, too, was ill, apparently dying. To Godet, in July, he mentioned an accident, which had had "the most tiresome consequences: flu; shingles, which attacks the nerves frightfully; in the end, for four and a half months I've done precisely nothing! Naturally these things cause miserable domestic worries and times when one can hardly see any way out but suicide."

> For a long time—it has to be admitted—I've felt lost, and terribly diminished! Ah! the "magician" you loved in me, where is he? All he is now is a builder of gloomy towers, who will soon break his back in a final pirouette devoid of beauty.[30]

Then, early in August, there came the ultimate depressant for the world at large.

For Debussy, the outbreak of war merely aggravated a mood that had been bearing down on him for several months. "You know I lack sang-froid," he told Durand, "still less the military spirit—having never had occasion to handle a gun; add to that my memories of 1870, which prevent me from giving way to enthusiasm." He felt small and useless. He envied Satie, he said, who was "seriously involved, as a corporal, in the defence of Paris." "My age and military aptitudes make me at most good for guarding a palisade."[31] Then there was Emma, beside herself with terror since both her son, Raoul, and her daughter Dolly's husband were in the army and off to the front. Her fears were, after all, perfectly justified. In the first month of fighting the Germans advanced far into France and more than a hundred thousand French soldiers died. At the start of September, with the German army at Senlis, a mere twenty-five miles north of Paris, the French government abandoned the capital and installed itself at Bordeaux. Not surprisingly, many Parisians also left, and the Debussys, too, packed their bags and took the train to Angers, far to the west on the River Loire.

Debussy himself had not wanted to go; the journey, he informed Durand, had been expensive and disagreeable, and although barely two months earlier he had told his publisher that he was hating Paris more and more, the truth was that he preferred it to anywhere else. In Angers the decent hotels were completely full, and they had to put up in what he called "a sort of inn for cattle merchants, distinguished by its absolute disdain for any kind of comfort and by its not very nice bugs."[32] By the beginning of October they were back in Paris, and the Germans, having destroyed Leuven and its historic university library, had been held back at the Marne. The ruthlessness of their advance and the barbarous behaviour of their troops had created general horror, but for musicians it had an additional nuance, in view of the nature of their repertoire. "I think we'll pay dearly," Debussy wrote to his former pupil Nicolas Coronio, "for the right not to love the art of Richard Strauss and Schoenberg."

> As regards Beethoven, it's just been happily discovered that he was Flemish! As for Wagner, there will be exaggeration! He will retain the glory of having gathered centuries of music into a formula. That's quite something, and only a German could have attempted it. Our mistake was to try for too long to follow in his footsteps . . . In other respects, our generation will hardly be able to change its tastes, any more than its forms! What may be curious and contain a few surprises is what the generation that has made the war—in a word, the generation that has "marched—will do and think." French art has a score to settle, just as serious as the other! It has had its Rheims Cathedral for longer . . .[33]

Despite all these woes, personal and public, he managed to work on one significant piece over the terrible summer months. It was not a completely new work, but a series of extensions of half a dozen of the short pieces he had composed in 1900 for the *tableaux vivants* staging of Louÿs's *Bilitis* poems. He had planned to compose the pieces up into an orchestral suite under the title *Six Épigraphes antiques*, but, as he remarked sadly to Durant, "the times are hard, and life for me is harder still," and he never got beyond the version for piano duet that has come down to us.[34]

Each epigraph takes one of the twelve movements of the *musique de scène* and, on a reading of the relevant poem, extends it from the (on average) forty-five or fifty seconds of the original to a two- or three-minute keyboard piece. I am merely speculating that Debussy read each poem before composing the music. Neither he nor practically anyone else has ever said so, and the pieces are certainly not programme music.[35] But it would have been odd of him not to, and there is some internal evidence. For instance, the first epigraph, "Pour invoquer Pan," based on the piece that accompanied Louÿs's "Chant pastoral," seems to respond to the poem's form, with its final repeat of the opening line, and its swifter music for Selenis running in search of grasshoppers and its winding music for Bilitis spinning. In No. 4, "Pour la danseuse aux crotales," the piano (*primo*) sounds the "crotales" (antique, small cymbals) as a sudden gesture, exactly as in the poem. On the other hand, the final epigraph, "Pour remercier la pluie du matin," keeps the image of the morning rain almost throughout, though the poem abandons it after two verses, and the return, at the end, of the music of the first epigraph is a device from the *musique de scène*, not from the poem.

Musically, the epigraphs build on the slightly wan charm of the original pieces in the harmonically enriched context of Debussy's later music. But they are not all enriched. "Pour invoquer Pan" is entirely diatonic in the Dorian mode (that is, no sharps or flats except in the key signature), a model of cool antiquity; however, the second piece, "Pour un tombeau sans nom," stays with the pure whole-tone colouring of the original only for as long as it quotes it, but then switches dramatically into more dissonant music for (perhaps) Bilitis's shiver of horror when Mnasidika shows her "the tomb of my mother's lover." No. 3, "Pour que la nuit soit propice," also derives from whole-tone material in the original, but then moves on through a range of contrasting ideas that seem to reflect Bilitis's journey (in Louÿs's poem "Chant"), down into the plain, beside the river, along the white road to the city of Sardis and its great palace ("night" is not mentioned). The crotale dancer then leads to the fifth piece, "Pour l'Égyptienne," the most remote of the six from its supposed source, and tonally the most remote as well, in E flat minor, with chromatic swirls and suitably exotic scales for the Egyptian courtesans, who sit motionless, their hands on their knees, speak bad Greek but do not understand the Lydian tongue of Bilitis and her friends.

Composing these pieces for piano, Debussy is often converting harp and celesta music, and one can hear the twang and tinkle of those instruments and the swirl of the flutes in his delicate writing for piano. One could almost wish, though, that he had composed the *Épigraphes antiques* for the original Bilitis ensemble, and perhaps it was some intimation of that possibility that led him a year or so later to write his Sonata for flute, viola and harp, which has an antique flavour of its own. One thing that can safely be said about these duet pieces is that they are not war music; anti-war perhaps, but really music that inhabits a world where war is not so much as spoken of or even thought. The naked-by-preference Bilitis in uniform is an image as ludicrous as *Parsifal* on ice. But Debussy had his own way with oxymoron, and the one other piece he composed in 1914 was a short march for piano with the improbable title *Berceuse héroïque* (Heroic Lullaby), commissioned by the London *Daily Telegraph* for a volume called *King Albert's Book*, in honour of the king of Belgium, the first country to be invaded by the Germans in August 1914. Debussy based his piece on the Belgian national anthem, "La Brabançonne," quoting it literally at one point, and borrowing its solemn, somewhat plodding tempo for his own march in (yet again) E flat minor. But he wrote without enthusiasm, finding the task (he told Godet) "very hard, all the more because 'La Brabançonne' pours no heroism into the hearts of those not brought up with it."[36]

His own heart, he knew, was short on heroism of the virile kind, and in any case at fifty-two he was too old to fight. There was a sort of heroic virtue in the way he composed his music, meticulously and without compromise. But even that seemed now to be failing him. To Godet he confessed to "having gone for months no longer knowing what music was . . ."

> Pythagoras doing his mathematics up to the moment when a soldier did him in; Goethe writing his *Elective Affinities* during the French occupation of Weimar—these are admirable minds. I can only note my inferiority—and do my own mathematics.[37]

In his case, "mathematics" meant editing Chopin's piano music as part of a new edition of classical works that Durand had set in train in October 1914 as a Gallic counterblast to the heavily footnoted German editions, which were in any case unobtainable on account of the war. Curiously enough, he seems to have undertaken this work willingly and in a truly critical spirit. Years before, he had praised Chopin's "elegance, his facility at 'finding' at each step marvellous flowers, with an air of saying: 'This is of no importance, and if you like we'll pass on to something else.'"[38] Now he notes the problem of deciding between the variant autograph manuscripts of certain works of Chopin, and prefers to adhere to proof copies corrected in the composer's own hand. More to the point, perhaps, will have been the impact on his own piano music of this prolonged contact with music that he regarded as "among the most beautiful that has ever been written." Among the works he was editing were the two books of studies, Op. 10 and Op. 25, and almost as soon as he had finished editing the Chopin he was embarking on a set of twelve studies—*études*—of his own. It seems obvious that his twelve were prompted, if not directly inspired, by Chopin's twenty-four, even though it turns out he had sketched music that went into the ninth *étude*, *Pour les notes répétées*, as well as an abandoned version of *Pour les arpèges composés* on the train to Angers back in September. The sketches are fragmentary and not yet expressly for *études*.[39]

He and Emma were both constantly ill. In February he had flu, was coughing "enough to break the heart of old oak trees," and felt, he told Durand, "like a little village after a visit by the Boches."[40] Victorine, his mother, was in the final stages of her long illness and died on 23 March, at the age of seventy-eight. Chouchou had had chickenpox, but by June was a picture of good health, like a peony, her father said. This year she got her way about the seaside—or was it the sea that got its way with the Debussys? In any case, off they went to Pourville on 12 July and, avoiding the hotels and their horrid patrons, stayed in a quiet villa with a garden lent them by friends and appropriately named *Mon Coin* ("My Retreat"). Pourville, Debussy told his conductor friend Désiré-Émile Inghelbrecht, "hasn't changed. The sea is still in the same place, the calm is extraordinary . . . The people are confident in their ugliness: thieves for sure, but the home-baked bread is excellent."[41] But a few days later the sea "is agitated, wants to encroach on the land and bite the rocks, and has tantrums like a little girl, odd for a person of such importance."[42]

The admirable thing is the garden . . . it's unkempt and hasn't that proud orderedness of gardens designed by Le Nôtre, but its wildness is well behaved, very nice for those who have no ambition to play at Robinson Crusoe. When you get to the top, you discover a fine extent of sea, enough for you to imagine more—I mean, the infinite sea![43]

They hardly dared open a newspaper. "I think of that youth of France, stupidly mown down by the merchants of culture—culture of which we have lost forever the glory it ought to bring to our patrimony."

> And now they're talking of an intervention by the Japanese. Why not by the Martians, while they're about it? All this can only increase the self-importance of the Boches, who—God knows—don't need it. And what a terrible reckoning-up afterwards! Why so many guests to eat a cake that isn't yet cooked?[44]

To Pourville he brought with him his first completely new work of any substance since *La Boîte à joujoux*, a two-piano suite called *Caprices en blanc et noir*, a title apparently inspired by the appearance of the keyboard itself, and by extension the restricted tone colours of the piano. Before leaving Paris he had signed a contract with Durand which included movement titles: "Qui reste à sa place" (from Capulet's call to the dance in Gounod's *Roméo et Juliette*), "Prince porté des serfs Eolus" (from Villon's "Ballade contre les ennemis de la France"),[45] and "Yver, vous n'estes qu'un villain" (the first line of a poem by Charles d'Orléans that Debussy had set as a chorus in 1898). In the end the titles were abandoned, then reappeared as part of longer epigraphs at the head of each movement. But the music itself was suddenly flowing, and within less than a fortnight of his arriving at *Mon Coin*, the suite, now called simply *En blanc et noir*, was finished—fifteen minutes of music composed in barely a month.

Out of the blue, it announces a new phase in Debussy's work. Not only is it his first multi-movement piano work since *Pour le piano*, but the individual movements are structured in a way that refer back, not to the *image* idea that has dominated his music since at least the turn of the century, but beyond, to the classical sonata tradition of evolving and contrasting themes presented as a balanced discourse. Debussy told Godet not to worry his head over hidden meanings in *En blanc et noir*. "These pieces," he said, "aim to derive their colour, their emotion, purely from the piano—along the lines of the 'greys' of Velázquez."[46] The exuberant first movement is, most strikingly, a rhythmic study, but with varied themes and textures worked into a kind of trace sonata form, a point one would not bother to make if it were not indicative of a specific change in Debussy's attitude to his material. Exactly as in a conventional sonata movement, one is aware of a process of contrast and resolution. The piece is in triple time throughout, but this is disguised at first by the way the arpeggios force their way across the barlines into what amounts to quadruple time, then into a slow three (across two bars—so-called hemiola), so that when the metric fog finally clears and we realise the piece is a quick waltz, we at the same time register a change in the formal texture—a new moment. Debussy then proceeds to play with this metric conflict with superb energy and control. Not a trace here of the "builder of gloomy towers" of a year ago. This is a music of pure release, bright morning after dark night.

In the second movement, however, night returns, and so, to some extent, do ideas beyond the pure black and white of the keyboard. We may choose to read the epigraph to the first movement ("He who stays put, and does not dance . . .") as a slight on those who, like Debussy himself, were taking no part in the war; there is no support for this in the music. But the epigraph to the slow movement, as well as its dedication to Durand's nephew Jacques Charlot, who had died in March leading his men into battle, relates directly to the music's content. The piece is openly an image of war: it has threatening military noises, fanfares, sinister marches (the enemy), a joyous march (our chaps); it has fragments of the "Marseillaise" and of other similar tunes that might or might not be patriotic songs, and most famously and prominently of all it has the Lutheran chorale "Ein feste Burg ist unser Herr" ("A Stronghold Sure is our God"), treated—somewhat ambivalently—as an image of German culture on the march. Debussy had trouble with this movement, mainly over the issue of how much of the chorale to include. "It was getting too black," he told Durand, "and almost as tragic as a Goya *Capricho*." He altered this aspect two or three times, but eventually declared himself happy with the piece. "It is," he said, "perhaps the most original [*trouvé*]."[47]

The finale reverts to the coruscating abstraction of the first movement, with little obvious reference to its Charles d'Orléans superscription, except perhaps to the wit of the whole poem, which accuses winter of being nothing but snow, wind, rain and ice, and wants it sent into exile (perhaps to England, where the poem's author spent twenty-four years as a prisoner of war). Here the writing for two pianos is of exceptional verve and brilliance, with great variety of texture, but also some lovely melody that at times, oddly, recalls Fauré. Although the harmony, in all three movements of *En blanc et noir*, hardly goes beyond what Debussy had already established as his personal vocabulary (even the bitonal treatment of the fanfares and chorale in the second movement has a precedent in *La Boîte à joujoux*), there is a freedom of utterance here that proclaims the mastery of the mature genius, who, even as his body is giving out, can still hit mental targets that, in Schopenhauer's wonderful image, others can't even see.

13

Indian Summer, Stygian Winter

A t Pourville, while Debussy was still struggling with the middle movement of *En blanc et noir*, he already had two other substantial projects on the boil. The first of them he announced to Durand in what he called a prospectus enclosed with a letter of 22 July, ten days after their arrival at *Mon Coin*. It was a cycle of "Six *Sonatas* for various instruments composed by Claude Debussy, *musicien français*; the first one: cello and piano." The other was a set of *Études* for solo piano begun, it seems, the day after the announcement about the sonatas. Bearing in mind Claude de France's track record on the non-fulfilment of ambitious projects, and especially in view of his recent illness and depression, Jacques Durand could have been forgiven for taking all these proposals with a huge grain of salt. He may indeed have done so. But for once there would be no backsliding, no shuffling pretence that works not yet actually begun were nearing completion. Debussy had suddenly found his stride, and within three months not only the Cello Sonata and a dozen *Études* were in the publisher's hands, but also a second sonata, for the beautiful and unusual combination of flute, viola and harp. There might even have been more, such was the explosion of creative energy, had his rectal cancer not broken out with comparable force in November and been at last diagnosed. On the 26th it laid him "lower than the earth," since when—he told Gabriel Fauré—"I've suffered like a dog."[1] Eleven days later, in terrible pain, he was operated on for the first time; and thereafter it was clear, though nobody told him, that his condition was incurable and his time almost up.

None of this is so much as intimated in any of the Pourville works. The Cello Sonata, apparently composed in two or three weeks at the end of July and the start of August, is cool and laconic and above all compact, barely twelve minutes of succinct dialogue. A few months before, Debussy had agreed, in addition to his work on Chopin, to edit a series of works by Bach, including the six violin sonatas with harpsichord (BWV 1014–19), the flute sonatas (1030–35), and the trio sonatas (1037–39). By July he had done nothing on this, as he confessed to Durand, as he had ideas of his own that he wanted to pursue, and it seems plausible to suggest that his own plan for six chamber sonatas may have been prompted by the thought of the Bach sets, without too much consideration of their actual music. The Cello Sonata has, certainly, a baroque lightness of touch but little trace of baroque style or technique. He himself described it as "almost classical, in the good sense of the term": that is, presumably, lucid, economical and well-proportioned. But its actual material is somewhat cartoon-like—brief, self-contained ideas, strongly characterised, then presented in balanced arrangements. The *Prologue*, for instance, has a clear ABA form, but little development as such, while the *Sérénade* second movement, like the *Sérénade interrompue* in the first book of *Préludes*, has a flavour of *commedia dell'arte*, an element of the grotesque in its whimsical pattern of themes and playing techniques, none of which seem to work for very long.[2] The *Finale*, linked to the *Sérénade* without a break, then brings a more decisive continuity to these ideas without questioning their mercurial wit. This is the most classical of the three movements, a rondo with a certain airy lyricism. But as a whole the sonata is a neatly designed patchwork: a "late work" in its preference for the understated and elliptical, and classical more in what it leaves out than in what it includes.

In a sense the *Études* are easier to place, being technical studies in the grand tradition of that particular genre. Debussy's obvious model here, as mentioned in the last chapter, was Chopin, not least in the desire to create works of the imagination out of the mechanical disciplines. "You'll agree," he suggested to Durand, "that there's no need to make technique any gloomier in order to appear more serious, and that a bit of charm has never spoilt anything."[3] In this respect, the *Études* are closer than one might expect to the earlier piano sets, which include several pieces that could easily be reclassified as studies, for instance, *Reflets dans l'eau*, *Mouvement*, *Poissons d'or*, *Les Tierces alternées*, or *Feux d'artifice*. Picturesque titles could readily be added to the *Études*, perhaps deprecatingly at the end, as in the *Préludes*. The fact that Debussy seems not to have considered this recourse is perhaps an indication of that classicising tendency that he himself noted in the Cello Sonata. Casual remarks hint at the way his titling might have gone. *Pour les agréments*, in book 2, "borrows the form of a Barcarolle on a sea that is a bit Italian"; another unidentified *étude* (Paul Roberts suggests "Pour les accords") "breaks in the left hand to an almost Swedish gymnastics";[4] in the case of *Pour les sixtes*, he describes what the sixths emphatically do *not* portray, "the effect of pretentious young ladies sitting in a drawing room, glumly doing tapestry, and envying the scandalous laughter of the mad ninths" (but sadly there is no "Pour les neuvièmes").[5] The irony of this description is that Debussy's sixths do sometimes recall Chopin's third Moscheles study in A flat, which is admittedly very superior tapestry music.

Imagery may be in short supply, but imagination certainly is not. The musical richness and variety that Debussy derives from what effectively start out as limitations is nothing short of astonishing—and not only richness of colour and idea, but richness also of wit. Already in the first study, *Pour les "cinq doigts"—d'après Monsieur Czerny* ("For the 'five fingers'—after Monsieur Czerny"), he concocts a dazzling satire of Czerny's book of *24 Five-Finger Exercises*, Op. 777, in which the great nineteenth-century pedagogue devised a series of ways of terrorising young pianists such as Debussy's own nine-year-old daughter, who had herself been suffering from an inadequate piano teacher in Paris.[6] *Pour les tierces* ("For thirds") superficially recalls *Les Tierces alternées*. But where the prelude was a study in sonority and character, and relatively easy to play (the notes, at any rate), *Pour les tierces* is a challenging technical study in the performance of parallel thirds in both hands, and at the same time a test of ear and touch in the balancing of inner voices without crowding the texture. In fact all six studies in the first book are more or less tests of the pianist's ability to climb technical mountains while engaging with the musical scenery. *Pour les quartes* ("For fourths") is not only exceedingly awkward, not least because successions of this particular interval are not a normal part of the classical repertoire; it is also a stunningly beautiful exploration of the strange, gamelan-like colourings that patterns of fourths can reveal.

Debussy dodges "les quintes" (not, presumably, because the Conservatoire outlawed them) and, after the sixths, proceeds to the octaves in the shape of a grand waltz, which to some extent feeds off, to some extent parodies, the way in which popular pianists of Debussy's day and earlier enhanced every melodic and chordal gesture by doubling it at the octave. Finally, in book 1, *Pour les huit doigts* ("For the eight fingers") seems a conscious advance on the opening five-finger exercises, less varied but more delicate and no longer satirical. The title indicates, as Debussy points out in a footnote, that "in this *étude*, the changing position of the hands makes the use of the thumbs inconvenient." But his pupil Marguerite Long decided otherwise. "Temptation," she wrote, "became too strong for me and, as I found the effect of using the thumbs satisfactory, I hastened to disobey . . . Confronted with the success of this *fait accompli* the composer could only applaud. He thereupon decided to authorise the use of the thumbs."[7] But he didn't change the title.

Aside from the question of technique, the first book of *Études* displays in a very pure form the consequences of Debussy's harmonic revolution. Where specific intervals or melodic shapes are predicated by the exercise in question, the particular shapes take precedence over correct harmony. An extreme case is *Pour les quartes*, which treats as a stable item of vocabulary a chord that in classical harmony is regarded as an unstable dissonance that needs to be resolved.[8] Debussy ignores this rule, as he always has done, and he also combines fourths in ways that generate more complex dissonances, without ever creating the jarring effect of other "advanced" music of his day where fourths are prominent, for instance Mahler's Seventh Symphony or Schoenberg's First Chamber Symphony. He had for years cultivated parallel chords and the effect they have of dissolving the sense of harmonic motion, even when the chords themselves are perfectly consonant, as in *La Cathédrale engloutie*. The *Études* merely turn the procedure into a principle, literally for the purpose of study, but in the process they underline the modernity of Debussy's style, a modernity none the less modern for avoiding the worst horrors of "earless" dissonance, the sort of dissonance that results from other processes without necessarily having been "heard" for its own effect.

The other side of Debussy's modernising, his emphasis on colour and texture, comes to the fore in the second book, without displacing the technical aspect. The seventh *étude*, *Pour les degrés chromatiques* ("For the chromatic steps"), is partly a study in chromatic fingering, but above all an exploration of the *leggierissimo*—the lightest possible—touches and colourings of which the piano is capable when the sustaining pedal is used either very sparingly or not at all. Debussy was well aware, of course, that chromaticism in the new music of his day meant post-Wagnerian harmony, the heavy expressionism of Strauss's *Salome* (which he knew and admired) and perhaps even the atonality of Schoenberg (which he didn't). He must have taken a mischievous delight in concocting a mostly linear chromaticism, feather-light, mercurial and witty, whose only counter-melody is a simple fragment of faintly oriental song, like something overheard on the breeze on the road to Mandalay.

In a similar way, No. 8, *Pour les agréments* ("For the embellishments"), starts with the individual decorative figure, refined, articulate, tonally fluid, ornamenting a counter-melody of an essentially simple cut. But Debussy also recalls that, in the music of Couperin and Rameau, ornamentation was not cosmetic but a means of expression, not only for superficial pleasure (*agrément*) but also for subtler and more inward and even more passionate feeling. So his embellishments gradually expand into music of a certain complexity and range, and a variety of texture perhaps greater than in any of the preceding *études*. No. 9, *Pour les notes répétées*, is the piece first sketched on (and conceivably inspired by) the Angers train. But there is nothing mechanistic about this needlepoint scherzo, and again the variety of colour and texture Debussy derives from this simple—not to say simplistic—keyboard device is utterly astonishing.

The tenth *étude*, *Pour les sonorités opposées* ("For opposed sonorities") stands somewhat apart from the other eleven, being a study not in any normal keyboard technique, but in the more nebulous issue of sound perspective—a crucial matter, admittedly, in all Debussy's mature piano music, but here treated as a specific object of investigation. Instead of the single types that dominate the other studies, the whole point here is the confrontation and layering of different kinds of idea, the weighing up and balancing of contrasted textures. In its form, the piece comes close to the montage of certain of the preludes, an anecdotal sequence of musical images. But there is also a kind of vertical montage between the hands, which cross for significant stretches, and on one occasion double the melody in unison—that is with the two thumbs on the same keys, an apparently pointless device. As for hand crossing, normally there is an obvious reason. A well-known example is in the first movement of Beethoven's "Pathétique" Sonata, where the left hand has a continuous accompaniment while the right hand plays in dialogue with itself below and above. But in *Pour les sonorités opposées* the crossing is technically unnecessary and seems motivated purely by the opposite anatomy of the hands, turning little-finger left-hand melodies into right-hand thumb melodies. In bar 40, for instance, the effect is marked *expressif et pénétrant* and the right hand, with the thumb melody, is marked *piano* against the left hand's *pianissimo*. One would love to have heard Debussy play this *étude*, with its deep registral contrasts, its subtleties of touch, and its "offstage" effects, the distant trumpets and ornithological twitterings. It is music that suggests a new kind of "difficulty": not how to get the fingers round the notes but what to do with them once you've done so.

Pour les arpèges composés, No. 11, is a replacement for another piece Debussy sketched on his laissez-passer on the train to Angers (the original title was "Pour les arpèges mélangés"—for mixed, rather than composed, arpeggios). It starts out as a serious, if extremely graceful (*lusingando*—enticing) arpeggio study, but soon throws off a suave left-hand melody that quickly turns into a sequence of music-hall parodies, almost quotes *Minstrels* and *Général Lavine*, then straightens its face, more or less, and ends as the serious study it was at the start. Finally, the Swedish gymnast flexes his muscles in the spectacular arm exercises of *Pour les accords* ("For chords"). But the piece is also a study in contrasts, with a middle section that expressly denies the brutality of the opening and turns inward to examine chords, not as missiles but as exquisite organisms to be placed under the Debussy microscope, before the gymnast reappears and brings the *études* to a close with a bang.

Debussy completed the second book towards the end of September, and to Durand he confessed himself "happy to have successfully concluded a work that, without false vanity, will occupy a special place. On the technical side, these *Études* will usefully prepare pianists to understand better that they shouldn't go in for music without formidable hands."[9] Yes, but they also prepare pianists for the much harder lesson that formidable hands do not a great musician make. They prove that technique is the first, not the last, requirement of the performing artist, a necessary but by no means sufficient condition for unlocking the secrets of this extraordinary music—a fact that, in the end, perhaps marks the boundary between art and gymnastics.

While still finishing off the *Études*, Debussy had already sketched the second of his six sonatas, a trio originally for flute, oboe and harp, but with a viola substituted at an early stage for the oboe. On the face of it, it would be hard to imagine a sharper contrast than between this agreeable, transparent three-movement work in the Attic pastoral vein of *Syrinx* and the *Épigraphes antiques*, and the ostentatiously brilliant piano *études*. But it may not be insignificant that the last of the *études* to be composed was *Pour les agréments*, where the concentration on ornament and a decorative kind of virtuosity does invite comparison with the airy filigree of the flute and harp writing in the sonata. There are textural and even thematic parallels; the opening gestures are similarly conceived. And after hearing the sonata, it is by no means a huge stretch to imagine at least parts of the *étude* rescored for the trio combination.

One could hardly, though, imagine the sonata as a piano study. Some modest bravura there is, but the mood is unforced, and the form open and somewhat improvisatory. Frequent tempo changes create an easy, almost opportunistic atmosphere, constrained by formal reprises at crucial moments: the sonata-form moments in the first movement *Pastorale*, the rondo moments in the *Interlude*, and the cyclic, back-to-the-first-movement moment near the end of the *Finale*. But it would be faintly absurd to describe this elegant, wistful music in textbook language. Debussy had naturally liked the sonata while writing it and found in it a paradigm of his existence at Pourville. "All present-day life," he explained to Durand, "was far away, harmonious times unfolded, oblivious of the tumult so near, and [the sonata] ended up so beautiful that I almost have to apologise for it."[10] But after hearing it played at Durand's office fifteen months later, with a chromatic harp played by a lady from Munich who "resembled one of those priestess-musicians you see on Egyptian tombs," he expressed himself more ambiguously. "It's not up to me to speak to you about the music," he wrote to Godet. "I could do so without blushing, as it's by a Debussy I no longer know! It's frightfully melancholy, and I don't know if one should laugh at it or cry? Perhaps both?"[11]

The family returned, reluctantly, to Paris on 12 October, at the

end of what must have seemed a miraculous yet strangely millen-
nial summer. Debussy brought back with him, figuratively speaking,
four works, two of them certainly masterpieces, all four suggestive of
new avenues, new creative possibilities. Yet it had been like writing
on the edge of a volcano: like André Chénier, he told Inghelbrecht,
still composing poetry as he mounted the scaffold. At Pourville, he
informed Godet, "I rediscovered the possibility of thinking musically, something I'd no longer been able to do for a year."[12] But there
was to be no continuation of this *annus mirabilis*. Within a month his
cancer had taken hold, and suddenly the whole perspective of his life
narrowed down to the need to survive and the diminishing hope of
recovery.

> I had been ill for a long time: not enough exercise, with the usual
> consequences, but I could live with that without needing to stop. All
> of a sudden it all got worse, and so: surgery; nasty moments, painful
> after-effects, etc. . . . . Ironically, this incident caught me working at
> full tilt. As someone said: that doesn't happen every day. One has to
> take advantage of the good moments to make up for the bad hours. I
> was about to finish—or near enough—*The Fall of the House of Usher*,
> but the illness has blown out my hopes. It's obviously of little impor-
> tance on Aldebaran or Sirius whether I write music or not, but I don't
> like being contradicted and I take this twist of destiny very hard! And
> I'm suffering the pains of hell.[13]

The supposed near-completion of *The Fall of the House of Usher*
was to be his last great self-deception. He had begun to recast the
libretto at Pourville, but probably had composed no new music by
the time he went into hospital. Instead, on the eve of his operation, he
composed two short pieces in aid of the war effort, "my only way," he
said, "of making war."[14] The first of these was a short *Elegy* for piano
solo, composed for a collection called *Pages inédites sur la femme et
la guerre* ("Unpublished pages on women and war"), to be sold for
war relief, and notable mainly as a rare example of almost continuous
left-hand arabesque. With one small, semi-private exception, it was
to be his last completed work for the instrument whose repertoire and
technique he had revolutionised in the previous dozen years.
    The other piece, altogether more remarkable, was a song or chil-

dren's chorus with piano called *Noël des enfants qui n'ont plus de maisons* ("Christmas Carol for Homeless Children"). Debussy's own text began:

> Nous n'avons plus de maisons!
> Les ennemis ont tout pris,
> Jusqu'à notre petit lit!

> [We no longer have homes!
> Our enemies have taken everything,
> even our little beds!]

The words, which continue in the same vein for a further dozen or so lines, might have inspired an outpouring of mawkish sentiment, but Debussy, in pain himself, sounded a very different tone, a tone of anger and desperation at the horrors that were daily reported but that he himself had not had to suffer. The piano accompaniment drives forward as if genuinely in flight from some murderous enemy, and the children chatter away with an urgency enhanced by the rapid note-per-syllable setting. More than anything, the style recalls Yniold's music in *Pelléas et Mélisande*, or even at times Mélisande's, in her moments of terror, as Debussy himself pointed out, for instance after the ring given her by Golaud has fallen into the well.[15]

Debussy made two versions of the *Noël*, one as a solo song, one for two-part children's chorus, both with piano. To judge by recent recordings, it has been more normal to perform it as a solo. But Debussy, having sketched an orchestral version (presumably for concert use with an adult choir), admitted that he had dreamt of children's voices for this music. "Women's voices," he said, "quickly become falsely dramatic. Or else—which is worse—they imitate little girls!"[16] François Lesure tells us that Debussy became irritated at the popular success of this touching piece, and was aware of "son caractère un peu racoleur" ("its slightly tacky character").[17] But he also recognised, not wholly without irony, its uncomplicated power to move. "Victory to the children of France," he quoted to Paul Dukas. "It's as simple as that. But that goes straight to the citizen's heart."[18]

As the war dragged on into its second year, he increasingly saw it exemplified in the condition of music, and even in his own sickness.

These last years [he wrote to Stravinsky soon after returning from Pourville], while I've felt the Austro-Boches miasmas spreading over art, I should have liked to have more authority to cry out my disquiet, to avert the danger towards which we were running so trustingly. How could we fail to guess that these people were attempting the destruction of our art, just as they had prepared the destruction of our countries? And above all, this racial hatred that will only come to an end with the last of the Germans? Will there ever be a last German? For I remain convinced that German soldiers reproduce by themselves!

Art, he thought, should fight back. "You," he told Stravinsky, "are certainly one of those who will be able to counter successfully these other 'gases' [other, that is, than the ones the Germans had begun to use on the battlefield], as lethal as the other sort, against which we had no 'masks'."

Dear Stravinsky, you are a great artist! Be, with all your force, a great Russian artist! It's so fine to be of one's country, to be attached to one's soil like the humblest of peasants! And when the foreigner tramps over it, how bitter is the cant of the internationalists.[19]

Stravinsky would certainly have agreed with him on all these points. At that very moment, October 1915, he had two of his greatest folk-based Russian works, *Renard* and *Svadebka* (*Les Noces*), on his desk. And only the previous year he had expressed himself no less forcibly than Debussy about the Germans. "My hatred of the Germans," he wrote to Bakst, "grows not by the day but by the hour, and I'm all the more burning with envy at the fact that our friends— Ravel, Delage, Schmitt—are all in the war."[20] And he told Romain Rolland that "Germany is not a barbarous country, but decrepit and degenerate." In his case, Germanophobia led to an abstract theory about the post-war renewal of the world through the healthy new seeds of Russian barbarism. But then, the foreigner had not yet tramped over Russian soil.[21]

Meanwhile, poor Debussy, having survived his operation but without much comfort, was undergoing radium treatment, a new and disagreeable process with a high risk of genetic and other undesirable side-effects. The treatment involved sitting on a rubber ring and being given tincture of opium to cause constipation and avert bowel motions, which could result in the loss of the expensive, not to say dangerous, radium. "All this," he wrote to Godet, "is surrounded by mystery, and they ask me to have patience . . . Lord! where to find it? After sixty days of assorted tortures."

Finally "je croupis dans 'les usines du Néant'" [I'm rotting away in the factories of Nothingness], as our Jules [Laforgue] says; I rotate in a rubber ring, watching the unchanging hours pass and only too happy if they are not too painful . . . The war goes on—as you know, no longer making any sense . . . I'm well aware that the end is hard to find, but this kind of warlike nonchalance has something aggravating about it and I'm afraid it plays into the hands of Messieurs Boches, who have the tenacity of vermin! Death continues no less to levy its blind tribute . . . So when will hatred end? And even in this business is it really a question of hatred? When will they stop entrusting the destiny of nations to people who regard humanity as a means of self-advancement?[22]

The treatment continued until early July, at which point it appears that Debussy simply decided to "walk out and work and not take any more orders from a rather too authoritarian rectum."[23] Since February he had also had regular morphine injections, "which turn you into something like a walking corpse and suppress any kind of willpower."[24] In that same month he had signed a contract with Durand for the third of his sonatas, the one for violin and piano, but he had been unable to do any work on it. Then in mid-July came what felt to him like the final blow. A Paris Tribunal of First Instance found against him in a case brought by Lilly for the payment of maintenance which he had discontinued in 1910, and ordered him to lodge a 30,000-franc deposit at the Caisse des Dépôts as a guarantee of her 3,600-franc annuity. Within days, Emma and Chouchou both went down with whooping cough, and nights that had for months been agony for him became agony for them all. "Destiny," he told his lawyer, "is treating me like the Atreidae . . . it's an honour I would willingly do without." He seriously contemplated suicide. "If I didn't have the worry, as much as the duty, of finishing the two little Poe dramas, I'd have done it already."[25]

The House of Atreus saved by the House of Usher! The justice would have been poetic indeed if it had actually led to the completion of the opera in question. But it was not to be. During the summer of 1916 he completely recast his *Usher* libretto, the only work, apart from proofreading, of which he was capable. But exactly how much of it he composed, or recomposed, is by no means clear, the sketches for the most part being undated. Much of the first scene between the sinister doctor and the unnamed friend was written in draft form, though still with a lot of detail missing or unclear, and there survived also a good running sketch of the first part of Roderick's monologue, now placed at the start of the second scene. But Debussy seems to have managed hardly any solid music for the middle section of the opera, from the moment of Roderick's recognition of his friend, through their first dialogue and the doctor's announcement to the friend of Madeline's death and burial, up to the point where the friend attempts to calm the increasingly deranged Roderick by reading from the ancient book about Sir Ulrich and the dragon. Instead, he seems to have worked at the final pages of the opera, where the reading of the story provides an unintended accompaniment to Madeline's breaking out of her tomb, mounting the stairs, and crashing through the door, killing her brother and literally bringing down the entire house.

One might suppose that, for Debussy, this was the scene that presented the most crucial challenge. It was the only scene that contained actual incident, but that incident was so drastic and awe-inspiring that it might threaten to overpower everything that preceded it unless paced with enormous skill. Even here his draft is no more than a skeleton, with the voices mainly in *mélodrame* (speech over music), and the actual ending, with the house disintegrating and the friend rushing away, is still handled in a somewhat perfunctory, incomplete fashion. The upshot of all this is that, so far from having at any time nearly completed *Usher*, he had actually sketched no more than a quarter of it, and most of that was in a shorthand, unrealised state. Listening to Robert Orledge's extremely skilful "realisation" of this material, one gets a fair glimpse of the musical intentions: the brooding harmonic and melodic atmosphere, the vocal idiom (largely an extension of the recitative style of *Pelléas*), even something of the orchestral colouring, with its melancholy cor anglais solos and exquisite string chord voicings, for which there are indications in the sketches. But how Debussy would have handled the characterisation and the all-important dramatic pacing remains, *pace* Professor Orledge, as uncertain as it probably remained, to the end, in the composer's own mind.

By September 1916 he must have been feeling at least marginally better, well enough, at any rate, to travel four hundred miles to Arcachon for a month's holiday on the south-west coast. The irony of this trip was that they were going, not for him, but for Emma, who, without ever being (like him) critically ill, always had something wrong with her that obstinately refused to get better in the hospital atmosphere of their Bois de Boulogne apartment, with trains whizzing past their back windows, the train guards constantly sounding their bugles, and the incessant rumours of war nearby. All the same, photographs of Debussy taken in the woods at Le Moulleau on this trip, including a well-known one of him with Chouchou (why wasn't she at school?), resemble all too closely the gaunt image he painted of himself after four months of morphine injections. It is the image of a dying man.

Their hotel at Le Moulleau, though Grand by name, was "a model of discomfort." It had neither gas nor electricity, but it did have a piano on every floor, often all being played simultaneously. "I don't think I've ever heard so much bad music played at the same time," Debussy said. "The total effect is curiously like St[ravinsky] rewritten by that bloody Hungarian anarchist whose name my memory refuses to retain."[26] There was a girl in the room opposite who played César Franck all afternoon on the piano. He detested both the hotel itself and hotel life, not alleviated by the smell of pines and the vigorous west wind off the Atlantic. "It's probably my fault," he confessed to Godet, "but I'm a sick old man who has increased his collection of manias—some of them worrying, like the horror of those little hotel tables seventy-five-centimetres wide . . . You'll see that I shan't bring anything worthwhile back from this trip apart from regret at having made it."[27] But then one day he surprised himself. On an excursion to Cap Ferret, across the bay from Le Moulleau, "I found the 'cellular' idea for the finale of the Sonata for piano and violin. Unfortunately the first two movements no longer want to know . . . As I know myself, you can imagine that I'm not going to force them to put up with a disagreeable neighbourhood."[28]

There must have been some work done on the sonata before Arcachon. Back in June he had told Arthur Hartmann that he had prepared to write it but had lost the impulse. Clearly he had been searching in vain for an idea for the *Finale*, but how much all this amounted to is impossible to say. Back in Paris towards the end of October, things must slowly have begun to go better. By now he seldom went out, "for fear of frightening the children and the tram drivers."[29] On 14 December Walter Rummel played four of the *Études* at a soirée at Countess Orlawska's, but there is no clear evidence that Debussy attended, though he had heard a private performance of the trio sonata at Durand's office a few days earlier. Then on the 21st he actually took part in a concert in aid of clothing for prisoners of war, playing *En blanc et noir* with Jean Roger-Ducasse and accompanying Jane Bathori in the *Noël des enfants qui n'ont plus de maison* and some other songs. By the end of January 1917 the first movement of the Violin Sonata was probably finished; at any rate, at about that time he sent Durand "the first instalment [*morceau*], duly polished." *Dûment verni*: a good description of this movement, one of the most classically perfect pieces he had ever written, in a clean sonata form, beautifully balanced and concise, every detail clear, and not one note too many. A more impressive illustration of the power of mind over body would be hard to find. Yet Debussy had painted a lurid picture of his brain to Godet. "There are some ruins," he remarked, "that are better kept hidden."[30]

After this, things did not go so easily, and the last of the three movements gave him more trouble than anything since *Gigues*. Dukas may have been speaking hyperbolically when he referred to "your six versions of the finale,"[31] but there were undoubtedly at least two completely unrelated finales, between which Debussy oscillated before deciding on the eventual movement but then being unable to find a satisfactory ending. The solution to the basic problem of what sort of finale to write was the characteristically French one of quoting and varying the main first movement theme, but he also incorporated a snatch of tarantella-like music that had perhaps belonged to the discarded first version (which Durand, who liked it, had dubbed "Neapolitan"), and that created an interruption somewhat in the manner of the *Sérénade interrompue* or *Le matin d'un jour de fête*. At last, in April, after keeping Durand at bay for more than a month, Debussy completed the sonata, and on 5 May he himself played the piano in the first performance in the Salle Gaveau, with Gaston Poulet, a young violinist who, he thought, "looked like a gypsy, even though born calmly in Paris."[32] It would be Debussy's final appearance on a concert platform.

As so often with the last works of great composers who die young, it is hard to say whether they are the start of a new phase that tragically remained unconsummated, or merely represent the stripping down of the existing style at a time of mental or physical frailty. With Schubert there is no frailty, and we can confidently detect a new manner in his last songs; the case of Schumann, who died in an asylum, is more complicated, but there is good evidence that his music was heading in new directions when he was struck down by mental collapse. With Debussy the evidence is mixed. The late piano works, *En blanc et noir* and the *Études*, are masterpieces that show no trace of decline, though it used to be fashionable to talk them down. The sonatas are a slightly different matter. Taken as a group—and in conjunction with the unfulfilled plan to write six of them—they were surely born of an intention to return to classical or pre-classical forms. They may have been prompted by the idea of Bach's sonatas, but probably not by their music, which, when Debussy actually got round to editing it, he found "truly pitiless . . . bearable only when admirable."

> If he had had a friend—maybe a publisher? [Debussy is writing to Durand]—who could gently have advised him not to write one day a week, for example, it would have saved us several hundred pages where we have to walk down a hedgerow of joyless bars that process without mercy and with always the same little rascal of a "subject," then "counter-subject."[33]

This was never his idea of a sonata. From the very start, the Cello Sonata, partly composed while he was also at work on the *Études*, adopts a nineteenth-century kind of discourse, with contrasting themes, strongly characterised rhythms, and a narrative approach to form. The piano texture, it's true, is generally light, as if with Rameau or Couperin in the back of its mind, and there is a "fantasque," Watteauesque colouring here and there, especially in the middle movements of the violin and cello sonatas. The *Intermède* of the Violin Sonata is actually marked *fantasque et léger* (fantastic—in the old, strict sense—and light), subtly evokes the eighteenth-century world of masked courtiers in landscaped parks, but also momentarily recalls General Lavine and the music hall.

These movements, though, dodge the need for contrasting slow music. The cello and trio sonatas start at slow tempo, but these are not really slow movements. One might even argue that the problem with the last movement of the Violin Sonata sprang partly from the fact that the *Intermède* pre-empted the kind of brilliant detailing that would normally have been a finale property. A slow movement here—an *Hommage à Rameau* or an *Et la lune descend*—would have provided a platform for a genuinely conclusive finale. The *Finale* Debussy eventually wrote is a sparkling, enjoyable piece (and by the way a difficult one: Poulet trembled when he saw it, and this in turn gave Debussy gooseflesh). But it might be thought disappointingly short, and in a curious way it leaves this work that started so marvellously with a somewhat perfunctory exit. Perhaps the shortwindedness is the evidence of frailty. But if so, the music itself is by no means frail, as Debussy himself noted with a certain pride after the performance:

> By a very human contradiction, it's full of joyous tumult. In future don't trust works that seem to soar into the open sky; they have often lain rotting in the darkness of a morose brain. Like the finale of this very sonata, which passed through many curious deformations, to end up with the simple play of an idea that turns back on itself. Like the serpent that bites its own tail—a diversion whose pleasure I take leave to dispute.[34]

The winter of 1916–17 was the coldest in Paris within living memory; coal and hence electricity were in short supply because of the German occupation of France's north-eastern coalfields, and such supplies as there were were strictly rationed in favour of the elderly and the families of soldiers. Debussy was reduced to begging Durand not only for cash advances but for firewood or coal, though the tone of his request ("Could you really not let me have . . .") suggests that a previous answer had been negative.[35] Instead he turned to his own supplier, a M. Tronquin, and in return for what he hoped would be regular deliveries of coal, he composed a short piano piece entitled *Les soirs illuminés par l'ardeur du charbon* ("Evenings lit by the heat of the coal"), which is a line from Baudelaire's poem "Le Balcon," set by Debussy thirty years before. In writing this intriguing two-minute piece, he had one further joke at kindly M. Tronquin's expense but no doubt without his knowledge, and based it musically on another piano piece of his that had derived its title from Baudelaire, *Les sons et les parfums tournent dans l'air du soir*. Sounds and perfumes turn in the evening air, needless to say, only in nice warm weather. M. Tronquin did respond and did deliver, and it would be pleasant to think that he profited, if not spiritually, at least materially from the autograph manuscript that Debussy gave him, which would today be worth several hundred deliveries of coal. He had at least the pleasure of knowing that he had made one little girl happy. "My daughter," Debussy told him, "jumped for joy when she read your letter—these days little girls prefer bags of coal to dolls!"[36]

Somehow the Debussys survived this terrible winter with nothing worse than colds. The composer was even comparatively active, though composition was not going well. He attended performances: the ballet *Les Abeilles*, based on Stravinsky's *Scherzo fantastique*, in January; the premieres of his own trio sonata and the *Épigraphes antiques* at war-relief concerts in March; Satie's *Parade* at the Ballets Russes in May. For some reason, he and Satie had fallen out, and when he finally went to see *Parade* at the Châtelet on 25 May (having missed the premiere on the 18th), he wrote to congratulate Diaghilev on the evening, but studiously avoided mentioning *Parade*. Something had happened between them in February or early March, to judge from a letter from Satie to Emma on 8 March, quaintly worded, as usual with him, but with a genuinely wounded flavour:

Dear Madame—decidedly, it is preferable that the "Precursor"* stay at home—far away—from now on . . . P.S. What snow! I hope you are all well. I shall write often. Love you all—very much.

* Painful teasing—& at rehearsal, still! Yes. Very unbearable, in any case.[37]

Debussy may well have disliked *Parade*, but if the cause of the
break was some sharp remark of his at an early rehearsal of the ballet,
its effect on the hypersensitive Satie will have been out of proportion
to the intention. Their friendship had always included a patronising
element on Debussy's part, and if Satie's Diaghilev commission had
altered that balance (bearing in mind the failure of *Jeux*), Debussy,
unwell and in pain, may have said something satirical or mildly offen-
sive that Satie took to heart. The breach, in any case, was not healed
during the remaining year of Debussy's life, and Satie's letter—with
a single exception, now lost—was the last between them.

Debussy himself had not abandoned all projects, but they were
assuming a degree of unreality. There was a plan for a choral-
orchestral work at first to be called "Ode à Jeanne d'Arc," then, more
simply, "Ode à la France," dreamt up with Laloy, and intended as a
more substantial sequel to the *Noël des enfants qui n'ont plus de maisons*. Laloy completed the poem, and later wrote that Debussy had
"found the time, before leaving us, to compose the music of this work
in its entirety, music that proceeds from the same inspiration as the
Martyre de Saint Sébastien, in a style no less pure and a sentiment even
more poignant."[38] Perhaps he did compose it, but all that survives are
a few pages of sketches in short score.

Then, in June, after seeing Firmin Gémier's production of *The
Merchant of Venice* at the Théâtre Antoine, Debussy suddenly
thought of resuscitating his old idea of incidental music for *As You
Like It*, using, as he hoped, the old translation by Paul-Jean Toulet,
to be staged by Gémier. Toulet, living now at Guéthary, on the far
south-west coast near Biarritz, was enthusiastic but quite out of touch
with Paris life. He had derived some hint from one of Debussy's letters that his health was not all it might be, and wrote to a doctor friend
of Debussy's seeking information. "Is he well enough to undertake
such a task? I'm sorry you weren't able to tell me what was wrong
with him (his wife mentioned an operation, but with no details. It
seems to me it may have been her)."[39] The matter had become urgent
because Debussy had taken a chalet at Saint-Jean-de-Luz, only a
few miles from Guéthary, for the summer, and was showing every
sign of treating the project seriously. Yet what followed was one of
those Kafkaesque chain of events in which the participants continu-

ally avoid the resolution implied by their stated intentions. Toulet, whom Debussy described as "a celebrated humorist, chronic alcoholic, with a face like a Van Dongen sunset,"⁴⁰ woke up one morning with rheumatism of the leg and was unable to leave the house, and when the Debussys passed through Guéthary the next day they refrained from calling in on that account. There is in fact no sure evidence that they met at all during the three months of Debussy's stay, though barely three miles apart. Had Toulet seen Debussy, he would surely have known at once that their project was hopeless. Instead, having heard rumours about his health, he wrote again to Debussy in early September discreetly enquiring if Saint-Jean was doing them good. As for their collaboration, the correspondence hardly mentions it. Debussy admitted the truth only to Durand:

> As for my work, I'd rather not talk about it now. I'm still having to battle with too many troubles and I still don't know how to write music in a bad mood—still less, in a bad state of health . . . as soon as I sense a break in the clouds, you can be sure that I'll try to make the best possible use of it.⁴¹

But he must have known there would be no break, no more sunshine, only the endless rain that seemed to fall on them, even in the south of France in the settled month of September.

Back in Paris in October he was still making plans. He and Laloy were theoretically working on an operatic version of *Le Martyre de Saint Sébastien*, a project that went back to 1916. But there was a predictable difficulty. "In these 3995 or so verses," he told Durand, "there is hardly any material. Words, words . . . I think we'll manage something all the same."⁴² They of course did not. *As You Like It* was still there in his mind, but it was all make-believe. The truth was, he admitted to Durand, that he could hardly leave the house without risking what he called "le fait divers"⁴³—the incontinence associated with his cancer. As for Godet's suggestion that he might travel to Switzerland, it would have to be in some sad "blague-bateau"—a fantasy boat.⁴⁴ Music, meanwhile, had completely given him up.

His "fait divers" letter of 1 November was the last he wrote to Durand and the last, apparently, to anyone else except his wife. To

Emma he wrote barely decipherable, barely completed notes: New Year greetings, enquiries about her health, simple words of affection. "If love is stronger than death . . . How will it not be . . ." "Forgive my more and more limited capabilities . . ." "Year follows year ever the same." "If you are no worse, nothing will be worse, and we shall be able to count on more flamboyant new years . . ." Meanwhile, she handled his correspondence, and her letters chart his decline. From 6 November he was bedridden, made some slight improvement, but still could not leave his bed, could not even sit up in bed, exhausted as he was by the incessant diarrhoea. In mid-January he was well enough to get up for short periods, his appetite improved, but he remained weak. Poor Emma was herself not strong physically, and even emotionally she was not altogether made to endure the prolonged suffering of others. "There are moments (numerous) when I'm at the end of my tether," she wrote to Caplet. "To see suffering is more horrible than anything if one can't get the means to allay it . . . what haven't I tried these two years?"[45]

In February she again reported some improvements, but they were slight, temporary and probably, in her letters, exaggerated. Early in March she wrote to Charles-Marie Widor, who had relinquished his Académie *fauteuil* in 1914 in order to take up the post of full-time secretary to that institution, and had suggested to Debussy that he apply for the vacancy. Partly because of the war, and partly no doubt because of an intervention by the eighty-year-old Saint-Saëns, who had written to Fauré anathematising *En blanc et noir*, nothing had been done. Emma now, perhaps on her own initiative, wanted to restart the process. Debussy certainly knew about it, whatever he really thought or hoped. On 17 March Emma wrote a formal application to Widor, in her hand but signed by her husband. But it was his final stroke of the pen. On the 24th a similar letter, signed "Claude Debussy" in Emma's hand, winged its way to the President of the Institut de France, Alfred Croiset.

The next day, in the evening of 25 March 1918, the composer— France's greatest perhaps since the Rameau he had so adored—died of the horrible disease that had ruined his existence for the past several years—yet miraculously not until the very end his genius.

A German artillery bombardment had begun two days before and continued all week.

Condolences flooded in, from musicians and non-musicians, from the great and the small. Perhaps one only learns how much one is loved and admired—or the reverse—when one is past learning. The most moving letter was written by twelve-year-old Chouchou two weeks later to her half-brother Raoul Bardac, away at the war:

Dolly [Raoul's sister] came because I asked her, seeing poor Maman's completely stricken face! As soon as she left, Maman was called in to Papa, as the nurse found him "very bad"! They quickly called two doctors who both said to give him an injection to ease the pain. Do you think I couldn't understand? Roger-Ducasse was there and said to me: "Come here, Chouchou, embrace your papa." Then I immediately realised it was over. When I came back into the room Papa was asleep and breathing regularly but very short—He stayed asleep like that until 10.15 in the evening and at that time he sweetly, angelically fell asleep for ever. What happened next I can't say. A flood of tears wanted to come from my eyes, but I forced them back at once for Maman's sake—All night, alone in Maman's double bed, I couldn't sleep a wink. I had a fever and my dry eyes gazed at the walls and I couldn't believe it was all real!!! . . .

The next day far too many people came to see Maman, who by the end of the day had had enough—then there was a break for her and me—Thursday came the Thursday when they were to take him from us for ever! I saw him again one last time in that horrible box—He looked happy, oh so happy and this time I hadn't the courage to hold back my tears and almost collapsing I couldn't kiss him. At the cemetery Maman naturally couldn't control herself any better than she did, and as for me all I could think of was "I mustn't cry because of Maman." I plucked up all my courage from I don't know where. I didn't shed a tear—tears held back are as good as tears shed, and now it's night for always. Papa is dead! Those three words, I don't understand them, or rather I understand them too well—And to be alone battling with Maman's indescribable grief is really terrible—but this made me forget mine for several days but now I feel it more bitterly still—oh—you there so far away think a little of your poor little sister who would so like to embrace you and tell you how much she loves you—Can you understand everything I feel and can't write?[46]

The funeral service was on the 28th, the burial in Père Lachaise Cemetery on the 29th. The funeral cortège crossed Paris from the Bois de Boulogne to the cemetery, still to the accompaniment of the German guns. Laloy described the scene:

In the garden of his house some fifty people were present, but the majority peeled off on the way, and barely more than twenty of us arrived [at the cemetery]. Through the streets of Paris—uneasy feeling for all its calm appearance—Camille Chevillard and Gabriel Pierné walked the whole way, in this way paying to the musician and friend their most faithful homage.[47]

Sixteen months after her father's death, Claude-Emma (Chouchou) Debussy contracted diphtheria and died, aged thirteen, on 16 July 1919.

14

What the Modern Made of Him

By dying in 1918, Debussy unintentionally located himself at a turning-point of history. The war still had more than seven months to run and, in March, was by no means settled in its outcome. But years have a numerical force independent of months, and in any case the artistic antennae were already out—had been out for some time—feeling for the war's end and its aftermath. The previous May Debussy had attended Satie's ballet *Parade* but had pointedly failed to mention it in his congratulatory letter to Diaghilev, partly no doubt because of his recent feud with Satie, but perhaps also because he sensed something in the piece—with its surreal fragments of modern life reimagined as a vulgar circus performance—that foretold his demise. Within weeks of his death, a little book came out—not much more than a pamphlet—that would have told him the same story in words of not many syllables; it was written by the author of the scenario of *Parade*, twenty-eight-year-old Jean Cocteau. The pamphlet was called *Le Coq et l'Arlequin*, and while punning with approval on its author's name ("the cock says Cocteau twice and lives on his farm"), it identified Harlequin with fuzzy nocturnal romanticism and proceeded to dismiss, with or without qualification, the music that he, Cocteau, chose to associate with that image. "The nightingale," it said, "sings badly."[1]

Debussy was a prime target, along with Wagner, Schoenberg ("blackboard music"), other assorted Germans, with some cautious side-swipes at Stravinsky. The pamphlet's unequivocal hero is Satie. "Satie," it announced, "teaches the greatest audacity of our time: to be simple."

The profound originality of a Satie teaches young musicians a lesson that doesn't mean abandoning their own originality. Wagner,

Stravinsky, and even Debussy, are beautiful octopuses. Anyone who goes near them will have trouble extricating himself from their tentacles. Satie shows us a white road on which anyone can freely leave his own footprints.[2]

As the war dragged on, the romantic past, with its epic symphonies and grand operas, its Xanadus and Ozymandiuses, not to mention its octopuses, seemed to recede further and further into irrelevance. "Enough of clouds," said Cocteau, "waves, aquaria, of ondines and perfumes of the night; we need a music on solid ground, *a music of every day*. Enough of hammocks and garlands and gondolas! I want someone to build me a music I can live in like a house."[3] Musical Impressionism, he alleged, was merely a backlash (*contre-coup*) from Wagner. *Pelléas* was "still music to listen to with your head in your hands. All music to be listened to head in hands is suspect. Wagner is the prototype of music to be heard through the hands."[4] And what was it that would sweep Impressionism away? It was "a certain American dance that I saw at the Casino de Paris." And there follows a description of an American band made up of banjos and "large nickel pipes" and a "noise barman" in evening dress with a battery of bells, metal bars, planks and motorbike horns, to which a M. Pilcer and a Miss Gaby Deslys danced a kind of wild pre-Charleston Charleston.[5] Cocteau's account of this experience is curiously reminiscent of Debussy's account of the Annamite Theatre; but Cocteau also seems unaware how interesting and suggestive Debussy would himself have found his American band, and that he might well have turned it into a prelude.

Cocteau turned out to be both a trendsetter and a prophet. His "music I can live in like a house" became the pattern for Satie's *Musique d'ameublement* ("Furniture Music"), an arty term for background music, one example of which, *Tapisserie en fer forgé* ("Wrought-Iron Tapestry"), was meant "to be played in a vestibule," and another, *Carrelage phonique* ("Sonic Tiling") could be played "at a lunch or a marriage signing." More generally, Cocteau was in effect predicting the 1920s rejection of excessive solemnity in the arts, its preference for fun over reflection, and its return to the superficial virtues of classicism, its clarity and simplicity and its sense of order. Cocteau himself published a set of essays in 1926 under the somewhat schoolmasterly title *Rappel à l'ordre*, the "Recall to Order." Debussy would certainly have taken no interest in the studied silliness and vacuity of *Musique d'ameublement*; in any case most of his music would have been inaudible at a 1920s lunch. But as for the classicising tendency of the best 1920s music, his own late works were tending that way, and there is no reason to suppose that, had he survived, he would not have exploited this new atmosphere at least as well and productively as Ravel did in his string sonatas and piano concertos. On the other hand, the intended purveyors of Cocteau's "everyday music," the group of young composers he fostered as Les Six, were all admirers of Debussy, did not truly see themselves as a group, and soon shuffled off the ill-fitting fancy dress that their patron had designed for them.

It would be another thirty years before Debussy's intellectual prestige fully recovered from the timing of his death. His music remained generally popular, especially the main keyboard works, the *Prélude à l'après-midi d'un faune* and *La Mer*. But it would have been thought eccentric to place him in the very front rank of composers. One of the reasons for this comes out in an article by the critic Ernest Newman published in the *New Witness* soon after the composer's death. Newman is discussing the issue of form in Debussy's music, and after excoriating what he calls "the invincible feeble-mindedness [of the Russian Five] wherever form was concerned," he turns on Debussy and invites us "to recognise frankly that the constructive sense of Debussy also, so far as the larger forms are concerned, was no more than that of a child . . . For my own part, much as I admire the imaginative qualities of the best parts of *Pelléas*, I have never been able to see it, so far as regards its form, as anything but a confession of artistic bankruptcy."[6]

The giveaway here is the phrase "so far as the larger forms are concerned." A specialist in Wagner and to this day his greatest biographer, Newman is incapable of separating the concept of form from the concept of forms. For him German music remains the touchstone and musical form will always be judged in terms of the specific formal types and processes it perfected. He is not ready for the idea that form is an idea *sui generis*, which emerges as an organic part of the creative process (even though this is by and large how it emerges in Wagner). And he fails completely to reckon with the fact that the Russian Five and Debussy were consciously seeking routes away from the Ger-

man tradition. Typically, he denounces *Boris Godunov* as "merely a
collection of fragments that the architect has dumped down near each
other on the same plot of earth,"[7] a description that he might just as
well have applied to *King Lear* or *The Winter's Tale*. The idea that
there might be different ways of creating beautiful and satisfying aesthetic objects seems not to have entered his head.

Debussy's intellectual reputation began to recover in the 1930s,
but it was only after 1945 that it reached the point at which the
young Pierre Boulez could ask, "Should we then set up a Debussy–
Cézanne–Mallarmé axis as the root of all modernism? If it were not
rather too chauvinistic, one could happily do so."[8] Constant Lambert had devoted a substantial section of his brilliant if idiosyncratic
1930s study of early twentieth-century music, *Music Ho!*, to a reas-
sessment of Debussy that managed characteristically to belittle all
the works normally regarded as masterpieces (*Pelléas*, "one of his
weakest and most mannered works"; *La Mer*, "cold and detached pictorialism"; much of what came next "definitely inferior in quality"),
and to elevate the later orchestral *Images*, *Jeux*, *En blanc et noir* and
the trio sonata—works that were much less played—to the summit
of his achievement. Lambert's discussion of Debussy's importance is
shrewd, but his choice of masterpieces is consciously off-piste.

> Had Debussy died after writing *La Mer*, he would have remained a
> great historical figure who had revolutionised the technique of music
> in a way that no one man had ever done before; but he would hardly
> have been remembered as an intrinsically great composer.[9]

Curiously enough, the same perversity apparently afflicted the
judgement of Boulez and Co. after the war. For Lambert the key
work was the *Images*; for the post-war avant-garde it was *Jeux*. But
the point about *Jeux* in this case was not that hardly anyone actually
knew it, but that it could be taken as a case study *contra* Schoenberg,
whom Boulez was wanting to dethrone from his position as inventor
of modern music, not because he was Austro-German, and certainly
not because he was Jewish, but because in Boulez's opinion he had
not taken his modernism nearly far enough. Schoenberg had evolved
a technique of continuous variation of his material, a dense, unin-
terrupted weave in which every line participated: no differentiation

between sections, no accompaniment as such, only a kind of fluctuation "in the course of which the various constituent elements take on a greater or lesser functional importance."[10] In fact this is Boulez's description of *Jeux*, leaving Schoenberg as a might-have-been who never faced up to the consequences of his own ideas. Three or four years later Boulez clarified this account in an encyclopedia article he wrote on Debussy.

> Far from being feebly fragmented, the structure is rich in invention and shimmeringly complex, and introduces a highly ductile way of thinking based on the notion of irreversible time; in order to *hear* it, one's sole recourse is to submit to its development, since the constant evolution of thematic ideas rules out any question of architectural symmetry . . . *Jeux* marks the arrival of a musical form which, since it involves *instantaneous* self-renewal, implies a way of *listening* that is no less *instantaneous*.[11]

These points were elaborated in great and arcane detail by the German theorist Herbert Eimert in a twenty-page analytical article in the new-music journal *Die Reihe*, the ultimate platform of the postwar musical avant-garde. Thus by way of *Jeux*, Debussy entered the pantheon of contemporary music in its severest phase, alongside Anton Webern and, with considerable qualification, Schoenberg and Stravinsky.

Is it possible for a creative artist to be both radical and popular? Modern art has conditioned us, on the whole, to expect the answer no to that question, but oddly enough history gives a different answer. In music, who are the great radicals before, say, the end of the First World War? Monteverdi, Haydn and Beethoven, Berlioz, Liszt and Wagner, Musorgsky, Schoenberg, Bartók, Stravinsky, Webern and . . . Debussy. Of course there are other radicals: Gesualdo, Louis Couperin, C. P. E. Bach, Berwald, Glinka, Alkan, Ives, Pratella, and probably a lot more; but if these composers are not popular, or even in some cases remembered at all, the reason is probably not that they were radical but that they were minor. Only Schoenberg, Webern,

Bartók and possibly Stravinsky in the "great" list, and Ives among the "minors," might be said to resist popularity because they are "difficult." It hardly seems much of a coincidence that these five composers were all born within a decade of each other, between 1874 and 1883.

Radical movements in art are often a response to a general feeling of ossification or over-academicism in the mainstream art of the day. But they can also be a reaction to a change in the market or the audience. Monteverdi was, among other things, a symptom of the gradual secularisation of music at the end of the sixteenth century; Beethoven, like Wordsworth, responded openly to the French Revolution, but he was also part of its social consequences, the rise and enrichment of the bourgeoisie, the growth in education, expansion of public concerts, and so forth. The explosion of what we now, rather confusingly, call modernism probably had similar causes. But where Beethoven wrote enthusiastically, at least in some of his music, for post-revolutionary man—"Alle Menschen werden Brüdern"—modernism devoted itself, openly or otherwise, to antagonising him.

Broadly speaking, modernists were in rebellion against everything that the educated common man stood for towards the end of the nineteenth century. They hated mass production and the suburbanisation of taste; they disliked the urge to explain and classify. So far from wanting to make clear, they wanted to make strange; where modern life was sophisticated and comfortable, they espoused the primitive and the impenetrable. Simply, they wanted to shock, as the French say, *épater le bourgeois*. And they apparently succeeded, although there was perhaps something ritualistic—a certain scriptedness— about the 1913 scandals, *The Rite of Spring* in Paris and the Schoenberg *Skandalkonzert* in Vienna. The bourgeoisie knew its part and played it to perfection, and modernism has never looked back. To this day Schoenberg and Webern, to a lesser extent Stravinsky and Bartók, and their many successors have successfully warded off mass bourgeois appreciation. Schoenberg may be the first "great" composer in modern history whose music has not entered the repertoire almost a century and a half after his birth.

Debussy was and is a subtly different case. With him *épater le bourgeois* was never an issue; on the contrary his watchword was beauty, and he honestly felt that attentive listeners would be able to hear and appreciate this quality if only they could shake off their attachment to the familiar and predictable in the standard repertoire. It turned out that they could. His music never seems to have created significant problems for audiences, although, as with his beloved *Boris Godunov*, critics were wary of it because it didn't meet their normal criteria of elucidation or assessment. Debussy's main enemy, as we have seen, was the Conservatoire, and the books of rules that were supposed to tell you what you could and couldn't do as a composer trying to respond to an inner voice. Just as the Impressionist painters had declared war on the Académie, with its mantra about drawing, colour and subject matter, so Debussy, a comparative latecomer to a discipline that gifted children could master almost before they could talk, was bewildered by the apparent need to obey precepts that were unable to accommodate his ideas. Study them, by all means; master them; but never let them take control of your thoughts. After all, the rules had been extracted in the distant past from the work of geniuses who were themselves probably stretching conventions that didn't meet their needs. Yet now these rules were taught like the Ten Commandments, or like algebra, as Delacroix had grumbled about the teaching of the beautiful at the École des Beaux-Arts.[12]

Debussy's music criticism shows that he was always equivocal about the accepted great music of the past, and more inclined to praise composers outside the Paris mainstream: composers such as the polyphonic masters Palestrina, Victoria and Lassus, whose music you would encounter only if you went to particular churches at particular times; or the *clavecinistes*, Rameau, François Couperin, Daquin, whose work had, in his opinion, been bullied out of the repertoire by German keyboard music from Bach onwards; or maverick figures such as Musorgsky, whom it was safe to admire because he had never obeyed a Conservatoire rule in his life and apparently hadn't known any. Debussy was perfectly well aware that the classical masters were secure on their plinths, but he sometimes resented their influence. His in-and-out attitude to Wagner is a case in point. It illustrates to perfection Harold Bloom's theory about precursors and the artist's desperate need to escape their influence in order to achieve anything remotely worthwhile of his own. To invent out of nothing is not so much impossible as feckless, the equivalent of banging stones together or cutting holes in reeds. The serious artist has no choice but to draw on his precursors, and everything hangs on his ability to do this without merely repeating or parroting their work: to be, in Bloomian terms, a "strong composer," who takes what he needs, reshapes it in his own image, deliberately "misreads" it.

This misreading, paradoxically, is the key to Debussy's approachability for modern audiences. Where Schoenberg saw his work as the logical outcome of the German classical tradition, and pursued that logic as a moral calling, regardless of, or even with conscious disregard for, the complexity and impenetrability of the results, Debussy treated existing music like a young child with a picture book, singling out this or that picture, this or that character, and ignoring the actual story. His enjoyment of particular sounds and his love of making patterns out of them were juvenile in a sense, except that, unlike a child, he never ran riot with the sounds, never crashed around on the keyboard. His starting-point was what he found, serendipitously, in the music around him: in Wagner, in Massenet, even in Bach or Chopin. This was music whose beauty was both sensual and architectural. From start to finish it held up, made sense, but slice it where you liked, and you would find something beautiful and worth examining for itself, regardless of its "meaning" in the context from which you had extracted it.

Of course, this is an over-simplification. In taking rich tonal chords out of context, Debussy was perfectly aware of their function, which still formed a part of their latent character for any Western listener or musician. So, in pieces such as *Hommage à Rameau* or *Les sons et les parfums tournent dans l'air du soir*, which contain strings of such chords, the effect is hybrid, partly tonal, partly anecdotal. The harmonic idea is, so to speak, stolen and misread: a problem for the theorist, but for the unconcerned listener a fascinating, unthreatening journey through a semi-familiar soundscape.

For Debussy, however, all this was merely a beginning. He was, after all, a composer, and a composer's job is to put things together. A piece of music occupies time, and it has to do so not idly but coherently. Debussy, as we've seen, brought a highly refined ear to the fashioning and voicing of individual sonorities, but he also had an acute sense of musical form and timing. Though he loved Wagner, he had no ambition to compose on a Wagnerian scale. His longest work by far, *Pelléas et Mélisande*, is really a succession of short scenes linked by orchestral interludes, while his longest single movements, his three ballets, are to some extent pre-formed by their scenarios.

More typical are the piano pieces, mostly between three and six minutes long, and almost without exception beautifully and convincingly designed, yet hardly ever in one of what Newman would have called "the larger forms." The history of musical analysis is full of expressions like "a kind of sonata form," "a sort of rondo," which reveal the desperation of the programme-note writer to fit any and every piece into a predetermined form. But in any decent work of art, form is a by-product of material, subject matter and workmanship, not a process of filling a template, like a dot-to-dot drawing or a do-it-yourself tapestry. "*Jeux*," Eimert remarks, "is a formless work in the traditional sense, without symphonic architecture, without thematicism by attraction, without contrapuntal evolution, not working out motives loaded with significance and relation-functions. What sounds at any moment is constantly adapted to what follows . . ."[13] Eimert calls this process "vegetative," in the sense of growing and spreading, throwing off shoots and suckers, but never returning or repeating (*Jeux* has brief, modified recapitulations, but they are almost swallowed up in the growth).

Jeux is an extreme case, which is one reason why it was singled out by Boulez. But something similar happens in *La Mer* and the solo piano pieces, often mixed up with hints of recapitulation, more or less varied, and new ideas emerging from the old. In its origins this is a form of improvisation, and we know that Debussy was addicted to improvising, because when, at Pourville in July 1915, he did not yet have a piano, he told Durand that this "would concentrate the emotion by stopping it dissipating itself in improvisations, in which one too often gives way to the perverse charm of telling oneself stories."[14] Improvising can be a wonderful source of ideas, but it needs disciplining, and Debussy obviously felt this was best done away from the piano, where he could stop and reflect, just as a painter standing back from his canvas could see a work whole, refine and exclude. In this activity he was a ruthless perfectionist, and if one sometimes feels that his treatment of the people in his life—the teachers he mocked, the women he ruined, the friends he lied to and sponged off—was not all it might have been, we can go to the music for an explanation, if not for an excuse.

Above all, it is this perfectionism that separates him from his many imitators. Anyone can find a vagrant chord or two, repeat them a few times, perhaps with slight changes (what Eimert called "organic inexactness"), add a flute-like arabesque and some silences, mark the whole thing *pianissimo*, and pretend it sounds like Debussy. But it won't, because it will lack that precision of the inner ear that makes the harmonies in *Danseuses de Delphes* or the orchestral voicings in *Nuages* or *La Mer* so unforgettable simply as musical moments, and it will lack that feeling for the touch and resonance of the piano, the mysterious functions of the two pedals, so rarely indicated by Debussy because he refused to generalise details that were of such refinement, yet so crucial to the character of his work.

Much of what happened to music—and to art in general—in the twentieth century marked a break, conscious or unconscious, with the nineteenth. The past was an orphan parent, rejected by its children, despised by its grandchildren. Debussy, too, found fault with his forebears and tried to do things differently from them. But while he questioned their methods, he never doubted their fundamental intention, which was to create beauty and to share sensibilities, to communicate wonder at the richness of the world around us and the various ways our senses give us of responding to it. His music is without ideology and without doctrine. Like the world, it simply is, take it or leave it.

Acknowledgements

L ike any book that combines facts with ideas, mine is the outcome of years of contact with other musicians, composers, pianists, fellow critics, and straightforward music lovers, who often come out with suggestive thoughts about music from direct experience, uncluttered by theories of music history. This is particularly true of Debussy, a composer loved by many who respond instinctively to the beauty of his music without it occurring to them that he might seriously be regarded as one of the very greatest, which is roughly speaking my view. Luckily the brain is a sponge that absorbs without remembering, which is why this list of credits is short. My most obvious debt is to the authors of the books cited in the footnotes and bibliography, often supplemented and enriched by personal conversation, especially with Paul Roberts and with Roger Nichols, always a generous adviser on matters French. In general, Debussy is a composer other composers talk about, and I have learnt a great deal from conversations with Anthony Powers, Robin Holloway, George Benjamin, and others too numerous to list. Colin Matthews read the manuscript and made a number of acute observations, most of which I have incorporated. On painters, I have been enormously helped (though it may surprise them) by Charles MacCarthy, Susannah Fiennes, and my cousin-in-law Richard Dorment, whose writings on art are an object lesson in how to combine aesthetic criticism with the discussion of techniques and materials.

The book is a biography, but the biographical materials are mainly from published sources, all I hope duly acknowledged. It has not involved endless trekking from foreign archive to foreign archive, but could not have been written without the generous and efficient help of, in particular, the music librarians at Cardiff University, who have never hesitated to track down, copy and send vital materials to this remote and now ineffectual don. It has been a huge pleasure to work once again with Jill Burrows, a perfect, meticulous, but unpernickety copy editor, and with Belinda Matthews at Faber, an attentive publisher who knows how to make pressure look and feel like encouragement. My gratitude to Chuck Elliott, Knopf's long-standing commissioning editor in the UK and a dependable sounding-board on all aspects of what is and is not required of a book of this kind, is I hope adequately recognised in the dedication.

I have taken the opportunity afforded by the slightly later publication date of this American edition to make a small number of corrections. I am grateful to Roger Nichols for his suggestions in this respect. Needless to say, I take full responsibility for any errors that remain.

STEPHEN WALSH
Welsh Newton, March 2018

Notes

ABBREVIATIONS

CDMC: François Lesure (ed.), *Claude Debussy: Monsieur Croche et autres écrits* (Gallimard, Paris, 1987)

Corr.: François Lesure and Denis Herlin (eds), *Claude Debussy: Correspondance (1872–1918)* (Gallimard, Paris, 2005)

DoM: Richard Langham Smith (ed. and trans.), *Debussy on Music* (Secker & Warburg, London, 1977)

LCD: François Lesure, *Claude Debussy* (Fayard, Paris, 2003)

PRELUDE A BIOGRAPHY OF SORTS

1 Pierre Boulez, *Relevés d'apprenti* (Editions du Seuil, Paris, 1966); *Stocktakings from an Apprenticeship*, trans. Stephen Walsh (Clarendon Press, Oxford, 1991), 275.

2 Martin Cooper, *French Music from the Death of Berlioz to the Death of Fauré* (Oxford University Press, London, 1961), 1–2.

3 *Gil Blas*, 2 February 1903, in *CDMC*, 91; *DoM*, 111–12.

4 *Gil Blas*, 8 May 1903, in *CDMC*, 169; *DoM*, 193.

5 Letters of "Thursday," February 1893, to André Poniatowski, *Corr.*, 115; and mid-September 1903, to Charles Levadé, *Corr.*, 784.

6 *Gil Blas*, 26 January 1903, in *CDMC*, 85; *DoM*, 101.

7 Friedrich Nietzsche, *Der Fall Wagner* (C. G. Naumann, Leipzig, 1895), 16.

8 Letter of 27 August 1906 to Louis Laloy, *Corr.*, 967.

I THE PRISONER AND THE PRODIGY

1 As a child and young man, Debussy always went by the name of Achille. He switched to Claude only in 1890.

2 Letter to Jacques Durand, 1 September 1915, in *Corr.*, 1926–27.

3 Annie Joly-Segalen and André Schaeffner, *Segalen et Debussy*, quoted in *LCD*, 20.

4 *LCD*, 18.

5 *LCD*, 19.

6 Léon Vallas, *Claude Debussy: His Life and Works*, trans. Maire and Grace O'Brien (Dover, New York, 1973), 9.

7 *LCD*, 35.

8 Roger Nichols (ed.), *Debussy Remembered* (Faber, London, 1992), 6.

9 Edward Lockspeiser, *Debussy: His Life and Mind*, vol. 1 (Cassell, London, 1962), 16; *LCD*, 13.

10 *Le Temps*, quoted in *LCD*, 26.

11 *LCD*, 31.

12 *LCD*, 33.

13 *LCD*, 28.

14 Lockspeiser, vol. 1, 37.

15 *LCD*, 60.

16 *LCD*, 42–3.

17 Letter of 7/19 August 1880, in V.A. Zhdanov and N.T. Zhegin (eds), *P.I. Tchaikovsky: perepiska s N.F. von Mekk*, vol. 2 (Academia, Moscow and Leningrad, 1935), 394.

18 Ibid.

19 *LCD*, 47.

20 Letter of 10 August 1880, in Zhdanov and Zhegin (eds), 389.

21 *LCD*, 46.

22 *Gil Blas*, 13 April 1903, in *CDMC*, 149, *DoM*, 173.

23 Quoted in Lockspeiser, vol. 1, 33.

24 Ibid., 65. See also François Lesure, "Debussy et le Chat Noir," *Cahiers Debussy*, 23 (1999), 35–43.

25 *LCD*, 49–50.

2 SONGS FOR MARIE

1 The phrase is Paul Vidal's, in a letter of 12 July 1884 to Henriette Fuchs. Vidal, for a time a close friend of Debussy, sided with his parents over the Vasnier affair. See Roger Nichols (ed.), *Debussy Remembered*, 24.

2 *LCD*, 51, 53.

3 *LCD*, 51.

4 Nichols, 17–18.

5 Ibid., 10.

6 Ibid., 18–19.

7 Letter of 23 June 1908, *Corr.*, 1098.

8 Nichols, 16.

9 *LCD*, 57.

10 *LCD*, 61.

11 *LCD*, 68.

12 *Gil Blas*, 10 June 1903, in *CDMC*, 188–9; *DoM*, 211.

3 UP AT THE VILLA

1 Letter of early February 1885, *Corr.*, 22–3.

2 Roger Nichols (ed.), *Debussy Remembered*, 8.

3 *LCD*, 75.

4 Letter of "Tuesday" [February/March 1885], *Corr.*, 25.

5 Letters of 4 June, [late June], and 19 October 1885, respectively, *Corr.*, 29, 32, 43.

6 *LCD*, 498.

7 Letters of 19 October and 24 November, *Corr.*, 42–3, 45.

8 *LCD*, 500.

9 John Rewald, *The History of Impressionism* (Secker & Warburg, London, 1973),

323, 320. See also Richard R. Brettell, *Impression: Painting Quickly in France 1860–1890* (Yale University Press, New Haven and London, 2000), *passim*.

10 *LCD*, 87.

11 *LCD*, 84.

12 Letter of early August 1889, *Corr.*, 78.

13 *Le Figaro*, 18 September 1886.

14 Letter of 4 June, *Corr.*, 29.

15 Ibid.

16 Richard Langham Smith, "Debussy and the Pre-Raphaelites," *19th-Century Music*, v (1981–82), 95–109.

17 Ibid., 99.

18 For a detailed discussion of the parallels between *La Damoiselle élue* and *Parsifal*, see Robin Holloway, *Debussy and Wagner* (Eulenburg, London, 1979), 22–42.

19 *LCD*, 502.

20 Emmanuel Chabrier to Ernest Van Dick, quoted in *LCD*, 97.

21 For more on Godet, see Edward Lockspeiser, *Debussy, His Life and Mind*, vol. 1, 103–7.

22 Bernard Lazare, quoted in *LCD*, 100.

23 "L'Art romantique," in H. Lemaitre (ed.), *Baudelaire: Curiosités Esthétiques* (Paris, Garnier, 1962), 697.

4 NEW RULES, OLD MORALS

1 See Annegret Fauser, *Musical Encounters at the 1889 Paris World's Fair* (University of Rochester Press, Rochester, New York and Woodbridge, 2005); also Anik Devriès, "Les Musiques d'Extrême-Orient à l'Exposition Universelle de 1889," in *Cahiers Debussy*, 1 (1977), 24–37.

2 Letter of 22 January 1895, *Corr.*, 237.

3 *S.I.M.* bulletin, 15 February 1913, in *CDMC*, 229–30.

4 Ibid., 229.

5 Letter of early August 1889, *Corr.*, 78.

6 The literal transcription of Maurice Emmanuel's notes is in *Inédits sur Claude Debussy* (Les Publications Techniques, Paris, n.d. [1942]), 27–33. A grammatically tidied up English translation is in Edward Lockspeiser, *Debussy: His Life and Mind*, vol. 1, 204–8.

7 Letter of 10 August 1909 to Edgard Varèse, *Corr.*, 1204.

8 Richard Mueller, "Javanese Influence on Debussy's 'Fantaisie' and beyond," *19th-Century Music*, x/2 (autumn 1986), 157–86.

9 Letter of 21 April 1905, *Corr.*, 904.

10 Letter of 30 January 1892, *Corr.*, 103.

11 Robert Orledge, *Debussy and the Theatre* (Cambridge University Press, Cambridge, 1982), 19.

12 Undated note, *Corr.*, 93.

13 See Marcel Dietschy, *A Portrait of Claude Debussy*, trans. William Ashbrook and Margaret G. Cobb (Clarendon Press, Oxford, 1990), 71–2, for these and other details.

14 Roger Nichols (ed.), *Debussy Remembered*, 135.

15 By way of the second line of the song, "Les lauriers sont coupés"—"The laurels are cut." A laurel branch above the porch was the sign for a brothel. See *Confidentielle*, http://www.confidentielles.com/r_9235_nous-n-irons-plus-au-bois-les-lauriers-sont-coupes.htm, for a detailed account of this ban and its causes.

16 Letter of 12 February 1891, *Corr.*, 95.

17 *LCD*, 458.

18 Quoted in Nichols, 37.

19 According to the pianist Marcel Ciampi, quoted in Jean-Michel Nectoux, *Harmonie en bleu et or* (Fayard, Paris, 2005), 132.

20 Quoted in Nectoux, 78.

21 Letter of 15 July 1905, in Rollo Myers (ed.), *Richard Strauss & Romain Rolland: Correspondence, Diary & Essays* (Calder and Boyars, London, 1951), 35.

22 André Suarès to Romain Rolland, quoted in *LCD*, 122–3.

23 Letters of 9 September 1892 and "Thursday February 1893," *Corr.*, 110, 117.

24 Letters of 22 September 1894 and 13 October 1896, *Corr.*, 222–3, 326.

25 Letter of 10 April 1895, *Corr.*, 249.

26 Quoted in Roy Howat, *The Art of French Piano Music* (Yale University Press, New Haven and London, 2009), 41. Grayson is writing about the later *Chansons de Bilitis*.

27 Letter to Ernest Chausson, 3 September 1893, *Corr.*, 154–5.

28 Letter to Ernest Chausson, 2 October 1893, *Corr.*, 160.

29 Letter to Ernest Chausson, 3 September 1893, *Corr.*, 154–5.

30 Letter of "dimanche après-midi" [2 July 1893], *Corr.*, 140.

5 MALLARMÉ AND MAETERLINCK

1 Roger Nichols (ed.), *Debussy Remembered*, 40. The Théâtre Guignol on the Champs-Élysées was (and is) a puppet theatre, named after the stock hero of French puppet shows.

2 Stéphane Mallarmé, *Divagations* (Fasquelle, Paris, 1897), 221.

3 *LCD*, 140.

4 See Denis Herlin, "*Pelléas et Mélisande* aux Bouffes-Parisiens," in Jean-Christophe Branger, Sylvie Douche and Denis Herlin (eds), *Pelléas et Mélisande: Cent ans après* (Symétrie, Lyon, 2012), 43, for the argument that he had not read the play until after he saw it. But the argument is inconsistent, depending on a handwritten note by Debussy of unknown date and now vanished, and partly on Louis Laloy's report that Debussy confided his plan to Pierre Louÿs, to whom Debussy was not close until October 1893. Debussy was certainly at work on the opera by August, a fact that effectively invalidates Laloy's memory.

5 Letter of Debussy to Georges Jean-Aubry, 25 March 1910, *Corr.*, 1261.

6 Letter of 22 May 1893, *Corr.*, 130.

7 Letter of 7 May 1893, *Corr.*, 127.

8 Letter of 10 October 1895, *Corr.*, 278.

9 Ibid.

10 *La Tribuna*, 23 February 1914, quoted in François Lesure, "Une Interview Romaine de Debussy," *Cahiers Debussy*, 11 (1987), 5.

11 Letter of "Thursday," February 1893, *Corr.*, 116.

12 Quoted in *LCD*, 134.

13 Letter of 22 May 1893, *Corr.*, 130.

14 Letter of 24 May 1893, *Corr.*, 131.

15 Letter of 4 June 1893, *Corr.*, 133–4.

16 Jean-Michel Nectoux, *Harmonie en bleu et or*, 52.

17 Letter of *c.*24 February 1894, *Corr.*, 196–7.

18 Letter of 25 February, in Nichols, 43.

19 Letter of 28 February, in Nichols, 44.

20 *Corr.*, 200.

21 *Corr.*, 202.

22 Quoted in Nectoux, 58.

23 Interview in the *Daily Mail*, 28 May 1909, quoted in Annie Labussière, "La mélodie dramatique dans *Pelléas et Mélisande*," in Branger et al., 215.

24 Letter of 2 October 1893, *Corr.*, 161.

25 Stefan Jarocinski, *Debussy: Impressionism and Symbolism*, trans. Rollo Myers (Eulenburg, London, 1976), 38.

26 Letter of 17 August 1895, *Corr.*, 268.

27 Letter of "Friday" [20 July 1894], *Corr.*, 215.

28 Letter of 28 August 1894, *Corr.*, 219–20.

29 Letter of 22 January 1895, *Corr.*, 237–8.

30 Letter of 17 August 1895, *Corr.*, 268.

6 BILITIS AND OTHER WOMEN

1 *Gil Blas*, 20 April 1903; in *CDMC*, 153; *DoM*, 177.

2 Letter of 16 November 1893 to Ernest Chausson, *Corr.*, 176.

3 *LCD*, 151–2.

4 Letter of 29 July 1894, *Corr.*, 217–18.

5 Letter of 10 December 1894, *Corr.*, 227.

6 Ibid.

7 Marguerite Long, *At the Piano with Debussy*, trans. O. Senior-Ellis (J. M. Dent, London, 1972), 23.

8 Letters of "Vendredi" [April–May 1895] and 12 May 1895, *Corr.*, 254–5, 257 (italics Louÿs's).

9 Letter to Louÿs of 8 May 1896, *Corr.*, 313.

10 Letter of 13 October 1896, *Corr.*, 326.

11 Roger Nichols (ed.), *Debussy Remembered*, 57.

12 Ibid., 59.

13 Roger Nichols, *The Life of Debussy* (Cambridge University Press, Cambridge, 1998), 96.

14 For René Peter's play Debussy eventually produced a short *Berceuse* for unaccompanied voice, but not a note otherwise.

15 The *Trois Chansons de Charles d'Orléans* were made up to three in 1908 by a brilliant setting of "Quand j'ay ouy le tabourin," with the lower voices imitating an instrumental dance accompaniment. Sadly, these are Debussy's only pieces for unaccompanied choir.

16 Nichols (ed.), *Debussy Remembered*, 34.

17 Letter of "Tuesday evening, 9 [February] 1897," *Corr.*, 342.

18 Letter of 27 March 1898, *Corr.*, 394–5.

19 Quoted in Henri Bourgeaud (ed.), *Correspondance de Claude Debussy et Pierre Louÿs* (Librairie José Corti, Paris, 1945), 109n.

20 Ibid.

21 Dietschy, *A Portrait of Claude Debussy*, 105; Pierre Louÿs, *Les Chansons de Bilitis*, No. XXXVII.

22 Letter of 25 October [1900], *Corr.*, 571.

23 Some of the pieces were later reconstituted as the *Six Épigraphes antiques* for piano duet. See below, chapter 12.

24 Letters of 9 September 1892 and "Thursday," February 1893, *Corr.*, 110, 117.

25 Letters of 25 June and 14 July 1898, *Corr.*, 408, 412.

26 Letter of 16 September 1898, *Corr.*, 419.

27 *Corr.*, 510; my italics, but the emphasis is implied by Debussy's change of tense.

28 Letter of 24 September 1899, *Corr.*, 518.

29 Letter of 22 September 1894, *Corr.*, 222–3.

30 Reprinted in Brettell, *Impression*, 233–5 (trans. Susan Barrow).

31 Quoted in Jean-Michel Nectoux, *Harmonie en bleu et or*, 218 (italics Kandinsky's).

32 These two songs, "Nuit sans fin" and "Lorsqu'elle est entrée," remained unpublished until 2000.

33 Letter of 25 August 1912 to André Caplet, *Corr.*, 1540; *La Revue blanche*, 1 July 1901, in *CDMC*, 49; *DoM*, 45.

34 Quoted without date in François Lesure (ed.), *Claude Debussy: Correspondance 1884–1918* (Hermann, Paris, 1993), 161, n. 79.

35 Quoted in Nectoux, 106.

36 Letter of 18 November 1858 (Old Style) to Balakirev, quoted in Stephen Walsh, *Musorgsky and His Circle* (Faber & Faber, London, 2013), 57.

37 Letter to Poujaud in Lesure (ed.), *Claude Debussy: Correspondance 1884–1918*, 161, n. 79.

38 He also later begged Gabriel Pierné not to conduct *Jeux de vagues*, the second movement of *La Mer*, on its own. See his letter to Pierné of 22 October 1907, *Corr.*, 1036–7.

39 Nectoux, 139.

7 LILLY VERSUS THE PIANO

1 Dietschy, *A Portrait of Claude Debussy*, 107.

2 He had once gone to San Sebastian, ten miles over the border, to attend a bullfight.

3 Howat, *The Art of French Piano Music*, 115.

4 *CDMC*, 23–4 ; *DoM*, 13.

5 *DoM*, 10.

6 *CDMC*, respectively, 25–6, 51, 36, 59–60, 52, 46, 28–9; *DoM*, 15, 28, 47, 56–7, 48, 41, 20–21.

7 "L'Entretien avec M. Croche," *CDMC*, 48–53; *DoM*, 44–9.

8 Ibid., 50, 46.

9 Hugh Wood, *Staking Out the Territory* (Plumbago, London, 2007), 5.

10 *Le Figaro*, 14 April 1902, quoted in Orledge, *Debussy and the Theatre*, 350, n. 19.

11 Quoted in *LCD*, 218.

12 Henri Busser, quoted in Orledge, 63.

13 *LCD*, 220, n. 14.

14 Gustave Bret, quoted in *DoM*, 81, n. 1.

15 *CDMC*, 275–7; *DoM*, 79–81.

16 Roger Nichols, entry on Debussy, in Stanley Sadie (ed.), *The New Grove Dictionary of Music and Musicians,* vol. 5 (Macmillan, London, 1980), 296.

17 *LCD*, 242.

18 Letter to Paul-Jean Toulet, 25 October 1902, *Corr.*, 697.

19 Letter to André Messager, 8 June 1903, *Corr.*, 742.

20 *CDMC*, 169; *DoM*, 193.

21 *CDMC*, 153; *DoM*, 177.

22 *CDMC*, 91; *DoM*, 112.

23 *CDMC*, 148; *DoM*, 172. The play he refers to was Eugène Sue's *Le Juif errant*. In a characteristically fascinating footnote (*DoM*, 176, n. 2), Langham Smith suggests that Debussy may also have been remembering Henri Rivière's shadowplays at the Chat Noir, which had also featured Sue's melodrama.

24 *DoM*, 109, n. 3. Langham Smith explains that Colette failed to get *pipi* past her sub-editor. It was restored by her husband, quoting her in an article in 1927.

25 *DoM*, 162, n. 2.

26 *CDMC*, 138–9; *DoM*, 161.

27 *CDMC*, 196, 192; *DoM*, 218, 215.

28 *Corr.*, 758–9.

29 *Corr.*, 757.

30 *Corr.*, 759.

31 See above, chapter 4 and n. 15 for another reason for not going to the woods any more.

8 TAKING TO THE WATER

1 Letter of 27 March 1898 to Pierre Louÿs, *Corr.*, 395.

2 Letter of 16 July 1904, *Corr.*, 852–3.

3 Letter of 19 July 1904, *Corr.*, 853.

4 Letter of 11 August 1904, *Corr.*, 861.

5 See Eric Jensen, *Debussy* (Oxford University Press, Oxford, 2014), 214, for the latest incarnation of this error—untypical, however, of a mostly very reliable and useful study.

6 Letter of 12 October 1904, *Corr.*, 869.

7 *LCD*, 189, n. 5 (emphasis in the source).

8 *Corr.*, 872, n. 2. Bardac's phrase, "elle vient de se payer le dernier musicien à la mode" (literally "she's just paid herself the latest musicien à la mode") puns on Bardac being the one with the actual money, but doesn't translate well.

9 *LCD*, 266–7.

10 Letters of late August 1903 to Colonne, *Corr.*, 773; 12 September 1903 to Durand, *Corr.*, 779.

11 Letters of 19 July, 30 July 1904, *Corr.*, 854, 856.

12 Letter of 12 September 1903, *Corr.*, 780.

13 Letter of 31 July/4 August 1904, *Corr.*, 859, quoting Manon's aria, "Je suis encore tout étourdie," in Act I of Massenet's opera.

14 Letter of 28 July 1915 to Désiré-Émile Ingelbrecht, *Corr.*, 1913–14. The somewhat obscure allusion to the old captain is perhaps a reference to Huysmans's "old skipper of the line . . . who sloshes the sediment of his absinthe while dripping into his glass, drop by drop, iced water from a carafe" ("Les Quartiers de la rive gauche," *La Revue indépendante*, 11 September 1887).

15 Letter of 24 September 1904, *Corr.*, 868.

16 Letter of January 1905, *Corr.*, 882–3.

17 As in Erik Satie's well-known jibe: "There was especially a little moment between half-past ten and a quarter to eleven that I found amazing." Quoted in Robert Orledge, *Satie the Composer* (Cambridge University Press, Cambridge, 1990), 245.

18 The Scotch snap is a strongly accented short–long rhythm, typical of the Scottish dance the Strathspey. Well-known examples occur in the songs "The Road to the Isles" ("As step I wi' my cromak to the Isles"), and "Comin' thro' the rye."

19 Louis Schneider, *Gil Blas*, 16 October 1905, quoted in *Corr.*, 927, n. 1.

20 Pierre Lalo, *Le Temps*, 24 October 1905, quoted in *Corr.*, 927, n. 3.

21 Letter of 25 October 1905, *Corr.*, 927–8.

22 January 1904. Quoted in *LCD*, 255.

23 Lesure's argument, however, is based on a Will drawn up in 1906, whereby the uncle left most of his money to the Pasteur Institute. This would seem not to disprove the theory that the uncle disinherited Emma because of her elopement. Lesure makes no reference to any earlier Will. It's true anyway that she was not wholly disinherited. He left her a competence of 5,000 francs per annum, equivalent to about £200 or $1,000 at 1907 values.

24 Letter of 26 July 1905, *Corr.*, 912–13.

25 Letter of 18 August, *Corr.*, 914.

26 Letter of 11 September, *Corr.*, 919. The last four words are in English, presumably a reference to Shakespeare's play, which Jean-Paul Toulet had turned into a libretto for Debussy in 1903. No music for it was ever composed.

27 Marguerite Long, *At the Piano with Debussy*, 25.

28 Richard Boothby, *Freud as Philosopher: Metapsychology after Lacan* (Routledge, New York & London, 2001), 23.

29 *Gil Blas*, 2 February 1903; *CDMC*, 91; *DoM*, 112.

9 IMAGES IN NAME AS WELL AS FACT

1 Louis Laloy, *La Musique retrouvée* (Librairie Plon, Paris, 1928), 120–21.

2 *LCD*, 251.

3 Letter to Laloy of 4 January 1903, *Corr.*, 712.

4 Letter to Laloy of 14 April 1905, *Corr.*, 900–901. The *Roman chez la portière* was a vaudeville of the 1850s about the omniscience of the janitress who watches everybody else's life go by and so is never able to finish the novel she's reading.

5 Laloy, 141.

6 Letter of January 1905.

7 Letter of 13 September 1905, *Corr.*, 921.

8 Letter of 16 May to Jacques Durand, *Corr.*, 908. *Valse* is followed by a question mark.

9 Letter of 3 September 1907, to Durand.

10 Letter of 6 January 1909, *Corr.*, 1145.

11 Letters of 29 September 1905, 7 July 1906, and 8 August 1906, *Corr.*, 923, 960, 962.

12 Robert Orledge, *Debussy and the Theatre*, 250. Orledge has also discovered and made a performing version of a "Death of Cordelia."

13 Letter of 26 August 1907, *Corr.*, 1027.

14 Letter of 27 August 1908, *Corr.*, 1110–11.

15 Laloy, 175.

16 Quoted in *Corr.*, 1021, n. 1.

17 Letter of 7 July 1906, *Corr.*, 960. The French is "faire remuer les voix"—"making the voices move"—something more specific, surely, than Roger Nichols's "writing for voices," or Orledge's "to treat voices." Debussy is dealing with crowd scenes and was perhaps thinking of something along the lines of Musorgsky's choral chatter in *Boris Godunov*, or perhaps, as Andrew Porter suggested in *Music of Three Seasons, 1974–1977* (p. 534), "a vocal counterpart to the texture of *La Mer*." Some years later Debussy elaborated this idea in a letter to Godet: "For *The Devil in the Belfry* . . . I should like to achieve an extremely simple, yet extremely mobile choral writing . . . Understand me . . . the veneering of *Boris* doesn't satisfy me any more than the relentless counterpoint in the Act 2 finale of *Meistersinger*, which in the end is nothing but cold disorder . . . There's certainly something else to be found: some clever *trompe-l'oreille*, for example" (letter of 6 February 1911, *Corr.*, 1385). Sadly, he never found it.

18 Letter of 5 July 1908, *Corr.*, 1100–11, and n. 1 (part quoted also in Porter, 532).

19 Letter of 18 June 1908, *Corr.*, 1097.

20 Letter of 18 July 1908, *Corr.*, 1102.

21 Letter of 13 July 1909, *Corr.*, 1195.

22 Letter of 18 April 1906 to Durand, *Corr.*, 951. "Je croupis dans les Usines du Négatif," from Jules Laforgue's *Dragées grises*. This was a favourite quotation of Debussy's; see, for instance, chapter 13, n. 22.

23 Letter of 15 August 1908, *Corr.*, 1109.

24 Letter of 24/25 February 1906, *Corr.*, 940.

25 *CDMC*, 29; *DoM*, 21.

26 Letter of 24/25 February. Debussy's attitude anticipates Stravinsky's remark, "I can wait as an insect waits."

27 Letter of 31 December 1905 to Durand, *Corr.*, 933.

28 Letter of 23 May 1907, *Corr.*, 1009.

29 Letter of 24/25 February.

30 Letter of 22 February 1907, *Corr.*, 996.

31 Letter of 23 May.

32 Letter of 8 August 1906 to Durand, *Corr.*, 962.

33 Letter of 27 August 1906 to Laloy, *Corr.*, 967.

34 Conversation between Victor Segalen and Debussy, reprinted in *Corr.*, 2199.

35 Quoted in Marcel Dietschy, *A Portrait of Claude Debussy*, 150.

36 Letter of 3 September 1907, *Corr.*, 1030.

37 Paul Roberts, *Images: The Piano Music of Claude Debussy* (Amadeus Press, Portland, Oregon, 1996), 293.
38 Letter of late September/early October 1907, *Corr.*, 1034.
39 Letter of 6 August 1907, *Corr.*, 1024.
40 After Albéniz's death in 1909, Debussy was asked by his widow to orchestrate some of his piano pieces, but Debussy declined. See *LCD*, 323–4.
41 Edward Lockspeiser identifies this as a translation of a canzona by the fifteenth-century Tuscan poet and dramatist, Poliziano: "Ben venga Maggio"; *Debussy: His Life and Mind*, vol. 2 (Cassell, London, 1965), 30.
42 Letter of 5 February 1909, *Corr.*, 1149.
43 Lockspeiser, 31.

10 A CRUMBLING HOUSE AND A SUNKEN CATHEDRAL

1   Letter of 15 January 1908, *Corr.*, 1054–5.
2   *Comoedia*, 20 January 1908, quoted in *LCD*, 296.
3   Letter of 31 January 1908, *Corr.*, 1062–3, n. 6.
4   Henry J. Wood, *My Life of Music* (Gollancz, London, 1938), 228–9 (italics Wood's).
5   Louis Laloy, *La Musique retrouvée*, 93.
6   Letter of 25 February 1910, *Corr.*, 1252–3.
7   Letter of 25 August 1909, *Corr.*, 1206–7.
8   Letter of 22 December 1911, *Corr.*, 1472–3.
9   Letter of 21 September 1909, *Corr.*, 1215.
10 *Azest*, 6 December 1910, quoted in Robert Orledge, *Debussy and the Theatre*, 119.
11 Andrew Porter, *Music of Three Seasons, 1974–1977* (Farrar Straus Giroux, New York, 1978), 534.
12 Letter of 26 June 1909, *Corr.*, 1193. The phrase "enough to make the stones weep" is sung by Golaud at Mélisande's deathbed in Act 5 of *Pelléas et Mélisande*. "Est-ce que ce n'est pas à faire pleurer les pierres!"
13 Letter of 18 December 1911, *Corr.*, 1471.
14 Letter of 12 June 1909, *Corr.*, 1191.
15 Letter of 20 January 1910, *Corr.*, 1240.
16 Louisa Shirley Liebich, "An Englishwoman's Memories of Debussy," *Musical Times*, LIX (1 June 1918), 250.
17 Paul Roberts, *Images: The Piano Music of Claude Debussy*, 245.
18 The perils of Wikipedia are nicely illustrated in its assertion that Debussy was a regular visitor to Anacapri. He may conceivably have visited with the von Mecks in 1880, during his only stay in Naples, but no such visit is recorded.
19 Although Debussy had disliked the Fauves when he saw their work at the Salon d'Automne in October 1908.
20 Letter of 3 September 1907, *Corr.*, 1030.
21 *La Sérénade interrompue* is one of the three undated preludes in the first book, but Debussy told Durand that the set was complete on 5 February, while *Ibéria* was first performed only on the 15th.
22 Roberts, *Images*, 193–4.
23 Hans Christian Andersen, *Forty Stories*, trans. M. R. James (Faber, London, 1930), 175.

24 Robert Godet, "Weber and Debussy," *The Chesterian* (June 1926), quoted in *DoM*, 106.

25 Letter to Jacques Durand, 15 July 1910, *Corr.*, 1302. The sight-reading test piece was published in December 1910 as "Petite pièce pour clarinette et piano."

26 Letters of 30 March and 8 July, *Corr.*, 1263, 1299.

27 Undated letter of, probably, 1910, *Corr.*, 1366.

11 THEATRES OF THE BODY AND THE MIND

1 Letter of 21 November 1910, *Corr.*, 1331–2.

2 Letter of 3 December 1910, *Corr.*, 1344.

3 Letter of 1 December 1910, *Corr.*, 1341.

4 Letter of 12 September 1912, *Corr.*, 1545.

5 Letter to Jacques Durand, 1 February 1912, *Corr.*, 1491.

6 Robert Orledge, *Debussy and the Theatre*, 145–7.

7 Letter of 25 November 1910, *Corr.*, 1335–6.

8 Letter of 30 November 1910, *Corr.*, 1339–40.

9 Letter of 29 January 1911, *Corr.*, 1380; also to Emma Debussy, 3 December 1910; *Corr.*, 1344.

10 Quoted in *Corr.*, 1392, n. 2.

11 *LCD*, 339.

12 Henry Bidou, *Journal des débats*, 29 May 1911, quoted in Orledge, 227.

13 Louis Laloy, *La Musique retrouvée*, 207–8. The 1912 concert performance, conducted by Désiré-Émile Inghelbrecht, used a heavily abridged version of the play.

14 Letter of 13 April 1912, *Corr.*, 1503. The *Firebird* quote is in Igor Stravinsky and Robert Craft, *Expositions and Developments* (Faber, London, 1962), 131.

15 Letter of 7 November 1912, *Corr.*, 1554.

16 Letter of 25 June 1911, *Corr.*, 1432–3.

17 Letter of 13 July 1911 to Durand, *Corr.*, 1436.

18 Letter of 15 August 1911, *Corr.*, 1445. But it was Hamlet who said, "There are more things in heaven and earth, Horatio, than are dreamt of in your philosophy." Perhaps Debussy's mistake was triggered by a sudden thought about Chouchou and his own virtue.

19 Letter to André Caplet, 17 November 1911, *Corr.*, 1463.

20 See Orledge, 206–16, for more details of this project, including a transcription of the main sketch.

21 Interview in *La Tribuna*, 23 February 1914, quoted in *Corr.*, 1585, n. 1.

22 Vaslav Nijinsky, *The Diary of Vaslav Nijinsky*, trans. Romola Nijinsky (Quartet, London, 1991), 123.

23 See Diaghilev's letter to him of 18 July 1912, *Corr.*, 1530–31.

24 Probably just the first part. The myth that Debussy participated in this play-through still persists in the literature on both composers. At that stage there cannot have been a usable four-hand score of any of the music. Laloy himself correctly describes a four-hand play-through by Stravinsky and Debussy, also at his house, in May 1913, a few days before the premiere, but Laloy's report has routinely been questioned because of Debussy's reminiscence, quoted here in the main text. See

Laloy, 213; also Stephen Walsh, *Stravinsky: A Creative Spring* (Knopf, New York, 1999), 181 and 593, n. 63.

25 Letter of 7 November 1912, *Corr.*, 1554–5. See also n. 2, which falls into the trap outlined in my n. 24 above. After quoting Laloy's invitation to Stravinsky to bring *The Rite of Spring* to his house on 2 June 1912, the editor then quotes Laloy's description of the May 1913 run-through as if they were the same event.

26 Letter of 18 July (emphases Diaghilev's). The idea of the man on points was eventually discarded. See Lynn Garafola, *Diaghilev's Ballets Russes* (Oxford University Press, New York, 1989), 60.

27 Letter of 25 August 1912, *Corr.*, 1540.

28 Letter of 9 August 1912, *Corr.*, 1537.

29 The theatre had actually been inaugurated with a concert six weeks before, in which Debussy had himself conducted his *Prélude à l'après-midi d'un faune*.

30 Robin Holloway, *Debussy and Wagner*, 160–94.

31 Henri Quittard in *Le Figaro*, quoted in Richard Buckle, *Diaghilev* (Weidenfeld and Nicolson, London, 1979), 251.

32 Tamara Karsavina, *Theatre Street* (Constable, London, 1948), 237.

33 Letter of 9 June 1913, *Corr.*, 1619, also n. 2.

34 This rather convincing idea is Robert Orledge's. See, for instance, Orledge, 183.

35 I'm grateful to Colin Matthews for drawing my attention to this similarity.

36 *Corr.*, 1503.

37 René Puaux, "Notes indiennes: Amber," *Le Temps* (10 August 1912), 4.

38 Jann Pasler, "Timbre, Voice leading, and the Musical Arabesque in Debussy's Piano Music," in James R. Briscoe (ed.), *Debussy in Performance* (Yale University Press, New Haven and London, 1999), 225–55.

12 WAR IN BLACK AND WHITE

1 Letter of 29 May 1913 to André Caplet, *Corr.*, 1609. Debussy had probably attended the previous day's dress rehearsal, which went off without disturbance, and he had also played through the four-hand arrangement with Stravinsky at Louis Laloy's house a few days earlier, as described by Laloy himself in *La Musique retrouvée*, 213. The four-hand edition was published in June, so the run-through will have been either from a proof or from a pre-publication copy. See also chapter 11, nn. 24 and 25.

2 I like the American composer Carl Ruggles's alleged, typical frontiersman's judgement: "Nothing wrong with Debussy that a few weeks in the open air wouldn't cure."

3 See Eric Jensen, *Debussy*, 115–18, for more on this.

4 Letter of 15 July 1913, *Corr.*, 1641.

5 Letter of 18 January 1913, *Corr.*, 1580.

6 *CDMC*, 244.

7 *CDMC*, 223.

8 *CDMC*, 232.

9 *CDMC*, 247.

10 *CDMC*, 229.

11 *CDMC*, 247.

12 There is some evidence that Debussy initially also planned a new setting of "Apparition." See Paolo dal Molin and Jean-Louis Leleu, "Comment composait Debussy: les leçons d'un carnet de travail (à propos de *Soupir* et d'*Éventail*)," in *Cahiers Debussy*, 35 (2011).

13 Letter of 8 August 1913, *Corr.*, 1651–2.

14 See his letter to Robert Godet of 14 October 1915, *Corr.*, 1948; also ibid., note 1, quoting a remark of Debussy's to Michel-Dimitri Calvocoressi.

15 Undated letter, 20 February 1909, *Corr.*, 1155. There is some disagreement over the letter's date, which Robert Orledge places in 1913. In any case the project was in principle in the wind in the latter part of that year.

16 Letter of 24 November 1913, *Corr.*, 1702.

17 Letters of 25 July 1913 to Jacques Durand and André Hellé, *Corr.*, 1646.

18 Letters of 7 and 11 August, and 5 September, *Corr.*, 1651, 1653, 1662.

19 Letter of 7 August.

20 "Claude Debussy nous dit ses projets de théâtre," *Comoedia*, 1 February 1914, in *CDMC*, 329–30; *DoM*, 311–12.

21 Footnote in the score. This is the music that might possibly be the discarded prelude, "Tomai des éléphants." See above, chapter 11.

22 Letter of 9 October 1914, *Corr.*, 1852.

23 See Robert Orledge, *Debussy and the Theatre*, 186–94 and 200–205, for these and many other details.

24 Letter of 13/26 February 1914, in Viktor Varunts (ed.), *I. F. Stravinskiy: Perepiska s russkimi korrespondentami*, vol. 2 (Kompozitor, Moscow, 2000), 229.

25 Letter of 5/18 July 1913, *Corr.*, 1643–4.

26 *Corr.*, 1723, n. 3.

27 Letter of 7 December 1913, *Corr.*, 1716.

28 Letter of 8 December, *Corr.*, 1717.

29 Letter of 11 December, *Corr.*, 1721.

30 Letter of 14 July 1914, *Corr.*, 1836. What the accident was is not known.

31 Letters of 8 and 18 August 1914, *Corr.*, 1842–4.

32 Letter of 5 October 1914 to Paul Dukas, *Corr.*, 1851.

33 Letter of late September 1914, *Corr.*, 1849–50.

34 Letter of 11 July 1914, *Corr.*, 1834. He later made a transcription for solo piano.

35 An exception is Frank Dawes in his useful handbook *Debussy Piano Music* (BBC, London, 1969), 52–4. Some of his identifications are wrong, but this is because at that time he did not have access to the unpublished *musique de scène*.

36 Letter of 1 January 1915, *Corr.*, 1863.

37 Ibid. He means Archimedes, not Pythagoras.

38 Letter of late November/early December 1901 to Paul Robert, *Corr.*, 627–8.

39 They are reproduced in facsimile and discussed in exhaustive detail in Paolo Dal Molin, "Une 'note de service des chemins de fer couverte d'esquisses musicales'," *Cahiers Debussy*, 33 (2009), 61–79.

40 Letters of 24 and 18 February, *Corr.*, 1877, 1874.

41 Letter of 28 July 1915, *Corr.*, 1913–14.

42 Letter of 12 August 1915, *Corr.*, 1920.

43 Letter of 14 July 1915 to Durand, *Corr.*, 1909.

44 Letter of 5 August 1915, *Corr.*, 1915.

45 The contract misspells "serfs" as "Cerfs."

46 Letter of 4 February 1916, *Corr.*, 1972. He actually advised Godet, "Ménagez vos méninges"; that is, "Control your meninges" (i.e., "Give your brain a rest").

47 Letter of 1 November 1915 to Durand, *Corr.*, 1955. For a detailed discussion of the creation of this movement see Jurjen Vis, "Debussy and the War: Debussy, Luther and Janequin: remarks on Part II of *En blanc et noir*," *Cahiers Debussy*, 15 (1991), 31–50.

13 INDIAN SUMMER, STYGIAN WINTER

1 Letter of 28 November 1915, *Corr.*, 1957.

2 However, the subtitle "Pierrot fâché avec la lune" ("Pierrot fed up with the moon") that is sometimes attached to this movement was an invention of a certain Louis Rosoor, a cellist who visited Debussy at Arcachon in 1916 and played the sonata with him. Debussy detested the subtitle and Rosoor's playing more or less equally. See his letter to Durand, 12 October 1916, *Corr.*, 2036.

3 Letter of 28 August 1915, *Corr.*, 1925.

4 Letter of 12 August 1915, *Corr.*, 1920–21. See also Paul Roberts, *Images: The Piano Music of Claude Debussy*, 314.

5 Letter of 28 August.

6 The original title of *Pour les cinq doigts* was "Pour le Gradus ad Parnassum," which (like the prelude to *Children's Corner*) suggested a parody of Clementi rather than Czerny.

7 Marguerite Long, *At the Piano with Debussy*, 45.

8 Technically the fourth is dissonant only when it is with the bass note.

9 Letter of 27 September 1915, *Corr.*, 1939.

10 Letter of 16 September 1915, *Corr.*, 1933.

11 Letter of 11 December 1916, *Corr.*, 2056–7.

12 Letters of 9 October 1915 to Désiré-Émile Inghelbrecht and of 14 October to Robert Godet, *Corr.*, 1945, 1947.

13 Letter of 4 January 1916 to Godet, *Corr.*, 1963–5.

14 Henri Busser, *Souvenirs*, quoted in *Corr.*, 2040, n. 1.

15 Letter to Jane Bathori-Engel, 2 November 1916, *Corr.*, 2042.

16 Letter to Henri Busser, 28 October 1916, *Corr.*, 2040. Busser had suggested orchestrating the piece himself, but Debussy said no. "I want this piece to be sung with the most discreet piano accompaniment. One mustn't lose a word of this text inspired by the rapacity of our enemies." *Corr.*, 2040, n. 1.

17 *LCD*, 394.

18 Letter of "early April 1917," *Corr.*, 2093.

19 Letter of 24 October 1915, *Corr.*, 1952–3.

20 Letter of 7/20 September 1914, in Viktor Varunts (ed.), *I. F. Stravinskiy: Perepiska s russkimi korrespondentami*, vol. 2, 290.

21 For these and other details, see Stephen Walsh, *Stravinsky: A Creative Spring*, 244–5.

22 Letter of 4 February 1916, *Corr.*, 1972, misquoting Laforgue's "Usines du Négatif." See also chapter 9, n. 22.

23 Letter of 3 July 1916 to Jacques Durand, *Corr.*, 2006.

24 Letter of 24 June to Arthur Hartmann, *Corr.*, 2004.

25 Letters of 27 July to his lawyer and of 21 July to Durand, *Corr.*, 2010, 2008. The Atreidae were the family of King Atreus of Mycenae and his sons Agamemnon and Menelaus, whose wife, Helen, was the cause of the Trojan War.

26 Letter of 19 September 1916 to Paul Dukas, *Corr.*, 2027–8. Presumably the Hungarian anarchist is Bartók.

27 Letter of 6 October 1916, *Corr.*, 2032–4.

28 Letter to Durand, 17 October, *Corr.*, 2037–8.

29 Letter to Godet, 11 December 1916, *Corr.*, 2056.

30 Ibid.

31 Letter of 6 April 1917, *Corr.*, 2096.

32 Letter to Dukas, 19 May 1917, *Corr.*, 2111.

33 Letter of 15 April 1917, *Corr.*, 2099. Perhaps he had in mind Verlaine's "L'Échelonnement des haies," the procession of hedges that roll to infinity, which he had set in 1891.

34 Letter to Godet, 7 May 1917, *Corr.*, 2106.

35 Letter of late January 1917, *Corr.*, 2075.

36 Letter of 1 February 1917, *Corr.*, 2076.

37 Letter of 8 March 1917, *Corr.*, 2083. The Precursor was Satie's name for himself.

38 Louis Laloy, *La Musique retrouvée*, 228.

39 Letter of 9 July 1917 to Louis-Pasteur Vallery-Radot (grandson of the inventor of vaccination and pasteurisation), *Corr.*, 2129, n. 2.

40 Letter of 28 July 1917 to Godet, *Corr.*, 2133.

41 Letter of late August 1917, *Corr.*, 2147.

42 Letter of 1 November 1917, *Corr.*, 2159–60.

43 Ibid.

44 Letter of 31 October 1917 to Godet, *Corr.*, 2158.

45 Letter of 6 February 1918, *Corr.*, 2182.

46 Letter of 8 April 1918, *Corr.*, 2195–6.

47 Laloy, 229.

14 WHAT THE MODERN MADE OF HIM

1 Jean Cocteau, *Le Coq et l'Arlequin* (Stock/Musique, Paris, 1979), 46. Cocteau may have been particularly annoyed with nightingales because his passionate desire to collaborate with Stravinsky on his Diaghilev project, *David*, had been thwarted in part by Stravinsky's need to finish his opera *The Nightingale*, which was itself then staged by Diaghilev.

2 Ibid., 60, 59.

3 Ibid., 61.

4 Ibid., 79.

5 Ibid., 53.

6 Reprinted in Herbert Van Thal (ed.), *Testament of Music* (Putnam, London, 1962), 199.

7 Ibid., 198.

8 "Corruption in the Censers" (1956), in Pierre Boulez, *Stocktakings from an Apprenticeship*, 20.

9 Constant Lambert, *Music Ho! A Study of Music in Decline* (Faber & Faber, London, 1934), 19–21.

10 ". . . Near and Far" (1954), in Boulez, *Stocktakings*, 155.

11 *Encyclopédie Fasquelle de la musique* (1958), in Boulez, *Stocktakings*, 274 (italics Boulez's).

12 Quoted in John Rewald, *The History of Impressionism*, 22.

13 Herbert Eimert, "Debussy's *Jeux*," trans. Leo Black, *Die Reihe*, 5 (Theodore Presser, Bryn Mawr, Pennsylvania, 1961), 16.

14 Letter of 22 July 1915, *Corr.*, 1912.

Select Bibliography

Andersen, Hans Christian, *Forty Stories*, trans. M. R. James (Faber & Faber, London, 1930)

Boulez, Pierre, *Relevés d'apprenti* (Éditions du Seuil, Paris, 1966); *Stocktakings from an Apprenticeship*, trans. Stephen Walsh (Clarendon Press, Oxford, 1991)

Bourgeaud, Henri (ed.), *Correspondance de Claude Debussy et Pierre Louÿs* (Librairie José Corti, Paris, 1945)

Branger, Jean-Christophe, Sylvie Douche and Denis Herlin (eds), *Pelléas et Mélisande: Cent ans après* (Symétrie, Lyon, 2012)

Brettell, Richard R., *Impression: Painting Quickly in France 1860–1890* (Yale University Press, New Haven and London, 2000)

Briscoe, James R. (ed.), *Debussy in Performance* (Yale University Press, New Haven and London, 1999)

Buckle, Richard, *Diaghilev* (Weidenfeld and Nicolson, London, 1979)

Cocteau, Jean, *Le Coq et l'Arlequin* (Stock/Musique, Paris, 1979)

Cooper, Martin, *French Music from the Death of Berlioz to the Death of Fauré* (Oxford University Press, London, 1961)

Dal Molin, Paolo, "Une 'note de service des chemins de fer couverte d'esquisses musicales'," *Cahiers Debussy*, 33 (2009).

Dal Molin, Paolo, and Jean-Louis Leleu, "Comment composait Debussy: les leçons d'un carnet de travail (à propos de *Soupir* et d'*Éventail*)," in *Cahiers Debussy*, 35 (2011)

Dawes, Frank, *Debussy Piano Music* (BBC, London, 1969)

Devriès, Anik, "Les Musiques d'Extrême-Orient à l'Exposition Universelle de 1889," *Cahiers Debussy*, 1 (1977), 24–37

Dietschy, Marcel, *A Portrait of Claude Debussy*, trans. William Ashbrook and Margaret G. Cobb (Clarendon Press, Oxford, 1990)

Eimert, Herbert, "Debussy's *Jeux*," trans. Leo Black, *Die Reihe*, 5 (Theodore Presser, Bryn Mawr, Pennsylvania, 1961)

Emmanuel, Maurice, "Transcription littérale des notes au crayon du carnet de Maurice Emmanuel (1889–1890)," *Inédits sur Claude Debussy* (Les Publications Techniques, Paris, n.d. [1942])

Fauser, Annegret, *Musical Encounters at the 1889 Paris World's Fair* (University of Rochester Press, Rochester, New York and Woodbridge, 2005)

Fulcher, Jane F. (ed.), *Debussy and His World* (Princeton University Press, Princeton, 2001)

Garafola, Lynn, *Diaghilev's Ballets Russes* (Oxford University Press, New York, 1989)

Holloway, Robin, *Debussy and Wagner* (Eulenburg, London, 1979)

Howat, Roy, *The Art of French Piano Music* (Yale University Press, New Haven and London, 2009)

Jarocinski, Stefan, *Debussy: Impressionism and Symbolism*, trans. Rollo Myers (Eulenburg, London, 1976)

Jensen, Eric, *Debussy* (Oxford University Press, Oxford, 2014)

Karsavina, Tamara, *Theatre Street* (Constable, London, 1948)

Kautsky, Catherine, *Debussy's Paris* (Rowman and Littlefield, London, Boulder and New York, 2017)

Laloy, Louis, *La Musique retrouvée* (Librairie Plon, Paris, 1928)

Lambert, Constant, *Music Ho! A Study of Music in Decline* (Faber & Faber, London, 1934)

Langham Smith, Richard, "Debussy and the Pre-Raphaelites," *19th-Century Music*, v (1981–82), 95–109

—— (ed. and trans.), *Debussy on Music* (Secker & Warburg, London, 1977) [*DoM*]

Lesure, François, "Une Interview Romaine de Debussy," *Cahiers Debussy*, 11 (1987)

——, "Debussy et le Chat Noir," *Cahiers Debussy*, 23 (1999), 35–43

——, *Claude Debussy* (Fayard, Paris, 2003) [*LCD*]

—— (ed.), *Claude Debussy: Monsieur Croche et autres écrits* (Gallimard, Paris, 1987) [*CDMC*]

—— (ed.), *Claude Debussy: Correspondance 1884–1918* (Hermann, Paris, 1993)

Lesure, François, and Denis Herlin (eds), *Claude Debussy: Correspondance (1872–1918)* (Gallimard, Paris, 2005) [*Corr.*]

Lesure, François, and Roger Nichols (eds), *Debussy Letters* (Faber & Faber, London, 1987)

Liebich, Louisa Shirley, "An Englishwoman's Memories of Debussy," *Musical Times*, LIX (1 June 1918)

Lockspeiser, Edward, *Debussy et Edgar Poe* (Éditions du Rocher, Monaco, 1961)

——, *Debussy: His Life and Mind*, 2 vols (Cassell, London, 1962, 1965)

——, *Debussy* (Dent, London, 1980)

Long, Marguerite, *At the Piano with Debussy*, trans. O. Senior-Ellis (J. M. Dent, London, 1972)

Mueller, Richard, "Javanese Influence on Debussy's 'Fantaisie' and beyond," *19th-Century Music*, X / 2 (autumn 1986)

Myers, Rollo (ed.), *Richard Strauss & Romain Rolland: Correspondence, Diary & Essays* (Calder and Boyars, London, 1951)

Nectoux, Jean-Michel, *Harmonie en bleu et or* (Fayard, Paris, 2005)

Nichols, Roger, entry on Debussy, in Stanley Sadie (ed.), *The New Grove Dictionary of Music and Musicians*, vol. 5 (Macmillan, London, 1980), 292–314

——, *Debussy* (Oxford University Press, London, 1972)

——, *The Life of Debussy* (Cambridge University Press, Cambridge, 1998)

—— (ed.), *Debussy Remembered* (Faber, London, 1992)

Nichols, Roger, and Richard Langham Smith (eds), *Claude Debussy: Pelléas et Mélisande* (Cambridge University Press, Cambridge, 1989)

Nijinsky, Vaslav, *The Diary of Vaslav Nijinsky*, trans. Romola Nijinsky (Quartet, London, 1991)

Orledge, Robert, *Debussy and the Theatre* (Cambridge University Press, Cambridge, 1982)

——, *Satie the Composer* (Cambridge University Press, Cambridge, 1990)

Porter, Andrew, *Music of Three Seasons, 1974–1977* (Farrar Straus Giroux, New York, 1978)

Puaux, René, "Notes indiennes: Amber," *Le Temps* (10 August 1912)

Rewald, John, *The History of Impressionism* (Secker & Warburg, London, 1973)

Roberts, Paul, *Images: The Piano Music of Claude Debussy* (Amadeus Press, Portland, Oregon, 1996)

Tresize, Simon, *Debussy: La Mer* (Cambridge University Press, Cambridge, 1994)

—— (ed.), *The Cambridge Companion to Debussy* (Cambridge University Press, Cambridge, 2003)

Vallas, Léon, *Claude Debussy: His Life and Works*, trans. Maire and Grace O'Brien (Dover, New York, 1973)

Van Thal, Herbert (ed.), *Testament of Music* (Putnam, London, 1962)

Varunts, Viktor (ed.), *I. F. Stravinskiy: Perepiska s russkimi korrespondentami*, vol. 2 (Kompozitor, Moscow, 2000)

Vis, Jurjen, "Debussy and the War: Debussy, Luther and Janequin: remarks on Part II of *En blanc et noir*," *Cahiers Debussy*, 15 (1991)

Walsh, Stephen, *Stravinsky: A Creative Spring* (Knopf, New York, 1999)

——, *Musorgsky and His Circle* (Faber & Faber, London, 2013)

Wenk, Arthur B., *Claude Debussy and the Poets* (University of California Press, Berkeley, 1976)

Wood, Henry J., *My Life of Music* (Gollancz, London, 1938)

Index

ILLUSTRATIONS

A NOTE ABOUT THE AUTHOR

Stephen Walsh is Emeritus Professor of Music at Cardiff University and author of a number of books on music including *Musorgsky and His Circle* and the prizewinning biography of Igor Stravinsky, selected as one of the ten Books of the Year by *The Washington Post*. He served for many years as deputy music critic for *The Observer* and writes reviews for many journals. He lives in Herefordshire, England.

A NOTE ON THE TYPE

Pierre Simon Fournier le jeune, who designed the type used in this book, was both an originator and a collector of types. His services to the art of printing were his design of letters, his creation of ornaments and initials, and his standardization of type sizes. His types are old style in character and sharply cut. In 1764 and 1766 he published his Manuel typographique, a treatise on the history of French types and printing, on typefounding in all its details, and on what many consider his most important contribution to typography—the measurement of type by the point system.

Composed by North Market Street Graphics, Lancaster, Pennsylvania

Printed and bound by Berryville Graphics, Berryville, Virginia

Designed by Iris Weinstein